An Encyclopedia of

SMALL
ANTIQUES

An Encyclopedia of
SMALL ANTIQUES

James Mackay

Harper & Row, Publishers
New York, Evanston, San Francisco, London

AN ENCYCLOPEDIA OF SMALL ANTIQUES

FIRST U.S. EDITION

ISBN: 0–06–012795–3

LIBRARY OF CONGRESS CATALOG CARD
NUMBER: 75–4145

Designed by Andrew Shoolbred

Published in Great Britain by
Ward Lock Limited, London

Contents

Colour plates

Introduction

This encyclopedia has been compiled primarily for the collector of average means with an average amount of storage space. The exigencies of modern urban living mean that many people who have the means to pursue an acquisitive hobby have only a limited amount of space available for their collections. The emphasis is laid therefore on small items, and larger articles (including most furniture) have been excluded. Until recently an antique could be defined as anything dating from the dawn of history until 1830, but this has been considerably relaxed, first by the hundred years' rule adopted by customs and taxation authorities, and latterly by the decision of the British Antique Dealers' Association to bring forward their date criterion from 1830 to 1930.

It would have been impossible, within the scope of a single volume, to encompass every aspect of small antiques. I have therefore concentrated on areas and periods which offer the greatest opportunity to the collector, particularly the applied arts of western Europe and Northern America over the past three centuries. Of course, other areas and periods are not overlooked, but their treatment has necessarily been less comprehensive.

This book is designed to offer suggestions to the beginner as well as the collector with a certain amount of knowledge. The alphabetical entries are devoted to antiques classified as subjects. Cross-references are given to related subjects to enable the reader to pursue a particular line of interest through several entries. In addition there are several generic subjects which will point the way to more specific articles, and separate entries on the important media, such as bronze, brass, glass, porcelain, pottery, silver and treen, in which the applied arts have found expression.

The fine arts – painting and sculpture – have been excluded, and this omission has been extended to watercolours, drawings and most classes of prints. Technical terms are not covered by separate entries and where they have occurred in the text it is hoped that their use is self-explanatory. It would require a volume of similar size to do adequate justice to the many and varied terms now used in the world of antiques. For the same reason names of individual manufacturers, craftsmen, artists and designers have been omitted from the alphabetical listing although, of course, they are mentioned in the context of the articles with which they were involved.

AERONAUTICA

Collectable objects in this category may be divided between those associated with balloons and heavier-than-air machines. Although the history of man's attempts at flight can be traced back to the legend of Daedalus and Icarus, practical expressions of these ambitions date from the Renaissance and the writings of Leonardo da Vinci and Francis Bacon. References to the feasibility of man-powered flight are also to be found in the works of Fleyder of Tübingen (1617) and G.A. Borelli (1680). Man's conquest of the air began in 1782 with the first experiments by the Montgolfier brothers in France. In September 1783 they sent aloft a hot-air balloon manned by a sheep, a cock and a duck. The balloon, which was extravagantly decorated with oil painting, attracted a huge audience and captured the popular imagination. The exploits of Pilâtre de Rogier and J.A.C. Charles, piloting hot-air and gas-filled balloons respectively, made them the heroes

Tortoiseshell snuff box with a ballooning scene in silver *piqué*; French, late 18th century.

of the hour. News of the French flights spread rapidly all over Europe and formed the topic of general discussion. The ballooning craze – or 'aerostation' as it was originally termed – had a tremendous impact on the fine and applied arts of the late eighteenth and early nineteenth centuries. Balloons and ballooning became fashionable subjects for depiction in prints, fan-leaves, watch cases, snuff boxes, enamelled objects of vertu, porcelain plaques and pottery. Balloons were worked in marquetry panels and, at a comparatively late date (*c.* 1870) were a popular motif in embroidered silk book markers.

Although heavier-than-air machines are a product of the twentieth century, the forerunners date back to Leonardo's ornithopter and subsequently to the experiments of Sir George Cayley between 1796 and 1820. The nineteenth century provides the collector with a surprising number of model aircraft produced by such inventors as Penaud (France), Henson and Stringfellow (England), and Langley, Manly and Maxim (United States). Around the turn of the century and up to the beginning of World War I, balloon ascents and aviation meetings were popular in Europe and America, either on their own or as a feature of carnivals and fairs. Posters, placards, postcards, stickers, printed handkerchieves and other souvenirs of these events are all highly desirable items of aeronautica. Military aviation, beginning with the French balloons from the sieges of Metz and Paris in the Franco-German War of 1870–1, is a vast field in itself; uniforms, flying equipment and the primitive instruments of World War I now have a keen antiquarian interest. Dirigible airships, beginning with the early experiments of Zeppelin and Parseval in the

1880s and culminating in the spectacular world flights of the Twenties and Thirties, have yielded a vast amount of collectable material, from the fund-raising postcards of the 1900s to the flown covers of the *Hindenburg* and *Graf Zeppelin*. Early brochures, flying timetables, menu cards and ephemera associated with the infancy of the commercial airlines are now much sought after, as well as personal items associated with the pioneer aviators and air aces, from Richthofen and Rickenbacker to Amelia Earhart and Amy Johnson.

Other categories of aeronautica which afford considerable scope include airline badges and insignia, medals and decorations of air forces, and vintage model aircraft. Aerophilately is a huge subject in itself, ranging from the *papillons de Metz* and the *ballons montés* of Paris down to the latest rocket mail experiments. Aerial propaganda leaflets date from Gabriele d'Annunzio's epic daylight raid on Vienna in 1918, and range chronologically through World War II and many minor campaigns, to the safe conduct passes dropped on the Viet Cong by the USAF.

ALMANACS AND EPHEMERIDES

Books or tables containing calendars, astronomical and navigational data, and registers of events began to appear in Europe in the sixteenth century, although their origins can be traced back to the astrological tables of the Egyptians and the *fasti* of the Romans. Long before almanacs were produced in printed form, the peoples of Scandinavia and northern Germany used a primitive type of calendar known as a clogg almanac. These consisted of blocks of hard wood about eight inches in length, with the days and months of the year indicated by notches of varying shapes and sizes along the four edges. Subsidiary symbols indicated saints' days, festivals and lunar phases. Wooden almanacs of this kind were commonly used in certain parts of England until the late seventeenth century.

Printed almanacs seem to have originated in France, where they circulated freely among the lower classes as early as the mid-sixteenth century. They took the form of a compendium of superstitions and sundry 'predictions and prognostications'. They were frowned on by the authorities and were subject to bans imposed at various times from 1579 onwards. Among the more reputable was the *Almanach Liègeois*, first published in 1625 at Liège by Matthieu Laensbergh. From the middle of the seventeenth century onwards the French almanacs began to publish calendars of public and royal events and gradually assumed the appearance of official yearbooks, of which the *Almanach Royal* (first published in 1679) is the best known.

The early English almanacs also concentrated on astrological matters. The best known of these, the *Vox Stellarum* (voice of the stars), was first published by Francis Moore in 1700, and still appears annually under the title of *Old Moore's Almanac*. The character of British almanacs changed in 1828, when the Society for the Diffusion of Useful Knowledge published the first edition of its *British Almanac*. The rival *Englishman's Almanac* was published by the Stationer's Company. Joseph Whitaker began publishing his *Almanack* in 1868 and this has appeared annually down to the present day.

The first American almanac was probably that published by Bradford of Philadelphia in 1687. Benjamin Franklin began publishing *Poor Richard's Almanack*, under the nom de plume of Richard Saunders in 1732, and this appeared annually for a quarter of a century. Subsequent American works of interest to the collector include *The American Almanac and Repository of Useful Knowledge* (published at Boston from 1828 to 1861) and *The Old Farmer's Almanac*, which has been published over many years. Among the European almanacs pride of place goes to the *Almanach de Gotha* (published since 1763), which is particularly noted for its detailed section on the royal and aristocratic houses of Europe. Although the majority of almanacs were produced in book form, a few Continental examples are known in tabular form, intended for suspension on a wall like a calendar.

The Illustrated Phrenological Almanac; American, 1851.

Individual items are usually T-shaped with a decorative vertical crossbar and a long foot sloping backward into the fireplace. Logs were slung across between the feet of two such rests. The earliest andirons were in wrought iron, but by the sixteenth century cast iron was being used for the ornament on the crossbar and subsequently this was greatly enriched with brass, bronze, silver or even gold inlay work. By the end of the seventeenth century the decoration on andirons was becoming even more lavish, with much use of cast bronze figures and gilding. The finest andirons were produced in France and England in the early eighteenth century, replete with rococo ornament. They continued to be produced with lavish ornament in France until the time of the Revolution; but the growing use of coal in Britain, necessitating iron grates and smaller fireplaces, led to the decline of andirons by 1750. Purely decorative andirons continued to be made throughout the Victorian period, particularly during the Gothic Revival in the 1840s. These reproductions were often made of wrought iron, with steel facings, beaten copper or brass plates and pseudo-medieval brass or bronze ornament. However, the majority were produced as a kind of Queen Anne revival in the late nineteenth century. Functional andirons, known as firedogs, were retained in Victorian kitchens. They were relatively plain, and may be recognized by the ratcheted uprights for the spits. Andirons of American manufacture were produced until the early 1900s and were generally less ornate than those of French or English origin.

Ephemerides are a type of almanac consisting of principally of astronomical tables calculated on a year-to-year basis, and intended for the use of navigators and astronomers. The first ephemeris of note was the *Connaissance des Temps ou des Mouvements Célestes*, published by J. Picard at Paris in 1679 under the auspices of the Bureau des Longitudes. The earliest British ephemeris was the *Nautical Almanac*, produced in 1767 at the instigation of Nevil Maskelyne, the Astronomer Royal. The principal European work was the *Astronomisches Jahrbuch*, first published in 1774. The American *Ephemeris and Nautical Almanac* dates from 1852 and now ranks among the best ephemerides published anywhere in the world.

ANDIRONS

Decorative iron bars, furnished in pairs as supporters for burning logs in open fires.

Protective covering on the backs of chairs and sofas, designed to prevent the Macassar hair-oil from staining the upholstery. Antimacassars date from the introduction of oils and pomades at the beginning of the nineteenth century, in place of the powdered wigs formerly worn by men. The earliest antimacassars were made of stiff, white crochet-work, but by the middle of the century a wider variety of materials was being employed. Soft cloth of various colours was extensively worked in embroidery, Berlin woolwork (q.v.) or patchwork. Towards the end of the century antimacassars gradually went out of fashion in the homes of the upper classes, though they survived in the front parlours of the lower classes in Europe, and were always more widespread in America, where they were often known simply as 'tidies'. Tidy-making was one of the social accomplishments required of mid-Victorian ladies and many different techniques of needlework may be found in this medium. Geometric or floral patterns predominated, but the most interesting examples are those which have woven inscriptions and dates, figure compositions or even landscapes. The antimacassar enjoyed something of a revival after World War I. Twentieth-century examples are almost invariably made of white lace or crochet-work and lack the variety and interest of the late nineteenth-century styles.

See also *Lambrequins*

Small bronze figures of a dog and panther; Eastern Greek, 5th century BC.

Term applied rather loosely by dealers and auctioneers to cover a wide range of objects which cannot be conveniently categorized in any other way. There is thus a degree of illogicality about a term which in saleroom parlance embraces Greek terracottas, Maya jade figures and Polynesian war-clubs, with a splendid disregard for time and geography, but omits Chinese and Japanese artefacts solely on the grounds that, because they are reasonably plentiful, they merit separate categories. The individual collector, however, may find a different method of grouping more acceptable. It is logical to regard as antiquities those objects which are the relics of ancient civilizations irrespective of the place of origin. For practical purposes, moreover, the fourteenth century and the beginning of the Renaissance in Europe provide a convenient division between antiquities and antiques.

The range of antiquities available to the collector is vast, encompassing the artefacts associated with Egyptian, Greek, Western Asiatic, Roman, Byzantine, Celtic, Teutonic, Scandinavian, Indian, pre-Columbian, African and Far Eastern cultures, from the second millennium BC up to the end of the Middle Ages. Within the scope of this work it would be impossible to do more than outline the field of antiquities. For obvious reasons certain media are better represented than others. Pottery vessels and figurines are among the most widespread forms of antiquities, and examples from Asia and Europe dating back 4,000 years can still be picked up for a relatively small outlay. Bronze antiquities include Celtic harness and shield ornaments, Egyptian and Etruscan statuettes, Western Asiatic decorated axe-heads and the curious barter currency of China, which used bronze replicas of knives, spades and saddles in exchange for goods, whose value was equal to the real thing. Silver items include brooches and penannular rings, small vessels and figures. Glass, apart from a number of Roman vessels, Egyptian and Greek beads and early examples of Islamic decorated flasks, is virtually non-existent in antiquities, while objects of wood or leather have not survived in any appreciable quantity.

Culturally, Africa may be divided between the ancient civilizations of the north, of Carthage, Roman Africa, Egypt and Ethiopia, and the more primitive regions south of the Sahara and the Nile basin. The implements and ornaments of the latter are considered under the heading of Primitive Art. The antiquities of northern Africa reflect the imposition of successive alien civilizations by the dominant Mediterranean powers – Phoenicians, Greeks, Romans, Vandals, Byzantines and Arabs. The bulk of the Punic antiquities now extant consists of grotesque terracotta masks, personal trinkets and jewelry recovered from stone coffins dating back to 700 BC. Phoenician art was rapidly hellenized, by contact with the Greek colonies in Sicily, long before Carthage fell to the Romans in 146 BC, and Graeco-Phoenician pottery and metalwork have been recovered from archaeological sites all over North Africa, from Numidia and Tunisia to Tripolitania and the Greek colonies in Cyrenaica. Terracotta figurines, painted vases, decorated oil-jars and small bronze statues comprise the bulk of Cyrenaic antiquities available to the collector.

While spectacular prices are paid for Egyptian Saite bronze cats, Shang Dynasty food vessels and ornately decorated Attic amphorae, there are still countless examples of humbler artefacts in the price bracket up to £100 ($250), ranging from Roman terracottas to Tibetan and Nepalese bronze figurines of the Middle Ages.

APOSTLE SPOONS

Spoons decorated with the figures of Christ and the Twelve Apostles, fashionable in the fifteenth and sixteenth centuries as baptismal gifts. This custom of giving spoons was largely confined to western Europe, and especially England. In most cases the godparents would give the child a single silver spoon, the stem of which was mounted by the tiny figure of a saint (in honour of whom the child was named, or perhaps the patron saint of the donor). The wealthier godparents, however, would give a set of thirteen spoons whose figures represented Christ and His Apostles, and many who were not so well-off would give a half-set of six. The custom survived rather longer in England than in western Europe, and only went into decline during the reign of Charles II. Hone's *Every Day Book*, written in 1666, notes that the custom was rapidly dying out. Silver apostle spoons of the latter half of the seventeenth century are, therefore, comparatively rare, particularly those with provincial hallmarks. Attempts have been made to revive this custom from time to time, and apostle spoons of more recent date may be found.

The composition of sets varies surprisingly. St Luke and St Mark occasionally replace St Simon and St Matthias; Judas Iscariot is often omitted; and St Paul is another frequent substitute. Other saints are also depicted and, like the Apostles, designated by objects or symbols associated with them. These tiny objects (such as Andrew's saltire cross or Peter's keys) were cast separately and subsequently riveted into place; as a result they often came adrift and have been lost.

ilver apostle spoons;
nglish, 1537–85.

Individual spoons of the Tudor and Stuart periods are scarce, for much English silver was melted down during the Civil War. Complete sets of spoons are now major rarities, whose appearance in the saleroom would be an outstanding event. Individual spoons from the early eighteenth century onwards vary greatly in value according to size, condition and date. Unusual features, such as a provincial hallmark, coat of arms or engraved inscription, may add considerably to the value.

Apart from spoons featuring Christ and His Apostles there are two other types which are generally considered in this category. Spoons with an effigy of the Virgin Mary are commonly referred to as maidenhead spoons and appear to date from the mid-fifteenth century to the time of the Reformation and even beyond. They do not, however, attract the same interest as apostle spoons. Another device found on spoons is a sejant lion, popular on christening spoons in Elizabethan and Jacobean times.

APOTHECARY JARS

Otherwise known as drug jars or drug pots, these vessels were designed to hold dry drugs and ointments. The earliest form was the *albarello* (an Italian term of Arabic derivation) which was introduced to Italy and Spain

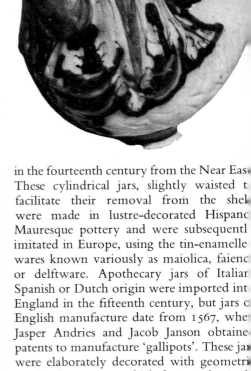

Maiolica apothecary jar with spout and handle; Italian, c. 1670.

in the fourteenth century from the Near East. These cylindrical jars, slightly waisted to facilitate their removal from the shelf, were made in lustre-decorated Hispano-Mauresque pottery and were subsequently imitated in Europe, using the tin-enamelled wares known variously as maiolica, faience or delftware. Apothecary jars of Italian, Spanish or Dutch origin were imported into England in the fifteenth century, but jars of English manufacture date from 1567, when Jasper Andries and Jacob Janson obtained patents to manufacture 'gallipots'. These jars were elaborately decorated with geometric or floral patterns, which betray the early Islamic influence. They often bore the names of drugs, many of which are otherwise lost

Left Maiolica aquamanile in the form of a mermaid; Spanish or Portuguese, late 19th century.

Right Brass aquamanile; German, 15th–16th century.

teristic form they appear as lions with their tails arched across their backs to form handles. The ewer was filled through an opening in the back and the water poured through the open mouth. Other heraldic beasts have been recorded and even knights on horseback are known. The majority of aquamaniles were cast in bronze using the *cire perdue* process. Rare examples were cast in silver or gold and ornamented with precious stones. Conversely, a few are known in other base metal alloys such as pewter. Rare English aquamaniles of the fourteenth century were fashioned in lead-glazed earthenware. These late medieval vessels were gradually superseded in the sixteenth and seventeenth centuries by water jugs and ewers (q.v.) of conventional form.

in oblivion. In addition to jars, barrel-shaped containers for dry compounds were developed in the mid-seventeenth century, while large spherical vessels with a tap near the foot were produced about the same time for liquid medicines. Later forms of decoration included angels and cherubs, acanthus leaves, satyrs and motifs derived from classical Greek and Roman designs. Earthenware drug jars of this sort continued to be manufactured, both in Britain and America, until the mid-nineteenth century when glass became increasingly common. Associated with these jars, both in substance and decoration, were delftware tiles and slabs used by apothecaries for rolling pills. Creamware was substituted for delft in the late eighteenth century (Wedgwood was a prolific producer of such jars), and these continued to appear until about 1860.
See also *Medicine Bottles and Instruments, Pill Slabs*

AQUAMANILES

Type of jug used to hold water for washing the hands, fashionable in Europe from the thirteenth to the sixteenth centuries. Aquamaniles were intended to stand on the dining table and from the outset were imbued with a decorative quality which enabled them to double as a centrepiece. In their most charac-

ASHTRAYS

Containers for tobacco ash developed in the latter half of the nineteenth century, as cigarette-smoking became more popular. A few early examples were designed specifically for pipe-smokers, but the great majority were used for cigarettes. These small objects may be found in almost every substance from precious to base metals, in wood, early plastic materials such as bakelite, pottery, porcelain and glass (usually pressed or moulded). At the lower end of the scale ashtrays were (and still are) stamped from sheet metal; examples in brass, tinware or toleware were frequently decorated with the advertisements of brewers or tobacco companies, while many of the glass and pottery

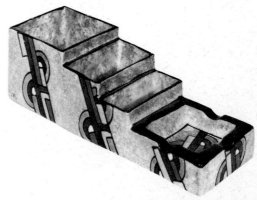

Right Enamelled pottery cigarette holder and ashtray by A. Dubois, 1920.

15

ashtrays were also produced as firm's advertisements. By the early twentieth century, however, this form of advertising was being extended into all kinds of businesses and many of these examples of company promotion have elaborate designs, featuring products, house symbols and views of factories. Ashtrays with regimental crests, naval and military insignia form an important category of particular interests to collectors of militaria (q.v.).

While the better quality of ashtray may be found in the prevailing styles of the applied arts (from Art Nouveau at the turn of the century to the *moderne* styles of the 1930s), the greatest interest lies in the novelty and souvenir ashtrays. Many of these have a somewhat Rabelaisian flavour, in keeping with the atmosphere of the bar-room, or the smokers' concert of the Edwardian era. Miniature chamberpots (q.v.) and toilet bowls with appropriate inscriptions typify the lavatorial humour of the 'joke' ashtray found in many countries. Pocket ashtrays, in the form of miniature warming-pans, may be found in brass, burnished copper, silver, enamel-ware or porcelain and, as a modern form of object of vertu, are worthy of study.

AUTOMATA

A more adult form of clockwork toy, which developed as a sideline from the clock and watch industry in the eighteenth century. The techniques of movement perfected for clocks were applied to mechanical figures which could be made to perform antics, dance, and play musical instruments. Birds and animals were similarly animated. Not surprisingly automata were first manufactured commercially in Switzerland, the Jaquet-Droz family of Geneva being the most prominent producers from the mid-eighteenth century onwards. Automata were also widely produced in Germany (particularly Nuremberg), the Low Countries and England. James Cox was the best-known manufacturer in England in the late eighteenth century and many of his clockwork confections were given by the Honour-

able East India Company to native potentate as presents. Subsequently Cox even opene an emporium in Canton, where his clock and automata enjoyed a certain vogue in th early nineteenth century.

In France the leading makers include Lazare Duvaux (specializing in musical bir in cages) and J. de Vaucanson (noted for h pictures with moving parts), both flourishin in the period immediately before the Revo lution. Automata were revived in France i the mid-nineteenth century, the leadin exponent being Charles Bontemps, wh produced clocks incorporating birds whic hopped from branch to branch. Later nine teenth-century automata became mor elaborate, and the more extravagant ex amples were composed of an entire orche tra. The monkey bands of Vienna were th mid-nineteenth-century equivalent of th porcelain groups modelled by Meissen, an are among the most highly prized forms automata today. The majority of nineteenth century and later automata incorporated mechanism for playing music and are mor fully described under the heading of music boxes (q.v.).

right Apothecary's
pocket scales; English,
mid-18th century.

below Pocket balances for
weighing guineas and
sovereigns; English, 18th
and early 19th centuries.

BALANCES AND SCALES

Instruments for weighing objects can be
dated back to the fifth millennium BC when
the Egyptians invented the equal-arm
balance. In its earliest form the balance was
a beam suspended at its middle point, with
pans attached by cords to either end. A later
refinement, devised by the Romans at the
beginning of the Christian era, was the use
of a pin through the centre of the beam for the
central bearing. This remained the basic
principle of weighing-machines until the
eighteenth century, when the invention of
the knife-edge balance led to the development of the modern precision balance.
Mechanical scales developed alongside the
science of dynamics from the middle of the
seventeenth century. In 1669 Gilles Personne
de Roberval invented the *énigme statique*,
deriving its name from the fact that he could
offer no explanation for its operation! It was
not until 1821 that the French mathematician
Poinsot was able to relate the workings of
Roberval's 'enigma' to the theory of couples.
From this developed the counter scales,
patented and improved on by Phitzer in
Germany, Beranger in France and the
Fairbanks brothers in the United States.

Steelyards, used nowadays for larger
weights, were invented by the Romans and
underwent numerous changes in size and
style over a period of 2,000 years. Many of
the smaller steelyards of the eighteenth and
nineteenth centuries are exceptionally decorative. Self-indicating weighing-machines,
with a calibrated segment and a pointer
activated by the weight of the object, were
invented by Leonardo da Vinci, but not
developed commercially until the eighteenth
century. A miniature form of this instrument, with a pincer mechanism, was devised
in the mid-nineteenth century for weighing
letters. The same principle led to the modern

dial scale and the computing counter scale used by grocers, in which a chart revolves against a fixed indicator and enables the operator to read the cost of commodities of varying prices.

Pocket scales for weighing gold coins date from the seventeenth century and range from simple sovereign balances to elaborate folding scales capable of weighing a number of different coins. Several patent devices appeared in the 1840s, following the establishment of uniform postal rates computed by the weight of letters rather than the distance travelled. Letter balances for the desk-top appeared about the same time, and may be dated fairly accurately by the tables of postal rates engraved on them.

BANDBOXES

Decorative boxes used in the United States during the nineteenth century for the storage and transportation of clothing, hats and other personal effects. They developed from the hat boxes used in Britain and Europe from the mid-eighteenth century onwards, but the American bandbox was invariably brightly coloured and elaborately ornamented, whereas its European counterpart was never anything other than a purely functional object without any form of decoration.

The boxes themselves were made of very thin, plain wooden sheets cut and curved to shape, with a shallow lid which fitted over the top. To protect them from wear and tear they were covered with stout paper, which was glued to the outer surface. By 1820, however, it had become fashionable to print pictorial motifs on the paper, to form a continuous panorama round the sides of the box, and provide an oval or chamfered rectangular vignette for the lid. The papers were specially block-printed for the purpose and extremely attractive effects were achieved by combining up to five or six different blocks. The colours were usually strong, primary shades and the subjects, which included landmarks and scenes from everyday life, have a naïve charm often associated

with the nineteenth-century primitiv painters. More sophisticated designs ap peared in the 1840s, with classical motifs an chinoiserie (q.v.) borrowed from conten porary European applied arts. A few banc boxes of the mid-nineteenth century portra celebrities of the period, such as the Swedis singer, Jenny Lind, who toured the Unite States from 1850 to 1852. Bandboxes de clined in popularity after the Civil War ar were gradually superseded by the mo utilitarian trunks, portmanteaux and cas of the late nineteenth century.

See colour plate page 34

BASKETS

The more collectable types of basket a those intended for the dining table or sid board and fashioned in precious metal Sheffield plate, electroplate or polished har woods. Metal baskets began to replace th more homely wooden variety, for brea cake, biscuits and fruit, in the seventeen century, and immediately their decorativ potential was realized they were subjected all the forms of elaboration fashionable different periods from the early eighteen century onwards. The earliest types wer usually oval and shallow in form; later baske were rectangular, with rounded or chamfere corners. At first twin D-handles were use but by the early eighteenth century a fixe central handle became more popular an this, in turn, gave way to a swing handle. B the end of the eighteenth century the prevai ing influence of the rococo resulted extravagantly decorated baskets, with the tall, vertical sides pierced and fretted wi rustic motifs and providing an attracti contrast with the deep purples and magent of the cloth liners. In the Regency peric baskets were intricately woven using silv wire studded with foliage and flowers. Wi the advent of electroplate in the 184 baskets became increasingly stereotyped form and were virtually mass-produce though examples in sterling silver continu to be a popular subject for presentatio Although the larger baskets were produce

Victorian oval cake basket with swing handle, designed in 18th-century taste; English, 1874.

individually, small baskets for sweetmeats were manufactured in pairs or sets in uniform or complementary designs.
See also *Cake Stands*

BEADS AND MARBLES

These two otherwise unrelated classes of objects are grouped together because they manifest the oldest techniques of glass manufacture. Glass beads have been dated as far back as the second millennium BC in Egypt, although pottery beads are thought to be of ever greater antiquity. In the centuries immediately before the Christian era the Egyptians had perfected several techniques for producing beads, the most distinctive being the so-called 'eye' beads, in which a dab of coloured translucent glass was bedded in a matrix of opaque glass. Other forms include thread spirals, rings, coils and the complex *millefiori* style, which was later to become associated with paperweights (q.v.). Glass beads were developed to a high art in Roman times, disappeared from Europe in the Dark Ages and in the twelfth century were re-introduced from the Near East to Venice, where they subsequently became one of the principal products of that city. The Venetians specialized in several kinds of beads, from the tiny, lustrous beads used for embroidery and the dark beads used in rosaries, to the large, brown beads used for jewelry. The Venetians revived the art of making marbles (practised in Roman times), and introduced techniques for encapsulating patterns and spirals in coloured and opaque glass.

Both beads and marbles spread to Bohemia and Silesia in the fifteenth century and thence to France, the Low Countries and England, where they were produced for a variety of purposes – for beadwork, jewelry (qq.v.), for export to different parts of the world (where they were often used as currency), and as children's playthings. Marbles reached the height of their popularity in the mid-nineteenth century and ranged in size from tiny beads to giant marbles of up to two inches in diameter, which were known as bouncers. Marbles may also be found in various kinds of pottery and even porcelain, but these are scarce. Plain pottery marbles were called taws or alley taws, while those streaked with red were called blood alleys. Large pottery marbles with a distinctive black and white glaze were known as Chinamen. Dutch stonies was the name given to German marbles made from Coburg slate.

Beads of stone and shell were produced in great quantities by the early civilizations of North and South America. Beads of this type, including complete shells as well as beads cut to shape from large shells, have been recovered from burial mounds in North America. In Latin America the use of beads was widespread, from the turquoise beads of the Incas to the stone, amber and gold beads of Colombia.
See also *Toys*

BEADWORK

Tiny beads in opaque glass were used to simulate pearls in the embroidery of sumptuous costume from the late Middle Ages onwards, and this form of decoration may be found in Middle Eastern countries to this day. Beads stitched to cloth to form mosaic patterns have been used extensively as decoration for all manner of small articles, from boxes to book covers, cushions and purses. There was a certain vogue for beadwork in England in the eighteenth and early nineteenth centuries but examples from that period are scarce. Beadwork was revived in the mid-nineteenth century, largely as a result of German enterprise. Beads of a large, cylindrical form known as 'Bohemian' were exported in great quantities from Germany to other European countries and also North America, together with stencilled sheets of canvas, not unlike those used in Berlin woolwork (q.v.), with which they were con-

temporary. These German beadwork samplers were used as table mats, lambrequins (q.v.), vase covers and, mounted between sheets of glass, firescreens. Beadwork decoration of this period was also applied to pincushions, napkin rings, slippers and a wide variety of other domestic articles. The beadwork craze flourished in Europe and America throughout the second half of the nineteenth century, but died out by World War I. Because of its stout construction, and the fact that such a tedious operation merited care and respect, beadwork has been relatively well preserved and there are still numerous examples to be found from England, from Europe and North America.

From the seventeenth century, many of the trade beads imported to North America were threaded together and woven by the Indians into belts, bracelets and other articles of personal adornment. These items often had a recognized monetary value and were used as a form of barter currency.

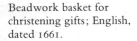

Beadwork basket for christening gifts; English, dated 1661.

American Indian beadwork pouch; 19th century.

BELLS

Among the earliest and most expensive forms of bells are those cast in bronze by the Chinese from the tenth century BC, if not earlier. Many of these bells, standing almost a foot high, were elaborately decorated with all-over patterns, and mounted with ornaments in human or animal form. Prayer bells and gongs are widely used by many of the world's religions in temples, monasteries and churches, and the smaller, hand-held varieties afford great scope for the collector.

Victorian table bell with ebonized plinth, 1872.

These bells may be found in various copper alloys – bronze, brass and bell-metal – iron or even pottery, and vary enormously in shape, size and decoration.

Bells have been used extensively in Europe and Asia by shepherds and cowherds to help them find stray animals. The bells, fastened to the necks of cattle by leather collars, vary from country to country, and even from one district to another, their decorative qualities exhibiting the prevailing styles in folk art.

Aesthetically, the most interesting and attractive bells are those which were designed for domestic use. Elegantly fashioned silver hand-bells were used in the eighteenth and nineteenth centuries to summon servants, and their handles were often beautifully cast or wrought. Larger bells, up to ten inches in height, were used in the American plantations to summon the slaves from the fields. Another common domestic variety on both sides of the Atlantic was the sleigh bell (often known in the United States as a rumbler bell) consisting of a pierced sphere containing a metal ball which rattled around inside. Many of the early rumblers were manufactured by Robert Wells of Aldbourne, Wiltshire, in the late eighteenth century, and the extent of his export trade may be gauged by the number of bells with his RW monogram which are to be found in the United States to this day.

BERLIN WOOLWORK

Variously known as Berlin-work, canvas-work, crewel-work and worsted-work, this form of textile ornament was immensely popular in Europe and America in the latter half of the nineteenth century. Indeed, it was a craze which soon got out of hand, both in the extent to which it was applied, and in the unimaginative quality of so many of its designs. Pre-printed designs or stencilled patterns on sheets of coarse canvas were produced in Germany for export, and relatively few enthusiasts branched out on their own and devised their own patterns or compositions. Consequently, Berlin woolwork is often regarded as the epitome of Victorian taste at its most vulgar.

21

Printed design for a Berlin woolwork picture of a hunting scene; English, late 19th century.

The decorative motif or picture was worked by knotting short thrums of brightly coloured wool through the canvas, using a rag-rug technique, and the result was a piece of tapestry with a rich, thick pile. Although floral patterns predominate, the more ambitious tried their hand at portraits (the poets Burns and Byron were great favourites), or simplified renditions of fashionable paintings of the period, such as the works of Sir Edwin Landseer. Biblical subjects, characters from Shakespearean plays or the novels of Sir Walter Scott were among the popular themes woven in this manner into cushion covers, firescreens and wall-hangings. Like bead-work (q.v.) this product of German enter-prise had died out by World War I.

BIBLE BOXES

Boxes, usually of oak, constructed to hold the massive family bibles which were fashion-able from the seventeenth century onwards. Although English bible boxes, with ornate Jacobean carving on their sides, are known from the mid-seventeenth century, the majority of extant examples hail from New England, where they developed into a distinct form of folk art in the late seventeenth and eighteenth centuries. They were hinged at the back and secured by a stout lock at the front. The sides and front of the box were intricately carved with floral or biblical motifs, and often bear dates and sets of initials. Similar boxes, with a sloping top, are known as desk boxes and were used in Europe in the seventeenth and eighteenth centuries as portable writing desks. Analogous to the bible box was the Hadley chest, which derived its name from the Massachusetts town of Hadley. These small chests were elaborately carved with floral patterns (the tulip was a popular motif), had one or two narrow drawers underneath and stood on four very short legs. They were popular as dowry boxes in New England in the late seventeenth and eighteenth centuries, particularly in Massachusetts and Connecti-cut, but examples are rare outside museum collections.

New England bible box with initials of Ruth Plummer; late 17th century.

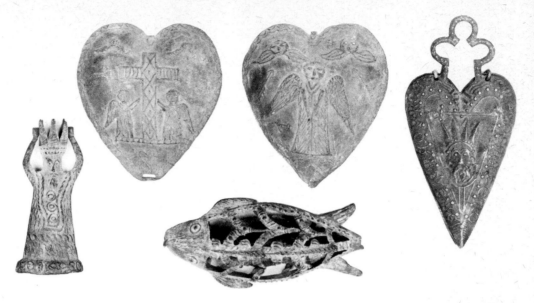

BIDRI WARE

A type of inlaid metalwork thought to have originated in the former Indian state of Bidar, but usually applied nowadays to any form of small metal object, in brass, bronze or a pewter alloy, inlaid with silver or, rarely, gold. The Islamic technique of damascening – inlaying a base metal with a precious metal – was applied to the article, which was then darkened chemically and the silver areas polished up to form an attractive contrast. The motifs found on this 'silver and black ware', as it is sometimes termed, were mainly derived from Arab or Persian originals, introduced to India by the Mogul invaders in the eleventh century. Bidri ware was, and is, one of the most popular forms of decorative artefact to be found in the bazaars, and its manufacture continues to form the backbone of the tourist industry in India, Pakistan and Bangladesh to this day. Although large objects, such as table tops, trays and salvers, may be found with this type of decoration, the majority of items include small boxes, vases, bells, bowls and other utensils. A great deal of Bidri ware came to England in the days of the British Raj and can still be picked up relatively cheaply. It went out of fashion in the 1930s, but it is now once more beginning to attract the serious attention of collectors.

BILLIES AND CHARLIES

Bogus medieval antiquities perpetrated by two Thames mudrakers of Tower Hill, London, in the mid-nineteenth century. The objects derive their name from William Smith and Charles Eaton, who, while scavenging on the mud-flats of the Thames, actually discovered a genuine fifteenth-century medal, which they subsequently sold to the British Museum for a considerable sum. Inspired by this stroke of good fortune, they began manufacturing spurious antiquities – amulets, medallions, badges, daggers, figures and seals and for a short time they succeeded in selling these items to collectors as genuine antiques.

How the public was ever taken in is a complete mystery, since the objects in question were poorly cast in lead or cock metal (a lead alloy), were utterly ludicrous in design and bristling with errors of inscription. Many of them, for example, bore medieval dates in Arabic instead of Roman numerals. It has been estimated that they sold over a thousand of these objects before their fraud was detected. Billies and Charlies, from being an object of curiosity, have now risen in status. Not only are they eminently collectable, but they are now almost as expensive as the objects they sought to imitate.

Large leather vessels made in Europe, Britain and Colonial America from the sixteenth to the eighteenth centuries. The majority of extant examples are thought to belong to the seventeenth century, before either pottery, pewter or glass were widely used. In general, black jacks had a large capacity, ranging from a quart to over a gallon. The seams were often reinforced with brass or even silver mounts or studs. Leather bottles and jugs continued to be used in rural areas well into the nineteenth century, but examples in good condition are rare.

BONBONNIÈRES

Little boxes intended for scented cachous or some other form of breath sweetener, carried on the person like snuff boxes and vinaigrettes (qq.v.). Larger boxes were probably intended for the table and held bonbons or sweets – hence the alternative names of sweetmeat box or comfit box. In construction, materials and decoration bonbonnières were often similar to snuff boxes, though the absence of the characteristically tight-fitting lid indicates the former. They may be found in gold, silver or silver-gilt, richly chased and engraved, in ivory, hardwood or even porcelain. Bonbonnières decorated with enamels (q.v.) were often made in novelty shapes, a speciality of the eighteenth- and early nineteenth-century Swiss enamellers. These boxes may be found in the shape of birds, fishes, animals and human forms.

Enamel-painted porcelain bonbonnière; Worcester, c. 1770.

The earliest bindings, found on manuscript as well as printed books, were of wood, vellum or leather, often ornamented with silver or copper mounts and fastenings, inlaid with ivory, mother-of-pearl or semi-precious stones, or covered in brocades richly embroidered in silk or gold wire. From the fourteenth century onwards bindings, particularly of sacred books, were richly decorated with low reliefs of biblical scenes carved in ivory or hardwood or painted in enamels. Rare examples had bindings entirely worked in precious metals. By the seventeenth century, however, leather predominated and although the decoration was seldom as ostentatious as the earlier examples, greater attention was being paid to the tooling of the leather in gold *au pointille*. Elaborate patterns, achieved by means of special punches and roulettes, continued to be fashionable well into the nineteenth century.

An important landmark in the publishing world was the introduction of wholesale binding by the publisher before the book reached the retail bookseller. All copies of an edition were case-bound in the same design and materials. This practice began about 1820 and was well established by the beginning of the Victorian era. It seems to have been adopted as an alternative to the paper wrappers in which publishers had previously issued their books, and which was originally intended as a temporary expedient before the book was properly bound to the customer's own taste. Cloth on board rapidly established itself as a cheap and effective method capable of mechanization, and by 1840 had virtually ousted the traditional methods of binding in Britain and the United States, though not to the same extent on the continent of Europe.

Around the middle of the century gift and prize books appeared in an astonishing array of bindings, with panels of vellum, silk, tortoiseshell, wood and even porcelain. Improved machinery revolutionized methods of binding and decoration. Bind

Right Pericles and Aspasia, designed and bound under the supervision of T.J. Cobden-Sanderson, 1903.

ings became increasingly pictorial, and the cloth covers were die-stamped in gilt or silver, often with elaborate vignettes. The use of metal embossing gradually gave way in the early 1900s to die-stamping in different colours, but this practice died out with the advent of colourful dust-jackets after 1918.

A reaction against the stereotyped and mechanical processes of bindings led to the revival of fine handmade binding by private presses. This was largely inspired by William Morris, whose Kelmscott Press was responsible for some outstanding book binding. At the beginning of this century T.J. Cobden-Sanderson founded the Doves Press and bindery, which exercised great influence on the development of the private presses and artistic binding in Britain, Europe and the United States. Other English bindings of the early twentieth century which are highly prized include the work of Douglas Cockerell and Charles Ricketts of the Vale Press. The leaders of the artistic revival in the United States were Theodore De Vinne and

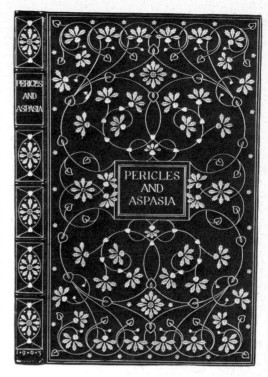

Right Binding for the *Rubáiyát of Omar Khayyám*, designed by Mary Houston, 1899.

Walter Gilliss at the end of the nineteenth century, while the bindings of Daniel Updike's Merrymount Press and Bruce Rogers at the Riverside Press represent the finest work in the early years of this century.

BOOK ENDS

Objects developed in the late nineteenth century to keep a row of books upright on a shelf or table top. They may be found in a wide variety of materials – cast iron or bronze, often gilded, being early favourites. In view of their function, solid construction was imperative, but at the turn of the century book ends with a cantilevered base, on which books themselves rested, came into fashion. By utilizing the weight of the books themselves this type of book end permitted a much lighter construction, and therefore greater scope in the design and materials. Book ends of this type may be found with a thin metal base, a wooden upright and a decorative motif carved in wood or fashioned in por-

celain. The ornamental designs frequently incorporated imitations of books, sometimes scattered 'artistically', but increasing use was made of tiny portrait busts of authors, poets and composers. Wrought metal book ends were popular in the early 1900s and examples in beaten pewter or copper enjoyed a certain vogue in the period when Art Nouveau was all the rage. In the 1920s new materials, such as bakelite and chromed metal, were often used in Art Deco book ends, though the inter-war period favoured a return to simpler motifs, human and animal figures predominating. Rustic book ends, largely of wood with imitation thatch, and examples in art pottery were fashionable in the same period. Book ends with ebony and ivory carvings of elephants were popular in the early twentieth century.

BOOK MARKERS

Book markers became popular in the mid-nineteenth century, when rising standards of literacy coincided with the advent of cheap books. Many of the early silk woven pictures produced by Stevens (see *Stevengraphs*) took the form of book markers, and although the majority of these were made in the late nineteenth century they have continued to appear to this day. Book markers were popular too with Sunday Schools and other religious organizations, which gave them away as prizes and incentives to deserving pupils. Occasionally these were silk markers, but mostly they were stout cards with chromolithographed pictures of biblical character and scenes, inscribed with the appropriate text. Trade cards, especially those produced by booksellers and publishers, often took the form of book markers, approximately six inches in length and an inch in width, and a one time they were inserted into every book sold.

Perforated card book markers became popular about 1850. Bristol board punctured with tiny holes set closely together wa worked with embroidery, resulting in miniaturized versions of those samplers with piou mottoes popular in an earlier age. Statione sold perforated cardboard in small format ready cut and often edged with fancy gilded or coloured borders. Embroidering book markers on perforated cardboard rivalled Berlin woolwork (q.v.) as a pastime fo young and old alike. Queen Victoria recorded in her journal (1872) a conversation with a old lady 'who worked me a book marker' From about 1870 American manufacturer even went so far as to print patterns on th cardboard, thereby minimizing the effort and imagination required.

The more permanent forms of book markers include those fashioned from thi slips of ebony or ivory. Pokerwork (q.v. book markers were popular in the earl years of this century, and leatherworl examples were produced in many parts o Europe as tourist mementoes. Book marker in sterling silver, brass or electroplate wer popular in the 1890s.

BOOKS, MINIATURE

Books under three inches in height com under this heading, their value depending more on the quality of binding, illustratio and type-setting rather than the actual con tent, although such well-defined categorie as miniature bibles, almanacs, children books and dictionaries each have their ow following.

Tiny editions of books first became popu lar in the seventeenth century and were in tended for carrying in pockets, which bega to appear in coats about this time. Miniature almanacs (q.v.) were among the first books of this sort, and in the eighteenth century there were many editions of these pocket-sized reference works. Tiny bibles were also fashionable, particularly in the mid-nineteenth century, when miniature bibles and prayer-books were printed in many languages in different parts of the world.

By the early nineteenth century the need for handy-sized books was of secondary importance to the typographic novelty of seeing who could exercise the greatest ingenuity in reproducing type and illustrations in minuscule dimensions. Books as small as a quarter-inch in height, with microscopic texts, have been recorded. Many of these were published specifically for furnishing dolls' houses. Miniature dictionaries and phrase-books for the traveller are produced to this day, but examples of miniature railway guides and steamship timetables in pristine condition are scarce.

BOTTLES

Blown-glass and earthenware bottles have been recorded since Roman times. The earthenware variety was predominant in the Middle Ages and examples are to be found from almost every part of Asia and Europe. With the revival of glassmaking in Europe from the fifteenth century onwards, glass gradually ousted pottery vessels, although earthenware bottles continued to be used for certain liquids (such as ginger or root beer) until recent times. Glass bottles were first made in England in the mid-seventeenth century and were very dark brown or green in colour. Many examples from this period onward bore a circular impressed device identifying the maker or the person for whom the bottle was made. Sealed glassware (q.v.) is a collectable subject in its own right.

The shape of bottles changed during the seventeenth and eighteenth centuries, the earlier types having squat, onion-shaped bodies and long, slender necks. Bodies became taller and necks shorter from about 1680 onwards. Early eighteenth-century

bottles had slightly curved bodies and square shoulders, while the present cylindrical form came into use about 1830. Machine-moulded bottles first appeared about 1840 and culminated in the fully automated processes patented by Owens of Toledo, Ohio, in the 1890s.

Glass bottles for wine were being made in Italy and southern Germany from the thirteenth century. Early bottles were usually tall and cylindrical or square-sided with a very short neck. By the sixteenth century the manufacture of wine bottles had spread to France and the Netherlands and more distinctive shapes had begun to appear. While the square-sided bottle remained popular, globular bodies had come into fashion and necks had become much longer. Considerable variety may be found in the wine bottles of the seventeenth and eighteenth centuries, particularly in the shape of the body, which was usually much fatter than most wine bottles of more recent manufacture. Relatively few bottles had flat bases; the majority had a pronounced basal kick or cavity so that the lees could gather in the narrow

27

trough round the inside of the bottom. With the advent of glass-moulding about 1820 the wine bottle industry was revolutionized and the tall cylindrical forms now universal came into use. Apart from their shapes, wine bottles of the period from 1650 to 1820 can often be dated by glass seals impressed on their sides.

Mineral-water bottles developed from about 1820 and evolved their own special shapes, dictated largely by the need to keep the contents airtight. Corks were used to seal bottles at first, and to ensure that the corks were kept moist and airtight the bottles had elliptical sides and pointed bottoms so that they could not be stood upright. The egg-shaped bottle, patented by William Hamilton in 1814, was widely used for this purpose throughout the nineteenth century, but was gradually superseded when improvements such as the screw stopper (1872), marble stopper (1875), swing stopper (1875) and crown cork (1892) were introduced. Beer and mineral-water bottles of the turn of the century were produced in pressed or moulded glass, which often bore elaborate inscriptions or pictorial motifs on the sides, neck and bottom. The distinctive Coca Cola bottle, which dates from this period, is an outstanding example of conservatism in packaging, for the shape has hardly altered in one hundred years. American bottles from the mid-nineteenth century onwards often appeared in fancy forms, of which the vertical ribbed and swirling spiral patterns were the most popular. Pictorial bottles with relief moulded patterns were also fashionable in America from 1830 to about 1870, and hundreds of different designs have been recorded. Fancy styles, epitomized by Jim Beam bottles, have been revived in recent years.

See also *Medicine Bottles, Scent Bottles, Snuff Bottles*

Below Amber glass bottle in the shape of an Indian princess, by Whitney Brothers, Glassboro, N.J.; late 19th century.

Below right Group of beer and mineral-water bottles; English, late 19th century.

BOULLE

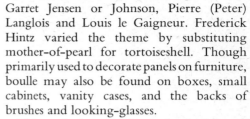

A form of marquetry, using tortoiseshell and brass, perfected by the French *maître ébéniste*, André-Charles Boulle (1642–1732). It is also known as Buhl work, which seems to have been a German phonetic version of the term. The technique was probably invented in Italy, and was practised by Italian craftsmen brought to France by Cardinal Mazarin about 1650, but it was developed into its present form by Boulle in the 1670s after he was appointed *ébéniste* to Louis XIV. Boulle work consists of thin sheets of brass and tortoiseshell fitted into the space left after cutting out the corresponding piece of brass, and *vice versa*. The inlaying of brass into tortoiseshell was known as *première-partie*, while the inlaying of tortoiseshell into brass was *contre-partie*. Both were used together, in contrasting bands on the same piece of furniture, or separate in matched pairs. Though brass was the alloy most commonly used, ivory, hardwoods, pewter and even silver were occasionally substituted.

The techniques spread to the Low Countries and thence to England at the beginning of the eighteenth century. Significantly most of the leading exponents of boulle in England were of Dutch or French origin and included

Garret Jensen or Johnson, Pierre (Peter) Langlois and Louis le Gaigneur. Frederick Hintz varied the theme by substituting mother-of-pearl for tortoiseshell. Though primarily used to decorate panels on furniture, boulle may also be found on boxes, small cabinets, vanity cases, and the backs of brushes and looking-glasses.

This technique attained the highest of perfection in the mid-eighteenth century, being particularly associated with Louis Quinze furniture. The first, and most expensive examples belong to the period from 1730 to 1780. Though this sumptuous form of decoration died out in France at the time of the Revolution, it was revived in the early nineteenth century. By that time, however, the rising costs of materials and craftsmanship precluded the use of boulle on a large scale for furniture, but it was applied extensively to small decorative items.
See colour plate page 87

BOXES

The collectable varieties of box range in size from the diminutive pill and patch boxes, through snuff boxes, matchboxes and pounce boxes, to the larger forms such as knife boxes, work boxes, bandboxes and bible boxes (qq.v.). Boxes classified by their materials are described more fully under Mauchline, Pontypool and Tunbridge wares (qq.v.), while the more mechanical or novelty boxes are discussed under money boxes and musical boxes (qq.v.).

Other categories not listed separately which are of interest to the collector, include trinket boxes of all kinds, the slim boxes used formerly to contain gloves, and small presentation silver items such as cigarette boxes. Boxes for rings, collar studs and other forms of jewelry were often constructed of silver, and decorated with semi-precious stones or enamelling in keeping with their elegant function. Small boxes with sloping bottoms and one, two or three compartments were designed to house postage stamps and were popular between 1840 and 1910; they may be found in silver, brass, ivory, wood or

Above Style of Coca-Cola bottle in use from 1901 to 1916.

Below Casket with boulle decoration of brass on tortoiseshell, with ormolu mounts; French, early 18th century.

Above Pennsylvania German bride box made of cedar with painted decoration; late 18th century.

Right Group of stamp boxes in Tunbridge and Mauchline ware and silver; 19th century.

porcelain and many have tiny glass apertures in their lids.

In recent years novelty tinware boxes for tobacco, chocolate, sweets and biscuits have attracted the attention of collectors. The more common shapes include hearts and octagons, but those in the form of books, bells and even coaches are worth looking for. Many of these tinware boxes were presented to schoolchildren in celebration of coronations, jubilees and other royal events. Less decorative, commercially produced boxes, inscribed with the names and advertisements of patent medicines and countless mundane consumer goods of yester-year are now being avidly collected. Special gift boxes bearing regimental insignia or naval crests, or the portraits of royalty on the lids, were prepared in connection with 'troop comforts' in both world wars, and are an important branch of militaria (q.v.). Boxes were also used extensively in America as souvenirs of

presidential inaugurations. Tinware cand boxes with patriotic motifs were also popul at the time of the Spanish-American W (1898–99).

BRASS

Although horse brasses (q.v.) are the bes known and most popular form of antiqu in this alloy of copper and zinc, there a many other examples of small brass objec which are highly collectable. Copper allo were widely manufactured from ancie times and brass is best associated with th monumental plaques found in mediev churches. Brass objects were mainly produce by casting, using the *cire-perdue* process, b the use of sheet brass for stamping o articles spread gradually during the secon half of the eighteenth century. In Englan the Worshipful Company of Founders w in existence by the fourteenth century, not earlier, and their members were engaged in the manufacture of saddlery equipment, candlesticks, ewers and pots. The Company of Braziers, formed at a similar date, manufactured brass objects by the application of heat and hammering. By the early eighteenth century brass manufacturing was carried out in the London area, Bristol and, at a later date, in Birmingham, which eventually became the world's largest producer in the nineteenth century, following the introduction of revolutionary techniques of mechanization by Boulton and Watt. Much of the brassware used in Colonial America was imported from Bristol or Birmingham, but by the 1760s braziers from Birmingham were setting up business in New England, and this indigenous industry grew rapidly in the aftermath of Independence. Connecticut and New Jersey were the centres of the American brass industry by the late eighteenth century, but articles which can definitely be attributed to the period before 1850 are very scarce.

Collectable items include a wide range of implements associated with the hearth. Brass andirons (q.v.) and firedogs were often highly ornate, with coats of arms, baluster columns and animal or human figures. Trivets, fenders, pokers, dustpan-and-brush sets, coal scuttles and those elaborate coal-boxes known as purdoniums come into this category. Bells (q.v.) provide numerous examples of brassware, from hand-bells and rumblers to cow bells. Bell-pulls were often cast in brass and many of them are attractively designed. Elaborate door-knobs and knockers may be found worked in brass, as well as numerous examples of small furniture mounts, such as handles, locks and hinge-plates. From the mid-eighteenth century onwards buttons (q.v.) were often cast or stamped in brass, and their designs often incorporate heraldic devices or insignia.

Lighting equipment of all kinds is a rich field, which includes candlesticks (q.v.), snuffers, wax-jacks, bougies, lamps (q.v.), lanterns and wick-trimmers. There are numerous examples of brassware which relate to the kitchen, such as mote skimmers, ladles, and pots and pans, ranging in size from diminutive saucepans to jelly pans. The more decorative items include kettles and sets of measures (qq.v.). Meat jacks or spit jacks were invented in the late seventeenth century and enabled meat to be rotated slowly by means of a simple clockwork mechanism. The late eighteenth- and nineteenth-century examples had ornate brass casings and are often very decorative. Warming pans, pipe stoppers, writing cases and balances (q.v.) are other collectable items in which brass is largely employed.

BRAZIERS AND FOOD WARMERS

The problem of keeping food reasonably hot must have been a serious one in the vast baronial castles and mansions of the Middle Ages. By the time the food was brought all the way from the kitchens to the dining table it was getting cold and the gravy was congealed. It was necessary, therefore, to have various devices for re-heating food or keeping it warm. Small portable stoves and braziers, which stood on a sideboard or even on the dining table itself, were usually made of brass, as their name suggests, though copper

Brass teapot by C.F.A. Voysey, c. 1896.

or iron may also be found. A bowl containing
charcoal was pierced to let the heat radiate,
and many decorative patterns were used in
the fretted sides and lid. A later and more
elegant version of this was the chafing dish,
also found in brass or copper with similar
pierced ornament. Chafing dishes had long
handles of polished hardwood or even ivory
and had wide rims on which pewter serving
dishes could be kept hot. A few have been
recorded in silver and these date mainly from
the mid-eighteenth century.

Braziers were also employed for general
heating purposes, usually in the form of a
portable heater, which could be carried around
from one room to another. The smallest
examples were used as foot warmers, often
mounted in special wooden cases and placed
in carriages in cold weather (hence the
alternative name of carriage warmer). Their
construction and decoration follow the same
patterns as braziers in general, but they often
incorporated upholstery and had short turned
wooden legs like footstools.

Apart from braziers, food warmers include small spirit lamps, in copper, brass o
silver, with matching trivets and crosses
and these were fashionable from the middl
of the eighteenth century onwards. Othe
warmers included an inner receptacle con
taining hot water to maintain the food at a
even temperature. The veilleuse was a ta
beaker made in porcelain or earthenware
used to warm gruel and other invalid foo
These should be collected with matchin
gruel bowls which were placed on to
Similar warmers, with ceramic beakers o
top, were fashionable in the late eighteent
century as tea warmers, when tea wa
stewed rather than brewed. Among th
smaller items which were briefly popular i
the nineteenth century were patent eg
warmers and spoon warmers and a wid
variety of individual hot plates using spir
lamps.

BRISTOL GLASS

The manufacture of fine quality glass wa
established in the town of Bristol in th
eighteenth century, and although a wid
variety of glass was produced there, and i
the neighbouring villages of Nailsea an
Stanton Drew, the name has come to b
applied to certain types of opaque white o
translucent coloured glass, much of whic
had no actual connection with Bristol.

In the mid-eighteenth century tea caddie
vases, cruet sets, jars and even candlestick
were produced in this form of opaque whit
glass, which resembled porcelain. Many o
these items were decorated with chinoiseri
motifs, but the most highly prized object
are those painted with enamels by Michae
Edkins, one of the finest Bristol craftsmer
The most characteristic type of Bristol glas
was the very deep blue or magenta glas
used in the manufacture of decanters, whic
were inscribed with the names of wines an
spirits in gilded lettering. Scent bottle
(q.v.), finger bowls, vases, dishes and pos
holders (q.v.) were also produced in this glass

The term 'Nailsea' is used rather loosely t
describe a type of mixed coloured glas

bells, as well as animals and birds. The more elaborate examples include lighthouses, full-rigged ships and fountains, complete with birds and flowers. Many of these novelty items were inscribed with mottoes such as 'Be true to me', 'Forget me not' or 'Ever thine', and decorated with lovers' knots and hearts.

BRONZE

Alloy of copper and tin, though zinc and lead are often added to produce greater durability and fusibility respectively. Articles of bronze are widely distributed throughout the world and are known to have been produced in Europe and Asia as far back as 2500 BC, if not earlier. Bronze is almost entirely used for cast metal objects (apart from its application to coins and medallions, die-stamped from metal flans and strips). Before the advent of iron, bronze was used for weapons and utensils, as well as a wide range of useful articles, such as lamps, basins and mirrors. Because of the poisonous nature of copper oxides, bronze, in its pure form, could not be used for vessels associated with food or drink, but this problem was overcome by lining bronze utensils with a thin deposit of tin or silver. Bronze was also used extensively in the casting of door handles, knobs and knockers, drawer handles, wall brackets and sconces, which were usually given some form of ornamentation. Smaller bronze items of collectable interest include bells, book ends, lamps, napkin rings, buckles, inkstands and inkpots, buttons and pipe stoppers (qq.v.).

Bronze is usually associated with figurines, which were cast in a number of ways. The oldest technique is *cire perdue* (lost wax), which was practised by the Sumerians, Egyptians and other eastern Mediterranean civilizations. This required a model of solid wax over which a mould was formed of some refractory material. Molten bronze was poured into the mould to melt out the wax and, after cooling, the mould was broken away from the cast. This was a comparatively expensive method, since only one cast could

known as marble glass. It is sometimes called slagware or end-of-day ware, for the workers in the glasshouses made use of the waste glass or slag at the end of the day in order to produce toys and novelties, which their wives and families could then sell to supplement their meagre wages. It describes also various kinds of fancy glass, ranging from the coloured glass with white flecks or streaks to the distinctive smoky-green glass fashioned into many different types of ornament.

Glass rolling-pins (q.v.) and walking sticks, hung over the fireplace as a form of good-luck charm, were especially popular in Bristol or Nailsea glass. Another kind of talisman was the witch ball (q.v.), made in coloured glass with the inner surface coated with contrasting colours. A wide variety of useful articles was produced in Bristol glass, including mugs, vases and flasks, toilet articles, such as jugs and ewers, biscuit barrels and oil lamps. The toys and novelties comprised miniature bellows, hats, slippers and

Cast bronze head of a queen mother (*iyoba*) from Benin, Nigeria, where highly sophisticated bronze castings had been made since the 14th century; *c.* 16th century.

make further moulds. The moulds wer lined with wax, with a refractory core in th centre. The wax was melted out as the molte bronze was poured in, producing hollov casts. Theoretically, innumerable casts coul be made from one mould, but in practice th moulds deteriorated rapidly and the cas required a considerable amount of afte work, in the form of chasing, chiselling an filing. This method, which is still used, therefore applied to limited editions.

A cheaper process was developed in th nineteenth century using fine sand instead c plaster moulds. This permitted the bronz founders to cast small figures in much large quantities, though they lacked the technic: perfection of bronzes cast by the mor traditional method. The industry was revc lutionized in the mid-nineteenth century b the adoption of electrotyping, by whic relatively thin bronze deposits could b applied to a mass-produced mould coate with plumbago. The resulting bronzes ar much thinner than cast figures, have a mor even surface and lack the 'ring' of the ca metal. This method was used widely in th manufacture of *bronzes de l'ameublemer* (bronzes used in interior decoration).

Nineteenth-century *bronzes d'édition*, prc duced in large quantities using the sand-ca: method, are still fairly plentiful. Thes figures fall into several categories: reduction of large and well-known pieces of statuary reproductions of classical figures; sentiment: compositions and allegorical groups. The were produced in Europe and North Americ to supply the rising middle-class market an were thus higher in the social scale than the ceramic counterparts, such as Rogers group and Staffordshire flat-back figures (qq.v. Groups featuring birds and animals ar particularly popular with collectors. Ani malier bronzes take their name from th French school originally known contemp tuously as *les Animaliers* and headed b Antoine-Louis Barye. These bronzes wer immensely popular between 1830 and th end of the nineteenth century, and althoug the majority were produced in France the were also produced in Britain, German

be taken from each mould and model, and the resulting bronze was solid and therefore wasteful of metal. The first improvement consisted of using refractory cores over which the wax was modelled and the mould then formed round the wax. The wax was melted out as before and the mould was broken after casting, but considerable saving of metal was achieved by producing hollow casts in this way. A third method consisted of making models in clay or terracotta (q.v.) and forming moulds in two halves over the model, which could then be preserved to

Right Painted wooden bucket; American, early 18th century.

Italy, Russia and the United States to a lesser extent. The revival in the fashion for animal sculpture in recent years has led to a marked re-appraisal of the work of the nineteenth-century Animaliers. The bronzes of Barye, Rosa Bonheur and a few others were produced in limited editions but most of the others were sand cast. Similar figures were cast in England in iron, and in Berlin using a zinc alloy (q.v.). Figures of cowboys, Indians and cavalrymen, evoking the spirit of the Wild West were sculpted by Frederic Remington in the Animalier tradition and cast in limited editions.

Bronze acquires a surface colouring known as patina which, though in effect a form of rust, should not be removed since it protects the surface from further corrosion and is usually a most attractive feature. The patina varies from dark brown to bright green, depending on the presence of salts, oxides and sulphides in the atmosphere or the soil, but other effects may be artificially induced by various pickling processes. Bronzes have also been silvered or gilt, the latter being especially fashionable in eighteenth-century France under the name of ormolu (q.v.).

Bronze vase featuring Loie Fuller by H. St Lerche and stamped Louchet, *c.* 1900.

BUCKETS

These utilitarian objects yield a surprising amount of scope for collectors. Leather buckets with copper or brass studs were widely used in the seventeenth to nineteenth centuries and, when highly polished, are attractive items. More decorative, however, are those buckets, of leather, wood (bound with copper bands) or metal (usually copper or brass) bearing painted or engraved insignia. Royal coats of arms and monograms, civic emblems and naval or military insignia greatly enhance the value of such items. Silver ice buckets became fashionable in the eighteenth century; later examples were manufactured in Sheffield plate, while electro-plate became popular from about 1840.

At the other extreme are children's sand buckets, produced from the late nineteenth century. The earlier examples in tinware and toleware had relatively formal floral painted decoration; those with Art Nouveau motifs are the most highly prized. Later examples bore gaily coloured seaside scenes or pictures of children and animals at play. Of particular interest are those buckets featuring Mickey Mouse and other cartoon characters, and authenticated early examples in this genre are now very desirable.

37

Group of shoe buckles in brass, iron and cut glass; English, late 18th century.

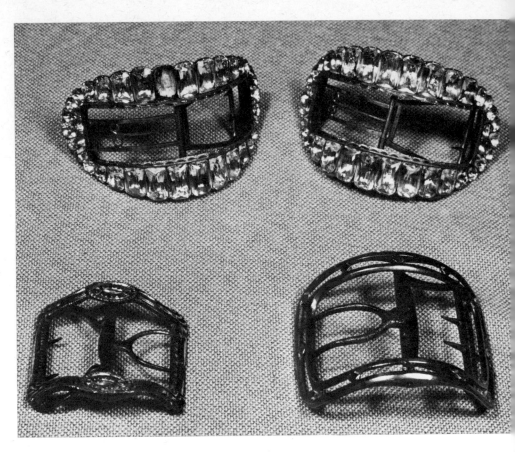

BUCKLES

These fastenings for belts and straps date back to Roman times and, as important dress accessories, often reflected contemporary styles in the applied arts. Examples can be found which exhibit almost every technique of construction and ornament known to metalworkers over the past 2,000 years and may be found in every kind of metal from gold and silver to brass, bronze and iron. Buckles of non-metallic substances include wood, bone, horn, tortoiseshell and ivory. Shoe buckles, fashionable from the seventeenth century, form a large group in themselves. Among the novelty buckles popular in the late nineteenth century were small garter clips and suspender buckles, often embellished with *risqué* motifs or good-luck charms. Tiny buckles for watch-straps, hat-bands, sashes and veils often had decorative guards in electroplate or sterling silver. Faceted steel buckles were fashionable in Europe from the late eighteenth century. Belt-buckles with regimental badges are among the most popular forms of militaria (q.v.) but other highly collectable groups include those with the emblems of fire services, police forces and youth movements. The belt-buckles worn by Wells Fargo drivers and guards were unusually large and elaborately engraved or cast with animal and human figures, scenery and early American landmarks.

BUTTER ITEMS

Several types of collectable object have been produced in connection with butter, either in its manufacture or in its use, and range from churns and coolers to moulds and butter-pats. The churns in which the cream is converted into butter vary in size from the large, slightly conical variety favoured in many European countries, to the tiny table models in which the barrel is rotated by a handle. Butter churns were frequently decorated with carving, poker-work or hand-painted floral patterns and are a distinct branch of European folk art. Various patent devices were produced in the nineteenth and early twentieth centuries for home butter-making, and those with polished wood surfaces and brass working parts make attractive ornaments. Special earthenware vessels were produced as butter coolers and may be recognized by the matching dish in which they stood. Water poured into the outer dish seeped through the porous walls of the vessel by capillary attraction and the resulting evaporation reduced the temperature of the interior. These butter coolers may

be found with patterns scratched in their surfaces. Slabs of wood with designs carved intaglio, or pottery plaques of a similar appearance, were used as butter moulds, to impress a pictorial motif in relief on the pat of butter. Traditional designs vary from country to country and a very large number of different patterns can be assembled. As butter moulds are made to this day, they form an interesting and unusual tourist souvenir.

Silver dishes with pierced and fretted sides and shallow glass liners were used from the mid-eighteenth century as butter dishes. Appropriate pastoral decoration (cows and dairymaids were popular subjects) on the sides or lids of these vessels indicate their purpose. These elegant dishes were also made in Sheffield plate or electroplate. Later butter dishes were made of pressed or moulded glass, and may also be found in every kind of pottery and porcelain. The latter offer a

Worcester porcelain butter dish and cover; 18th century.

Pennsylvania German
ceramic butter mould;
19th century.

stores, and the examples in this category are
eminently collectable, since they exhibit a
wide range of ornamentation on their
handles. Flowers and foliage predominate,
but novelty types featured animals, birds and
human figures. Classical poses were popular
in the 1890s. They were produced in electroplate, bronze, silver or brass, in ivory or wood
inlaid with ivory, bone, horn or mother-of-
pearl. A few may be found incorporating
small penknives, toothpicks and other
gadgets.

BUTTONS

Small knobs or discs originally attached to
clothing or other articles for decorative effect
but later employed to secure garments. In
their original function buttons were known
to the Egyptians and Persians, who ornamented their clothes with small buttons of
gold, silver, glass or earthenware. In *Piers
Plowman* (1377) there is a reference to a knife
whose scabbard was with 'botones ouergylt',
while the original English translation of
Froissart's *Chronicles* (1525) mentions a book
covered with crimson velvet with 'ten
botons of syluer and gylte'. Purely decorative buttons have continued to this day,
particularly on women's dress; but functional
buttons were beginning to appear in Europe
by the late thirteenth century, and the
expression 'not worth a button' was in use
in England a century later. Buttons of gold
conferred as a mark of approbation, are
referred to in the Old Testament and are the
ancestor of today's medals and decorations.
In China a button on the hat denoted an
official of high rank, and different grades of
mandarin were distinguished by buttons of
different colours and compositions – the
original of Foote's 'grand Panjandrum himself, with the little round button at top'.

Numerous varieties of button have been
produced in connection with clothing, but
they may be divided into two categories. In
one they are provided with a shank (either
a metal loop or a tuft of material) through
which the thread is passed to secure them to
the cloth; in the other they are pierced with

reasonably inexpensive medium for collecting a wide range of ceramics from different
countries and manufacturers. Tub-shaped
butter dishes with matching lids were also
made in pottery (similar examples with a
bee motif on the lid were intended for
honey).

Small butter-knives with scimitar blades
were introduced in the eighteenth century,
sometimes with porcelain handles matching
butter dishes, but more often found with
ivory, ebony or mother-of-pearl handles.

BUTTON HOOKS

Slim metal hooks, somewhat similar to
crochet hooks, with handles about six inches
in length, were indispensable when high
buttoned boots were fashionable. Smaller
hooks of a more delicate construction, were
used to secure the buttons on gloves. Both
kinds were extensively used in Europe and
America in the second half of the nineteenth
century but died out by the time of World
War I. They may be found in two distinct
categories. Trade items were given away
with purchases by haberdashers and boot-
shops, and were either plain or had the firm's
name engraved on the handle. Button hooks
were also sold by jewelers and fancy goods

two or more holes, for sewing directly on to the cloth. Further variation consists of simple or composite buttons, the latter comprising two or more layers sandwiched together. Until the early nineteenth century composite buttons were laboriously sewn together but about 1807 B. Sanders, a Dane resident in Birmingham, devised a method of producing them mechanically. The Sanders buttons consisted of twin metal discs locking together and enclosing a piece of card or cloth. At first they had rigid metal shanks but from about 1825 flexible shanks were used. Sanders revolutionized the Birmingham button trade, which captured the world markets with buttons of infinite variety of shape, material and decoration. These ranged from gold, silver, filigree work, inlaid silver on brass, the use of semi-precious stones and glass paste

cameos, to more utilitarian buttons in ivory, bone, shell, horn, mother-of-pearl, glass, porcelain, wood, card and early attempts at plastic substances derived from bull's blood and milk casein. Faceted steel buttons were produced in Birmingham from the 1760s. Glass and porcelain buttons of exquisite workmanship were a speciality of Bohemia, while enamelled buttons were produced in France. Glass-topped buttons enclosing tiny pictures, became fashionable about 1775, while cameo buttons, carved from shell or some other nacreous substance, were produced in Italy in the early years of the nineteenth century. The mechanical production of cloth-covered buttons spread from England to the United States in 1827. Early manufacturers whose buttons are now very collectable include Samuel Williston of Easthampton and the Haydens of Haydenville.

Although brass buttons were first produced in Birmingham in 1689, it was not until the improvements introduced by Matthew Boulton Senior in the 1740s that brass buttons became widespread. In this category come heraldic buttons impressed with the coats of arms of gentleman and worn with the livery of their servants. After 1740 brass buttons were used increasingly for the coats and tunics of soldiers and sailors, and these form an important aspect of militaria (q.v.). Zinc buttons were used by German troops in World War I and various kinds of plastic buttons were used by combatants in World War II, but the more traditional brass form is still that most widely employed.

Buttons are also worn as a form of miniature badge in the lapels of coats and jackets. This practice, of European origin in the nineteenth century, is now world-wide, both to denote the holder of a decoration and to indicate membership of a political faction. The latter aspect has long been particularly popular in the United States and an enormous collection of political buttons, portraying leading politicians and presidential candidates, or emblems of the political parties, can be formed for a reasonable outlay.

election of 19th-century rench and English uttons.

CADDY SPOONS

Silver spoons used in conjunction with tea caddies (q.v.). They seem to have originated in eighteenth-century England and, on account of the English tea-drinking habit, have always been a predominantly English item, though examples may be found in other European countries and America. Eighteenth- and early nineteenth-century examples were made of silver or occasionally silver-gilt, since tea-drinking was very largely the prerogative of the wealthier classes. Later examples were made of Sheffield plate and from about 1840 electroplate was common.

The styling of caddy spoons has varied over the years, though the unusually large bowl has remained a constant feature. The earliest caddy spoons had leaf-shaped bowls, often highly ornate with foliate patterns, but later bowls were scallop-shaped, rectangular or formed like miniature ladles. On the earliest spoons the handle was short and narrow ending in a point, the purpose of which was to clear tea-leaves clogging the strainer holes in the teapot. Later spoons had short handles with rounded ends. Novelty spoons in unusual shapes became popular at the end of the nineteenth century and spoons with enamelled crests and coats of arms sold as tourist mementoes date from the same time.

Design for a silver caddy spoon, based on the wild anemone, by Higgins of London; from the Great Exhibition *Catalogue*, 1851.

CAKE STANDS

Wooden or metal stands holding cake plates evolved in the second half of the nineteenth century as part of the ritual of afternoon tea in the drawing room. Many of the earlier examples were over-ornamented in the pre-vailing florid styles, but by the 1870 functionalism triumphed and lighter, mor elegant cake stands predominated. Th majority consisted of one or more upright supported on tripod legs, with brackets fron which cake plates were either suspended o held. The usual arrangement was in tiers, on above the other, but the more elabora types had groups of two, three or four pla holders on the same level radiating from central pole. They were produced *en sui* with tea trolleys and other pieces of furnitur or as individual items. They were admirab suited to such materials as bentwood an bamboo, which were immensely popular the turn of the century. Other variation include stands with circular or rectangula wooden platters, or stands with silver c silver-plated handles and frames.

CAMEOS

Strictly speaking, this term may be applie to any small, two-dimensional sculpture low relief, in any precious, semi-precious beautiful substance. The earliest-know cameos were produced in Egypt 4,000 yea ago and numerous examples of these gen have survived to this day. Cameos we fashioned from glass by the Romans, a glass of various colours and degrees opacity has remained a popular medium f cameos down to the present time. U doubtedly the greatest stimulus for this a was provided by James Tassie in the mi eighteenth century; Tassie's improved glas paste, coupled with the high artistic quali of his gems, revolutionized the art of t cameo, and Tassie gems are among tho most highly esteemed nowadays.

Cameo glass medallion of William Pitt the Younger by James Tassie; late 18th century.

Cameos in shell, cut in such a way as to reveal the different layers, colour variations and textures of the material, did not become fashionable until the fifteenth century. Although cameos have possessed an enduring popularity over the centuries, they seem to have been particularly fashionable in the Middle Ages, during the Renaissance and in the period from 1740 to 1850. There has been a revival of interest in cameos as jewelry in the past two decades, but their antiquarian interest has always been considerable.

In gem-engraving only soft stones and metals can be worked freehand without cutting tools, whereas the harder stones require the use of the wheel technique. Early cameos were worked with variously shaped drills ending in balls, discs and cylinders, which were made to rotate with the aid of a wheel. Later the stone to be engraved was fastened to a handle, and was held to the head of a rotating drill and moved as the work required. The actual cutting was not done by the drills direct but by the abrasive action of the powder which was rubbed on the stone with the drill. Usually diamond powder mixed with oil was employed, but in the earliest times emery powder is thought to

Gold-mounted shell cameo brooch, carved in the Cinquecento manner, 1865.

have been used. After cutting, the gem was polished.

Although the glass-paste cameos of Tassie and his imitators went into eclipse by the middle of the nineteenth century, cameos in gem-stones of various kinds became extremely fashionable in Britain from 1855 onwards, when Thomas Cook began offering cheap Continental holidays. Many tourists returned from Italy with cameos, especially those cut from lava. Consequently Italian cameos of the latter half of the nineteenth century are relatively plentiful.

Cameos were also moulded in pottery, the best-known examples being the jasperware cameos of Josiah Wedgwood, which are produced to this day.
See also *Intaglios*

CANDLE ITEMS

Apart from candlesticks (q.v.) there are several collectable items which are associated with the old-fashioned candle. Special boxes, with sloping lids and an attachment for suspension from a wall, were used to hold candles, and were widely produced all over Europe and North America until the advent of gas and electric lighting in the nineteenth century. The earlier examples were made of wood and resemble knife boxes (q.v.), but they do not have the tell-tale lining and interior apertures. From the late eighteenth century candle boxes were made in metal, and the surfaces were often japanned. These boxes were a speciality of Pontypool (q.v.). Candle boxes were also produced in brass or copper sheet, in cylindrical form with a flattened back for hanging from a wall.

Douters and snuffers are related classes of object, which often appear similar to the uninitiated and are often confused in popular parlance. Douters or extinguishers resemble pairs of scissors with flattened, spade ends which gripped the candle wick and put out the flame. Snuffers, despite their name, were intended to make the flame more efficient rather than put it out. They also look like scissors, but have pointed ends and an ingenious trap arrangement (like a small lidded pan) which secured the burnt end of the wick and prevented it from falling into the molten wax below. Other extinguishers were simple cones with a knob at the pointed end (held between finger and thumb) and a square-section hook projecting from one side for anchoring the extinguisher to the candle-stand when not in use. These objects were made in silver, pewter, brass or bronze to match the candlesticks.

Bougie boxes were small, drum-shaped containers in which coils of wax tapers were held. The end of the taper projected through an aperture in the lid. These boxes were usually fitted with a handle and an extinguisher. The sides and lid were often richly decorated, with engraving, chasing or piercing, sometimes incorporating an inner glass vessel. They were made in Europe of silver or brass and were also fashionable in Britain in the late eighteenth and early nineteenth centuries. A similar device was the wax-jack (known in America as a pull-up), consisting of a small reel on a stand with a circular opening at the top. A key was provided at one side to wind or unwind the wax taper, and a conical extinguisher at the other side. Wax-jacks and bougie boxes have also been recorded in Sheffield plate, though silver was more commonly used.

Group of candle items: adjustable candle holder, wooden rush-light holder, metal rush-light holder, candle mould, rush-light holder with extinguisher, and snuffers; English, 17th–19th centuries.

Silver candlestick and snuffers by Joseph Lownes, Philadelphia; late 18th century.

CANDLESTICKS

Candlesticks were made in Europe from about the tenth century, if not earlier, mainly for church use. The earliest authenticated English example, dating from the early twelfth century, was made for the Monastery of St Peter, Gloucester, and is a remarkably fine example of medieval cast brass. The earliest candlesticks were of the pricket type, having a spike set in the top to impale the candle. This type survived into the middle of the seventeenth century, but as candles became slimmer the familiar nozzle variety of candlestick was evolved. From the fifteenth century onwards, candles became widespread in domestic use; examples may be dated according to the shape of the rim, the presence and positioning of the grease-pan, the shape of the column (fluted, plain, baluster or knopped). By the beginning of the eighteenth century the grease-pan had been replaced by an enlarged socket rim. The shape of the base also varied from one generation to the next, from plain rectangular, to pyramidal, to polygonal and finally, in the eighteenth century, to the scrolled columns and foliate decoration of the baroque and rococo styles. There was a return to simpler forms in the early nineteenth century, betraying classical influence, but more florid styles predominated in the Victorian period. Art Nouveau candlesticks from the late nineteenth century occasionally had female figures cast as the support, with the socket held in an outstretched hand.

Candlesticks were originally cast in sections but from the mid-eighteenth century sheet-metal die-stamped candlesticks were more common. A wide range of metals was used for cast candlesticks, from gold and silver to brass, bronze and pewter. Silver candlesticks were popular with the wealthier classes in the eighteenth century, while Sheffield plate was used extensively for the less expensive models and brass was a perennial favourite. The use of pewter died out about 1720, was revived around 1800 and finally declined in the latter half of the nineteenth century. Gun metal was occasion-

Right Glass candlestick with dolphin shaft by Sandwich Glass Company; American, 1840.

Right Cane handles in red agate with malacca and ivory shafts and silver mounts; English, late 19th century.

ally used from the late eighteenth century onwards. Relatively few candlesticks were made of non-metallic substances, though glass was popular in the eighteenth century and many examples were fashioned in pottery and porcelain, paralleling the styles found in metal.

Miniature versions are known as taper sticks and were fashionable in the eighteenth century for use on writing desks. While bracket candlesticks (attached to pianos and writing bureaux) are fairly common, wall candlesticks, or sconces, are rare, having gone out of fashion in the early eighteenth century. Chambersticks or chamber candlesticks had short, stubby sockets with broad, saucer-shaped pans and a ring or handle at the side. They may be found in silver, brass, Sheffield plate, electroplate or pottery and were widely used until the advent of electric light.

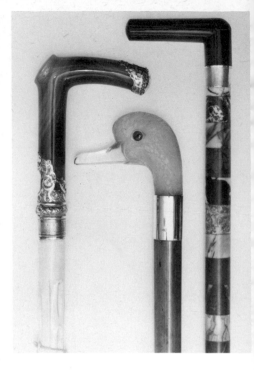

CANES AND WALKING-STICKS

Walking-sticks and canes became fashionable in the eighteenth century as the wearing of swords by non-military gentlemen went into decline. Many early examples combined the functions of a walking-stick with an edged weapon by concealing within their shaft a slender steel blade. Rare nineteenth-century walking-sticks of both European and American manufacture even concealed a small pistol in the handle. Air canes were dual-purpose sticks and firearms, using compressed air to discharge a small bullet. There seems to have been no limit to the ingenuity and gadgetry incorporated in nineteenth-century walking-sticks. Some may be found with a built-in torch, a concept which seems to date back to about 1785, as an aid to the gentleman 'walking abroad' after dark in the poorly lit streets of that period. Comparatively plentiful are canes and sticks with detachable heads which open to reveal small spirit flasks.

From the collector's viewpoint the most interesting items are the canes of the mid-eighteenth to late nineteenth centuries, designed for use by both sexes and often highly ornate. The handles, which are collectable on their own, were made of gold, silver-gilt,

silver, brass, ivory, horn, porcelain, ebony and glass, with inlay or filigree decoration. The more elaborate examples had human and animal figures cast on the handles or were intricately carved or chased with floral and foliate patterns.

Although wood or cane were the most common materials used for the shafts of walking-sticks some unusual materials may be encountered. Dried kale-stalks preserved by varnishing were used in Scotland to produce surprisingly light but strong walking-sticks. Glass walking-sticks were not intended for actual use, but served as lucky charms hung over fireplaces. These were a speciality of the Bristol (q.v.) glass-houses. Canes and sticks whose gold or silver heads are decorated with regimental badges form an important branch of militaria (q.v.).

CARD CASES

Cases fashionable in Britain in the eighteenth and nineteenth centuries, when the ritual of calling and leaving one's card was strictly

Silver card case engraved
with a goldfish in Japanese
style by Deakin & Francis,
London, 1882.

CARICATURES AND CARTOONS

The art form known as *caricatura*, or portraits in which characteristic features have been ludicrously exaggerated, can be traced back to classical Greece; but in its modern form the caricature originated early in the seventeenth century in Italy, where it was widely used in satirical medals and political broadsheets. It spread to France and Germany and thence to the Low Countries, England and America, where it reached the height of popularity in the late eighteenth and early nineteenth centuries. Playing cards (q.v.) bearing caricatures of public figures were popular in the eighteenth century. Gentlemen such as Lord Bute and Charles Fox were frequently caricatured in the form of jackboots and foxes with human physiognomy, but the majority of caricatures were less extreme. Conversely, nineteenth-century caricatures humanized animals (the British lion by Tenniel is a prime example) or inanimate objects.

Some idea of the extent of caricatures may be gained from the fact that F.G. Stephens catalogued over 4,000 satirical prints in the British Museum dating before 1770 alone, and those produced in the ensuing two centuries run into hundreds of thousands as this medium was universally applied. Hogarth, Sandby, Rowlandson, Cruikshank and Gillray are among the acknowledged masters of the British caricature, while George Townshend took the playing-card cartoon and developed satirical cards as a separate medium in the 1760s. S.W. Fores of Piccadilly pioneered the series or folio of caricatures and extended the range of subjects to cover every aspect of life. The pictorial Mulready envelopes of 1840–41 were parodied extensively by many publishers and these Mulready caricatures are of particular interest to philatelists and postal historians. Victorian caricature was dominated by the works of Richard Doyle and Robert Seymour, whose lithographic cartoons were published in monthly sets by McLean. Other caricaturists whose works are now sought after include John Leech, 'Phiz'

observed. The custom seems to have arisen in the seventeenth century and was derived from the habit of leaving one's name and address written on the back of a playing card. This determined the rather large format of calling cards for almost 200 years, and hence the size of the card cases. With the reduction in the size of visiting cards to their present format the fashion for card cases declined.

As an indispensable object of vertu, however, the card case attracted the attention of jewelers and craftsmen, and although their shape was strictly limited on account of their purpose, an infinite variety of materials and decorative styles may be found. Silk- or leather-covered card was the most common type, but card cases were also made of silver, Sheffield plate, Britannia metal, mother-of-pearl, ivory, hardwoods and lacquered papier mâché. Many of the late eighteenth-century examples were beautifully decorated with vignettes in polychrome enamels. Silver card cases with elaborate borders and views of famous landmarks and identifiable scenery are among those most prized today.

Satirical cartoon by
William Charles;
American, early 19th
century.

THE GHOST of a DOLLAR or the BANKERS SURPRIZE

(Hablot K. Browne), 'Ape', 'Spy', and Max Beerbohm in the early years of this century.

Caricature was widely practised in Europe, France being in the forefront with such exponents as Honoré Daumier, Gustave Doré and Gavarni, and the most prolific artist of them all, Charles Philipon, founder of *La Caricature* and *Le Charivari* as well as other satirical or humorous papers. Satirical cartoons and caricatures may be found from every European country from the early nineteenth century onwards. Although a rather crude form of cartoon was prevalent in America in the late Colonial period, its more sophisticated brands originated with the works of William Charles, an émigré Scot, who was a brilliant propagandist for his adopted country during the War of 1812. Charles's cartoons were in the savage vein associated with Gillray, but a more refined style of caricature was evolved by Thomas Nast, whose cartoons dominated the American scene during the second half of the nineteenth century and reached their peak during the Civil War. Many outstanding political cartoons were produced by Bernhard and Victor Gillam.

The cartoon, often satirizing topical events of a social or political nature, developed with the rise of the popular press in the mid nineteenth century. The tabloid newspapers reviews and periodicals gradually took over the role of the broadsheets and tracts of earlier centuries and expanded with the technical progress in printing. By the end of the nineteenth century the cartoon, either as an individual picture or as a comic strip was well established in Europe and America, though it is in the latter country that it has enjoyed its finest and most prolific flowering. The practice of syndication has stimulated the growth of cartoons of an international nature, reproduced in even the smallest and most obscure newspapers all over the world. From the collector's viewpoint the chief interest of caricatures and cartoons lies in the original artists' drawings or in works produced separately, as hand-coloured prints or chromolithographs. Though they are mainly published in newspapers or magazines, cartoons may also be found on picture postcards and posters (qq.v.). The rise of the movie cartoon and, to a lesser extent, the strip cartoon, has created a wide range of ancillary articles – dolls, badges, mascots and ephemera – featuring such well-known characters as Mickey Mouse, Popeye and Andy Capp.

H. G. Wells and his Ball Game

Group of children's plates
and mugs with Mickey
Mouse decoration, c.
1930.

CARNETS DE BAL

Small, slender cases containing leaves, usually of ivory, but latterly of card, on which ladies inscribed the names of their dancing partners at balls. The cases were suitably decorated, often fitted with a thin chain for attachment to the wrist or evening purse, and provided with a tiny lead pencil held in a side compartment. *Carnets de bal* were a popular form of bibelot in the eighteenth and nineteenth centuries and may be found in polished hardwoods, ivory, mother-of-pearl, silver or gold with enamel or filigree work. Miniatures (q.v.) were sometimes bedded into the lid. Nineteenth-century examples were often inscribed with the words *Carnet de bal* or *Souvenir*. A variation on this theme was the *tablette* whose ivory leaf was not detachable. *Tablettes* were useful for making pencil notes, which could then be wiped clean with a damp cloth. The construction of *carnets de bal* varied considerably, and they may be found either in the form of a tiny book, with the leaves held in silk pockets concertina fashion, or, more commonly, with a frontal flap, hinged about a third of the way down so that the case could be opened to reveal the cards inside.

Left Cartoon of
H.G. Wells by David
Low; from the London
Evening Standard, c. 1930.

Right Ladies' writing
equipment including
carnets de bal; early
19th century.

CARPETS. See *Rugs and Carpets*

CARTONNIERS

Small pieces of furniture, containing several tiny drawers, intended to convert a table into a writing desk. Cartonniers, otherwise known as *serres papier*, were devised in late eighteenth-century France and were used to file papers and contain writing materials. In addition to the shallow drawers there were small compartments for wafers, sealing wax, ink, pens and pounce pot. The more elaborate cartonniers incorporated a clock or even small bronze ornaments, often decorated with ormolu (q.v.).
See also *Writing Cases*

CARTOONS. See *Caricatures and Cartoons*

CASSOLETTES

Small vases, usually of gilt-bronze or brass, with fretted lids. Cassolettes were first made in France in the late seventeenth century and employed as pastille burners (q.v.) to sweeten the air. They were produced all over western Europe in the eighteenth century, and vary widely in style and construction. A number of examples incorporate a spirit lamp, while others have a reversible lid which could also be used as a candle-holder. As the necessity for them diminished cassolettes became more and more ornamental and appeared in such materials as fine porcelain, which would not have stood up to the heat of burning pastilles. As an ornament, cassolettes survived well into the nineteenth century, the later examples being often produced as matched pairs to decorate mantlepieces and sideboards.
See also *Pastille Burners*

CASTERS

Small upright containers for sugar, salt, pepper and spices, manufactured mainly in silver, although pewter and Sheffield plate were also used. The characteristic feature of casters was the domed lid with perforations through which the contents were sprinkled.

Many different styles were followed, rangin from a simple cylindrical shape to elaboratel gadrooned, fluted or globular bodies. Th fretted lids were invariably decorated wit intricately pierced patterns. Casters may b found individually, though sets of three i varying sizes were fashionable in the eigh teenth century and are worth a premium Though the majority were made in metal,

few have been recorded in Chinese export porcelain. Muffineers were small casters made in England from the late eighteenth century onwards for sprinkling sugar and spices on toasted muffins. They are generally smaller than ordinary casters, with finer perforations.

CAUDLE CUPS AND POSSET POTS

Two beverages regarded as tonics for invalids and expectant mothers were caudle and posset, consisting respectively of thin gruel or curdled milk, laced with wine, sugar and spices, and usually heated before drinking. Special vessels designed for these mixtures were known as caudle cups and posset pots. The two are often confused, though purists distinguish them according to shape. Posset pots were relatively tall, baluster-shaped mugs with two handles and sometimes a teapot spout (if the invalid was too weak to sip the brew over the rim). Caudle cups were generally very much more shallow, with horizontal handles not unlike Scottish quaichs (q.v.), though usually much more elaborately decorated. Both cups and pots were fitted with high-domed lids, usually with decorative knops and finials. Caudle cups and posset pots were usually made of pottery or porcelain (though silver or silver-gilt examples are not unknown) and were often provided in pairs or sets as part of a coffee or tea service.
See also *Écuelles*

CHALKWARE

Ornaments popular in the United States from the mid-eighteenth century to about 1900. These hollow slip-moulded figures were made in plaster of Paris, and were usually filled with a heavier plaster to give them more weight and substance. They were produced in imitation of the more expensive porcelain but, because of their composition, could not be glazed. Instead they were hand-painted in oils or watercolours. Candle-smoke fixed with oil paints was a popular mode of decoration. The earliest chalkware figures were probably manufactured in

France and England for export to America, although an indigenous industry was established in New England before the War of Independence. Subsequently they became immensely popular all over the United States, occupying a position analogous to Staffordshire figures (q.v.) in England. Birds and animals predominate, but classical groups and portraits of contemporary personalities may also be found. Bowls of plaster fruit were also produced as sideboard ornaments. The import of cheap porcelain figures and groups from Germany in the late nineteenth century led to the demise of chalkware.
See colour plate page 51

CHAMBERPOTS

For at least two thousand years before the invention of the water closet the inconvenience of out-door privies was mitigated in some respects by these handy domestic utensils. They were known to the Egyptians and the Greeks of ancient times and the name by which they were known to the latter (*skaphé*, i.e. a skiff) indicates their original boat shape. The familiar rounded form with flattened rim began to emerge in medieval Europe, but oblong pots were popular in France until the early nineteenth century. The French oblong pots were usually made of porcelain and were often elegantly decorated as befitted their purpose. Their name, *bourdalou*, was derived from the seventeenth-century popular preacher, Louis Bourdaloue. His services were so well attended that it was necessary for the congregation to get to the church hours before worship commenced.

Ladies carried these slim-line chamberpots concealed in their muffs and slipped them unobtrusively under their skirts when required.

A very high proportion of the more mundane chamberpots were also decorated, and the styles varied from country to country and from one generation to the next. Delftware chamberpots were manufactured in northern Europe from about 1650 onwards. Blue-and-white scratched decoration was popular in Germany in the seventeenth and eighteenth centuries and spread to England and Colonial America. English chamberpots of the eighteenth century were frequently decorated with portraits of the reigning sovereign or his monogram. After the American Revolution the export of these chamberpots continued, but with the portrait of George Washington or the Great Seal of the United States substituted. So long as the portrait was featured on the outside no disrespect was intended. But examples are frequently encountered in which a portrait, or even a small pottery bust, appears on the bottom of the pot inside. Napoleon Bonaparte, King George III and the Duke of Wellington were singled out for this treatment, in Britain, America and France respectively.

Many chamberpots from the seventeenth century onwards were decorated with pious mottoes; others bore sets of initials and dates which suggest that they were given as betrothal or wedding presents. Two-handled bridal chamberpots were frequently inscribed with ribald verse. Other embellishments include a frog in the inside, a large eye on the bottom with the slogan 'Oh me, what do I see' or some similar sentiment; examples of the same genre, with inscriptions in French, German, Swedish or Italian, show the universality of this brand of humour.

Chamberpots were widely manufactured in various types of pottery and exhibit all the styles of decoration prevailing in successive periods. Many of them were issued unmarked but those bearing the mark of well-known potters are worth a premium. Chamberpots produced for special purposes are also worth looking for. Comparatively rare examples bear regimental crests or other military insignia on their sides. The old railway companies and hotel groups had chamberpots decorated with their monograms and emblems and many of these are highly ornamental. Stylistically chamberpots may be found with large flat rims, small slightly raised rims, or virtually no rim at all. Their handles may be oval in section, strapped or highly ornamented. Silver chamberpots are comparatively rare, though they were widely produced in the seventeenth and eighteenth centuries, and examples with armorial bearings engraved on their sides are now highly prized. Brass and pewter chamberpots belong mainly to the seventeenth century and are also relatively scarce. Other materials are very rare, though not unknown. Cardinal Mazarin had a glass chamberpot with a fur-lined rim!

As a rule chamberpots were produced without any form of cover, but lidded earthenware pots were made in the nineteenth century, complete with matching

Novelty chamberpot in enamelled ironware; English, 19th century.

light Chatelaine and
matching brooch in blue
jasper and cut steel, by
Wedgwood, 1780–1800.

wickerwork carrying basket, and were intended for the traveller. Novelty chamberpots, in various bird or animal shapes to disguise their function and assist the toilet training of young children, were a late Victorian invention which survives to this day in the many different plastic pots.

Decorative bedpans, close-stools and bidet bowls were fashionable in the eighteenth and early nineteenth centuries. Chamberpots may also be found in sets, either two or more chamberpots of ascending sizes, or singles or matched pairs as part of toilet sets which also include ewer, bowl, slop-pail, and soap-stand.

CHATELAINES

Roughly triangular ornaments from which hung several small articles attached by fine chains. Chatelaines had hook or brooch fittings so that they could be affixed to a waist-belt or sash. They were fashionable in eighteenth- and nineteenth-century Europe and were worn by both sexes. The earlier examples were often elaborately decorated in gold, silver-gilt, enamels and semi-precious stones, incorporating portrait miniatures (q.v.) and fitted with various useful articles in matching decoration. A wide variety of objects was attached to the chatelaine, and included a watch, scissors, clock or watch key, seal, étui, bodkin, button hook, vinaigrette, snuff box, needle case, looking-glass and pencil. Chatelaines will be found with rings or chain attachments for up to ten articles, though five seems to have been about average. The ornamental belt attachments were known as chatelettes and are quite collectable in their own right, though complete chatelaines with genuinely matching accoutrements are worth a premium.

It is often stated that chatelaines went out of fashion by 1800, but it would be more correct to say that they survived until World War I, albeit in a more utilitarian style. Later nineteenth-century chatelaines were usually made of silver and lacked the florid decorative qualities of the eighteenth-century examples. In addition to the various objects mentioned above, late nineteenth-century

chatelaines may be found with tiny silver envelopes, for holding postage stamps, and from the hallmarks found on these they seem to have been particularly popular between 1880 and 1910.

CHEESE DISHES

Special dishes and covers for cheese became fashionable in Europe in the mid-nineteenth century and although they declined after World War I they have never quite died out. The more functional examples have a distinctive triangular or wedge-shaped appearance, with an ornamental handle set on the lid. Although porcelain was occasionally used, the majority were made of earthenware or stoneware in a wide variety of glazes and decorative effects. Apart from the motifs, either transfer-printed or hand-painted on their sides, many cheese dish covers were produced in novelty shapes – cows' heads and milk churns being popular allusions to the dairying industry. Other forms include castles, cottages and a curious form of floral tea-cosy with a recumbent cow on top.

CHESS PIECES

The origins of chess have been much debated, but the consensus of opinion is that the game originated in India, where it was known as *chaturanga* (the four arms of an army), and spread from there to Persia in the six[th] century. The name was there corrupted [to] *shatranj*. In the ensuing centuries the ga[me] was developed in the Middle East and t[he] names of many of the pieces and the mo[st] important terms betray Arabic, Persian a[nd] Hindu origins. Thus the word 'rook' [is] derived from the Persian *rukh* (soldier), a[nd] 'checkmate' comes from the Arabic *Shah m*[at] (the King is dead). Chess found its way [to] western Europe by various routes. T[he] Moorish invaders of Spain brought it fr[om] North Africa to Iberia, while the Byzanti[nes] learned it from the Turks and subsequen[tly] introduced the game to Italy and the Balk[an] countries. It seems to have been fairly wi[de] spread by the eleventh century, judging [by] references to it in folklore and early reco[rds]

Carved bone chess set; Chinese, early 19th century.

Right Painted and
Decorated Windsor
highchair; American,
1765–1810.

The game was essentially for the upper classes and this explains the fact that many of the earliest surviving pieces were intricately carved in ivory or hardstone, decorated with gold or precious stones, putting them beyond the reach of most private collectors. By the end of the sixteenth century, however, chess was played at every level in society and pieces were manufactured to suit every purse. Thus the chess pieces of the seventeenth century range from relatively plain wood and bone to cast metal sets in lead, pewter or bronze. Pottery chessmen became popular in the early eighteenth century and porcelain enjoyed a certain vogue about fifty years later. Chess pieces in alabaster hailed from Italy in the late eighteenth century. At an early date the style of chess pieces began to diverge from traditional stereotypes, and the eighteenth century in particular witnessed a wide variety of pieces, many of which were designed to commemorate or illustrate important battles and campaigns. From this period date the many fine portrait pieces, a custom which has been revived in recent years with chess pieces portraying or caricaturing well-known political figures. From the eighteenth century onwards a vast quantity of carved ivory or jade pieces was exported from the Far East to Europe and America. Oriental chess pieces are often quite distinctive, with elephants and pagodas instead of knights and rooks, and the more intricately carved examples are highly regarded as individual collector's items. Complete sets of chess pieces, with matching case and board, are usually worth a considerable premium.

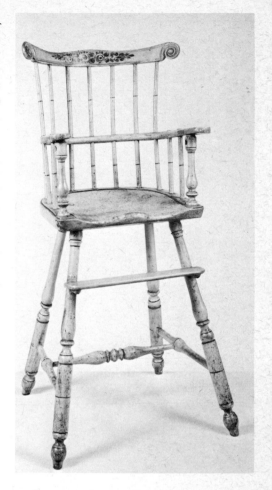

CHILDREN'S FURNITURE

Although furniture, on account of its size, is outside the scope of this book, miniaturized pieces intended for the nursery or kindergarten are worth considering as examples of contemporary furniture styles which take up much less room.

Children's furniture may be divided into two broad categories: items specifically made for children's use and items which are merely smaller versions of pieces in general use. In the first category come baby's cots and cradles, highchairs and pushchairs. Baby-walkers, designed to teach infants to walk, were in use by the mid-fifteenth century. The earliest examples consist of two wooden circles, the smaller placed above the larger, and joined by vertical struts. Short legs terminating in castors were placed at intervals round the underside of the lower circle. Highchairs, incorporating a small table and often having a recess to contain a chamberpot (q.v.), date from the late seventeenth century.

Small chairs, desks, stools and tables come within the second category. Early examples exhibit all the techniques of cabinet-making to be found in adult furniture; but from the

Child's washstand in
beechwood with bowl
and jug; English, mid-
19th century.

in a special bronze alloy containing lead, tin
and copper. Apart from the many different
styles of decoration, ranging from engraving
and chasing to cast relief and the addition of
animal, demonic or human figures cast
separately, the vessels themselves comprise
several distinctive types. The *chia* was a wine
cup mounted on a short tripod, based on
neolithic pottery and found only during the
Shang period. The *chien*, dating from the
fifth century BC, was a deep bowl with
intricately decorated handles and suspension
rings, and was probably used in ritual
purification ceremonies. The *chih* was another
type of wine cup, usually fitted with a high-
domed lid and having elegantly waisted
sides and an ornamental foot-rim. The *chüeh*
was a larger wine vessel, on tall tripod base,
fitted with an elaborate handle over one leg
and a wide, elongated spout on one side at
right angles to the handle. The *fang i* was
a bronze container of uncertain purpose,
shaped like a little house, with a ridged top
surmounted by a ridged knob. The *hu* was a
tall-shouldered vessel with round handles set
near the mouth and a high foot-rim. The *ku*
was a wine goblet found in the Shang and
early Chou periods, characterized by its
wide-flaring mouth and bell-shaped bottom;
like the *chüeh* it was possibly derived from

mid-nineteenth century children's furniture
was generally more robust and simpler in
line and construction. Towards the end of the
century it became fashionable to decorate
children's furniture with transfers or scraps
which were subsequently varnished over.
This, in turn, gave way to the use of light
pastel colours, coral-pink and duck-egg blue,
with transfer decoration, after World War I.

CHINESE RITUAL VESSELS

Utensils cast in bronze from at least the
fifteenth century BC were widely used in
religious ceremonies and were often interred
with the dead. Archaeological excavations in
the past hundred years have brought many
examples to light and a large proportion of
them has filtered through to the West since
1900. These objects were cast in clay moulds

58

some primitive horn vessel. The *kuang* was a mixing bowl, elliptical in shape, with an ornamental cover often rendered in the form of an animal. The term *tsun* was used to denote vases of many different shapes, often resembling animals such as the elephant, ram or rhinoceros. Both the *kuei* and the *yu* were bronze bowls mounted on high ring feet, the former used for serving food and the latter (distinguished by its expanding curved sides, lid and loop handle) for storing wine. Many objects of jade also had a ritualistic significance. These include the *huan*, *pi* and *yüan*, denoting discs and rings, with varying dimensions and patterns or carving.

Bronze vessels emulating Chinese originals were widely produced in Britain, France and Germany in the eighteenth and nineteenth centuries. They should present little difficulty in attribution since they generally lack the finish and patina of the genuine examples and in many cases bear inscriptions which are poor imitation of the true Chinese characters.

CHINOISERIE

Name given to Western adaptation of Chinese motifs and styles on furniture, ceramics, silverware and other aspects of the applied arts. The fashion for Chinese decoration began in the seventeenth century with the import into western Europe of Chinese porcelain, lacquerware and textiles by the Portuguese, Dutch and British. In its wider context chinoiserie stimulated the European development of soft-paste porcelain and the craze for japanning (q.v.) in the eighteenth century. It manifested itself in the predilection for piercing and fretting in furniture, distinctive Chinese shapes such as pagodas, dragons, mandarins, phoenixes and butterflies, and both geometric and naturalistic patterns based on Chinese originals. The fashion for chinoiserie reached a peak at the end of the seventeenth century, declined in the early eighteenth and was revived again about 1745. In its revived form chinoiserie went to greater extremes, in keeping with the extravagance of the baroque and rococo periods. Furniture in particular became much more elaborate in its carving, piercing and fretting, while chairs and cabinets generally simulated the forms of Chinese architecture. The late eighteenth century was the heyday of blue-and-white decoration on pottery and porcelain imitating Chinese styles, and this has continued to be popular to the present day. Chinoiserie figures were produced by most of the early European porcelain factories, and many of the more useful wares were modelled on Chinese patterns, especially tea bowls and caddies – even to the extent of applying fake or imitation regnal marks and other Chinese characters. Apart from a brief revival in Regency England, chinoiserie declined in popularity in the nineteenth century, though its position as one of the major stylistic influences on the applied arts has ensured that it has never quite disappeared at any time. In the mid-nineteenth century it manifested itself in papier mâché (q.v.), lacquered and inlaid with mother-of-pearl or ivory decoration with Chinese motifs, in the penchant for fan leaves, and in the Oriental style of drapes and upholstery. An important group of chinoiseries consists of miniature silver items (see *Silver, Miniature*) in the form of coolies, sampans, rickshaws, pagodas and other typically Chinese subjects, produced in Europe in the late eighteenth and nineteenth centuries.

See also *Japonaiserie*

CHIP CARVING

A form of decoration on wood which seems to have originated in Europe in the thirteenth century, reached its peak in the sixteenth and seventeenth centuries and was revived as a pastime in the nineteenth century. The decoration was often drawn on the surface beforehand, using geometric instruments to achieve a highly intricate pattern, and then the motif was incised by chipping away small particles of wood with a mallet and chisel. Although the finest examples of chip carving belong to the late Middle Ages, and may be

found on panels and furniture of the perio these are now of the greatest rarity. Late examples are inferior in craftsmanship bu more easily available, while there is n shortage of nineteenth-century boxes decor ated with chip carving, popular as a folk a in Europe and America.

CHOCOLATE AND COFFEE POTS

Pots for chocolate and coffee (both beverage being popular from the mid-seventeent century) were produced from about 167c They were made of silver, rarely Sheffiel plate, and in electroplate from the mid nineteenth century onwards. The principa difference between the two is that chocolat pots often had an aperture in the lid for stirring rod. The earliest forms for both po were cylindrical, tapering slightly toward the top, with domed lids surmounted by knop. Handles were set on the opposite sid to the spouts, but after 1700 handles wer often mounted at right angles to the spou Spouts were generally straight until the mid eighteenth century when curving was intro duced. At the same time the body becam more globular – first pear-shaped and late baluster-shaped. Various urn shapes becam

professional 'colourer' named Mason. The cards were sold for a shilling each and it has been estimated that fewer than 1,000 were sold. Of these, barely a dozen are now known to exist and most of these are in the United States, where the collecting of Christmas cards is an old-established hobby.

The design of the Cole-Horsley card seems quaint by modern standards. No one could object to the subjects of the side panels, which represent the spirit of Christmas charity, but the principal vignette, depicting a large Victorian family toasting the absent friend (the addressee) with glasses of wine, was severely censured at the time as being an incitement to drunkenness.

Other Christmas cards were produced in the 1840s (that produced by W.M. Egley having been a serious contender for the title of the first, on account of the difficulty of deciphering the date 1848 printed on it), but their popularity was restricted for many years. Many of the cards in the period before 1867 were made and painted by hand. They developed slowly alongside the more popular Christmas notepaper and envelopes. These envelopes were often gaily decorated and had ornately embossed flaps which could be cut out and mounted on a plain card. In this way the mid-Victorian Christmas card composed of scraps or several layers of embossed and perforated paper gradually evolved. Examples of these cards, from the 1850s and 1860s, scarcely larger than a playing card and intricately decorated with lace, silk ribbons or scraps, are very scarce, especially with matching envelopes. Animated cards, which were in vogue for a time in the period 1870–80, are also expensive nowadays.

The development of the techniques of die-sinking and embossing in the 1850s encouraged the firm of C. Goodall and Son to manufacture Christmas cards on a commercial basis in 1862. Marcus Ward, however, was the first publisher to develop the Christmas card beyond the somewhat dilettante approach of his predecessors. Great attention was paid to design, and leading artists of the time were commissioned to illustrate the cards. The first Marcus Ward

fashionable in the late eighteenth century, emulating Egyptian, Greek and Roman originals. Thereafter styles were mixed and eclectic, drawing on a wide range of styles and periods. Porcelain chocolate and coffee pots date from the latter half of the eighteenth century, but never enjoyed the same popularity as silver pots. Pewter coffee pots were made in the late nineteenth century.

CHRISTMAS CARDS

Greetings cards for the Christmas season originated in England. The first card was published in 1843 at Felix Summerly's Home Treasury Office, Bond Street, London, at the instigation of Henry Cole, and was designed by John Horsley. The Cole-Horsley card was lithographed by Jobbins of Warwick Court, Holborn, and hand-coloured by a

Christmas card of 1938
portraying Prime Minister
Chamberlain, 'who gives
a nation peace' – an
allusion to the Munich
Agreement with Hitler,
which guaranteed 'peace
in our time'.

"Who gives a nation peace,
gives tranquillity to all . . ."
(Horace Walpole)

Daily Sketch

With Best Wishes for
Christmas and the New Year
from

CHRISTMAS, 1938.   SHILLINGLEE PARK

ingenuity in combining the Christmas me
sage with the 'hard sell'. The early twentie
century was the heyday of the romant
Christmas card, often using real photograp
of animals and young children in a sent
mental context. Patriotic cards from Wor
War I are now highly prized as an adjunct
militaria (q.v.), and to this period also belor
the many finely embroidered silk Christm
cards displaying the national flags of th
Allies and other patriotic motifs.

See colour plate page 69

CIGAR AND CIGARETTE CASES

The increasing popularity of cigar-smokin
which spread from America to Europe at th
beginning of the nineteenth century, led
the development of the cigar case. Since th
earliest cigars were relatively small and slir
the cases were comparatively compact ar
held four or six cheroots. Leather, cloth
covered card and papier mâché were th
most popular materials for early cases, whic
were either hinged with a flap at the upp
end or had a sliding cover. The flat surfac
were ideal for decoration, and elabora

cards on a commercial scale appeared in 1867,
and in the ensuing decades they featured the
work of Walter Crane, Kate Greenaway,
Stacy Marks and other artists often associated
with the Arts and Crafts Movement in
England. Marcus Ward subsequently turned
away from Christmas cards in face of the
competition from Raphael Tuck, whose
first cards appeared in 1871. Tuck promoted
the Christmas card with public design
competitions offering vast sums of prize-
money, and held regular exhibitions of the
season's new designs. The introduction of
new postal regulations, from 1870 onwards,
which permitted the transmission of postcards and printed matter at reduced rates,
greatly increased the number of cards sent
each year. This coincided with the rapid
spread of Christmas cards in Europe and
America, and the custom was world-wide by
the end of the nineteenth century.

The later cards lack the charm of the mid-
nineteenth-century examples, but are not
without great interest. The commercial
Christmas card, sent out by business firms to
their clients, developed in the United States
in the 1890s and they display considerable

floral or geometric patterns were worked or embossed on them. The commercial production of cigarettes began shortly after the American Civil War and revolutionized the form and appearance of cigar and cigarette cases, which, from then onwards, were largely produced by mechanical means. Although leather continued to be the most popular medium, other materials, notably wood and ivory, were used increasingly, and cases were embellished with silver or gold mounts, clasps and hinges. Metal decoration increased gradually, until the end of the century when all-metal cases became fashionable. The cigarette case assumed the position held by the snuff box (q.v.) in previous generations, and became an object of vertu on which craftsmen and goldsmiths lavished all their skills. Cases may be found in most metals, from gold and silver to brass, gunmetal and even aluminium alloys. Decoration includes *guilloche* engine-turning, relief engraving, chasing and enamelling (the last-named being very fashionable in Russia and Central Europe at the turn of the century). The Russians in particular excelled in the decoration of cigarette cases, often using the inherent qualities of the metal, such as contrasting colours of gold and silver alloys, or the technique of surface pitting, known as *samarodok*.

CIGAR AND TOBACCO CUTTERS

Special knives and other devices for cutting plugs of tobacco or the ends of cigars became fashionable early in the nineteenth century. Pocket cutters were (and are) often highly elaborate, with gold-plated heads and ivory or porcelain handles. The handles were either beautifully decorated or assumed various fancy shapes – a lady's leg or a champagne bottle being typical motifs. Less elaborate, but usually ornamented to some extent, were the table models, which were screwed to shop and bar counters and operated by an elongated handle. These cutters were invariably decorated with human, bird or animal figures, or even constructed like miniature guillotines.

CLOCKS

From the French and German words for a bell (*cloche* and *Glocke*) it seems that the earliest mechanical clocks were intended to activate a church bell for the regulation of the services. The invention of this device is traditionally credited to Pope Silvester II in AD 996. The earliest clocks were usually somewhat inaccurate and required sundials (q.v.) mounted alongside for periodic correction. Springs, pendulums, weights, and finally the verge escapement were in existence by the fifteenth century, and the miniaturization of their mechanism led to the development of the watch.

There is a wide range of small clocks (such varieties as the longcase or grandfather clock being outside the scope of this encyclopedia). Coach clocks were popular in the eighteenth century and resembled outsize 'turnip'

ft Art Deco cigarette *se*; English, 1931. The *s*tumes show the *fl*uence of Bakst and the *llets Russes*.

ight Carriage clock with *amplevé* enamel *coration*; French, late *th* century.

Gothic clock; American, c. 1885. The case could be made at home from designs supplied, at 25 cents, by A.H. Pomeroy of Hartford, Conn., who also sold the movement at $3.50.

Ormolu-mounted marble repeating carriage clock by Tiffany, c. 1900.

watches. Travelling clocks were small clocks housed in glass cases which, themselves, were encased in wood or leather boxes to protect them in transit. Eighteenth- and nineteenth-century travelling clocks were often attractively decorated with ormolu and enamelling. Small clocks for the mantelshelf or wall-bracket were produced in many different forms, with hardwood cases, ormolu gilding and boulle (q.v.) decoration. Others were incorporated in bronze or porcelain figures. Astronomical clocks date from the late sixteenth century and took the form of globes, sometimes incorporating such instruments as an astrolabe. A curious globular clock was the falling-ball clock of German origin in the mid-seventeenth century; it was suspended by a fine chain and operated by its own falling weight. Horizontal, drum-shaped clocks, often decorated with hunting scenes and human figures, were fashionable in Central Europe from the late seventeenth century onwards. Clocks in the form of ships were known as nefs (q.v.), and were intended as table ornaments.

Novelty clocks include those in the form of miniature grandfather clocks, with marquetry decoration on their cases. The cuckoo clock originated in Switzerland in the early eighteenth century and has undergone many changes in form and decoration since then remaining a popular tourist souvenir to this day. Swiss and French horologists produced many other types of clock incorporating automata (q.v.) from the middle of the eighteenth century onwards. Children's clocks, with fairy-tale characters on the dials and some form of animation operated by the movement of the verge, became popular in the late nineteenth century and continue to the present in many shapes and sizes. Early examples of more modern form such as ticket clocks and digital clocks (pioneered in the United States at the turn of the century) are now attracting serious attention. Ships' chronometers, precision clocks and other forms used in scientific work have been developed since the mid-eighteenth century and are now much sought-after by collectors.

See also *Timepieces*

CLOISONNÉ

A technique of enamelling, practised in the Byzantine Empire in the Middle Ages but lost to Europe until about 1860, since when it has been revived in western Europe for decorating jewelry (q.v.). The technique was developed independently in China and is most closely associated with Chinese decorative wares. The name is derived from the small cells or cloisons which were formed by means of copper wires or strips soldered to a metal base. These tiny cells were then filled with molten coloured glass. This form of decoration could be applied to vessels of all kinds as well as two-dimensional items such as bronze mirrors and plaques.

Although occasional pieces of Chinese cloisonné enamels were known in Europe from about 1840, they did not make a significant impression in collecting circles until 1862 when the treasures of the Summer Palace reached western Europe. In the same

year Madame Desnoye opened a shop in Paris specializing in Oriental art, and the first flood of Japanese art and artefacts also arrived in France. It was Japanese, rather than Chinese, cloisonné that attracted the attention of collectors and industrialists such as Barbédienne, Christophle and Falize, and by the end of the 1860s both jewelry and objects of vertu were being manufactured in France using cloisonné techniques. Fresh impetus was supplied by the Exposition Universelle of 1867, and thenceforward over-wrought cloisonné vases, candlesticks and bowls became all the rage. Goblets, lamps, coffers, jardinières and clocks were decorated with gaudy enamels derived from Japanese lacquer and cloisonné originals. Much of this late nineteenth-century decoration was applied in the cheaper and less exacting champlevé technique. The finest cloisonné enamels were

produced by Fernand Thesmar, an employee of Barbédienne, who perfected this technique in the closing decades of the nineteenth century. Thesmar's enamels were usually signed with his monogram.

The English firm of Elkington began producing cloisonné enamels in 1862 and manufactured large numbers of salvers and vases enamelled with japonaiserie motifs. Though technically Elkington was superior to the Japanese, the quality of English cloisonné only improved after 1885 when Adrien Dalpayrat brought the French styles to London. The finest English cloisonné was produced by such artist-craftsmen as Alexander Fisher and Archibald Knox. Cloisonné enamelling was very popular with European jewelers at the turn of the century and was used extensively in the decoration of small boxes in Russia and the Baltic countries.

COASTERS

Small circular trays for wine bottles or decanters. They were made of metal with a wooden base, or occasionally entirely of wood, with a pad of cloth or felt on the underside, so that they could be coasted or slid along the highly polished surface of dining tables at the end of a meal when the tablecloth and extraneous ornaments were removed and the port was passed round.

The earliest coasters were of all-metal construction with a ridged base, and may be found in silver or silver-gilt but rarely in Sheffield plate. Rather later examples were also of metal construction, but were fitted with tiny rollers on the underside. The commoner form with a baize pad on a wooden base came into use by the middle of the eighteenth century. The bottoms of coasters were either completely lined with metal or had shallow rings cut in the wood to prevent the bottle or decanter from sticking. The raised rim or gallery was invariably decorated in the prevailing style, and ranged from the cast ornament and intricately pierced flowers and foliage of the rococo to the more austere forms of engraving and fretting popular in the Regency period. Coasters were usually made in matched pairs or sets. A more elaborate form, which enjoyed some measure of popularity in the mid-nineteenth century, was the wine wagon, consisting of a boat or wagon-shaped coaster, with spaces for two decanters, mounted on silver wheels so that it could be trundled round the table. A few examples are known in the form of loco-motives, complete with silver rails and steam engine.

COFFEE POTS. See *Chocolate and Coffee pots*

COMMEMORATIVE WARES

For centuries artists and craftsmen have been inspired to produce objects commemorating famous persons and historic events. Such objects were fashioned by the Greeks and the Romans, by the Persians, Indians and Chinese.

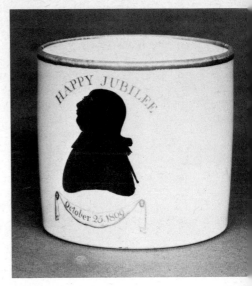

So far as Western civilization is concerned, commemorative pottery and silverware begins to be relatively plentiful from the seventeenth century onwards. The 'cult of the personality' was a feature of the Italian Renaissance of the fifteenth century, manifesting itself in the cast portrait-medal on the one hand, and in the *istoriati* earthenware bowls, dishes and vases decorated with scenes and personages from the Bible, mythology and medieval history. They established a trend which spread to other parts of Europe, and has continued down to the present day.

In Britain one may cite as typical examples the delftware platters commemorating the accession of William and Mary; Admiral Vernon medals and tankards celebrating his victory at Portobello in 1739; a vast range of pottery, glassware and medals marking the political struggle between John Wilkes and the Establishment of the 1760s; punch bowls honouring the French Revolution; and engraved glassware celebrating the opening of Sunderland Bridge. These objects differed in one sense from most of those which came after them: they were invariably produced in commemoration of an event after it had taken place. Although a few items were produced for the coronations of George III and George IV, the first occasion on which

left George III Jubilee
mug, 1809.

right Minton plaque
portraying Queen
Victoria, *c.* 1855.

objects were manufactured in anticipation of an event on a grand scale and cashing in on its topicality was the coronation of Queen Victoria in 1838.

Apart from the medals struck at the time, there were plates, vases and ornaments which alluded in their inscriptions or decoration to the event being celebrated. Once the coronation had taken place the production of these souvenirs ceased – unlike the items which marked the opening of Sunderland Bridge and which were produced continuously for some thirty years after. The souvenirs which greeted the coronation of the young queen were small in number compared with those produced in celebration of her Golden Jubilee in 1887 and her Diamond Jubilee ten years later. New series of stamps and coins also appeared at the time of the Golden Jubilee though neither was commemorative in the strict sense. There was, however, a plethora of commemorative medallions, plaques, dishes, mugs, boxes, paperweights and trivia of all kinds, produced for the Diamond Jubilee, much of which was aimed at the souvenir industry. From then onwards, royal occasions in Britain provided splendid opportunities for the souvenir manufacturers, although it is only in comparatively recent times that a conscious attempt has been made to produce objects of great aesthetic beauty and superlative craftsmanship worthy of the occasion.

The vast majority of souvenirs produced for special events have had little intrinsic value. In this class belong the countless thousands of earthenware mugs presented to schoolchildren all over the country in celebration of the various coronations from 1902 onwards. Nevertheless, early examples of this sort are now highly prized. Doulton's manufactured some 60,000 mugs for presentation to schoolchildren in commemoration of the Golden Jubilee of Queen Victoria. Many lesser potteries also produced their quota of Jubilee mugs and though they are often of inferior workmanship they are eagerly sought after.

Apart from the mugs presented to schoolchildren there were vast quantities of other

souvenir chocolate tin
commemorating the
coronation of 1902.

items, produced for sale to the general public. Plaques and plates, vases and figures, prints, posters and even bottles of specially brewed beer – all are now in great demand by collectors who specialize in the complete range of objects connected with a particular event. The kingdoms of Europe indulged in royal commemorative wares to a much lesser extent, a reflection perhaps on the comparative popularity of British and European royalty. Significantly, much of the pottery, glassware and objects of vertu commemorating European rulers, from Frederick the Great of Prussia to Napoleon III, was actually produced in England for the European market. The English potters even went so far as to produce plates and mugs commemorating American naval heroes of the War of Independence, even though they were on the opposite side! Early American statesmen, such as Washington, Franklin, Adams and Monroe, were also the subject of commemorative wares of English origin.

Later American commemorative items were centred mainly on the expositions and world's fairs, from the Centennial at Philadelphia (1876) to the Jamestown and Panama-Pacific Expositions prior to World War I. The Spanish-American War of 1898 sparked off a wave of memorabilia in which the depiction of the battleship *Maine* threatened to overtake the popularity of Washington's

67

Opposite Selection of Victorian Christmas cards; English, late 19th century.

Right Pressed glass bread dish in Liberty Bell pattern; made for the Centennial Exposition, 1876.

crossing of the Delaware. Political satire was the motive for many of the commemorative items of yester-year, from the seventeenth-century Popish Plot to the Great Reform Act of 1832, but the use of commemorative mugs and plates as propaganda declined with the rise of the popular press and political cartoons.

COMMUNION TOKENS

Metal discs originally intended as tickets of admission to the service of Communion in the Presbyterian and Calvinist forms of the Protestant churches. The sacrament of Communion, unlike its Anglican counterpart or the Catholic Mass, was celebrated much less frequently, either quarterly or annually, and preceded by a series of preparatory services including the catechizing of the congregation, a formal examination of the members in their knowledge of the Scriptures. The service of catechism, held on the previous Thursday, was accompanied by the distribu-

tion of tokens for the Communion service o Sunday. Elders of the church received th tokens from members of the congregatio before allowing them to enter the church Communion tokens were in vogue fo about 350 years. The earliest were made pasteboard (and the wheel has come fu circle, since modern Communion cards a of the same substance), but by the ear seventeenth century metal tokens were b coming common, since they could be us and re-used for years on end. They were ca in simple moulds or crudely struck with device on one side only. Later examples we cut from brass or pewter sheet and had di struck inscriptions on both sides.

Biblical quotations referring to the sacr ment of Communion or the catechism we widely used on tokens of the eighteenth a nineteenth centuries. The initials of t parish church appear on early examples, b by the early nineteenth century the name w usually rendered in full. Later in the centur

WITH BEST WISHES FOR A HAPPY NEW YEAR!

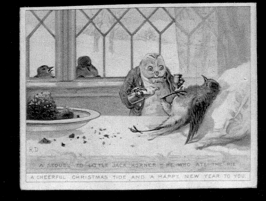

A SEQUEL TO LITTLE JACK HORNER ↔ HE WHO ATE THE PIE

A CHEERFUL CHRISTMAS-TIDE AND A HAPPY NEW YEAR TO YOU.

Remembrance

A Merry Christmas
and
A Happy New Year

Wishing you a Merry Christmas
and a Happy New Year.

A Christmas
Greeting
to you

more elaborate examples incorporated pictorial devices (Communion cup and plate), the burning bush emblem of the Scottish Presbyterian Church, or even a tiny vignette featuring a view of the church itself. Though the custom was most prevalent in Scotland it also extended to the English, Welsh and Irish Presbyterian churches, to the Dutch Reformed and French Calvinist churches and to churches of Scottish origin in the United States, Canada, Australia and New Zealand. Although the custom of metal tokens has now largely died out, they are still struck from time to time and examples commemorating important church anniversaries are produced in the United States to this day.

COPPER

Malleable metal found all over the world and widely used by mankind from prehistoric times. Copper in its pure form is unsuitable for general use since it corrodes quickly and forms dangerous oxides, and is too soft and easily worn for most practical purposes. It is most commonly found in combination with other metals, such as calamine or zinc to form brass (q.v.), with tin to make bronze, or with lead to form pewter (q.v.). The majority of items, both useful and decorative, described loosely as copper are, in fact, bronze alloys with varying proportions of lead or tin. Copper was used in the eighteenth and early nineteenth century as a base for enamels and Sheffield plate (q.v.) but in its plain, undecorated form, has been employed for a vast range of domestic wares. From the practical standpoint of the collector, copper wares become available in reasonable quantities from the seventeenth century onwards. Earlier examples are known but they are rare. Because of its corrosive properties copper was less widely used than brass for many articles. The majority of sheet-copper articles in domestic use, such as pots, pans, bins, jugs and buckets, were lined with tin or even silver (close-plating) to avoid the contamination of liquids and foodstuffs. Copper was also popular in Europe for kettles (q.v.) and even coffee pots, urns and

wine coolers. Many of the objects most often associated with copper are discussed elsewhere in this book, but other objects worth looking for include ale warmers and wine mullers, skillets and saucepans.

See also *Andirons, Aquamaniles, Bells, Buttons, Candlesticks, Door Furniture, Foot Warmers, Kettles, Measures, Medallions, Plaques, Pots, Spittoons, Warming Pans, Wine Coolers*

CORKSCREWS

Corks were introduced as bottle stoppers in the seventeenth century, and corkscrews were devised about the same time. The screw itself is invariably of steel, but the handle may be found in many different substances and shapes. Though gold was seldom used, silver-handled corkscrews were popular in the eighteenth and nineteenth centuries while bronze, brass, nickel and electroplate examples are fairly common. Many non-metallic substances were also used. Stag-horn, bone, ivory and mother-of-pearl handles may be found as well as wood handles, either plain, turned or carved. Pottery and porcelain handles are compara-tively scarce, but glass handles were popular earlier this century, sometimes incorporating *millefiori* ornament in the manner of paper-weights (q.v.). Novelty corkscrews often feature miniature bottles, golf balls or motifs associated with various sports. From the mechanical viewpoint, however, there are many different types of patent corkscrew, dating from about 1890, and incorporating other gadgets (such as can-openers, brushes and bottle openers). Some very complex corkscrews were devised at the turn of the century, the object being to ensure that a cork was cleanly drawn, and these are worth looking for as examples of late Victorian ingenuity.

COSTUME ACCESSORIES

Articles of clothing, though now widely collected, are mostly beyond the scope of this book, but there are many items associated with clothing which are collectable in their own right, either on account of the range of sizes and shapes which they present or because of inherent decorative qualities. From the fifteenth to the nineteenth cen-turies fashionable women wore a stout wooden busk inserted down the front of their stays to maintain an erect posture. These stay-busks were often intricately carved or hand-painted, and were traditionally given to wives and sweethearts as love tokens (q.v.). Also associated with corsetry, though of a much later date, are suspenders or garter clips, which became fashionable in the 1890s and continued until the advent of tights in the late 1960s. Apart from the numerous patented varieties there were novelty types which were often highly decorative. Other products of the late nine-teenth century include garters and sleeve-bands, whose clips were often decorated with good-luck charms, sporting motifs and erotic symbolism. The best examples were

fashioned in silver but many interesting item were electroplated and die-stamped. Gentle man's braces (suspenders) followed the adven of trousers in the early nineteenth century Mid-nineteenth-century examples often ha floral patterns or tiny decorative vignette woven or printed on the straps, while th adjustable clips (gilt, enamelled or plain were frequently ornamented with fanc designs.

Pins form an interesting group, fron handmade drawn-wire pins with solid head to the early types of safety pin patented in th 1870s. Studs for collars and shirt-front were often engraved or stamped with orna mental devices. The small boxes in whic they were kept were among the few con cessions made by gentlemen to person ornament and they may be found in man different materials and designs.

See also *Buckles, Buttons, Fans, Hair Ornament. Lace*

COW CREAMERS

Cream or milk jugs in the form of a cow, th tail curled to form a handle, a stoppere aperture in the hollow back and an outle through the cow's mouth. The cow creamer in fact, operates on the same principle as th medieval aquamanile (q.v.), though ther is no evidence of continuity. These curiou and much sought-after jugs seem to hav originated around the middle of th eighteenth century in the Low Countrie where they were modelled in delftware an silver. The idea was brought to England by Dutch silversmith, Johann (John) Schuppe who worked in London in the period 1753 73. Silver creamers were widely produce in the late eighteenth and nineteenth cen turies, in different sizes but with the sam basic design. As a rule the cow was fre standing, with a hinged lid (usually orna mented with a bee or a fly), and occasionall it was garlanded with floral decoration.

Cow creamers made in ceramics rang from the relatively coarse earthenware fron the Welsh potteries to fine Continent: porcelain with delicate underglaze flora

decoration. The majority of examples, however, were made in Staffordshire pottery, black gilded Jackfield ware, pearlware, creamware, stoneware and agate ware. Although European creamers (notably Dutch delftware in traditional patterns) have continued to be produced down to the present day, the greatest variety of shapes and sizes is to be found in the English creamers, which show the cow free-standing or on a base (either elliptical or chamfered rectangular), often with a daisy motif, occasionally with a matching calf and rarely with a seated milkmaid. The quality and colours of the glazes also vary enormously, from plain, natural colours, to fancy floral or chinoiserie motifs. Ceramic cow creamers were fitted with stoppers, and as these had a distressing habit of getting broken or lost their absence detracts from the value of the piece.
See colour plate page 70

...lass cream jug with ...obnail pattern by Hobbs, ...rockunier, *c.* 1886.

CREAM JUGS

Small jugs for cream came into fashion as coffee-drinking became a widespread habit in Europe in the early eighteenth century. The earliest examples were of silver and bore little decoration other than an elegantly curving handle and lip. Later eighteenth-century examples became increasingly decorative, echoing developments in the styles of silver ware, through the baroque, rococo and neo-classical forms. Shapes became more varied, inverted Greek helmets, shells and nautilus beakers being particularly popular. Elongated, low jugs resembling sauceboats were fashionable in the mid-eighteenth century, but later, vase shapes, often incorporating high foot-rims or ball feet, came into vogue. Novelty shapes included the cow creamer (q.v.) and the goat-and-bee jug, made in the form of a vessel with reclining goats at the bottom and a recurring bee motif (perhaps a reference to the Biblical 'milk and honey'). The prevailing silver shapes were repeated in porcelain from the middle of the eighteenth century onwards, and lower down the social scale pottery cream jugs have been widely manufactured in Europe and America to this day. In this medium there are countless examples worth considering, from transfer-printed mementoes to modern tourist souvenirs and crested jugs in Goss china (q.v.).

CRUETS

This term is often incorrectly used to denote salt and pepper sets (q.v.); from the collector's standpoint the term signifies a type of small glass bottle of Venetian origin, intended to hold vinegar or olive oil used in salad dressing. These bottles resemble tiny decanters (q.v.) and paralleled the larger vessels in development, style and decoration. The earliest examples in Britain date from the late seventeenth century and were produced in flint glass with a distinctive mallet shape. Eighteenth-century cruets were rather taller, with bulging bodies, though tapering cylindrical forms became fashionable by 1780. The most popular technique was cut glass,

Queen's ware cruet stand of English manufacture for export to France, c. 1786.

though wheel-engraving was also used. Opaque glass cruets with enamel decoration were a speciality of Bristol (q.v.). Cruet stands were fashioned in silver or Sheffield plate, and consisted of footed trays with a frame containing two or more rings which held the bottles securely. The earlier type had a large central handle, but eighteenth- and nineteenth-century examples often had twin handles mounted at the sides of the frame.

CUPS AND SAUCERS

Cups designed specifically for coffee, chocolate or tea began to appear in Europe in the seventeenth century when these beverages were first introduced. A reflection on the costliness of such drinks was the fact that the earliest cups were made of silver. As the quality of ceramics improved in the eighteenth century, silver cups rapidly declined and examples are now comparatively rare. Porcelain cups were used in China, and the earliest European ceramic cups followed Chinese patterns, being either fitted with twin handles or without handles at all. The early form of coffee cup was a straight-sided cylinder with a handle jutting at right angles from the body. Such coffee cans were fashionable in the second half of the eighteenth century. The single-handled teacup developed slowly in the same period and shallow cups without handles continued to be manufactured until the beginning of the nineteenth century and are often referred to as tea bowls (q.v.). Thereafter the general shape of teacups became standardized although providing an infinite variety of

Sèvres porcelain cup and saucer, 1769.

74

a circular stand with a central indentation to hold the cup steady. The saucer-dish with its high sides was often regarded as no more than an extremely shallow tea bowl, whose greater surface area permitted more rapid cooling of the liquid – hence the eighteenth-century custom of drinking tea from the saucer rather than the cup. The collecting of matched cups and saucers enables the student of ceramics to acquire typical examples of the wares of many different potteries for a modest outlay.

See also *Tea Bowls, Trembleuses*

designs and motifs, each pottery producing its own distinctive styles.

Saucers in their present form are relatively modern and evolved out of the Oriental saucer-dish, with its characteristic central depression and slightly upward-curving sides, and the teacup stand, originally no more than

CUTLERY

The layman's term for what the antique trade describe as flatware (forks and spoons) and knives (q.v.). The trade term is derived from

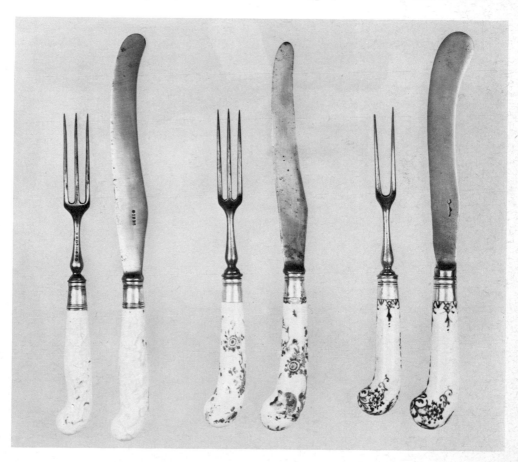

75

Two settings of silver cutlery by H. Van de Velde, c. 1900.

the fact that forks and spoons are manufactured from flattened sheets of metal (silver, gold, Sheffield plate), which is cut and stamped to the desired shape. The term cutlery, however, embraces all manner of small domestic items associated with eating and drinking, irrespective of their material or method of manufacture.

Apart from knives (which are discussed separately), domestic eating implements are relatively modern, but ordinary tableware, in silver or pewter, dates from the sixteenth century. Even a century later such items were by no means commonplace and examples in metal are rare before the eighteenth century. Forks were introduced to England from Italy in the early seventeenth century but were very slow to catch on, it being considered unmanly to use them. One's spoon and fingers, aided with copious chunks of bread, were long considered

adequate for all practical purposes. Fork were originally produced with two tines three-tined examples began to appear in th late seventeenth century and did not becom widespread until the eighteenth century Thus the majority of early specimens o cutlery will be found as isolated examples an matched sets with uniform patterns are rar before the mid-eighteenth century. There after there is immense scope in the man different styles of flatware, though some o the patterns (such as Queen's pattern, rat-tail fiddle-back and acanthus leaf) remaine popular long after their début and have bee revived at various times down to the preser day. Silver cutlery, of course, can be date by the hallmarks, but this guide does no apply to Sheffield plate or electroplate Larger items, such as slices, servers and ladle may be found in matching patterns as par of a service.

DAGGERS

Generic name for any edged weapon with a short blade, and covering a wide range of weapons for both military use and personal protection. Daggers were developed in medieval Europe as ancillary weapons to the sword, the earliest form being the *misericorde* or *panzerbrecher*, whose French and German names suggest that it was used for administering the *coup de grâce* to a fallen adversary or for piercing armour of opposing knights. From about 1350 daggers were sheathed in scabbards which were highly ornamented, and the blades, pommels and handles of the weapons themselves were often decorated. Other early versions of the dagger included the *anlace*, carried by judges and magistrates, and the *poignard* or poniard, used as a jabbing or parrying weapon in conjunction with the sword. The French *basilarde* or *langue de bœuf* had a broad ox-tongue-shaped blade and often had a smaller knife mounted in the side of the scabbard. This idea spread to Scotland and may be found in dirks and *sgian dhu* (literally 'black knife') of Highland dress down to the present day. Military-pattern dirks were carried by midshipmen of the Royal Navy and officers of Highland regiments. Similar dirks and daggers, suspended by hangers from the sword-belt, were also worn by many European armies and navies, the Imperial German and Nazi *Kriegsmarine* being a notable example.

From the sixteenth century onwards many European military daggers had a large thumb ring so that they could be mounted on a staff and used as a form of pike; this may have suggested the bayonet, thought to be named after the French town of Bayonne. The earliest bayonets had a solid circular shaft which could be rammed into the muzzle of a musket after it was fired, but the so-called plug bayonet was replaced by the modern ring bayonet in the eighteenth century, which enabled the weapon to be fired with the bayonet fixed. Twentieth-century bayonets have become progressively shorter, but present a wide variety of types, from the British spike bayonet to the elaborate American and European versions with saw-edged blades, and Commando knives incorporating knuckle-duster handles. Other types of dagger include the narrow-bladed stiletto, the toothed-edged *main gauche* used in duelling as a parrying weapon which could catch the opponent's sword-blade and snap it off. Oriental daggers include the curved *kukri* of the Gurkhas, the wavy-bladed *kris* of Malaya and the distinctive Hindu *katar* with its broad, triangular blade and H-shaped handle.

See also *Firearms Curiosa*, *Knives*

DECANTERS

The importation of wines in casks from Europe to Britain led to the development of the decanter in the late seventeenth century. Previously wine was served at the table in the original bottle. The practice of storing wine bottles in bins and cellars stimulated the growth of decanters, which were much more suitable for table use. The earliest decanters were made of heavy flint glass and had long necks, squat bodies, and a looped carrying handle near the top, with a wide rim to secure the cord tying the cork. Early eighteenth-century decanters had wider mouths and no handles, and by the late

A pair of carved and painted decoy ducks; American, mid-19th century.

Swirl-patterned decanter; Pennsylvania, 1800–50.

eighteenth century the shape used to the present day had become standardized. Glass stoppers gradually replaced corks from about 1750, though nineteenth-century examples with silver mounts, often in the form of vine-leaves and bunches of grapes, are known.

Coloured glass was widely used for decanters of the eighteenth century, the name of the wine being inscribed in gilt lettering on the side. Decanters often bore gilt decoration, with floral patterns, heraldic emblems and scenery predominating. In the latter half of the century, however, decanters were increasingly produced in clear, colour-less glass with cut or engraved patterns, and the extension of this decoration to cover the entire surface led to the development of the separate wine label (q.v.). The styles and techniques of decanters varied considerably and included barrels with concentric rings on the neck or deeply cut vertical ribbing, tall, cylindrical shapes with fluting on the sides and faceting on the shoulders and stoppers, all-over strawberry cutting on globular decanters with tall necks, and square decanters with deep relief engraving, wheel or acid engraving on the sides in intricate figure compositions (hunting scenes being parti-cularly popular). Nineteenth-century de-canters continued or revived earlier shapes, but increasing use was made of colourless glass, and pressed or moulded glass was a cheaper substitute for the heavy cut-glass

decanters of the Regency period. There was revival of free-blown decanters in the la nineteenth century, but pressed glass is st that most commonly used. Jug-shaped d canters, with silver handles, spouts and li became popular in the second half of th nineteenth century, mainly for clarets. Part cularly sought after are French and Englis decanters with *millefiori* decoration in th base and stopper, and American fancy gla decanters with Art Nouveau motifs.

DECOYS

Decoys are artificial ducks carved from woc and painted to simulate the plumage of real bird. These decoys are placed in th water as if feeding, to attract wild fowl to th spot and bring them within the range the concealed hunter. This practice is thoug to have been devised by the North America Indians, although in seventeenth-centu England and the Netherlands a special trained tame duck was used to entice oth ducks into a tunnel leading from the se marshes or estuary into a net-covered pon However, the use of artificial decoys or ginated in the United States and was lor regarded as a distinctive form of folk a Intricately carved decoys, with realistica chiselled feathers, beak and eyes, were pr duced in many parts of New England in th eighteenth and nineteenth centuries. T more elaborate examples incorporated glass eyes and even quacking devices which imitated the call of the wild fowl. The art of hand-carved decoys declined in the late nineteenth century with the advent of machine-made decoys and the increasing use of moulded rubber which, though more realistic, lacks the aesthetic qualities of the older wooden ducks.

DESK EQUIPMENT

There are many collectable items associated with writing and, in the broader sense, office administration. Fountain pens, inkstands and inkpots, paperknives, paperweights and writing cases (qq.v.) are discussed separately, but there are many other articles of lesser importance. Small boxes in Mauchline or Tunbridge ware (qq.v.) were popular from about 1820 onwards, first as containers for wafers and other sealing devices and, after 1840, for postage stamps. Many of

them have actual stamps mounted or set in their lids, but the sloping tops and stamp-sized compartments are tell-tale characteristics. Various gadgets were patented in the late nineteenth century for moistening stamps and envelopes. Blotters may be found in the form of elaborate binders and covers for blotting-paper sheets, as well as semi-circular roller blotters which sometimes have stamp boxes mounted in the flat upper side. Victorian paper clips were large, spring-loaded contraptions, their leaves heavily ornamented and often shaped like human hands. Patent devices for weighing letters became popular after the uniform postal reforms of the 1840s, and these are described under *Balances and Scales*.

Pencils are among the commonest and cheapest forms of tourist souvenir, with gaily painted decoration and inscriptions on their sides. More elaborate pencils had ivory or bone mounts, while some late nineteenth-century examples incorporated miniature

Desk set by Jacob Petit; mid-19th century.

peepshows at one end. Propelling pencils with adjustable lead date from about 1830 and may be found in gold, silver, white metal, pewter or brass. Pencil sharpeners range from desk models originating in the 1870s to the numerous novelty sharpeners whose function is disguised by their shape – animals, birds, locomotives, houses and aeroplanes being typical examples. Nineteenth-century erasers consisted of pieces of indiarubber mounted in ornamental holders of wood, ivory, porcelain or brass, many of which were quite decorative. Children's erasers were of brightly enamelled metal with fairy-tale or nursery-rhyme characters. Ferrules and rulers come in many different forms, both circular and two-dimensional, illustrating the different units of measure used in Europe before the advent of metrication. Other examples have tables of postal rates engraved on them, and there are even papier mâché rulers with chinoiserie (q.v.) decoration in inlaid mother-of-pearl and ivory.

From 1870 onwards the office equipment industry developed rapidly, especially in the United States. Early examples of staple-fasteners, letter-embossing gadgets, filing punches and string dispensers were lavishly decorated in the prevailing 'Beaux Arts' style. See colour plate page 87

DIARIES AND NOTECASES

Objects of vertu fashionable in the nineteenth century, when the diary became less of a private journal and more of an *aide-mémoire* or engagement book. For this purpose much smaller books were produced by stationers, with spaces for two or three days' entries to each page, headed with the dates throughout the year. The practice of inserting brief notes on important anniversaries, national events and holidays developed in the 1850s into useful tables of all kinds, attached to the diary proper, and combining it with the most practical elements previously confined to almanacs (q.v.). These commercial diaries were frequently bound in decorative cases, embellished with tartan covers, pokerwork

or embossed leather, and frequently had a small, slim pencil housed in the spine. By the end of the nineteenth century specialized diaries for various trades and professions were being published, their notes in keeping with the vocation of the person using them.

Decorative diaries were produced for ladies, and in this instance the content was reduced in favour of a more ornamental style of binding. In many cases the diary itself consists of no more than a few sheets of paper embellished with floral patterns, while the binding is lavishly carved in ivory or mother-of-pearl and inlaid with gold or silver. Diaries and notecases (as they are often called) were even produced with silver or silver-gilt bindings, chased or embossed with floral ornament, and fitted with silver or gold pencils to match. Notecases with fine leaves of ivory, which could be washed and re-used, were designed as engagement books. These attractive cases may also be found with bindings in horn, tortoiseshell, porcelain plaques or transfer-printed enamels. Semi-precious stones, amber, coral and jet were set into the bindings and were particularly fashionable in the late nineteenth century. These decorative diaries and notecases declined in Edwardian times and had all but disappeared by the time of World War I. Various attempts have been made to revive them in more recent years.
See also *Carnets de Bal*

DISHES

Shallow circular or oval objects, made in a
variety of materials and sizes and primarily
intended for the serving of food. Dishes
range from the medieval trenchers made of
wood, to the ornate gold and silver plate of
the wealthier classes, and encompass the
whole range of ceramics. Wooden platters
were commonplace in Europe and America
until relatively recently and many examples
may be found with carved or decorated
borders, often following traditional folk
patterns. The majority of ceramic dishes
available to the collector date from the
seventeenth century and range in size from
small side-plates to the large, usually oval
chargers and meat-servers. Individual items
may be collected to illustrate the different
glazes, bodies and styles of decoration
favoured by the potteries of different countries. The more decorative (and collectable)
forms include European delftware (faience

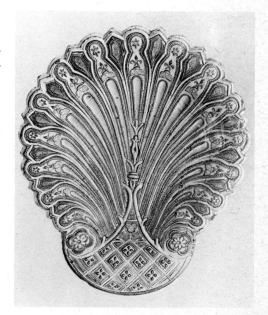

and maiolica) decorated with distinctive 'blue dash' tin-glazed ornament. These elaborate, though crudely decorated dishes and chargers were the forerunners of the many rack-plates and commemorative plates of more recent times. Electioneering plates were popular in England from the eighteenth century onwards, and dishes bearing portraits of famous personages and inscriptions marking outstanding events form a large group of commemorative ware (q.v.).

Associated with dishes are several collectable items. Dish covers were fashionable in the eighteenth and early nineteenth centuries for keeping food warm and free of dust and insects. They were made of domed or bell-shaped silver or Sheffield plate, with handles at the sides or on top. Early examples were ornately decorated but the early nineteenth-century covers were usually rather plain, relieved only by the coats of arms of the owners. They were often made in sets of varying sizes. Supports for dishes, either to keep them from damaging the surface of tables or so that small heating lamps could be placed underneath, may be found in the form of metal crosses or rings, the latter being especially popular in

Ireland. These supports were fashioned i pewter, silver, brass or Sheffield plate an often had ornamental features.
See also *Butter Items, Cheese Dishes*

DOLLS

The earliest dolls, dating back to the *ushab* figures of Egypt of the second millennium B were not children's playthings, but had socio-religious significance. The ban on th creation of human images, found in many the world's religions, shows the importanc attached to such figures in primitive societie Dolls, or more accurately, human figurine may be found in every part of the worl from the pre-Columbian ritual dolls of th Mayas and Incas to the fertility dolls of Afri and the carved wooden figures of Polynesi Many of these dolls belong more properly the realms of ethnography, and have lon been an object of serious study b anthropologists.

Children's dolls are modern by compariso and in Europe date from the end of th Middle Ages. Young girls would imitat their mothers by nursing a doll, and for th reason many dolls, especially the early one were in the form of babies. Indeed, the figures were known as babies until the lat seventeenth century when the term 'dol first came into use. Significantly the wor for doll in many languages – *pupa* (Latin *poupée* (French), *Puppe* (German) – mean baby (cf. the English words puppy an poppet). The French *bébé* and America baby-doll indicate the virtual synonymity dolls and babies to this day. For this reaso also, the majority of dolls were fashione like babies, with disproportionately larg heads and wide-eyed expressions. Even whe dolls were dressed to represent more matu figures, their facial expressions were ofte infantile. Likewise the majority of dolls a of the female sex, partly because the litt girls who played with them tended identify with their dolls, and partly becau girls' clothes have usually been more attracti and colourful than boys'.

Until the early nineteenth century, do

Dressed pegwooden dolls; European, late 19th century.

English wax doll, c. 1860.

dolls, the best being produced by the Montanari family, Pierotti and Marsh. These wax dolls were comparatively expensive at the time, being exquisitely modelled with individual strands of hair sprouting from their scalps in a lifelike manner. Conta and Boehme of Possneck manufactured heads in parian ware which were exported to France and England for assembly with dolls whose cloth bodies were produced locally. Many dolls, however, were completely assembled in Germany and those by such firms as Simon & Halbig, the Heubach brothers, Armand Marseille and Kammer Reinhardt are particularly sought after.

During the Colonial period the majority of American dolls were of English, French or Dutch origin, having been imported by the early settlers. The earliest documented doll of European origin in the New World was presented by Sir Richard Grenville to the Roanoke Indians in 1585, and the drawings of John White, who accompanied the expedition, show an Indian girl proudly clutching her Elizabethan doll. Philadelphia was an early centre of doll production on a commercial scale by the 1820s, the heads being imported from Germany and leather-covered bodies assembled locally. Thenceforward many American dolls were made up of European parts or followed European patterns closely. Nevertheless, most of the technical developments in doll manufacture took place in the United States. The earliest rubber dolls were produced by Benjamin Lee of New York in 1855 and the first celluloid dolls were produced by John Wesley and Isaiah Hyatt a decade later. Subsequently American manufacturers developed the first commercial rag dolls, stuffed dolls and plastic dolls. Distinctive types were evolved in the United States, including the Palmer Cox Brownies, the Kewpie doll and the Golliwog. Even the Teddy bear, one of the few humanoid animal figures to win acceptance in this medium, originated in the United States, being allegedly associated with President Theodore Roosevelt. Mechanical dolls, with moving limbs and eyes, talking dolls and

in Europe were virtually a cottage industry. The toy-makers of southern Germany were the first to commercialize the object, producing the so-called pegwooden dolls about 1820.

A decade later dolls with wax heads began to appear. They were popularly known as slit-heads on account of the technique of inserting tufts of hair into the scalp. By the middle of the century an important sideline of the Saxon porcelain industry consisted of making bisque heads for dolls, and these continued to dominate the quality end of the world market until World War I. Both France and Britain began producing fine dolls in the second half of the nineteenth century to compete with the German factories. The best French dolls were produced by Jumeau, Bru, Huret, Martin and Rohmer, and dolls with the names of these manufacturers impressed on them (usually on the base of the neck) are worth a considerable amount of money nowadays. The English manufacturers specialized in wax

have been recorded in France as far back as 1391, but they became an important adjunct of the French fashion industry in the eighteenth century when many of them were exported to England and Colonial America to demonstrate the latest styles in day and evening wear, night-dresses and underwear. Fashion dolls were also widely circulated within France itself in order that the provinces should be fully conversant with the latest Paris fashions. Such fashion dolls were often known as pandoras, after Pandora, the woman made from clay by Vulcan and endowed by the gods with every talent known to mankind. The fashion doll was largely superseded by the fashion plate (q.v.) though examples have been recorded dating from the early nineteenth century.
See colour plate page 88
See also *Furniture – Miniature, Toys*

DOOR FURNITURE

The fittings of doors include a wide range of items, from knobs and knockers to bell-pulls and finger-plates. Knobs and handles offer plenty of scope, being available in many different materials and shapes. Turned wooden knobs are the more common, but decorated porcelain knobs and handles date from the late eighteenth century. Metal knobs are fairly plentiful, brass, bronze and white metal alloys being readily obtainable. Apart from floral or geometric patterns, cast, engraved, stamped or pierced, there are novelty handles in the shape of human hands or animals' paws. Door knockers gradually

Kewpie dolls, c. 1920 by Rose O'Neill and c. 1940, and matching doll's china teaset, c. 1910.

crying dolls, were developed in the United States between 1880 and 1910.

In more recent years there has been a marked development in the art of costume dolls which are now regarded as an important aspect of tourism all over the world. A few of these tourist mementoes follow traditional designs, such as the Russian hollow wooden dolls with smaller dolls concealed within dolls of successively larger size, or the ubiquitous corn dolly found in many parts of Asia and Europe; but the majority of them are comparatively modern and consist of dolls dressed in national or regional costume. From the middle of the nineteenth century onwards clothing, accessories and a wide range of domestic equipment have been produced in miniature for dolls' use, and such items are also worth collecting.

Articulated wooden dolls have been recorded from France and Germany from about 1450 and were intended not as children's playthings but as models for artists. Such figures were known as mannikins and the idea was adapted in France in the eighteenth century to become the *mannequin* or *poupée modèle*. Exquisitely dressed dolls, emulating the real-life fashions then current,

Right Brass door ornament with head of George III; English, late 18th century.

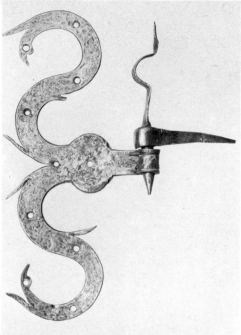

nnsylvania iron hinge
th stag-horn and bird's-
ad motif; 18th century.

soiling the woodwork, date from the eighteenth century and even to this day many ornamental examples may be found, in glass, pottery, porcelain, hardwoods, or beaten copper or brass sheet.

See also *Door Stops, Locks and Keys*

DOOR STOPS

The invention of the rising butt type of door-hinge about 1775, whereby doors closed automatically, gave rise to the door porter or stop. The object was to hold the door open when required, which meant a fairly solid construction to withstand the weight of the door. The earliest examples were moulded in earthenware and fitted with long handles so that it would not be necessary to bend down to move them around. Other early forms were cast in iron, bronze or brass and these often produced in fanciful shapes.

came into fashion in the late sixteenth century, and by the early nineteenth century were used widely at all levels of society. Brass, bronze, gun-metal and iron were commonly used for the purpose, both cast and wrought, and innumerable examples may be found in a wide range of decorative styles down to the present day. Door-bells became common in the nineteenth century, the earliest type consisting of brass bell-pulls operating a bell just inside the door. Rotary door-bells came into fashion about 1880 and many different types have been produced in the past century. Until comparatively recently door-bells were elaborately decorated with animal masks and foliate patterns. Plates and flaps of bronze, brass or iron for letter apertures are relatively modern, since there was no use for them before the advent of pre-paid postage in Britain (1840) or house-to-house delivery in the United States (1863). Lock-plates and covers from the eighteenth century onwards were frequently decorative in appearance and are worth looking for. Finger-plates, to prevent finger-marks from

ght Group of English
orstops; early 19th
ntury.

A common design resembled a solid bell sliced in half, surmounted by a long handle. Improved techniques of casting at the beginning of the nineteenth century led to bronze or iron door stops which resemble Staffordshire pottery figures (q.v.) in their characteristic 'flatback' appearance. Brass door stops were popular in the early nineteenth century, coated with a form of black lacquer which prevented corrosion. A mixture of bronze powder and turpentine, patented by Hubball of Clerkenwell in 1812, superseded this.

By the middle of the century cast-iron door stops featuring historic figures, Shakespearean characters and even famous contemporary personages such as Queen Victoria, the Duke of Wellington and Disraeli, were produced in vast quantities by the iron foundries of Carron and Coalbrookdale. Glass door stops known as 'dumpies' are thought to have been made in Bristol (q.v.), while the Kilner factory in Wakefield produced tall door stops in green bottle glass, often incorporating bouquets of flowers worked in tiny air bubbles.

See also *Door Furniture*

DRESSING-TABLE SETS

Sets of hair and clothes brushes, combs and looking-glasses with uniform decoration became fashionable in the second half of the eighteenth century and have remained in use to the present day. They provide the collector with a cross-section of many different materials and decorative styles,

from boulle and *piqué* (qq.v.) to pla tortoiseshell, gold, silver-gilt, or silver various techniques such as *martelé* (q.v raised relief and engraving, wood inlaid wi ivory, mother-of-pearl or bone, or wi enamel, glass or porcelain mounts ai decoration on the handles. Dressing boxe produced from the seventeenth centu onwards, contained a number of tiny cor partments and drawers to hold trinke jewelry, patches and other items, and gene ally had a mirror fitted in the underside of tl lid, which could be propped open. Speci trays, of silver, glass or porcelain, were pr duced in the eighteenth and nineteen centuries, sometimes with shaped depre sions to hold the brushes, combs and mirro These trays were often made in sets wi small matching stands for scent bottles (q.v and powder pots. Small branched objec usually made in silver or Sheffield plate, b occasionally in pottery, glass or wood, we used to hold rings when not worn, and we known as ring trees (q.v.). They were usual ornamented and shaped like miniature tre or a stag's antlers. Other small objects ass ciated with the dressing table or, mc accurately, the ladies' purse, include dori cases and powder compacts, a product of t late nineteenth century and a reflection changing social attitudes which permitt ladies to repair their make-up in public semi-public places. Tiny circular pots, f rouge or eye-shadow, were fashioned porcelain, enamels, Mauchline and Tunbrid ware or silver (qq.v.).

See colour plate page 291

ÉCUELLES

French term for a type of shallow, two-handled bowl with a close-fitting lid, popular in western Europe in the seventeenth and eighteenth centuries. The German name *Wöchnerinschüssel* (midwife's bowl) is more explicit, and refers to the fact these vessels were often used for feeding women in the last stages of pregnancy and early period after childbirth. Écuelles were fashionable in France, Germany, Italy and Spain but never seem to have caught on in British or Colonial America, where the rather similar caudle cup (q.v.) was used instead. They were usually made of silver or porcelain, often with matching stands which served as food warmers (q.v.).

EGGS

Glass, porcelain, alabaster or marble fashioned in the shape of large hen's eggs, popular from the mid-eighteenth century as hand-coolers. They were employed by young ladies attending dances and balls in order to prevent hot, sweaty palms. Similar objects in humbler materials such as earthenware or wood, were known as darners or darning eggs and their use is self-explanatory. More elaborate examples, dating from the 1870s, were made of turned wood with hollow interiors; the two halves unscrewed to reveal a compartment for needles, thimble and thread.

EGG BOILERS

Small metal vessels, usually in silver, Sheffield plate or electroplate, for boiling eggs at the dining table or sideboard. Egg boilers were fashionable in late eighteenth-century England, and though their use declined in the nineteenth century they have been occasionally produced down to the present day. They consist of a cylindrical can, with twin handles at the sides, tripod or four-footed stands with small spirit lamps underneath. The interior sometimes contains a horizontal plate with apertures for two, three or four eggs, and additional refinements include a glass and sand egg-timer mounted on the lid. Egg boilers were usually manufactured *en suite* with egg cups (q.v.) and spoons with a matching frame.

EGG CUPS

Small utensils designed to hold boiled eggs. Egg cups are thought to date back no further

ght Porcelain egg with *a*melled decoration; *ss*ian, late 19th century.

e Lucy, in a white *s*lin dress, with a *ri*c body and parian *d*, *c.* 1865; Marie, *a* blue dress, with kid *ly* and bisque head, *nch*, *c.* 1875; *wooden doll with *ri*c body and papier *ché* head, *c.* 1845.

than the late seventeenth century, but few examples are known prior to the early eighteenth century. They were generally produced in silver or Sheffield plate, often with matching spoons, frame and egg boiler (q.v.). Later, as the practice of using special cups for boiled eggs became more widespread, humbler materials were employed, such as brass or pewter. Turned wooden cups and pottery cups became very popular in the second half of the nineteenth century and exhibit a wide range of decorative styles and treatment. The earliest shape consisted of a shallow cup on a stem with a raised foot, but later versions had solid bases. Double egg cups were common from about 1850, often having cups of different sizes to accommodate small or standard hen's eggs or duck's eggs.

ELECTROPLATE

Generic term for objects of one metal or alloy whose surface is coated with another metal by electrolytic action. The process involves the immersion of the object to be plated in a bath containing an electrolytic solution. At the opposite pole (anode) the plating metal is suspended in the solution. When an electric current is passed through the bath particles from the plating metal are transferred evenly to the surface of the object. The thickness of the coating will depend on the length of time during which electrolysis takes place. The principle of electrolysis was perfected in the early nineteenth century, but received its most important commercial application when George Elkington of Birmingham filed patents on electroplating between 1836 and 1840. Thenceforward Elkington & Company revolutionized the mass market for silver objects, ousting Sheffield plate (q.v.) and mechanizing the processes for making hollow-ware resembling the more costly silver articles. The basic objects were produced in various copper alloys with tin, zinc or nickel and plated with silver or, more rarely, gold. The technique of electroplating freed the craftsman from the need to work directly in precious metals and stimulated the mass-

production of base-metal articles mechanically die-stamped out of copper sheeting rather than hand-wrought or cast. For this reason many examples of electroplate have a 'tinny' ring about them and a stereotyped quality which lacks the aesthetic satisfaction of genuine silver articles. As the original Elkington patents expired their processes were widely used and developed in the United States and European countries for tablewares, jewelry, costume accessories and many small, useful or decorative articles.

EMBROIDERY

The art of making needlework patterns on any textile base. Embroidery has been widely practised for countless generations, but on account of the fragile nature of the materials employed, the majority of items available to the collector date back no further than the seventeenth century. The quality and style of embroidery vary considerably, depending on the material on which it is based, from fine silks to coarse canvas, and the numerous types of stitches practised, varying in fineness from twelve to twenty-five stitches the inch.

The bulk of the embroidery now available to the collector was produced in the eighteenth and nineteenth centuries. The larger forms of embroidery include samplers and biblical texts (often stitched by young girls as a form

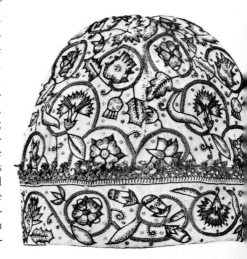

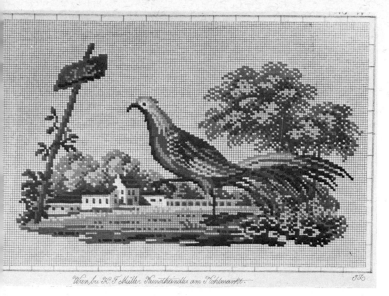

Wien, bei K. F. Müller Kunsthändler am Kohlmarkt.

inted embroidery
ttern; Austrian, mid-
th century.

'i Man's night-cap
broidered with black
k and silver-gilt thread
linen; English, late
h century.

of 'apprentice piece'), cushion covers, fire-screens, lambrequins (q.v.), mats, cosies and tidies. The more decorative forms of embroidery may be found on a wide range of articles such as book jackets, purses, book markers (q.v.) and costume accessories. Many forms of male apparel, from slippers to braces (suspenders) were elaborately embroidered by women and given to their men-folk as presents. The invention of the sewing machine and the improved techniques of weaving patterned fabrics led to the decline of home needlework from 1860 onwards.

Embroidery pictures were popular in the late eighteenth and early nineteenth centuries. Well-known paintings and prints were drawn on a linen base and then stitched laboriously in coloured threads to match the original. A short cut was devised whereby parts of prints were glued to pieces of cloth, and embroidery worked around them. Such pictures may be found with the faces of people taken from the original picture, while their bodies, clothing and surrounding scenery have been embroidered. Alternatively the finer details, such as human features, would be first applied to the silk or satin base in watercolours and the rest of the picture built up by fine needlework.

See also *Berlin Woolwork, Stumpwork*

ENAMELLED COINS

Coins on which the inscription and pictorial elements have been worked over in enamels of various colours. Enamelled coins were a product of the late nineteenth century when the working classes in France and Britain began to wear gaudy pieces of jewelry – large, brightly coloured and cheap. Gold coins mounted on watch chains or converted into brooches, pendants and cuff-links were fashionable at the time, and enamelled coins offered a cheaper and more flashy substitute. Gold coins with surface enamelling are not unknown but are comparatively rare. Conversely, very few bronze coins were enamelled, partly because the basic material had so little value, and partly because few base-metal coins of the period had designs suitable for enamelling.

The use of enamelling in jewelry was revived about 1884, in a modest way, by William Henry Probert, employed as a jeweler's painter in Birmingham. Probert confined his enamelling to two or three colours, and specialized in the larger coins, such as the crown featuring Pistrucci's splendid St George and Dragon. He built up a considerable business, supplying jewelers with enamelled coins up to 1892, though he continued in business until 1904.

Contemporary with Probert, but far surpassing him, was Edwin Steele, who inherited the family jewelry business in 1886. From then until his death in 1891, he produced some of the finest enamelled coins, noted for the intricacy of their decoration and the great number of different colours which he managed to incorporate in a single piece. No coin was too small for him and he excelled in enamelling groats and threepences mounted as earrings. Edwin Steele had no equal in the depth and delicacy of his craftsmanship and because of his brief career it is not surprising that examples of his work are very rare. His son carried on the business but he never attained the skill of his father, and with his death in 1900 the firm ceased production of enamelled coins altogether. Probert and the Steeles enamelled many

British coins other than contemporary issues, and most silver coins from the Great Re-coinage of 1816 onwards have been recorded in this manner. In addition they enamelled the coins of other countries, especially the United States, to which many examples were later exported.

The majority of European coins with enamel decoration, however, emanated from a number of jewelers working in France up to the end of World War I. To them is attributed the exotic Burmese rupee with a peacock reverse. These handsome coins, minted under Mindon Min and Thibaw, circulated throughout South-East Asia and were brought back to France at the turn of the century by troops serving in Indo-China. The best French enamelling is attributed to Louis-Elic Millinet who specialized in the subtle decoration of the peacock's tail feathers. Contemporary French silver coins, up to the 5 franc denomination, were also decorated in enamel.

ENAMELLED GLASS

The technique of decorating glassware by means of enamelling is of immense antiquity. Archaeological evidence has proved that the Egyptians in the tenth century BC practised this art, while numerous examples of Roman enamelled glass have survived.

The decoration was painted on to the glass with a mixture composed of powdered coloured glass and a binding substance. When the object had been painted it was placed in a kiln and fired at a very high temperature so that the enamel and the body of the object were fused together. This decoration, when properly applied, is extremely durable, and nothing short of marking with an abrasive substance or a sharp tool would remove it.

During the Dark Ages the art of enamelled glass died out in western Europe, but continued to flourish in the Islamic world, from Syria to Spain and North Africa. Enamelled glass was an important feature of Moorish art, lamps decorated in this manner being a common sight in mosques in the thirteenth

and fourteenth centuries. Syrian refugees a thought to have re-introduced the art enamelling on glass to Venice in the ear fifteenth century, and from there the proce spread to Bohemia and Germany. It w very popular in central Europe in the si teenth to eighteenth centuries and is main associated with the elaborately decorat beakers known as *Kurfürsten* glasses ar *Reichsadlerhumpen* (qq.v.), but it was al fashionable in France in the same period.

In Britain, however, enamelled glass w at its most popular in the latter half of t eighteenth century, and it was often used conjunction with a decorative techniq known as oiled gilding. The popularity enamelled glass in Britain coincided wi the spread of the rococo style from Europ

Left Enamelled glass
drinking vessel; German,
1609.

Right Glass chalice made
by Venetian workmen in
France; early 16th
century.

and the motifs employed in this form of decoration were often characterized by the asymmetrical lines of vine-leaves and tendrils.

Many of the artists employed in glass enamelling were equally versatile in applying this kind of decoration to porcelain and the small boxes and toys for which Battersea, Birmingham and the South Staffordshire area were famous in the mid-eighteenth century. There is a certain similarity between the fine translucent porcelain of Chelsea and Bow and the opaque white glass developed at Bristol about the same time. One of the finest of the Bristol enamellers was Michael Edkins (1733–1811), who began his artistic career as a decorator of delftware and progressed to the enamelling of Bristol glass about 1762. He is believed to have decorated

vases, cruet sets, bowls and even tea caddies in the Bristol blue-and-white glass. Items finely decorated with birds and Chinese figures have also been attributed to him. Edkins seldom, if ever, signed his work, and thus collectors should beware of attaching too much significance to the name. Nevertheless, there is now a great demand for enamelled Bristol glass, which has an uncanny resemblance to Chinese porcelain in form and texture, and which is decorated with chinoiserie (q.v.) motifs in soft greens and reds, with elegant birds and diaper borders.

In London, the outstanding craftsman in this field was James Giles (1713–80), who also began as a decorator of English and Chinese porcelain. Much of the best decorated Worcester porcelain of the 1760s came from his studio, and he is also known to have worked on Chelsea and Bow porcelain. He practised enamelling and gilding on glass, both opaque white and coloured varieties, and his motifs varied from chinoiseries to elegant classical designs of urns, flowers and pheasants. Examples of coloured glass scent bottles (q.v.) decorated by Giles are not uncommon, but larger items, such as bowls and decanters, are scarce.

In the eighteenth century Newcastle was the centre of a glass-making industry whose wares are now eagerly sought after on account of their superior quality and delicacy. While the best-known Newcastle glass is that which was shipped across the North Sea to be finely engraved in Germany and the Netherlands, the products of the town are also noted for the excellent enamelling and gilding applied by the Beilbys. William Beilby Jr (1740–1819) at first worked in Birmingham as a maker and decorator of enamel boxes, but about 1760 he moved to Newcastle, where he gained employment at the Dagnia-Williams glasshouse. His sister Mary (1749–97) joined him five years later and between that date and 1778, when they left the district, they were responsible for some of the finest enamel decoration ever applied to English glassware. The Beilbys were equally at home with monochrome white and with multicoloured enamel decora-

English wine glass with twist stem decorated by the Beilbys.

tion. Glass decorated with a very faint white enamel is comparatively rare and is believed to date from their earliest, experimental period. They seem to have specialized in the decoration of wine glasses, either with a fruiting-vine motif or with armorial bearings, but later examples of their work are noted for more ambitious decoration including landscapes, nautical scenes and some very rare chinoiseries. Among the most highly prized and expensive examples of their work are those glasses with a Jacobite flavouring, bearing enamelled portraits of Prince Charles Edward Stuart or decorated with the Stuart rose.

See also *Kurfürsten Glasses*, *Reichsadlerhumpen*

ENAMELS

Term used to denote objects decorated by various enamelling techniques. Enamel consists of compounds of silicates and metallic oxides (coloured glass), ground to a powder, applied as a paste to the surface of metal, and fused by the action of heat which melts the paste. Enamelling was known to the Egyptians, the Assyrians and the Celts and was widely practised in China, Japan and North Africa as well as the Mediterranean area. The oldest form of enamelling was champlevé, in which paste is applied to recesses in the metal base, then fused by heat. The cloisonné technique consisted of fixing the enamel paste in cloisons or cells, composed of thin strips of wires, arranged in a honeycomb pattern and soldered to the metal base. A form of this is known as *pliqué-à-jour* in which the base is removed, leaving a translucent, stained-glass effect. Other forms of decoration include *en grisaille*, in which white enamel is applied to a dark ground to give a tonal quality; and *basse taille*, in which clear enamel is applied to a metal base engraved and chased in low relief.

Enamelling was widely applied to all manner of objects of vertu in the eighteenth and nineteenth centuries. The French and the Swiss were the finest exponents of enamelling as the main or subsidiary decoration on watch cases, snuff boxes, étuis (qq.v.) and other objects fashioned in gold or silver and ornamented with precious stones. The Swiss enamellers, notably the Huaud family of Geneva, specialized in miniatures (q.v. painted in enamels. Enamelling on precious metals had been a speciality of Venice and Limoges since the Middle Ages, but example of these wares are now beyond the reach of all but the wealthiest. Less expensive, and affording many opportunities to the collector, are the English enamels which were in vogue in the second half of the eighteenth century.

English enamels were produced at Battersea, Birmingham and certain South Staffordshire towns. The industry developed to meet the demands of the rising middle classes who could not afford the gold bijouterie of the aristocracy, but needed a passable substitute Snuff boxes, patch boxes, étuis and bonbonnières were manufactured in enamelled copper in imitation of the expensive gold an

94

jeweled articles which the French and Swiss produced for the very rich. The art of enamelling on metal was in existence in London by 1747, and was well established in the Midlands by the same date. By 1750 John Taylor employed upwards of 500 persons in his Birmingham factory in the production of cheap enamelled boxes and buttons. Some idea of his output can be gained from William Hutton's *History of Birmingham* (1781), which records that one of Taylor's employees earned £3 a week by painting enamelled snuff boxes at a farthing each. At the same time there was a colony of French enamellers living in the South Staffordshire town of Bilston. They improved on the locally manufactured small japanned boxes by adorning their lids with painted enamel. Snuff boxes of japanned metal assigned to the decade 1740–50, have been attributed to these Bilston craftsmen, but they are too rare for definite identification to be made.

Although an embryonic enamel industry was in existence by 1753 in Bilston and Wednesbury, and just across the Staffordshire boundary in Birmingham, it is through the Battersea factory, established by Stephen Theodore Janssen in that year, that English enamel-ware rose to new heights. Battersea enamels far surpassed their predecessors in quality and design and indeed outclassed the later products of the Midlands. Though the Battersea enterprise lasted a mere three years, its output was tremendous and its products quite distinctive.

As Battersea went into decline, the enamel-ware industry in Birmingham and South Staffordshire prospered increasingly. It used to be fashionable to decry the products of these factories, but in recent years there has been a marked re-appraisal of them, with the result that the prices paid for the best Bilston boxes are comparable with those paid for Battersea. In general the pieces manufactured in the Midlands were much richer in colouring, partly as a result of the taste for gaudier articles as the century wore on, and partly because brighter colours became more

95

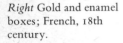

readily available to the enamellers as research into pigments progressed.

The best English enamels were produced over a period of barely thirty years. They are characterized by fine soldering and jointing of the copper plates; they are carefully enamelled with exquisite decoration, either painted by hand or transfer-printed and embellished or retouched by hand. It is difficult to differentiate items from the various Midland factories, although it is generally accepted that bonbonnières and novelty boxes in the shape of animals and birds emanated from Bilston. These should not be confused with the vast output of cheap, mass-produced trinkets in the late eighteenth and early nineteenth centuries. These little boxes, usually oval, badly hinged and lacking base rims, inferior in colouring and design, nevertheless enjoyed immense popularity as souvenirs of holiday resorts. They have a certain naïve charm, especially those depicting contemporary scenes, personalities and events.

Painted enamels were produced extensively in Berlin in the eighteenth century, the finest work being produced by the Fromery workshops. This combined enamel-painted motifs with gilded copper and silver mounts. In the early eighteenth century Augsburg

was the centre of an industry devoted to the production of finely enamelled boxes but this declined in face of the competition from the English factories. The Du Paquier porcelain works in Vienna also produced painted enamel objects of vertu in the mid-eighteenth century. Many of the German and Austrian enamelled boxes bore vignettes of a political nature, particularly before and during the period of the Seven Years' War (1756–63). Prior to about 1790 the Swiss enamelling industry had been geared primarily to the decoration of watches, but after that date diversified into the manufacture of boxes, first modelled in contemporary French style but gradually evolving distinctive styles including irregular or unusual shapes. Enamelling was also used extensively in the decoration of musical boxes and automata.

The art of enamelling languished in France during the revolutionary period and revived gradually in the early nineteenth century when craftsmen such as Julien Robillard of Paris began imitating the traditional Limoges enamels. The fashion for enamels in the Limoges style, however, gained momentum in the second half of the century when the Sèvres porcelain works produced enamelled boxes, candlesticks and *tazze*, designed to supply a rising demand which could not

Mame for money

Shall we sleep first, or how?

Savcumate opportunity

A long pull and a strong pull

Oysters Sir

Cursame

Some contributors to Punch

WHISKY

Oysters

Halleluja / JHS JHS JHS

17 82

Zu Meine Seele Singe,

Wohl auf, Und Singe schön, dem Welchem alle dinge, zu Dienst und willen stehn, Ich Will den Herren droben, hier Preisen auf der Erd, ich will ihn Herzlich lobe, so lang ich Leben Werd.

Ich will lieben und mich üben, daß ich Meinen Bräutigam Nun in allem, Mög gefallen, welcher an des Creuzes stam hat sein Leben, hingege- ben, so geduldig Wie ein Lamm.

Ich Will lieben, und mich üben, Meine ganze Lebens = zeit mich zu schicken und zu schauen, mit dem Weißen Hoch- zeit-Kleid zu Erschei- nen, mit den Rei- nen, auf des Lames Hochzeit-freud.

met by sufficient quantities of originals.
Reproduction Limoges enamels were also
produced by Samson of Paris, who is noted
for his forgeries of eighteenth-century porcelain. The taste for Limoges reproductions
reached its peak in the 1880s when enamellers
in England, Austria and Germany also
engaged in their manufacture. The fashion
declined in the 1890s in face of competition
from the entirely new styles of enamel
decoration produced by the Arts and Crafts
movement in Britain, and the Wiener
Werkstätte and the Deutscher Werkbund in
Austria and Germany, though enamel bibelots in the true Limousin tradition continue
to be produced in France to this day.

ENGRAVED GLASS

The art of engraving on glass by means of a
wheel or diamond point has been practised
since the seventeenth century, although rare
examples showing this technique of decoration have survived from Egypt and Rome at
the beginning of the Christian era. This art,
lost to Europe during the Dark Ages, was
tentatively revived in Venice in the sixteenth
century, fine diamond-point engraving being
applied to the relatively fragile soda-glass
produced at Murano. This technique spread
northwards, to the Inn and Tyrol districts of
the Habsburg dominions, and thence to
Bohemia and Silesia. By the mid-seventeenth

Right Engraved glasses;
Dutch, 18th century.

century diamond-point engraving on glass was practised in Germany and the Low Countries. The development of flint glass in England late in the seventeenth century led to the technique of wheel engraving, using a series of small copper wheels coated with emery powder mixed with oil to form a fine abrasive agent. The most elaborate engraved glass was that produced in Bohemia, which has never been surpassed for its subtle qualities of light and shade, depth and texture. The German craftsmen developed several allied techniques, such as *Hochschnitt* (high relief), *Tiefschnitt* (deep engraving or intaglio) and *Geschnitzt* (chipped). Coloured glass, with engraving in colourless contrast, was popular in Europe from the mid-eighteenth century onwards. Cameo glass was a nineteenth-century form in which layers of coloured and opaque glass were engraved so that the white layers contrasted with the coloured overlay. Engraving on drinking glasses and bowls often took the form of armorial bearings, floral patterns and scenery, but the most highly prized examples are those with commemorative inscriptions or scenes, and the important English group portraying the Old and Young Pretenders or featuring Jacobite emblems.

Allied processes involved the application of decoration by stippling with a sharp point, or by etching. The latter method used acid to eat away portions of the surface unprotected by a coating of wax in which the design was previously drawn with a stylus; but in the second half of the nineteenth century mechanical processes, using printed transfers, brought a mechanical, stereotyped quality to etched glass, lacking in genuine engraved glass. Fine engraved glass is still produced, but because it involves a high degree of skilled handwork it is usually confined to limited editions of commemorative items, which are always worth looking for.

EPHEMERA

Term embracing all manner of printed, two-dimensional items. As the name suggests, such items were of only passing importance

or usefulness, and the relative scarcity of many examples today is an indication that they were seldom considered worth preserving at the time of their currency. Even the most mundane form of printed matter, however, acquires a certain attraction with the passage of time, exhibiting the styles of design and typefaces of the past, not to mention the information it may provide for the social historian. The more decorative kinds of ephemera, such as Christmas Cards and Valentines (qq.v.), have long attracted the attention of collectors; these, along with specialized subjects such as aeronautica and militaria (qq.v.), are discussed elsewhere in this work. The most important branches of ephemeral printing are postage stamps (dating from 1840) and banknotes (dating, in Europe, from the late seventeenth century), but these are such large and highly specialized subjects as to be beyond the scope of this book.

Trade cards, carrying advertisements for businesses of all kinds, began to appear in the late seventeenth century and reached their peak of artistic excellence in the nineteenth century. They were frequently embellished with tiny vignettes illustrating the trade or profession concerned, and beautifully inscribed with copperplate engraving. The earlier examples were generally produced in letterpress, with crude line engravings, but their naïve charm compensates for their aesthetic shortcomings. Trade cards are, of course, printed to this day but are generally less exciting visually, and make up only a small part of the numerous leaflets, brochures and other promotional literature put out by many companies. Nevertheless, this type of commercial ephemera is worth considering today for its potential antiquarian interest in years to come.

Cigarette cards developed in the late nineteenth century from the earlier trade cards, being originally intended as stiffeners in the paper cigarette packs then in use. The best examples date prior to 1902, when the large tobacco combines came into being, but technically the later examples are often masterpieces of fine printing, often in full colour. They declined in America and most

European countries as monopolies were created, and died out in Britain at the beginning of World War II. Although now largely superseded by vouchers and coupons which can be exchanged for gifts, cigarette cards have their modern counterpart in the numerous picture cards given away with confectionery, foodstuffs and other consumer goods, and many examples of this type may be found all over the world.

Decorative notepaper was popular in the nineteenth century and led to such diverse forms of ephemera as commercial billheads (which, like the earlier trade cards, often featured firms' advertisements), and pictorial envelopes which reached the height of their popularity in the second half of the nineteenth century.

Security documents form an important branch of ephemera, dating from the early eighteenth century and including bonds and share certificates, insurance policies and cheques. The nature of such documents ensured that they were invariably printed to a very high specification, with such devices as engine-turned backgrounds and intricately engraved vignettes to defeat the would-be forger, and in many respects are analogous in design and execution to banknotes and stamps.

Another large group consists of tickets denoting prepayment for services, transportation and admission. Although early theatre tickets were produced in ivory, and some rail tickets (especially those issued to directors and officials of the railway companies) were made of brass or silver, the majority of tickets from the beginning of the nineteenth century were printed on pasteboard, card or paper, and often incorporate features derived from security documents. Similar types of ephemera include tokens, vouchers and coupons, exchangeable for specified goods or services in war or times of economic crises.

Paper labels on the packaging of manufactured articles date from the early eighteenth century. Amongst the more attractive categories of label are the highly ornate labels and packets formerly used for pins and needles. Patent medicines, dice and packs of playing cards, tobacco, wine and sauce-bottles, chocolate and candy, and matches are important groups whose labels offer enormous scope and have long attracted the serious attention of collectors. An unusual and now greatly sought-after form of ephemera was the watchpaper, a circular paper disc fitting inside the lid of watches to protect the workings from dust and dirt. These labels were generally engraved with the name, trademark and advertisement of the jeweler or watchmaker, and as a rule they were fine examples of minuscule typography. Publishers' and booksellers' labels, often found inside the covers of books, were often elaborately decorated, while bookplates (usually bearing the Latin inscription *ex libris*) exhibit a vast range of decorative style: intaglio, copperplate and letterpress printing, pictorial motifs and typefaces.

See also *Christmas Cards, Playing Cards, Postcards, Posters and Playbills, Valentines*

EPHEMERIDES. See *Almanacs and Ephemerides*

ÉTUIS

Small cases designed to contain personal articles such as sewing materials, scissors, manicure sets, drawing instruments and even cutlery. Étuis were in use from the early seventeenth century onwards, but the most collectable varieties were fashionable in the eighteenth and early nineteenth centuries when they were considered important objects of vertu. Their shape may be either cylindrical or flattened and rectangular, sometimes tapering slightly towards the bottom. Tops either fitted closely over the open end or were hinged. The later examples were smaller, and fitted with a ring for suspension from a chatelaine (q.v.). Great skill and artistry were lavished on the ornamentation of étuis, which may be found in gold, silver, enamels, ivory, semi-precious stones such as

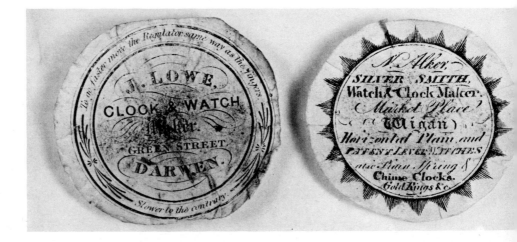

Watch papers bearing makers' trademarks and advertisements; English, late 18th century.

agate, malachite or lapis lazuli, leather or hardwood with inlays of mother-of-pearl or precious metals. Étuis were often mounted with jewels or miniatures (q.v.).

EWERS

Large jugs dating from the late Middle Ages and used mainly for pouring water for washing purposes. The characteristic form of ewer is tall and vase-shaped, with a high pedestal base, globular body, narrow neck and relatively small spout. Handles were often elaborately decorated, and lids, hinged at the handle side, were fitted to the metallic ewers. They were originally made in silver, bronze, brass or pewter but pottery ewers are known from the seventeenth century and many fine examples in porcelain were produced in the late eighteenth and nineteenth centuries, usually in conjunction with matching wash-bowls and other toilet articles. Highly decorative ewers in the form of inverted Grecian helmets on square or octagonal bases, were produced in France in the eighteenth century for ceremonial use and were fashioned in gold, silver or silver-gilt, and were richly decorated. Similar ewers in faience were produced during the same period in the Rouen and Moustiers districts of France.

See colour plate page 98
See also *Aquamaniles*

ove Silver egg-shaped ui; 19th century.

ght Worcester porcelain er with portrait of the st Duchess of vonshire; part of a set nted with 'The auties of the Court of ng Charles 11', by iah Rushton, 1869.

FAIRINGS

Small porcelain figure groups popular throughout the nineteenth century as prizes or mementoes of fairgrounds. They were especially popular in Britain, and although they were for the most part manufactured in Germany and latterly in Japan, they display a markedly British style of humour. The earliest, and now the most expensive fairings were produced by Springer and Oppenheimer of Loket in Bohemia. These were slightly larger in size and have a more solid appearance than the later fairings. The colours and glazing were of fine quality and the modelling was excellent. The subjects ranged from the faintly *risqué* to the frankly bawdy and manifest that low brand of humour which survives to this day in the seaside postcard. A high proportion of fairings feature domestic comedy, usually bedroom scenes. Timid newly-weds, drunken husbands and irate wives provide the material for these comic vignettes. Although more than 200 different titles have been recorded the commonest are those entitled 'Last to bed to put out the light', 'An awkward interruption', 'The Landlord in Love', 'Two months after marriage' and 'Returning at one o'clock in the morning'.

Fairings reached the height of their popularity in the period from 1860 to 1890 and suffered as a consequence. To this period belong the vast majority of the poor quality, mass-produced fairings, with flat bases, clumsy modelling and inadequate colouring. These mass-produced fairings were largely produced by one company

Conta & Boehme of Pössneck, well known for their bisque dolls' heads (q.v.). Although the inscriptions are always rendered in English there is often a Teutonic atmosphere about the lettering. At the turn of the century, even more slipshod fairings were produced by rival potteries in Saxony, undercutting Conta & Boehme and flooding the market with gaudy trifles which try to compensate for their poor quality by a too lavish use of gilding. These later fairings were hollow, made from mechanical moulds and lacking the bases found in earlier examples. The Germanic quality of these fairings is even more marked, though the majority of them have the inscription 'Made in Germany' impressed on them for good measure. The Rabelaisian humour of the earlier fairings gave way to humanized animals and rather quaint, grown-up looking children in sentimental poses, reflecting a banal quality present in much late Victorian art. A few rare fairings alluded to topical events, such as the British neutral stance in the Franco-German War of 1870–71, and these are now much sought after. Welsh tea-party scenes were common early this century and were imported into Britain from Japan.
See colour plate page 99

FANS

Important dress accessories widely used in China, India and the Near East since pre-Christian times. There are two principal types of fan – the rigid or screen fan and the folding fan. Rigid fans are characterized by their long handles and fixed leaves, either palmate or semi-circular, and were produced in many different materials including feathers, silk, parchment and straw-work. The majority of fans dating from biblical times and found to this day in Middle Eastern countries are of this type.

Folding fans are made up of sticks secured at one end by a rivet or pin; attached to the sticks are pleated leaves, which unfold as the fan is opened out. This type originated in China during the Ming period, and was introduced to Europe in the late sixteenth century by Portuguese traders. The sticks were ornately carved in wood or ivory and the leaves consisted of fine parchment made from chicken skin. Early European folding fans emulated the Chinese and had scenes painted across the leaves, featuring chinoiserie (q.v.), classical, mythological or biblical scenes. A variant on this was the *brisé* fan, in which the sticks themselves made up the

* left* Painted and carved ivory fan; Dutch, th century.

right English chapel fan th wooden sticks, 1796.

Opposite Fashion plate of
Jean Patou's mantles
from *Art-Goût-Beauté*,
1922.

overlapping fan-leaves. *Brisé* fans had painted
or incised decoration on the sticks, which
were held together by ribbons or threads
when fully extended. During the eighteenth
century distinctive fans with a form of
lacquering known as *vernis Martin* were
produced in France and exported to other
parts of Europe. Later eighteenth-century
fans varied considerably in shape and styling.
Some had two or three tiers of leaves, with
spaces between them with different scenes
painted on each tier and even across the sticks.
Italian fans with panoramic views across the
leaves were popular in the late eighteenth
century. In the first half of the nineteenth
century fan-leaves often featured topical
events or portrayed famous persons, while
others replaced the pictorial element by
purely ornamental forms. Mourning fans
were produced with an all-over black design
relieved only by mother-of-pearl inlay and
the intricate piercing of the sticks. Small rigid
fans were fashionable at the turn of the
century for interior decoration, attached to
drapes and screens in a style popularized by
the Aesthetic movement. Many of the fans
belonging to the nineteenth century were
commercially produced from printing plates,
with poorly registered colours. They often
bore firms' advertisements and were an early
form of sales gimmick, now prized more as a
curiosity rather than for any aesthetic quality.

FASHION PLATES

Improvements in the techniques of engraving, together with a heightened interest in
clothing for both sexes, resulted in the
fashion plate. This distinctive art form
originated in the middle of the eighteenth
century in France, then, as now, acknowledged leader of European fashion. The
estampe galante was produced in black-and-
white, the delicate lines of the engraving
matching the refinement and fastidiousness
of the subject. These fine prints, featuring the
costume and, to a lesser extent, the interior
decoration of the period, were produced in
great profusion during the reigns of Louis XV
and Louis XVI but came to an abrupt end in

1789, with the Revolution and the downf
of the *ancien régime*. It has been estimated th
by 1789 about eighty engravers and arti
were employed in the design of fashi
plates. The plates by Nicolas de Launay a
in a class of their own, but the work of oth
artists was also of a very high standard. The
prints were sold separately or in sets, the b
known being the sumptuous folio called
Monument de Costume, produced by Joha
Heinrich Eberts, an Alsatian banker domicil
in Paris, designed by the Swiss artist Sigmu
Freudeberg, and engraved by the leadi
craftsmen of the 1760s. A further series
twelve plates appeared in 1777 and a thi
set, supervised by J.M. Moreau le Jeur
appeared in 1783. No fewer than twenty-s
different engravers were involved in pr
ducing the thirty-six plates of *Le Monume*
including de Launay', J.B. Simonet, Nico
Ponce and the Swedish engraver Nico
Lafrensen (rendered in French as Lavreinc

Colour prints, using stipple engravin
were also produced in France as fashion pla
in the eighteenth century, but were surpass
by a technique, known as *manière de lav*
perfected by Laurent Guyot, which repr
duced the effect of watercolours. Fashi
plates in this technique were engraved
such artists as François Janimet, Char
Melchior Descourtis and Philibert Lo
Debucourt, the last-named being renown
for his twin folios entitled *La Galerie du Pal*
Royal (1787) and his swan song, *La Promena*
Publique (1792).

French fashion plates were in great dema
in England in the latter part of the eighteen
century, and it was to cater for the fashio
conscious that special periodicals we
launched. The most important of these w
The Lady's Magazine which occasiona
included a full-colour fashion plate. Folios
fashion plates were also produced, the b
known being the *Gallery of Fashion* (179
Towards the end of the century the numb
of fashion magazines increased, and t
practice of including plates devoted to t
latest styles grew significantly. These prir
were engraved in black-and-white ar
coloured by hand. They usually featured tw

* left* Miniature table with
lamp, miniature glasses,
cups and saucers, cards
and dominoes; English,
19th century.

No. 5.   Lady's Magazine.— May, 1813.

Morning Promenade & Evening Dresses.

right Evening and
Promenade dresses from
the Lady's Magazine,
1813.

Journal de la Mode et du Goût, *Le Moniteur des Dames et des Demoiselles*, *La Mode Illustrée* and *Mode et Lingerie*. American women were very fashion-conscious from the early nineteenth century onwards, often importing their ideas direct from France without the usual transmission via England, and this is demonstrated in the fashion plates which were incorporated in such periodicals as *Graham's American Monthly Magazine of Literature, Art and Fashion* (1826–58) or *Godey's Lady's Book and Magazine* (1839–98), both published in Philadelphia. The fashion capital shifted to New York in the aftermath of the Civil War, with the advent of *Harper's Bazaar* in 1867. In Britain, *Vogue* and *House and Garden* became the leading fashion journals and continue to this day. The elegantly engraved fashion plates of the early nineteenth century gave way to chromolithographed plates, surviving until the 1930s when the present practice of using photographs of models was universally adopted.

The best of the lithographic fashion plates were produced in France from the end of the nineteenth century until the mid-1920s. Foremost in this field was Paul Iribe who

or three dresses or suits grouped together, and the captions were relatively detailed, even including general comment on the prevailing fashion scene. On the fringe of fashion plates proper were numerous coloured engravings of the late eighteenth and early nineteenth centuries which caricatured and satirized the extravagances and caprices of contemporary fashions. *Le Bon Genre* and *Théâtre des Variétés* are excellent examples of this type, indicating that the French themselves were quick to perceive the ridiculous aspects of fashion. The coloured prints of A.C.H. Vernet were more subtle in their treatment and often incorporated a multitude of diverse fashions in a single plate featuring a group scene.

Fashion plates continued to appear in separate folios as well as in fashion magazines well into the nineteenth century, but gradually the latter predominated. This was the heyday of such French periodicals as

113

executed the magnificent plates for *Les Robes de Paul Poiret* (1908). This was followed four years later by a similar volume of plates entitled *Comoedia Illustré*. In 1911 Georges Lepape's fashion plates were published in book form as *Les Choses de Poiret*. Luxury magazines devoted exclusively to fashion and illustrated by exquisite plates reproduced on thick, expensive paper, flourished briefly in France, the best being the *Gazette du Bon Ton* (1912–25) which combined the talents of the leading couturiers with the skill of such outstanding fashion artists as Benito, Pierre Brissaud, Drian, André Marty and even Raoul Dufy. The coloured plate featured in each monthly issue ranks among the most sought-after items in this field.

FIGURES

Examples of human figures modelled in clay, or crudely carved from wood or stone, date back to the beginning of mankind and numerous examples may be cited under the heading of antiquities or primitive art (qq.v.). Figures in brass or bronze are known from China and India and even now examples dating back to the beginning of the Christian era are not uncommon. Medieval bronze figures from Italy and southern Germany range from the finely modelled statuettes of Giambologna and Filarete to the more whimsical works of Riccio and the Paduan School. Small bronze figures cast by the lost-wax process were also produced in France from the seventeenth century onwards, but sand casting was used extensively for *bronzes d'édition* in the eighteenth and nineteenth centuries and these are fairly plentiful. Rather crude brass figures were popular in England in the eighteenth and early nineteenth centuries as chimney ornaments. These followed the style of the contemporary earthenware Staffordshire figures (q.v.) and the primitive casting techniques entailed a considerable amount of finishing work – chasing, filing and the removal of flashing. Larger figures cast in brass or iron were often used as door stops (q.v.).

Glass figures were manufactured at Nevers

in France from the beginning of the seventeenth century, free-blown from rods different colours, and this established tradition which is now universally practise Moulded glass figures were extremely popular in nineteenth-century America, the best known being those produced by the Heisey Glass Company and re-issued in more recent years by the Imperial Glass Corporation Bellaire, Ohio (the latter identified by the IG monogram). Glass figures were produced by the late nineteenth-century French glass houses of Émile Gallé and Daum Frères and this has subsequently extended to the Swedish and Bohemian factories.

Undoubtedly the greatest variety exists ceramics, ranging from the homely Staffordshire figures of the eighteenth and nineteenth centuries to the elegant porcelain figurines of Robj and Capodimonte at the present day

ft Chelsea porcelain
gure of General
onway, c. 1765.

ght Pair of Minton
gures of gardeners;
nglish, c. 1835.

with the Derringer pocket pistol, supposedly the favourite weapon of ladies and gamblers (who concealed them in their sleeves), but there are many examples of pistol which are even smaller. Some miniature firearms are little more than an inch in length and discharge a shot the size of a small ball-bearing. From their generally decorative appearance it may be assumed that they were carried by ladies, and some were even mounted with a ring or clip so that they could be worn on charm bracelets or as brooches. The majority of firearms curiosa, however, consist of guns concealed in the handles of walking-sticks, swords or daggers (q.v.) and were intended to defeat an opponent whose sword-play might be superior. Other guns were concealed in pipe bowls, statuettes and even small books, the element of surprise compensating for inaccuracy and short range.

FIRING GLASSES

Type of English drinking glass, popular in the eighteenth century and distinguished by its large bowl, short, thick stem and heavy base. They were also known as bumping glasses or bumpers, from the custom of banging them on the table during toasts – the rattle also resembling the sound of gunfire. Because these glasses were favoured by social and political clubs they were often decorated with the emblems of freemasons, Jacobite clubs and secret societies and for this reason are very highly prized. Two styles of bowl were employed, either a rounded bucket shape or a taller, conical form. The latter is not unlike the sundae glasses used for serving ices at the turn of the present century, and collectors should beware of such modern glasses being offered as genuine firing glasses.

Figures were among the earliest decorative wares produced by the European porcelain factories, and fine examples of Meissen, Sèvres, Bow, Chelsea and Worcester are among the most expensive man-made objects. The early figures were strongly influenced by early Chinese imported porcelain and the characters of the Italian *Commedia dell'Arte*, but by the beginning of the nineteenth century the repertoire of porcelain figures had been infinitely extended to include military, pastoral, classical, biblical and allegorical figures. In the second half of the nineteenth century bisque porcelain or parian ware (q.v.) was very fashionable. Figures modelled in chalkware (q.v.) were very popular in the United States in the nineteenth century, and perennial favourites were the genre figures modelled by John Rogers which enjoyed a wide vogue in the 1870s.

FIREARMS CURIOSA

Generic term to describe unusual types of hand-gun as well as those incorporated in other objects or disguised in some way. In the first category come very tiny firearms. Aficionados of the Western will be familiar

FLASKS

Small bottles, usually distinguished by their very narrow neck, intended mainly for carrying spirits and other liquids around in a convenient form. Flasks may be found with a circular profile, narrow end-on, or roughly rectangular with a slight curvature to fit the

Porcelain flask with underglaze-blue decoration; Chinese, 14th century.

hip pocket. Travelling flasks were usually made in silver, Sheffield plate or electroplate, and the sides and stoppers were frequently ornamented. Pottery flasks were popular in Europe from the late Middle Ages and may be found in faience, maiolica or delftware with tin-glaze decoration. Some highly ornamental pressed-glass flasks were produced in Europe and America in the late nineteenth century and these are worth looking for.
See also *Pilgrim Bottles*

FLATWARE. See *Cutlery*

FOBS. See *Seals and Fobs*

FOOD WARMERS. See *Braziers and Food Warmers*

FOOT WARMERS

Small containers for glowing charcoal were first devised in the seventeenth century as foot warmers. They were generally made of copper or brass, less commonly in pewter or iron. The lids were pierced to allow the heat to escape and keep the charcoal embers glowing, and the piercing was invariably arranged in a decorative pattern. Foot warmers were provided with wooden carrying handles at the sides, or a single long wooden pole, in the same fashion as a warming pan (q.v.) Those used in churches and carriages were frequently provided with wooden cases (themselves elaborately carved), while examples from Norway and Sweden may be found consisting of wooden boxes with metal linings. Earthenware 'pigs' date from the eighteenth century and are used to this day as hot-water bottles, although they have largely been ousted by the rubber hot-water bag introduced at the end of the nineteenth century. Earthenware warmers were usually relatively plain, though some may be found with the names and trademarks of the manufacturers. A few examples were elaborately decorated (usually in underglaze blue-and-white or scratched ware). Copper hot-water bottles,

with contrasting brass stoppers, were wide used in the nineteenth and early twentie centuries, and may be encountered wi knitted or embroidered covers.
See also *Braziers*

FOUNTAIN PENS

Self-supplying pens operating on the princip of capillary attraction were first patented 1819 by James Lewes, though quill pens a steel-nibbed, non-automatic pens continu to be universally popular until the 188 Early fountain pens had a distressing hal of leaking, which prevented their wi acceptance, although a large number different mechanisms was patented betwe 1860 and 1884, when a New York busine man, Lewis Waterman, produced the fi really efficient fountain pen. At the sar time several German inventors produc reliable pens, and such brands as the Kollisc Oidtmann, Reisert and Schmackelsen domi ated the world market in the late ninetee century. In Britain and America such bran as Swan, Parker and Onoto became hou hold words. The styling of fountain pens not varied greatly over the past centu though examples in gold, silver, hardwo and early forms of plastic are worth looki for. The interest lies mainly in the techni features of the nib, reservoir and supp system. The more unusual pens include th made of glass, ivory or porcelain and nove types with built-in compasses, magnifi and other gadgets.

FRAKTURS

Name given to a form of German-Americ folk art, from the style of fractured letteri which is its most typical feature. Frakt writing was introduced by German settl in Pennsylvania and this unusual ornamen style was employed on birth, baptismal a marriage certificates as well as on elabor: family records. Examples of fraktur writi were embellished with floral patterns (usua rose and tulip motifs), birds and animals, a were glazed and framed for use as w

Right Miniature bed with quilted cover; American, 19th century.

decorations. Fraktur writing was mainly the work of itinerant scribes and schoolmasters from the mid-eighteenth century onwards. It reached its peak in the early nineteenth century when the Ephrata religious community developed it as an art form on the same lines as the illuminated manuscripts of the Middle Ages. Unfortunately the idea was taken up commercially, and debased by printed forms which could be hand coloured. Fraktur writing died out in the late nineteenth century and authentic examples in contemporary mounts are now relatively scarce. See colour plate page 100

FURNITURE, MINIATURE

Miniaturized versions of furniture were produced in Europe from the seventeenth century onwards for a variety of reasons. Initially these small pieces would have been made by apprentices learning their trade and often such items were required as the master piece before an apprentice joiner or cabinet-maker became a fully qualified member of his trade guild. For this reason many of these apprentice pieces exhibit all the virtuosity of skill and artistry which the young craftsman could command, and their finish was often superior to that found in many full-sized pieces. Miniature chairs, tables, dressers and bedsteads were produced in the late seventeenth and eighteenth centuries by journeymen cabinet-makers and turners as samples of the work they could produce. Even in the nineteenth century, when furniture-making had become largely mechanized, miniature pieces were still produced for the use of travelling salesmen, long before the advent of the modern colour brochure.

From the early eighteenth century, however, it became fashionable to collect miniature furniture, displayed in 'baby houses' and special cabinets, giving rise to an industry which concentrated on producing miniature pieces. These items may be considered almost as objects of vertu; they certainly received

the same lavish ornament and attention from jewelers, silversmiths, enamellers and gilders as the more familiar snuff boxes and étuis of the period. This branch of the furniture trade, specializing in trinkets and toys (as such pieces were often described at the time) declined about 1840, at a time when doll's houses for children began to increase in popularity and encouraged the commercial manufacture of miniature furniture. Although these nineteenth- and early twentieth-century items lack the artistry of the earlier pieces produced for wealthy connoisseurs, they reflect contemporary styles in furniture and interior decoration and are worth looking for. So-called dolls' furniture is generally much smaller and more representational than the earlier apprentice pieces and drawing-room display items. The finest examples were produced in Germany, France and the Low Countries in the late nineteenth century. Increasingly, however, dolls' furniture was die-stamped from sheet metal or crudely cast. Handmade wooden furniture has continued to be produced to this day and even contemporary examples of this art should be considered.
See colour plate page 110
See also *Children's Furniture, Toys*

GAMES

The heyday of games, puzzles and other indoor pastimes, was the late nineteenth and early twentieth centuries. This was a period when many more people enjoyed an increased amount of leisure time, before the advent of radio, motion pictures and television, which, from the late 1920s onwards, gradually stifled home entertainment. Many of these late Victorian games, designed for both nursery and drawing room, have survived in good condition, and may be divided into several major groups.

Jigsaws became fashionable in the late eighteenth century, the earlier examples having relatively simple shapes and large pieces. The object of early jigsaws was to disseminate useful knowledge in a palatable form, and the pictures which most often appear relate to history or geography. By 1840, however, the now familiar interlocking piece was coming into use, and the vogue for single pictures, often reproducing famou works of art, was established.

Numerous card games were a natur development from the traditional playin cards (q.v.) and likewise served an education purpose, treating various subjects themat cally. Towards the end of the nineteent century the concept of card games w considerably widened by the use of dic counters, elaborate boards and novelty fea tures, though there was still an underlyin educational purpose involved in suc popular games as Lotto, Bell and Hammer c L'Attaque (the last-named being the Frenc forerunner of war-gaming). The Traveller invented in 1842, was a geographical ra game which enjoyed immense popularity the mid-nineteenth century. Games loose based on chess and checkers included Asal (sometimes known as Officers and Sepoy reflecting the glories of the British Raj at height) and Fox and Geese. Many of the games enjoyed a brief popularity, but other

Didactic card game featuring the counties of Wales; English, dated 1818.

'Waterloo' war game by
Parker Brothers of Salem,
Mass., 1895.

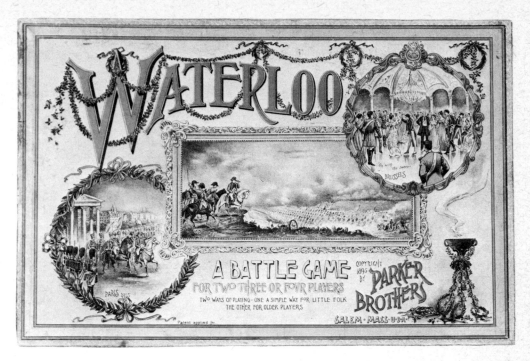

such as Halma (1880) and Ludo (1896) have become established favourites. Ludo was based on an Indian game called Pachisi and established a vogue for Oriental games, such as Mah Jong, which became popular at the turn of the century.

More traditional games, such as backgammon, cribbage, draughts and dominoes, yield numerous examples of boards and pieces which were beautifully fashioned in wood, ivory, bone and mother-of-pearl, and these have long been sought after by collectors. Dice and dice boxes, jetons, jacks, gaming counters and knucklebones associated with games of chance are also worth looking for.

GIMMEL FLASKS

Bottles or flasks produced like Siamese twins, blown separately and then fused together. Their necks curve in opposite directions so that only one may be poured at a time. These flasks came into use in the Low Countries and France in the seventeenth century and were used for salad oil and vinegar. Subsequently they were manufactured all over Europe and America and may be found with silver mounts and the various styles of decoration found on contemporary glassware.

GLASS

A hard, brittle substance, usually transparent or translucent, produced by the fusion of silica with carbonates of calcium (lime), sodium (soda) or potassium (potash). The molten liquid cools without crystallizing or changing its structure to any noticeable extent, and can thus be melted and re-used again. In its molten state it is extremely plastic and can be drawn, blown, moulded, pressed or even spun into fine threads. Glass was probably discovered by accident, from the fusion of wood ash on sand from open fires. It was known to the Egyptians and other eastern Mediterranean peoples long before the Christian era, but used mainly in the production of beads and jewelry (qq.v.). The technique of glass-blowing was invented in Syria during the first century AD and used in the production of bowls and beakers, often

Goblet and cover; Venetian, late 15th century.

Right Opaque white glass goblet with painted decoration; English, probably Stourbridge, 1845–50.

of a high degree of perfection, including double-walled vessels with gold leaf ornament. Glass-blowing was adopted by the Romans and used in the manufacture of both clear and opaque glass vessels decorated with small excrescences (prunts) or trailed strands of glass of contrasting colours. Blown glass was also carved, engraved and pierced. All subsequent decorative techniques stem from the two principles established in Roman times: incorporating the decorative effect in the glass at the molten stage; adding to or working on the glass in its cooled state. In the former category comes the application of coloured glass, either in combination with clear, colourless glass, with opaque white glass or glass of contrasting colours. Vessels built up of glass of different layers and compositions were decorated by carving away portions of the upper layers to produce a cameo (q.v.) effect. Patterned rods were drawn out and pressed into various shapes and then cut into short sections to provide the coloured canes used in the form of decoration known as *millefiori* (Italian for 'thousand flowers'). A technique used originally by the Egyptians for making beads, it was expanded by the medieval Venetians to form the basis of many decorative glass articles and is best known for its association with glass paper-weights (q.v.) of the nineteenth and twentieth centuries. *Latticinio* is a technique involving thin strands of opaque white glass drawn out in spirals or lattice-work in clear glass. This effect was also popular in paperweights, as well as the stems of wine glasses (q.v.). Moulded and pressed-glass techniques were developed in the nineteenth century and applied to commercial glassware as well as small figures and ornamental tableware.

Engraved glass (q.v.) was revived in the sixteenth century and given a wide variety of effects by using acid etching, stippling, wheel engraving, sand-blasting and diamond-point engraving. Enamelled glass (q.v.) was also produced during the same period.

Glassmaking was revived in Europe in the Middle Ages, the earliest form using plant ash (ferns or barilla being the commonest source), hence the terms *Waldglas* (wood

glass) and *verre de fougère* (fern glass) used i Germany and France respectively. Th Venetians used a very light form of glass using soda or lime, to produce some of th most extravagant forms ever blown. Th English pioneered lead or flint glass, usin red lead (lead oxide) from the late seven teenth century. This heavier and more sub stantial form of glass permitted deepe engraving and cutting, used extensively i the decoration of glasses, decanters, chande liers, salts and cruets (qq.v.). This form c glassware became very popular in the Unite States from the 1820s onward.

Coloured glass, which results from th presence of metallic impurities in the sub stances used, is of greater antiquity tha colourless glass. The presence of cobalt c copper, for example, produces a glass i various shades of blue; iron impurities pro duced colours ranging from olive and ligh green to pale blue, and manganese produce shades of red and purple. The deliberat introduction of these substances to produc coloured glass developed in the sixteent century and continues to this day. Colourle glass cased with coloured glass was ofte facetted or engraved to reveal the contrastin

Pomona, satin glass, Hobnail, Mother-of-Pearl (usually abbreviated to MOP glass). L.C. Tiffany produced Favrile glass, an iridescent form incorporating many different colours in Art Nouveau motifs. Iridescent glass was also produced in Austria and Bohemia. American art glass also influenced developments in France in the early twentieth century, notably the work of Émile Gallé, Daum Frères and René Lalique.

GLASSES

Drinking glasses were known in Roman times but did not re-emerge in Europe until the thirteenth century when the Venetians began producing them in their light soda-glass. Over the ensuing 300 years glasses were manufactured in Silesia, Bohemia, southern Germany and the Low Countries. Venice and Antwerp dominated the European market in drinking glasses up to the late seventeenth century. The earliest glasses produced in France and England were manufactured by Italian immigrant craftsmen. In England Giacomo Verzelini established a glass factory in 1571, closely imitating Continental models. Indigenous styles developed very slowly in the early seventeenth century under Verzelini's successors, Bowes and Zouche, but English soda-glass of this period was of a rather poor quality. The industry was revolutionized in the 1660s by George Ravenscroft, who worked on the problem of 'crizzling' (fine cracks in the body of glassware) and finally evolved the heavy flint glass used in English glassware from about 1676 onwards. English style flint or lead glass was established in the American colonies by 1690, and thereafter early American glass followed the contemporary English patterns. The development of this glass industry was crippled in the eighteenth century by heavy taxes. Ireland, however, was exempt from the glass excise, thus permitting the growth of the Waterford glass industry, which remains in the forefront of world production to this day.

American glassware began to develop its own distinctive styles following the establishment of the Amelung glasshouse in

areas of light and shade. Coloured glass with painted decoration, usually of children and animals, is often referred to as Mary Gregory glass (q.v.). Opaque glass, such as German *Milchglas* (milk glass) or French opaline was produced from the eighteenth century onwards as a substitute for porcelain. It may be found with enamel or painted decoration, or cased in combination with coloured glass. Various forms of glass simulating hardstones such as chalcedony and agate were developed in France and Italy in the mid-nineteenth century and spread to other countries.

Numerous types of art glass were developed in the United States in the second half of the nineteenth century, foremost being the famous Peachblow pioneered by the New England Glass Company and also produced by Hobbs, Brockunier. The NEGC also manufactured Agata, with its distinctive mottled surface, and Amberina, a glass shading from pale amber to deep ruby. This glass was also made by the Mount Washington Company, who pioneered the Burmese glass (made by Thomas Webb in England under the name of Queen's Burmese ware), noted for its delicate pastel shades. Other distinctive forms of glass were Kew Blas,

God bless Queen Ann.

Right Lead glass goblet with diamond-point engraved caption; English, *c.* 1705.

Below Wine glass with air-twist stem; English, mid-18th century.

Maryland immediately after the end of the War of Independence (1783). The Glass Excise Act of 1745 had the long-term beneficial effect of reducing the size and weight of glasses, and more elegant styles resulted. Glasses were delicately engraved or enamelled (qq.v.), but deep cutting was also widely practised. Glasses with engraved portraits and emblems relating to the Jacobite movement and other political factions are now eagerly sought after.

Glasses may be dated according to their shape as well as the style of decoration. In general the following styles outline the chronological development of glasses: heavy, inverted baluster stem (1590–1630); cigar-shaped stem (1620–50); ribbed knops with rigaree decoration at base of the bowl (1665–75); solid, truncated and inverted baluster stem (1675–85); quatrefoil stem (1685–1705); heavy inverted baluster containing a tear or air bubble (1690–1710); waisted and inverted baluster stem (1695–1715); solid, inverted baluster surmounted by a knop (1700–25); heavy, inverted baluster surmounted by a ball, both having elongated tears in hour glass fashion (1700–30); baluster with bal knops above and below (1700–20); large baluster separated from an annulated knop by a collar (1705–15); acorn knop containing tear (1705–25); large inverted baluster running into a ball below, with an elongated tear (1710–40); moulded, four-sided stem so-called 'Silesian' pattern (1710–20) octagonal 'Silesian' stem, with diamond cutting in high relief (1710–20); a similar but more fluted version (1720–50); drawn stem with greatly elongated tear (1725–60) straight stem with a small tear in the base of the bowl (1730–60); straight stem with small annular knop in the middle (1745–70) drawn stem with *latticinio* opaque glass decoration (1750–80); similar type with air twist stem (1735–70); straight stem with hexagonal faceting (1760–80); shorter stem with angular, sometimes blades, knop and stepped junction to faceted bowl (1800–30) Later styles were more eclectic and ofte combined disparate elements from previou styles. Distinctive types of glasses ar described individually.

See also *Firing Glasses, Kurfürsten Glasse Reichsadlerhumpen, Syllabub Glasses, Todd Glasses, Wine Glasses, Yard-of-Ale, Zwischen goldgläser*

GLASS, MINIATURE

Trinkets and toys made in spun glass (q.v were popular in Europe from the fifteent century when the Venetians began producin intricately fashioned little baskets, bouquet candlesticks and miniature figures of bird and animals. It is thought that the majority these items were produced by workmen i their spare time for sale at carnivals and fair This tradition subsequently extended t Germany and France, and was popular i England in the eighteenth century. Suc items were known as friggers. The fine examples came from the French glass factorie at Nevers and ranged from individual figure to elaborate centrepieces composed of tin human and animal figures, flower arbour and full-rigged sailing ships. By the earl nineteenth century, however, miniature glass items were being produced on a commercial basis. The best of these were hand-blown in the traditional manner, but by 1850 cheap glass toys were being mass produced in pressed or moulded glass – techniques which are still widely employed. Many distinctive styles of miniature glassware were produced by the Bristol (q.v.) and Nailsea glasshouses and these are now very desirable, but equally collectable are the glass trinkets from the Newcastle, Sunderland and London factories. Miniature wine glasses and decanters, for use in conjunction with miniature furniture (q.v.), are comparatively rare, the majority dating from the eighteenth and early nineteenth centuries. Tiny candlesticks and bells made of glass were popular novelties in the nineteenth century on both sides of the Atlantic, and may be found in coloured translucent or opaque white glass.

GLASS PICTURES

Pictures worked directly on to glass come into three main categories. The most common

type was painted by hand on the under side of the glass, the better examples being set in a curly maple frame. This technique has been practised in many countries for centuries, and such pictures vary greatly in quality and craftsmanship. They range from rather crudely delineated scenes of country houses and castles to finely executed portraits, the value of which may be enhanced if the subject can be identified.

A more ambitious type of picture was produced by a form of transfer printing on the reverse of the picture. The sheet of glass was coated with turpentine and allowed to dry. A paper print, usually a mezzotint, was then soaked in water and partially dried, before being placed, face downwards, on the glass. The back of the picture would be carefully sponged, soaked again and then pressed gently with the fingers so that no air bubbles remained. When the paper was carefully removed a dark outline of the picture would be deposited on the glass. After allowing the glass to dry out gradually, opaque colours were applied by hand. This painting in reverse on the back of the glass called for

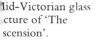
Mid-Victorian glass picture of 'The Ascension'.

Goss china cottages:
Manx, Shakespeare's
house and Burns'
cottage; 19th century.

considerable skill, and consequently such glass pictures now command comparatively high prices.

This type of glass picture is sometimes confused with a process known as *verre églomisé*. Strictly speaking, *verre églomisé* is a process of decorating glass by drawing and painting on the reverse side of the glass and then backing the decoration with metal foil, usually in gold or silver leaf. The term itself is confusing, since it is derived from a Parisian artist and print-collector named Jean-Baptiste Glomy, who lived in the latter part of the eighteenth century. Glomy is credited with having invented a method of framing prints with black and gold fillers painted from behind the glass, but there is no reason to suppose that he utilized a backing of metal foil. The term *verre églomisé* has been debased and has often been applied loosely to any form of glass picture involving painting on the reverse side.

Even the process of metal-foil backing which Glomy is said to have pioneered is of far greater antiquity, examples of this form of decoration having been recorded from the Middle East, whence it was introduced into Italy at the time of the Renaissance. This type of ornamentation became fashionable in the seventeenth century for the borders of mirrors, and numerous examples are extant from this period with *verre églomisé* decoration on a red, green or black ground, the gold arabesque designs being exceedingly ornate and quite enchanting.

This type of glass decoration was widely practised in France and seems to have been introduced into England during the reign of William and Mary by Huguenot craftsmen. Individual pictures in the true *verre églomisé* technique are comparatively rare, and yet are still surprisingly undervalued.

GOSS CHINA

Name given to a peculiar form of souveni porcelain ware, pioneered by William H Goss, who established the Falcon pottery Stoke-on-Trent about 1860. Goss produce the standard porcelain and parian wares the late nineteenth century, but is be remembered today for the miniature piec which he probably regarded as of secondar importance to his main business. Sma porcelain objects, originally replicas standard-sized useful and ornamental ware were produced in a plain white body an decorated with the crests and coats of arn of towns and cities. These articles were so for a few pence as tourist mementoes, main of seaside resorts, though they also exist fro large inland cities and industrial towns. E the turn of the century the Falcon potter was expanding its range of souvenir ware and producing novelties in the shape Grecian urns, Roman lamps, Etruscan vas as well as contemporary styles. Durin World War I this diversification went ev further and crested porcelain was produc in the form of soldiers' heads, tanks, airshi motor bicycles, Red Cross ambulances ar other martial subjects. Goss china continu to be popular in the inter-war period. In 19 the pottery was renamed the Goss Chi Company, to take note of the fact that the ceramic baubles were now their main sto in trade. The company went out of produ tion during World War II, when the seasi souvenir industry was severely hit. Althou, Goss china is no longer manufactured, th porcelain souvenirs were treasured and ma homes had cabinets full of them at one tin Though long disregarded by serious stude of ceramics, they have become very popu

Right Goss china
miniature of an
Etruscan lamp, with view
of the New Zealand
Auckland Exhibition,
1913.

with collectors in recent years. Goss had many imitators, in Britain, the United States and in other English-speaking countries as far afield as Australia and New Zealand. The name 'Goss' is now applied to these wares as a generic term.

GRATERS AND GRINDERS

Many of the domestic graters and food grinders produced in the past century are now being sought after by collectors as early examples of kitchen gadgetry. Many interesting and unusual types were patented in the late nineteenth century and the more decorative examples include those with copper or brass metal parts and polished wooden bases or casing. Several objects in this group have long been regarded as antiques in the original sense. Nutmeg graters, which were widely used in Europe from the mid-seventeenth century until the late Victorian period, were small boxes made of silver, or wood, with a steel rasping surface against which nutmeg and other spices could be grated. These boxes had hinged lids at the top and bottom, the latter to permit the grated nutmeg to be removed. Such boxes were carried on the person, and were popular in an age when meat was seldom fresh and required heavy seasoning.

Coffee mills were developed in Europe at the beginning of the eighteenth century and, though the basic principle has remained unaltered to this day, numerous variations in design have been evolved in the intervening

years. Coffee mills may be found with polished wooden, brass or lacquered metal cases and there are countless minor variants in the grinding mechanism. Small grist mills, meat and vegetable mincers and corn grinders are further examples of domestic or agricultural antiques. Prior to the late eighteenth century, before snuff was sold ready ground, it was necessary for individual snuff-takers to grind their own, and this gave rise to a special type of grater known as a snuff or tobacco rasp. The earliest examples of the mid-seventeenth century were of iron in a plain wooden case, but later types had steel rasps, with casings of brass, silver, copper, earthenware and even porcelain. The larger variety stood on the counter of tobacconists' shops, but tiny pocket rasps, about three inches in length, were cased in leather with silver mounts and often decorated *en suite* with snuff boxes (q.v.).

GROTESQUERIE

The excavation of certain grottoes in Rome, subsequently identified as the Golden House of Nero, in the late fifteenth century triggered off a fashion for decorative forms in which human, animal and even plant elements were combined. Raphael was the first to popularize grotesquerie, using a modified form of this classical style in the decoration of the Vatican loggia in the early 1500s. These designs were later published and were widely copied by other artists and designers. Grotesquerie became especially popular in the tin-glazed maiolica produced at Urbino. Sphinxes, satyrs, chimeras, centaurs and other mythological creatures formed the basis of grotesques, but sixteenth- and seventeenth-century developments of the theme also included birds and fishes with human or vegetable characteristics. The fashion for grotesquerie spread to Germany and France, where it remained popular until the nineteenth century. Because of its association with maiolica, itself based on Hispano-Mauresque wares, grotesquerie is sometimes referred to by the Italian term *arabeschi* (arabesques).

123

HAFNER WARE

Type of earthenware, mainly stove tiles, derived from the German word *Hafner* (stove-maker). Although it is thought that the elaborate tiled stoves of central Europe may date back to Roman times, the earliest surviving examples can be dated precisely to the late fifteenth century. Nuremberg, Salzburg and Lübeck were the chief centres of the hafner-ware industry, though similar tiles were also manufactured in other parts of Germany, Austria and Switzerland. The earliest tiles had relatively crude relief decoration and a green lead glaze. By the beginning of the sixteenth century other colours, predominantly yellows and browns, were being used, occasionally with a clear, colourless glaze over a white body to provide contrast. By the end of the sixteenth century these lead-glazed tiles were being produced in conjunction with tin-glazed tiles with decoration (notably yellow and blue) on a white ground. The motifs found on hafner ware were mainly biblical or historical, though heraldic emblems are also found. By the mid seventeenth century relief-decorated tiles of this type were being superseded by tin-glazed tiles, known variously as maiolica, delft or faience. Hafner techniques of glaze and relief were also applied to other forms of earthenware such as jugs and dishes, pot slabs and the panelling on tombs.

Hafner-ware tile from a Renaissance stove, from Vienna cathedral, *c.* 1500.

HAIR ORNAMENTS

The elaborate coiffures which were fashionable in the seventeenth and eighteenth centuries encouraged the growth of an industry devoted to the manufacture of objects of vertu connected with the hair. Brooches, clasps and slides were made of bone, horn, ivory, tortoiseshell or precious metals, with *piqué* and boulle decoration (qq.v.) or set with precious stones. Toward the end of the eighteenth century hair ornaments became most extravagant, incorporating tiny portrait miniatures, cameos, intaglio gems, and cast figures of animals and birds in silver or gold. Butterflies with richly enamelled wings and studded with precious stones were a popular form of decoration on barrettes, which held the strands of hair firmly in place. Different styles of comb were used for the back and sides of the coiffure and these were usually two-

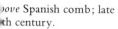

the end of the century novelty hatpins, with animal, bird, flower and figural decoration, became very popular. In addition to the jewels set in precious-metal mounts, hatpins were often decorated with glass paste, porcelain, wood, ivory or mother-of-pearl heads.

HANDKERCHIEVES

The habit of using a pocket-sized piece of fine cloth for blowing the nose was confined to western Europe, and to the more refined class of society. Moreover, it seems that they were mostly regarded as decorative rather than functional items, and it is the decorative aspect which now predominates in an age when paper tissues are commonplace. Handkerchieves were made of the finest linens and silks and were always relatively expensive, even when devoid of ornament. The theft of handkerchieves by pickpockets was a profitable part of their activities well into the nineteenth century – as readers of *Oliver Twist* will recall – and this explains why they were so often elaborately stitched with the name or monogram of the owner. Hand-embroidered handkerchieves ranked among the finest examples of needlework in the eighteenth century and were designed to be worn as important dress accessories. The fashion spread to the United States in the early nineteenth century, when Stewart's of New York sold them for $60 to $80 each, and they reached the peak of their popularity with the wealthier classes about 1850. In the ensuing decade there was a great export of embroidered handkerchieves from Ireland to America, needlework schools having been established to alleviate the hardships of the famine in the late 1840s.

For the less wealthy, however, printed handkerchieves or those woven on Jacquard looms were plentiful from about 1820 onwards. By the 1860s this medium was being widely used to commemorate events and personalities, or even for political or religious propaganda in the same fashion as the broadsheet of earlier generations. Printed handkerchieves with portraits of Queen Victoria,

three-pronged. Combs of this type remained popular throughout the nineteenth and early twentieth centuries, but were superseded by jeweled bandeaux in the 1920s, when hairstyles became shorter and simpler. Combs designed for grooming the hair did not become fashionable until the early nineteenth century – which, incidentally, explains the popularity in less fortunate generations of scratching-sticks, often surmounted by a hand or bird's foot carved in ivory or hardwood, with which ladies might surreptitiously relieve their itching scalps. Combs for combing hair were always more robust in construction, all-metal types being among the earliest to be produced. Bone, horn, tortoiseshell and wooden combs were also manufactured in the nineteenth century, often highly decorated along their sides and backs to match brushes, mirrors and other dressing-table articles (q.v.).

Hatpins became fashionable in the eighteenth century, when bouffant hairstyles made it necessary to anchor the hat firmly. Various techniques of decoration were applied to the pins themselves, which may be found with straight, polygonal, spiral or grooved blades; and a wide variety of styles may be seen in the ornamental heads of the hatpins. Throughout the nineteenth century elaborately jeweled pins were fashionable, using classical, gothic or rococo motifs, but towards

Gladstone and Disraeli were very popular
in Britain, while the patriotic motifs of the
American Civil War are among the most
eagerly sought after today. Printed handkerchieves of this type have continued to be
popular down to the present time, and include a vast range of tourist souvenirs with
landmarks and other scenic motifs from all
over the world.

HORN BOOKS

Alphabet primers used by children in Europe
from the sixteenth to the nineteenth centuries. They consisted of a back-plate, made
of wood, brass, pewter, leather or bone,
bearing a printed sheet covered by a thin
layer of horn, which was secured to its base
by metal studs. The printed sheet bore the
letters of the alphabet, sometimes accompanied by the Lord's Prayer or biblical texts.
Horn books often had wooden or metal
handles with a hole so that they could be
attached by a cord to the scholar's belt. More
sophisticated examples had an aperture at
the top which allowed the printed sheet to be
replaced by a more advanced text. The
earliest examples had sheets surmounted with
a large cross, the Christ Cross or criss-cross
(from which horn books derived their
alternative name of criss-cross books). This
was followed by the alphabet in capital and

lower-case lettering. The vowels were print[e]
underneath, and then their combinatio[n]
with the consonants in tabular form. A[n]
invocation to the Holy Trinity was follow[ed]
by the Lord's Prayer and a line of Rom[an]
numerals appeared at the foot. Hand-draw[n]
sheets of vellum are of the greatest rarit[y]
printed paper having become general by t[he]
late sixteenth century. Collectors shou[ld]
exercise care in purchasing horn book[s]
especially those made of pewter purporti[ng]
to be seventeenth- or early eighteent[h]
century English examples, since these a[re]
known to have been forged extensively at t[he]
time of the Gothic Revival in the ear[ly]
nineteenth century.

HORSE BRASSES

Talismanic decorations on the harness [of]
horses and other animals have been record[ed]
dating back to 1500 BC, and examples fro[m]
Mycenae and Nineveh are preserved [in]
museums. Italian pottery figures of the four[th]
century BC show rows of decorative di[scs]
about the heads and necks of horses. Ho[rse]
ornaments which have been preserved in[di]
cate that the custom in the British Is[les]
goes back as far as the Iron Age, and the[re]
are many examples of bronze orname[nts]
from the period of the Roman occupati[on]

Documentary evidence concerning brass ornaments is given in a fourteenth-century manuscript concerning the dress details for Knights of the Bath.

The purpose of horse brasses was talismanic. Symbols of fertility, power and prosperity – the wheatsheaf, the sun, the crescent moon – are commonly found on brasses from every part of Europe. In more recent times, however, the traditional symbols have yielded ground to more ornamental motifs. Fine horse brasses were made in Birmingham in the nineteenth century, especially in the period from 1850 to 1890. The great majority of these were sold by saddlers to farmers and horse-owners. These Birmingham brasses were cast, the edges and plain parts filed, and the fancy portions treated with aqua fortis and then roughly polished by hand.

These fine cast brasses, now greatly coveted by the collector, can be identified by the two small studs left on the back of the casting after the shanks have been cut away. The brasses worn by farm horses soon took the fancy of those who attended country shows and many other traders began to use them. The various guilds had their insignia incorporated in brasses, commemorative brasses were produced for popular events, and wealthy landowners began putting their family crests on their brasses.

A full set of brasses for a horse could total nineteen; one or two would appear on the brow-band, two on the ear-flaps, five or six on the martingale and four or five on each side of the pad saddle. Sets of harness with their brasses complete are seldom seen nowadays, though occasionally parts of saddlery with brasses mounted on them can be purchased in country antique shops. The decorative quality of horse brasses has long been appreciated and they are very popular as wall ornaments. Unfortunately, the majority of the brasses offered today have probably never been anywhere near a horse. They are usually poorly manufactured, having been stamped out of sheet brass, and they lack the qualities possessed by cast brasses. Many of them have been given an ageing treatment, but such spurious brasses may be detected by the absence of the casting studs on the reverse.

The more collectable items include engraved brasses, brasses from railway horses, some of which carry the names of old locomotives or defunct railroad and tramway companies, brasses with a nautical flavour depicting ships and anchors, brasses depicting animals (a rare example shows the famous elephant Jumbo), and those featuring the insignia of trade guilds (especially brewers and farriers) or bearing masonic emblems.

Among the commemorative brasses are those produced to celebrate royal jubilees and coronations. Other categories include the brasses from dustcart horses, bearing the emblems of cities and boroughs, patriotic brasses dating from the Boer War (1899–1902), and merit badges awarded to the Best Carthorse of the Year.

HOUR-GLASS. See *Clocks*

ICONS

Greek word meaning images, applied to small pictures which were intended to be hung in churches on the iconostasis, the screen separating the nave from the sanctuary, or borne in procession on religious festivals. To the Orthodox believer, the icon was no mere adornment but came to be invested with something of the divinity or sanctity of the person depicted.

Icons were nevertheless a central feature of worship in the Orthodox Church and examples may be found all over Eastern Europe. The Greek, Serb, Bulgar, Turkish and Russian Orthodox churches developed their own distinctive styles. Of these the Russian was the most widespread and, with the wholesale closure of churches and the export of ecclesiastical works of art in the early Twenties by the Soviet authorities, the best known to collectors in western Europe and America.

Although Russia was comparatively late in embracing Christianity, her contribution to this form of art over the centuries was outstanding. Russian Orthodoxy dates from the conversion of Vladimir, Prince of Kiev, in 988, and the subsequent mass baptism of his subjects, but the new religion spread rapidly across the vast country, ousting paganism. Kiev was rivalled in piety by Novgorod, Yaroslavl and Vladimir-Suzdal – all centres which were noted for the splendour of their church decorations, including icons. Few early pieces have survived, however, because of the Mongol invasion of Russia, though Novgorod retained its independence and developed a style of icon painting which differed from the Greek

tradition by adopting a more compassiona[te] less ascetic approach.

The Greek influence in early Russian [art] was very marked, nonetheless, and w[as] strengthened towards the end of the fou[r-] teenth century when Theophanes the Gre[ek] settled in Novgorod and raised religio[us] painting to a new level. Theophanes mov[ed] to Moscow about 1395, and by 1404 he w[as] being employed in decorating the Cathed[ral] of the Annunciation. His assistants were t[he] monks Prokhordof Gorodetz and And[rei] Rublev, the latter destined to become t[he] Fra Angelico of Russian art. Few works [of] Rublev or his successors, Danila Cherny a[nd] Dionysius, have survived, although they h[ad] a tremendous impact on the Muscovite ic[on] of the fifteenth and sixteenth centuries.

In this and the succeeding period, ico[ns] tended to become smaller, corresponding [in] size to the contemporary miniatures (q.v.) [of] western Europe. As Moscow grew [in] importance and its citizens prospered, th[ey] developed a need for small icons for use [in] private chapels and even in the home. A le[ad] was given by the Tsar, who established [a] studio for icon painters in the Palace of Ar[ms] in the Kremlin, while many of the nobil[ity] set up their own workshops, the best kno[wn] being that run by the Stroganov fam[ily] between 1580 and the 1620s. The princi[pal] artists of the Stroganov school were the f[our] Savins, Chirin and Ushakov, whose wo[rk] though formed in Novgorodian traditi[on] was influenced to some extent by cont[act] with Westerners. As these painters w[ere] forbidden by the Orthodox Church fr[om] humanizing the portraits of the saints [in] icons, they sought to express their indi[vi-] duality not only in the richness of the colo[ur]

used, but through the medium of elaborately ornamented allegory, in marked contrast with the simple and austere subjects which satisfied earlier generations.

To a large extent the styles of miniature painting absorbed from the West appealed to a new class of connoisseurs rather than to the devout. In addition, however, the westernizing policy of Peter the Great did little to prevent Russian art from being over-whelmed, and icon painting in the eighteenth and nineteenth centuries declined into an exercise which was largely mechanical. There are fine examples of icons to be found right down to the time of the Revolution, but the art was dead long before the Soviets put an end to it and directed its craftsmen into the production of those lacquered boxes and inlaid caskets which are so popular with tourists in Russia to this day.

Outside Russia the only flourishing school of icon painting was centred in Serbia, which maintained an uneasy independence from the Ottoman Empire. The strict control of the Orthodox Church in the Turkish dominions, and the periodic persecution of its adherents, has meant that little of significance was pro-duced by icon painters in the seventeenth and eighteenth centuries, while the general decline in standards in the nineteenth century has meant that the majority of items available consist of cast bronze or brass icons with enamel decoration, rather than the wooden panels finely painted in oils, preferred by earlier generations. Genuine icons are now subject to strict state control in most eastern European countries and the collector should beware of comparatively tawdry imitations produced specifically for the export market. See colour plate page 128

INKSTANDS AND INKPOTS

Inkstands, otherwise known as standishes or encriers, consist of trays or shallow boxes, often footed, with compartments to house inkpots, pens and other writing materials. They differed primarily from the portable writing case (q.v.) in that they were intended for permanent use on desks. Thus the inkpot was the principal component around which the other implements were arranged. Ink-stands may be found with two or more ink-pots, and rare examples with up to six pots have been recorded. Recesses were often provided for such items as pounce boxes (q.v.), hand-bells, taper sticks, quill pens, wafer box, desk seal, sealing wax and even lighting materials. They were made in polished wood, sometimes with glass liners, but all-metal stands, in silver or Sheffield plate, were also popular in the eighteenth and early nineteenth centuries. Fine porcelain inkstands were fashionable in eighteenth-century France. A novel type, popular in Britain from about 1770 to 1840, was globular in shape, supported by a baluster stem and moulded base, with a revolving lid which opened to reveal the inkpot, pounce box and other writing accessories. A more utilitarian type, first issued to officials at the Treasury in the reign of James II (1685–89), had a double lid and central handle. This form later became widely popular and remained in fashion till the late nineteenth century. During this period inkstands often incorporated long, narrow curved trays for pens and rulers, built-in stamp boxes, pin cups and even small timepieces.

Inkpots themselves are collectable, since many decorative forms were manufactured and sold separately. They may be found in

Right Bow porcelain inkwell in *famille verte* enamels; English, dated 1750.

pressed, moulded or cut glass, with silver, bronze, pewter or brass mounts. Some were mounted on heavy metal or marble bases for use as paperweights. Particularly prized are examples with coats of arms of government departments, military units or royal households on their lids. Small glass bottles, with rectangular or hexagonal sides, short necks and stoppered mouths, were used for ink from the mid-eighteenth century. The doubling of the glass excise in Britain during the Napoleonic Wars led to a revival of brown stoneware for ink bottles, either squat cylinders or wide-based cones, with stoppered mouths into which pens could be dipped. Many stoneware ink bottles of this type were exported to the United States. Larger bottles, in which the ink was sold, were also manufactured of earthenware and frequently had the maker's name and address impressed on the side. In the early twentieth century ink bottles were frequently moulded in shapes which would facilitate tilting, and novelty or patent forms, mostly of American origin, are worth looking for.

INRO

Japanese word literally meaning 'seal box', used from the fifteenth century onwards as a container for chops and ink with which documents were signed by important officials. Subsequently the inro became a fashionable object for carrying medicines, writing materials in general and, latterly, tobacco. Inro were constructed in separate compartments which fitted ingeniously into each other in tiers of two to five sections. These little boxes were fitted with a cord which was attached to the obi (sash) by netsuke (q.v.). The great majority of inro were made of wood, which was often lacquered or inlaid with gold, silver or mother-of-pearl in intricate floral patterns, scenery, bird or animal forms. Others were relatively devoid of decoration, relying on the figuring of the natural grain in the wood; and, at the other extreme, a few were elaborately carved and engraved. The best examples of inro were produced from the sixteenth to the early

nineteenth centuries. Thereafter the ar declined and became more stereotyped finally dying out as the Japanese adopte Western forms of dress in the late nineteent century. Like other traditional art form however, there has been a revival in the cra of inro in more recent years.

INTAGLIOS

Gem-stones with the design cut into them unlike cameos (q.v.) in which the decoratio stands out in relief. The art of intaglic cutting was practised in classical times an revived in the Middle Ages in the manu facture of seals. The technique was applied t glassware in Bohemia and Silesia in th seventeenth century and became very popula in central Europe in the eighteenth centur It is often found in decanters, vases, bow and tankards with the surface in coloure translucent glass and the intaglio-cuttin effected in such a way as to reveal th colourless layer underneath. This techniqu known as *Tiefschnitt*, was a speciality of th Potsdam glassworks from about 1680 or wards. French glassware was decorated wit rococo motifs in intaglio fashion during th eighteenth century. The term is also applie to deeply incised decoration in pottery an porcelain, in wood, silver and brassware.

IVORY

White substance from the tusks of the elephant, walrus, narwhal and mammoth and the teeth of whales and hippopotami, carved into decorative or useful objects all over the world since palaeolithic times. Examples of entire elephant or mammoth tusks decorated with intricate carving or used in the construction of quite large pieces of furniture have been recorded from India, Siberia, Africa and Alaska but these are rare and of immense value. The great majority of ivory carvings are no more than a few inches in size. Numerous examples of carved ivory have survived from the Stone Age and have been excavated in archaeological sites all over Europe; most of these carvings feature animals, but occasionally female figures, associated with fertility rites, have been discovered. Ivory was used extensively in Egypt, the elephant tusks being brought north from Ethiopia or overland from India. The Egyptians fashioned statuettes from ivory, and they also pioneered the technique of inlaying ivory on wood used in caskets and furniture. Ivory from the Babylonian, Assyrian and Mycenean civilizations is known, though comparatively rare. Very few examples of Greek ivory carving have survived though the craft is well documented

ove Ivory figure of an
mortal; Chinese,
ond half of 19th
tury.

ght Ivory mirror case
picting a medieval
urnament; French,
h century.

in contemporary writing. The art was widely practised in the Roman Empire and ivories dating from the beginning of the Christian era have been found in sites from Britain to Asia Minor. During the Dark Ages Christianity gave great impetus to ivory carving and examples range from tiny figurines and diptychs to the celebrated throne of Maximianus at Ravenna. The art of carving ivory was re-introduced to western Europe in the ninth century from the Byzantine Empire and numerous examples exist from the Carolingian and Romanesque periods. Thereafter there is an unbroken tradition of ivory carving in Europe which developed along distinctive lines in Spain (showing Moorish influence), Italy, France, Austria, southern Germany, Flanders and Scandinavia (the last-named producing some notable walrus and narwhal carvings in the seventeenth and early eighteenth centuries).

The finest carving has always been associated with the Far East, particularly China, where the supply of elephant ivory has been abundant without any break in continuity for over 2,500 years. By contrast Japan, which frequently had the supply of ivory cut off, preferred to work in wood, though in those periods when ivory was employed, some excellent work resulted. Ivory was mainly used in Japan for carving plectrums for *samisen* and other stringed instruments; both netsuke and okimono (qq.v.) were produced in this material in great profusion from the seventeenth century onwards.

Some of the most remarkable ivories have emanated from the far north of the American continent. Ivory carving was practised at some time within the past 2,000 years by the Eskimos of Alaska, who used mammoth tusks for the purpose. There is a considerable gap, chronologically and stylistically, between these early Bering Sea carvings and the ivory objects carved by the Eskimos of the present day. Carving on walrus and narwhal tusk dates from about the eleventh century, and is characterized by the profusion of geometric or stylized animal forms used to decorate ivory articles in everyday

133

Ivory figure of an archer; late 19th century.

Right Ivory okimono of Tadabonu, the young man wielding a table to slay his opponents; second half of 19th century.

hardwoods. Ivory carving continued to fi favour in Germany and France, reaching peak in those countries in the seventeer and early eighteenth centuries, Nurembe and Dieppe being notable centres of produ tion. Among the small objects which w largely, or wholly, carved in ivory w snuff boxes, étuis, cane-handles, pipe ca and work boxes (qq.v.). Finely carved iv handles were fitted to silver tankards, seventeenth-century speciality of the Neth lands, and ivory panels with intricate fig work were used in the bindings of pra books and other devotional works.

use, the famous needle-cases of Alaska and Greenland being the most distinctive examples. Pictographic carving became popular about 1750, and European influence is to be seen in the ivory carving of the present century, which caters to the growing tourist industry of the far North.

In western Europe ivory was never available in great abundance, depending on imports from the Middle East and North Africa, which were often subject to political and economic upheavals. From the sixteenth century onwards, first bronze and then porcelain ousted ivory as the favourite medium for figurines, but it continued to be widely used as a basis for portrait miniatures (q.v.), in the manufacture of small objects of vertu and, most of all, in inlay work, often in combination with ebony or other dark

JAPANESE SWORD FURNITURE

The Japanese propensity for investing utilitarian objects with artistry is seen at its best in the fittings of swords. To the *samurai* (warrior class) the sword was not only a weapon but an object of deep religious significance, and was accordingly treated with respect. From the eleventh century onwards swords were made of high-quality steel, and became increasingly ornate, without ever sacrificing their fighting efficiency. Several components are particularly noted for their decorative qualities, including the menuki (sword handle), kodzuka (handle of the small knife slotted into the side of the scabbard), fuchi-kashira (fitments attached to the sword belt) and tsuba (sword-guards). The menuki was made in wood or metal (often iron), and was lacquered and gilded or inlaid with ivory or precious metals. Similar decoration was applied to kodzuka.

The most interesting part of the sword furniture, however, is the tsuba. This was originally a simple metal disc, perforated with an elliptical aperture through which the blade and handle could be fitted. Smaller slits on either side accommodated the blades of the knife and a bodkin. During the twelfth century the manufacture of tsuba passed from the swordsmiths to the armourers, and thenceforward more elaborate forms began to emerge. Technically the workmanship in tsuba was always of an extremely high quality. The iron was well forged and subjected to a variety of treatments, involving hammering and pickling in solutions which imparted different colours of patina or textures of surface. These patinas and textures themselves served as the basis of ornament,

in contrasting layers or bands, though the bulk of the decoration was effected by piercing the discs to create branches of trees, delicate fern-like tracery, clusters of blossom, the pattern of dragonflies' wings or the fluting of sea-shells. By the sixteenth century more ambitious forms were appearing, including landscapes, elaborate flower compositions and heraldic devices. Inlays of gold and silver date from the late sixteenth century, reaching the peak of ostentation in the eighteenth century, when highly ornamental sword fittings became obligatory for *daimyo* (noblemen) attending the court of the Shoguns. To this period belong the intricate forms of weaving silver or bronze objects by means of silver or copper wires on to the basic iron plates. Enamelling in restrained colours was a notable feature of these court swords, but this ostentation caused a reaction at the beginning of the nineteenth century, and there was a return to more austere forms which relied on traditional patination for decorative effect.

JAPONAISERIE

Objects emanating from Europe or America, styled or decorated in the manner of Japanese originals, or in a form which Occidentals believed to be Japanese in concept. The earliest example of japonaiserie in Europe was the seventeenth-century Dutch lacquerware, which sought to imitate the fine, durable lacquers of the Far East and subsequently degenerated into the poor European imitation known as japanning. Articles in wood, metal and even papier mâché with japanned surfaces were frequently inlaid with mother-of-pearl or ivory figures and scenes in the Japanese manner. European porcelain of the late eighteenth century was also decorated in styles reminiscent of the pottery and porcelain of Kakiemon, Imari and Arita wares. These wares came to Europe via the Dutch, who maintained a precarious foothold in Japan at their trading post near Nagasaki. The forcible opening of Japan to western trade, following the visit of Commodore Perry in 1853, and the sweeping reforms of the Meiji Restoration in 1867–68, led not only to the rapid westernization of Japan but to the export of Japanese art and artefacts to Europe and America in vast quantities in the late nineteenth century, stimulating a craze for *Japonisme* from 1875 onwards. Initially this was satisfied by the genuine article, but as the supply began to dry up entrepreneurs in America, France, Germany and Britain began to develop decorative styles which often loosely imitated (and sometimes parodied) Japanese originals. This manifested itself in the Japanese motifs found in textile patterns, prints, screens, metalwork and furniture of the late nineteenth century, in the craze for bamboo furniture, the fashion for fans as a form of interior decoration (especially popular in the United States), in the peacock's feather motif found in Art Nouveau glass, and in many of the flower and bird designs advocated by the Aesthetic movement.

See colour plate page 98

JET

Hard black substance created by the fossiliing of driftwood found in bituminous shal Various types of jet have been found i coastal areas of western Europe, but th finest was that deposited in the Yorkshi cliffs between Peak and Boulby. The jet this district was described by the Venerab Bede in the eighth century, but beads ar rings made of jet from the Whitby area hav been recorded even earlier in Bronze Ag burial sites. Whitby jet jewelry, rosaries ar crucifixes were popular until the import precious and semi-precious stones in th fifteenth century led to its decline. The j industry was revived at the beginning of th nineteenth century by a retired naval offic named Treulett, who perfected a techniqu for manufacturing jet beads of a very hig polish. In 1808 Treulett established a facto in Whitby, and by 1830 several other firr were operating in the district. Jet beads, rin and combs made slow headway at first b received enormous impetus from the Gre Exhibition of 1851. Queen Victoria help

Earthenware dessert plate with japonaiserie motifs, 1873.

136

to popularize the fashion for jet jewelry and ornaments, especially after the death of Prince Albert, the Prince Consort, in 1861, when jet became very fashionable in mourning jewelry. During the period from 1860 to 1880, vast quantities of jet were exported, especially to the United States. Soft Spanish jet was used as a cheaper substitute, and black glass, known as French jet, was a passable imitation. At the height of its popularity jet was used in the manufacture of jewelry of all kinds: buttons, studs, clips, watch chains, fobs, seals and combs.

JEWELRY

Personal adornment dates back to the very beginning of mankind and is universal from the most primitive to the most advanced forms of society. An infinite variety of materials has been used from the earliest times, including seeds, bones, shell-discs, teeth, porcupine quills, birds' feathers, stones and fossilized wood, as well as all kinds of metal from gold, electrum and silver to copper and iron. The earliest jewelry served several purposes – primarily to enhance or beautify the person, but also to denote status or rank and serve as a token of good luck.

Jewelry in materials and forms still recognizable today dates back at least 4,000 years, to the necklaces, rings and pendants worn by the Egyptians and composed of coloured glass and precious metals. The range of jewelry was extended by the Greeks, who excelled in the crafts of metalworking and produced head-dress, bracelets, brooches and earrings delicately wrought in silver or gold with decoration in filigree or repoussé work. Similar forms of jewelry were adopted by the Etruscans and the Romans and their decorative styles developed to include cameos and intaglios (qq.v.) cut in shell and semi-precious stones. In north-western Europe jewelry consisted of rings, bracelets and torques wrought in native gold. The Celtic tribes favoured brooches with a gold or silver base, set with semi-precious stones or brightly enamelled. These fashions spread north to Scandinavia and east into Russia and have

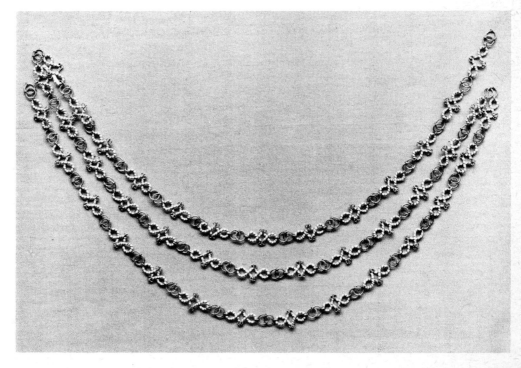

137

Art Nouveau gold
pendant; French, *c.* 1900.

survived, with numerous permutations, to
this day. The practice of interring jewelry
and other personal effects with the dead has
ensured that early European jewelry is
relatively plentiful. Imperial edicts in the
Middle Ages, however, forbade this practice,
and this explains the comparative dearth of
European jewelry from the ninth to the sixteenth century. The few surviving examples
show a predilection for enamelling figures
and architectural motifs, set with uncut or
cabochon gems.

Jewelry enjoyed a revival with the other
applied arts during and after the Italian
Renaissance, and some of the most elaborate
pieces ever made date from the sixteenth
century. Pearls were now widely used and
diamonds came into fashion. Antique (i.e.
classical Greek and Roman) forms of jewelry
were copied, cameos became fashionable
once more, and pendants, earrings, finger-
rings and brooches were cast, wrought or
hammered with designs based on classical
originals. Much of the jewelry of this period
had richly enamelled reverses. The increasing
popularity of diamonds and other precious

stones, however, had an adverse effect o
jewelry. The stones and precious met
became more important than the piec
themselves, which were invariably broken u
as fashions changed or the owners die
Thus authentic examples of sixteenth- an
seventeenth-century jewelry are scarc
Techniques of stone-cutting improve
dramatically in the seventeenth century an
the methods of faceting first applied
diamonds were later extended to all forms
gem-stones. Enamelled reverses went out
fashion at the end of the seventeenth centur
but enamelling as the principal form
decorating a piece of jewelry enjoyed
moderate revival at the end of the nineteen
century, often applied to copper, pewter
other base metals.

Diamonds have continued to form t
chief ingredient of fashionable jewelry fro
the seventeenth century to the present da
The need for cheaper substitutes led to t
development of glass paste in the eighteen

Gold jewelry set with
amethysts and pearls;
English, *c.* 1830–40.

century. It is interesting to note that at its inception glass paste was highly valued for its novelty and was often mounted in gold settings, unlike the nineteenth-century paste jewelry, which merely satisfied demand at the cheaper end of the market. The close co-operation of goldsmiths, enamellers and jewelers in the second half of the eighteenth century meant that the dividing line between jewelry and objects of vertu was often shadowy. Thus portrait miniatures, étuis, snuff boxes and patch boxes (qq.v.) were often elaborately decorated in styles parallel to the prevailing fashions in jewelry, and were regarded almost as forms of personal adornment. This is seen at its best in the development of buckles, chatelaines (qq.v.), fobs and watch cases.

During the nineteenth century jewelry became more eclectic, drawing on all previous fashions from different parts of the world for inspiration, often gloriously jumbled together in a mixture of Egyptian, pre-Columbian, Greek and Asiatic forms. Jewelry became more naturalistic, with animals, birds, flowers and butterflies modelled in precious stones. Jewelers became more adventurous in their use of materials, and worked in substances such as jet (q.v.), coral and amber, which had not been used since the Middle Ages. Prussian austerity during the closing campaigns of the Napoleonic Wars instituted the fashion for iron jewelry, popular for much of the nineteenth century. Later, cut steel jewelry came into vogue and has survived to this day. Increasing use of machinery after 1850 led to a decline in the quality of jewelry in the lower and medium price range, but this was countered by the development of craft jewelry at the end of the nineteenth century.

JUGS

Vessels fitted with a single handle and a pouring rim or spout, widely used for water, wine, beer, milk and other liquids from medieval times to the present day. The earliest jugs, from the eleventh century, were fashioned in stoneware, pewter or bronze.

Tall stoneware jugs were made in Germany in the sixteenth and seventeenth centuries with a distinctive mottled surface resembling the coat of a leopard, hence the incongruous name of tigerware. Tigerware jugs were imported into England in great quantities, and they were subsequently ornamented with silver or brass foot-rims, handles, spouts and lids. A few rare examples have been recorded with mounts in gold or parcel-gilt. The shape and size of jugs varied enormously from the seventeenth century onwards, from the diminutive silver jugs used for cream and milk to the outsize pitchers and ewers (q.v.) used for washing. In shape, jugs could be low and squat or tall with bulbous bodies and long, slender necks. Eighteenth- and nineteenth-century jugs were modelled in a wide range of pottery and porcelain, with an infinite variety of glazes and decorative techniques. Apart from ceramics and precious metals, jugs have also been made in leather, wood, copper or brass sheet in different parts of the world, and many of these styles are in use to this day.

See also *Cow Creamers*

KETTLES

The term was originally applied to cooking pots, especially cauldrons; this archaic usage survives in the specialized form of fish kettle. In its present, spouted form, the kettle first came into use in the seventeenth century, when boiling water became necessary for the infusion of tea. No dated examples of silver tea kettles have survived earlier than 1694, and it seems probable that copper and brass kettles are somewhat later, corresponding with the period when tea-drinking came within the reach of the lower classes. Copper kettles were manufactured in the Netherlands and exported to England and America in the early eighteenth century. The term Dutch kettle came to denote a vessel of the larger sort, with twice the capacity of a so-called Hollow kettle (about three pints). Brown kettles were those equipped with a stand and a lamp, the name being derived from a process of browning the exterior to protect it from the effect of the flames. Unfortunately most of the utilitarian kettles of the eighteenth century were scrapped once their usefulness was expended, and examples before 1820 are scarce. Brass and copper kettles were produced as chimney ornaments in the late nineteenth century.

KEYS. See *Locks and Keys*

KITSCH

German word signifying trash, gaudy trinkets or worthless daubs, but adopted in English in recent years as a generic term for objects of the late nineteenth and twentieth centuries distinguished solely by their lack of taste. More specifically, kitsch is characterized by poor design, garish colours, shoddy workmanship, cheap materials and, above all, by banal quality. Any or all of these criteria may be present, but there are also many fine examples of kitsch rendered all the more tasteless by the prostitution of excellent craftsmanship or the use of expensive materials. Alternatively, kitsch has been defined as the debasement of refined design in popular adaptation. Art historians are divided on what constitutes kitsch, some maintaining that it is essentially a product of the Jazz Age of the 1920s; others taking a rather wider view and laying the blame on the mechanization of the applied arts from 1860 onwards; while a few go to the extreme of including anything which, to them, betrays the mawkishness and sentimentality of much European art since the *Biedermeierzeit* of the 1830s. The term has also been applied to the pseudo-art qualities of utilitarian objects produced in the second half of the nineteenth century; thus the rococo gilding on a Singer sewing machine would be regarded as kitsch.

From the collectors' viewpoint, kitsch is virtually synonymous with the rise of the chrome-plated and plastic era in the applied arts, or Art Deco in its more popular, debased and vulgar manifestations. Interest in Twenties kitsch began as a light-hearted 'fun thing' but became tinged with nostalgia and, with the passage of time, has become respectable and the object of serious study. More than anything else, book ends and ashtrays (qq.v.) typify the kitsch of the interwar period, but other fertile media include cigarette cases (q.v.) and powder compacts, cocktail glasses and shakers, cheap mass-produced tourist souvenirs (especially those pandering to the universal lavatorial joke) and even the rather florid Teutonic propaganda pieces of the Nazi period. Far too much trash is being produced at the present day; the discerning collector will doubtless be giving it due consideration as the kitsch of the future. Such objects only gain antiquarian interest once they have acquired a certain period flavour.

KNIFE BOXES

Special cases for knives were made in Europe from the sixteenth century onwards, though the finest examples date from the eighteenth and early nineteenth centuries. The most common form was an upright box with a sloping top and a serpentine front. The sloping lid was hinged at the back, and lifted to reveal a honeycomb interior, often lined with velvet, into which the knife-blades were slotted. Knife boxes were mainly produced in various types of polished wood, but shagreen was also used extensively. Metal

ogany knife box
silver mounts;
lish, c. 1775.

boxes with japanned exteriors, often decorated with chinoiseries, were popular in the early nineteenth century and were a speciality of the Welsh factories in Pontypool (q.v.) and Usk. Knife boxes were usually produced in matching pairs to stand at either end of the sideboard, but some may be found with a ring at the back for hanging from a kitchen wall. Similar boxes, usually in tinware or brass, with the same sloping front, were used for candles; these boxes lack the characteristic interior slots of knife boxes. The boxes intended for use in the dining room were frequently decorated with boulle or marquetry (qq.v.), or fitted with silver hinges, handles and lock-plates in ornamental styles. A distinctive form, which was popular in the late eighteenth century, was designed by Robert Adam in the shape of a vase or Grecian urn, in accord with the neo-classical style of interior decoration then fashionable.

KNIFE RESTS

Small objects, resembling miniature dumb-bells or Oriental pillows, made in the late eighteenth and early nineteenth centuries for resting carving-knives. The majority of them were made of glass, ranging from deep-cut crystal to fancy coloured glass, sometimes incorporating *latticinio* or *millefiori* decoration. Knife rests were also made in earthenware, stoneware, pearlware or porcelain.

KNIVES

Bladed implements used in the preparation and eating of food have been recorded from prehistoric times to the present day. Cutlery (q.v.) in the modern form, with spoons and forks manufactured in matching patterns, first began to appear in the seventeenth century. Prior to the adoption of the fork the knife was the principal eating tool, and medieval knives were usually provided with a tapering blade and sharp point which could be used as a fork. After the introduction of forks in the late sixteenth and early seventeenth centuries the shape of table knives altered radically. Ends became rounded, and

English penknives; 18th century.

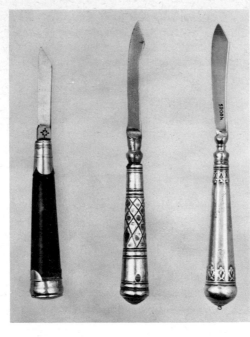

blades had parallel edges. These narrow, straight blades terminated at the handle end in a long solid haft, often faceted and inlaid with brass, silver or gold and set into a handle made of wood, bone, horn or ivory. During the seventeenth century the solid shoulders shrank in size and became slimmer, until they had all but disappeared and consisted of no more than a ring protecting the end of the handle nearest the blade. The ends of blades were often rectangular, as if the points had been broken off, but the chamfered or rounded edge became predominant by 1700. At the same time blades were curved slightly, and this gradually evolved into a blade resembling a miniature scimitar. Handles were correspondingly curved in the opposite direction to achieve symmetry and often terminated in a bulbous projection resembling a contemporary pistol-grip. Seventeenth-century knives had a metal spike as a continuation of the blade, running right through the handle and terminating in a flattened rivet or tang. Eighteenth-century knives often (though not always) substituted a flattened metal projection from the blade, sandwiched between two wooden or bone

plates pierced with rivets. Both types of blade and handle combination were revived in the nineteenth century and are commonly manufactured to this day.

Silver handles became fashionable in the eighteenth century, when entire suites of cutlery were *de rigueur*. These handles were not cast solid, but die-stamped from thin silver sheets or Sheffield plate. The interior was filled with a resinous material which gave knives the appearance of solidity without the accompanying weight. Unfortunately this composition was seldom satisfactory and care must be taken not to immerse such knives in hot water. Porcelain and earthenware handles, usually in the prevailing pistol-grip design, were manufactured in the second half of the eighteenth century. During the nineteenth century the variety of knife handles widened considerably, ebony, ivory, horn, mother-of-pearl and bone becoming fashionable, with plain polished or patterned surfaces or inlaid with other material. Electroplated handles became increasingly popular after 1840.

Steel was invariably used for the blades of knives, though rare examples had steel edges fitted unsatisfactorily to blades of gold or silver. As the blade was the most important part of a knife the bladesmiths dominated the cutlery industry. This explains the growth of knife manufacturing in such towns as Sheffield and Solingen, and their export all over the world. Moreover, the blades were usually marked by the cutlers jealous of their reputation, and early examples can be identified and dated almost as accurately as hallmarked silver. It should be noted that Sheffield cutlers often pirated the marks of their London rivals (whose wares were considered to be superior), and this led to the introduction of the London 'dagger' mark obligatory on blades manufactured by members of the London Court of Cutlers from 1606 until the mid-eighteenth century.

Knives designed for special purposes other than food preparation or eating form an interesting group. Penknives, with fixed or folding blades, developed in the seventeenth century for the cutting of quill-pens

142

amelled fruit knife
ntaining a musical box;
iss, early 19th century.

ver kovsch with gilt
nel decoration; Russian,
91.

Eighteenth- and nineteenth-century pen-knives were frequently ornamented in the manner of objects of vertu, with enamelled or carved handles. Silver handles with relief scenery, or decorated with landmarks, were popular in the nineteenth century, and were often produced as souvenirs of exhibitions or tourist resorts. Multi-bladed knives were among the *tours de force* of the Sheffield cutlers, and some exceedingly elaborate year-knives were produced, with a blade for each year of the Christian era, a new blade being added annually. These blades were decorated with minuscule engraving. Small pocket knives for ladies were produced with handles decorated to match étuis (q.v.) or sewing cases.

Hunting knives were large and broad-bladed and the surface of the blades was often engraved with hunting scenes, while the handles were made of stag-horn or consisted of a deer's foot. Decorative knives of this type were particularly favoured in the United States. The broad-bladed throwing

knife popularized by Jim Bowie was made by Rogers of Sheffield and exported to America in large quantities in the mid-nineteenth century.

KOVSCH

Russian drinking ladle with a boat-shaped body and short flat handle, made from the Middle Ages to the late seventeenth century and revived in the nineteenth century as a reflection of Romanticism in Russia. The earliest vessels were made of wood or horn and elaborately inlaid. Later examples were made of silver, with enamel or niello (q.v.) decoration, often in sets of different sizes. Gilding and mounting with precious stones characterize the nineteenth-century revivals, often emblazoned with the Imperial arms.

KURFÜRSTEN GLASSES

Enamelled glasses of German origin, popular in the sixteenth and seventeenth centuries. They were comparable in treatment, period of manufacture and popularity with the better-known *Reichsadlerhumpen* (q.v.), and their decoration consisted of portraits of the Emperor and the seven Electors (*Kurfürsten*). The figures in full panoply are either depicted seated at court or riding in procession.

There were many variants of this theme and since the portraiture was generally well conceived the *Kurfürsten* glasses provide a fascinating contemporary record of the important personages of the Holy Roman Empire in the sixteenth and seventeenth centuries. The majority of *Kurfürsten* pieces consist of beakers, though a few bottles, mugs and other vessels have been recorded.

See also *Enamelled Glass, Reichsadlerhumpen*

143

LACE

Reticella lace; Italian, 16th century.

The earliest attempt at lacemaking originated with the drawing of threads in linen fabrics, then dividing the existing threads into strands and working over them in various fanciful designs, either with a buttonhole stitch, or simply a wrapping stitch. A later development consisted of cutting away some of the threads and substituting them with others placed at an angle or in circles; this method was popular in English cottage lace-making from the sixteenth century onwards.

During the fifteenth century European lacemakers evolved a system of working with the needle point 'in the air', hence the term *punta in aria*, which describes the working over and connecting of patterns of thread in a geometric fashion on a parchment base which could then be cut away when the work was completed. This was the origin of the beautiful and costly Point lace, which was a feature of apparel for the well-dressed man or woman of the sixteenth to eighteenth centuries. The earliest form of Point lace was known as *reticella*, made in vast quantities by the nuns in the convents of Italy. They also developed Needlepoint, which, by the beginning of the seventeenth century, was exceedingly popular all over Europe. Some of the exquisite Old Point of this period is so fine that a powerful magnifying glass is required to discern how the marvellous *toile* and *gimpe* is formed.

A somewhat later development, though parallel with Needlepoint, was the so-called Pillow lace, which is thought to have originated in Flanders. It is possible that the fine flax thread spun in that region may, at the time of weaving, have suggested a looser and

more ornamental material, but this is a matter for conjecture. At any rate, an interchange of techniques very soon occurred, that Pillow lace was produced in Italy (notably in Milan and Genoa), while Needlepoint patterns appear in the Low Countries. Lacemaking was introduced to France by Catherine de Medici in 1585, when she induced Federico de Vinciolo to settle there and manufacture the fine lace for which the Venetians had been hitherto renowned. Imports of Italian lace were so great in the ensuing century that Colbert checked their importation and founded lace schools near Alençon, hence the magnificent fabric known as *point d'Alençon* and *point Argentan*.

Above Bobbin lace lappet;
French (Valenciennes),
mid-18th century.

Above right Fan mount
of Chantilly lace; French,
mid-19th century.

Left Milanese bobbin
lace; 17th century.

which for long were regarded as the acme of the lacemaker's art.

The persecution of the Huguenots and their flight to England brought the art of lacemaking to Britain at the end of the seventeenth century. Many of these laceworkers settled in Devon, and Honiton lace is still regarded as the finest produced in Britain. Lacemaking spread to Ireland early in the nineteenth century, being introduced as a cottage industry to alleviate poverty and unemployment. Carrickmacross, Youghal and Limerick were the best-known centres of this industry.

The manufacture of lace was intricate and tedious. Girls were initiated into its complexities at the age of three and the work was often carried out in very humid conditions in order that the fine threads should not become brittle and snap. The perfection of fine lace is all the more astonishing when it is remembered how poorly lit were the cottages and cellars where the work was carried out. Up to 800 bobbins might be required in the production of a wide flounce of bobbin lace, an inch of which could take more than a day's labour to produce. That this fine handmade lace was well produced is demonstrated by the fact that so much of it has withstood the ravages of time. Handmade lace, by virtue of the costliness of the thread used and the amount of work involved in its manufacture, was always an expensive material and, belonging only to the wealthiest classes, seldom came on to the market.

Curiously enough, there was little tradition of lacemaking in the United States. The Huguenots who settled in the Hudson valley introduced bobbin lace to that area but it remained a minority interest which never developed into an industry. Various styles of lace, following the patterns popular in the English Midlands, were produced as a cottage industry in the district around Ipswich, Massachusetts, in the latter part of the Colonial era. Unfortunately mechanization was applied to the American industry at an early date. Factories employing machinery were established at Medway and Ipswich between 1818 and 1824, and handmade lace rapidly disappeared thereafter. Machine-made lace in Britain and western Europe ousted the handmade product by the 1840s. Until the outbreak of World War I, lace (mainly machine-made) was popular in the trimming of women's clothing, but the austerity of the war years dealt the lace industry a heavy blow from which it has never recovered, despite isolated efforts to revive it. In the same way, the collecting of old lace, a popular pastime in Victorian and Edwardian times, passed completely out of fashion.

Lace has been largely neglected by dealers,

collectors and scholars, but interest in old lace has begun to revive in recent years, notably in the United States which now has the finest institutional collections.

LACE BOBBINS

Slender bobbins or sticks used in lacemaking to keep the threads at the requisite tension. Anything from twelve to several hundred bobbins were needed, according to the size and fineness of the lace being worked. Lace bobbins evolved in the eighteenth century out of the rudimentary sticks and pieces of bone previously used. The earliest types were comparatively short and thick, and were nicknamed bobtails and dumps. They had a balustroid shank and a slender neck on which the thread was secured. Later examples were rather longer and slimmer and often had several tiny beads attached to the end of the shank. A great deal of variation exists in these beads, pearls and spangles, as well as in the decoration of the bobbins themselves, since

it was essential that the lacemaker coul[d] identify individual threads by their bobbin[s].

The bobbins were often made of ivor[y,] bone or close-grained hardwood such as bo[x,] holly, beech or cherry. Metal bobbins a[re] relatively scarce but have been recorded i[n] brass, bronze, pewter, silver and even gol[d.] The names given to the different shapes a[re] as distinctive as their style of decoratio[n.] Butterflies and leopards denoted bobbin[s] with splayed wings and spotted shank[s] respectively. Plain bobbins were called ol[d] maids, while a cow-in-calf was a large bobbi[n] with a smaller one inside. Bobbins may b[e] found with minuscule inscriptions com[-] memorating family events, such as birth[s,] betrothals and weddings. A few have bee[n] noted with eighteenth- and nineteent[h] century political slogans on them. With th[e] decline in handmade lace the decoration [of] lace bobbins died out, but this vanished form of folk art was once widely diffused i[n] England, Ireland and America, and to [a] lesser extent in France and the Low Countrie[s.]

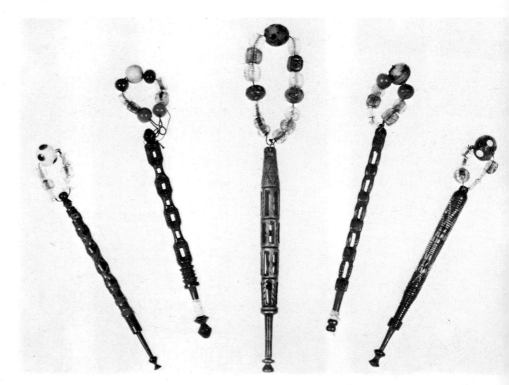

Group of lace bobbins; English, early 19th century.

LACQUER

The art of lacquering was practised in China and Japan for many centuries. In China its origins are obscure, although bronze vessels dating from the Shang dynasty have been found with lacquer protective coating, and its application to wood probably dates from the same period. By the beginning of the seventeenth century lacquer had been raised to the level of a fine art. The basis for Oriental lacquer consisted of ground varnishes derived from the resin of the *Rhus vernicifera*. The preparation of the ground was an expensive business involving a considerable amount of time. The essence of the process was the lengthy drying out of the successive coats. As much as three weeks might elapse between the hardening of one coat prior to rubbing down in preparation for the next. Anything up to three years could be spent in lacquering a single item, so it is hardly surprising that the best-quality Oriental pieces were seldom exported, and fetched enormous prices when they were.

Chinese and Japanese lacquers were imported into Europe in the latter half of the sixteenth century, first by the Portuguese and later by the Dutch. The majority of these articles consisted of small chests, cabinets and boxes, and by the middle of the seventeenth century the techniques of lacquer were being imitated in Holland and England. These imitators lacked the proper materials, but they developed a tolerably good substitute based on shellac. Western craftsmen, however, ignored the crucial time factor; drying processes were accelerated, no more than a single day being allowed for the drying of each coat. Inevitably 'japanning', as European lacquer is confusingly termed, lacks the brilliant lustre and durability of Oriental lacquer.

Both Oriental and Western lacquer was applied in black, red, green, blue or brown. Decoration was added in gilt, using a paste of gum arabic and whiting as the base on which gold leaf was laid. European gilding preferred base metal substitutes, such as bronze or brass powder, which had to be varnished to prevent tarnishing. The publication of Stalker and Parker's *Treatise of Japanning and Varnishing* in 1688 stimulated a craze for home-produced lacquer, and many small articles were decorated with lacquer and chinoiserie (q.v.) ornament in the early eighteenth century. It went out of fashion from 1740 till about 1780 when it revived again for a short time, and was also briefly in favour in the early 1800s.

LAMBREQUINS

This term was originally applied to the scarves worn over the helmets of medieval knights, but was revived in the mid-nineteenth century to describe decorative pieces of fabric designed to conceal any sharp structural edge in furniture or interiors. Tasselled or crocheted lambrequins were popular as valances or pelmets on curtains, and were also draped over the mantelpiece, the whatnot and the occasional table. They were made of plush, velvet, brocades, damask, felt, leather and other heavy materials, decorated with beadwork or Berlin woolwork (qq.v.). Fashionable in western Europe from the middle of the nineteenth century, they spread to the United States and were immensely popular from 1870 to 1900. In America they were often referred to as 'tidies' or 'lamberkins'. Geometric, floral and figural patterns were worked on cloth by the *appliqué* method, and écru twine was knotted into the form of pillow lace known as macramé to give lambrequins their distinctive irregular edging. Subsequent generations derided the lambrequin as the epitome of late Victorian fussiness, but they are now worth considering for their period appeal and as fine examples of the different techniques of needlework practised in the nineteenth century.
See also *Antimacassars*

LAMPS

The earliest type of lamp consisted of a small bronze or pottery cup in which the wick (often a piece of moss) floated free in a bath

of oil and gave off a very smoky, smelly and
flickering light. Lamps of this rudimentary
type are known to have been used in the
Mediterranean area 5,000 years ago. More
sophisticated lamps, consisting of enclosed
shallow vessels, with a pouring hole, a
handle and a narrow spout for the wick and
flame, were developed in Egypt during the
first millennium BC and had spread to Asia
Minor and Greece by the fifth century BC.
The small bronze or terracotta lamps of the
Greeks and the Romans were often intricately
decorated with incised patterns, ornamented
with cast or moulded human or animal
forms, and incorporated a wide range of
fanciful shapes. Lamps with covers, which
protected the flame from the wind when
carried out of doors at night, developed into
the lantern. Ornamental terracotta lamps
were a popular form of birthday present in
Roman Imperial times, judging by the
symbolism and inscriptions found on them.

The basic design of lamps and lanterns
remained unaltered throughout the Middle
Ages, but by the late seventeenth century an
important improvement consisted of the
double pan, which caught the drips of oil. By
the beginning of the eighteenth century the
wick-holder was re-styled and this obviated
the need for the double drip-pan. In many
parts of England and America the simple
earthenware cruisie was known as a betty
lamp. Although earthenware was the most
popular medium for small domestic lamps,
brass and copper were employed increasingly
during the eighteenth century. The science
of illumination was revolutionized in 1782
when Ami Argand invented a lamp surmounted by a glass chimney and fitted with
a tubular wick, which enabled a better flow
of air to feed the flame. Argand failed to
secure a patent for his invention and it was
rapidly copied by manufacturers on both
sides of the English Channel. Problems in
maintaining a steady flow of oil to the wick
were overcome by the Carcel lamp (1798),
which had a small clockwork pump in the
oil-container beneath the burner; and the
Moderator (1836) operated by a spring and
piston mechanism. The most popular type of

lamp in the United States in the late eightee[n]
and early nineteenth centuries was know[n]
the Agitable, patented by John Miles
Birmingham in 1787 and subsequently ma[nu]
factured in America, where it was adapte[d]
burn the whale oil so plentiful there. It ha[s]
very simple design which permitted m[ass]
production and it remained popular
many decades.

Technical advances in combustible [ele]
ments paralleled developments in the des[ign]
of lamps. Improvements in the method[s]
refining oil (making it less viscous), led
simpler, less cumbersome forms of la[mp]
relying on capillary attraction to feed
fuel to the wick. Both candle paraffin [and]
kerosene were patented in 1853, and n[ew]
types of lamps were manufactured to t[ake]
advantages of these fuels. The earliest
lamps were patented in 1779 but w[ere]

Wooden betty lamps and
holder; New England,
17th–18th centuries.

ft Pewter and brass
~~arking~~ lamp, with bull's
~~e~~ reflector; American,
~~th~~ century.

ght Iridescent glass and
~~etal~~ lamp by Lötz;
~~A~~strian, *c.* 1900.

relatively unpopular until the mid–nineteenth century, when a plentiful supply of coal gas became readily available. A dramatic improvement was the gas mantle (1885), which gave a steadier and brighter flame than was previously possible. Gas lamps of the late nineteenth century were invariably modelled on existing oil lamps. The first open arc lamp (ancestor of the neon light) was patented in 1878 and Edison's first electric light-bulb appeared a year later. Numerous improvements in electric and arc lighting were made between 1881 and 1914, but few of these may be considered collectable on aesthetic grounds. Few of the early light-bulbs have survived, but there are many examples of reading lamps and table lamps designed from 1890 onwards for use with electricity. Some of these combined the novelty of electricity with the spirit of Art Nouveau and are now highly prized. These include the bronze and frosted glass lamps produced in France between 1895 and 1910 in the form of the American danseuse, Loie Fuller, giving her interpretation of the Dance of the Seven Veils.

An infinite variety of glass bulbs and shades was produced from about 1870 in America

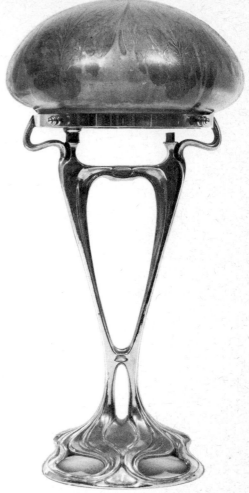

~~a~~ble lamp in the Tiffany
~~sty~~le; American, *c.* 1900.

and Europe, reflecting the diversity of the fancy glass of the period. Opaque, plated and translucent coloured glass was produced in great quantities by the American glasshouses and many of the more famous styles, such as Peachblow and Queen's Burmese ware, were subsequently manufactured in England, France and Germany. Fairy lights, night lights and other novelty forms were popular at the turn of the century, and are now attracting the serious attention of collectors. Other types worth considering include portable lamps, from coach lanterns to carbide lamps and early examples of battery lamps patented at the beginning of this century.

149

LEATHER

Animal hides and skins treated by the process of tanning to preserve them and convert them into a tough, pliable substance. The commoner hides used are those of cattle, sheep, goats and pigs, but many rarer animals, such as deer, walrus, camel and antelope, reptiles such as snake, alligator and lizard, and even birds, such as turkey and ostrich, have been used. Numerous techniques of tanning, dyeing, glazing and finishing give rise to a very wide range of leathers, varying in composition, colour, grain and texture, depending on the purpose for which they are intended.

Book bindings, black jacks, card cases and cigarette cases (qq.v.) are discussed under their individual headings, and examples of

leather will also be found in the categories of costume accessories and militaria (qq.v.) Decorative leather, with pierced or embossed motifs, has been used in the manufacture of purses, sealing cases and stud boxes. Belts, boots, shoes and gloves are among the small articles of dress principally produced in leather, and each offers a considerable amount of scope for the collector.

Prior to the late nineteenth century, when mechanization in the leather industry virtually eliminated hand-work, boots and shoes were largely handmade and many individual styles of construction and decoration were evolved in different parts of Europe and America. In general, footwear tended to become lighter and more elegant as the nineteenth century drew to a close. There was considerable variation in the height and shape of the heels in ladies' boots and shoes. In men's footwear boots gradually became lower, as top-boots went out of fashion and were replaced by ankle boots, half-boots and the modern shoe, which was evolved about 1900. Apart from the different kinds of leather used, principally for uppers, styles became increasingly elaborate in design and decoration and gave rise to the term 'shoe millinery' between 1911 and 1920. From then onwards, however, the manufacture of women's shoes became more standardized throughout the western world and ornament was reduced to a minimum. Among the leathers which were popular in the late nineteenth and early twentieth centuries

Leather picture frame by Elbert Hubbard's Roycroft shops; American, *c.* 1900.

the production of boots and shoes were box calf, willow calf and glacé kid, various types of patent leather, oil-dressed leather, leathers with exotic grains and colours from such reptile skins as Indian and Java lizards, python, shark-skin and ostrich skin.

LINEN SMOOTHERS

Household implements produced in the west Midlands of England in the eighteenth and early nineteenth centuries. They consisted of a glass mushroom with an elongated stock ending in a grooved or knopped handle. They were rubbed vigorously over linen sheets to smooth them out, but the advent of more efficient ironing devices led to a decline in their popularity. They may be found in clear colourless glass, or coloured green or brown bottle glass in different sizes and styles of decoration.

LITHOPHANES

Thin plaques of unglazed porcelain with relief ornament which becomes visible when held against the light. The name is a compound of two Greek words: *lithos*, meaning 'stone' and *phane*, meaning 'light'. Lithophanes require a relatively strong light immediately behind them to show up the decoration. They are frequently found in lampshades, small hand screens, candle shields and children's nightlights, or, in more recent years, in novelty panels with concealed electric light-bulbs. The process was patented in Paris in 1827, but the following year the Meissen porcelain factory in Saxony acquired the rights to produce translucent porcelain plaques and they were subsequently manufactured by the Royal Prussian porcelain works in Berlin until the middle of the nineteenth century. Grainger, Lee and Company are known to have made lithophanes in England and other potteries are also thought to have produced them, though no marked specimens have so far been recorded. Belleek, Minton and Copeland are known to have made lithophanes in the late nineteenth century.

They may be found in various sizes, from little more than an inch square to upwards of a foot, the larger types being mounted with a concealed light and hung on walls. The smallest lithophanes were sometimes set in the bases of glass tankards so that the decoration could be seen as the tankard was emptied, and a few have been noted in the bases of cups or mugs. Lithophanes were uncoloured, and usually white, though some with a faint pinkish tinge are known. The subjects depicted ranged from classical and biblical scenes to fairy tales and nursery rhymes, scenic views and floral compositions. They were immensely popular in the United States where attempts were made to simulate the process using opaque glass, the Hobbs, Brockunier Company being the leading exponent of this form.

LOCKETS

Small container for portraits or locks of hair, suspended on a chain or brooch fitment and worn as a form of jewelry. They were usually made in two parts hinged and secured by a clasp or catch, with one or both inner sides glazed to hold a portrait or other personal mementoes. Many different shapes may be found, though ovals and hearts are the most common. Lockets were widely produced from the seventeenth century in western Europe in a variety of materials including gold, silver, silver-gilt, pinchbeck, brass or copper, often decorated with chasing and filigree work, set with precious stones, or enamelled. Minuscule pictures or inscriptions worked in human hair were fashionable in the nineteenth century. Photography ousted portrait miniatures (q.v.) in lockets from about 1860.

See also *Jewelry, Mourning Items*

Iron key; Welsh, late 17th century.

LOCKS AND KEYS

Very few locks have survived from medieval or earlier periods, when only royalty, the nobility and the higher clergy had possessions which were valuable enough to require such security. The earliest locks were of wrought-iron construction in geometrical or plain designs and operated with enormous keys. By the fourteenth century the carcase of locks was sometimes covered with brass plates, often decorated in intricate motifs by engraving and piercing, embellished with the coats of arms of the owners, and sometimes enamelled or gilded. Latten, a form of brass alloy, was widely used on lock-cases from the sixteenth century. Seventeenth-century locks were made of steel in steel cases with a brass cover for ornamental effect. The foliate and floral patterns on lock-plates matched those on the door hinges and even the broad handle of keys. By the middle of the eighteenth century several different types of lock were in general use, the most important being stock-locks (on outer doors), spring-locks (on chamber doors) and trunk-locks on trunks, boxes and cabinets. Portable locks, known as secret or padlocks (fr pad, the common term for a thief), were popular from that period onwards. Fr about 1740 lock-plates were increasin produced by casting, which permitted m ornate relief decoration.

Mortice locks came into use in the 17 operated on the sliding-bolt principle, bu 1784 Joseph Bramah invented a lock ope ing by means of a rotating drum or cylin which enabled a great reduction in the siz keys. Linus Yale invented an impro cylinder lock in 1848 and many variant this are used all over the world to this Mortice locks were recessed into the wo work of doors, the only part visible being tongue on the narrow edge of the door w open. They were fitted with lock-plate either side of the door, with match handles, keyhole covers and escutch plates, usually in cast brass with chasing gilding. The finest of these were designed Robert Adam. Novelty locks, incorpora secret devices, were produced from the seventeenth century onwards. John Wi of Birmingham was noted for his pa devices, night-locks and detector lo many of which are highly ornamenta well as being technically ingenious.

The rim-lock, with the mechanism tirely contained in a metal box, develope the early nineteenth century, and was fected by James Carpenter in 1830. This ty with the Chubb patent detector mechan of 1818, has remained popular to this despite fierce competition from Yale similar cylinder locks. Many locks of Eng manufacture from the late eighteenth tury bear the maker's name and the cyp of the reigning monarch, which is a us guide to dating.

Padlocks have been in use since the fiftee century, if not earlier. The earliest form known as a barrel padlock, from the tub shape of the lock, with a hasp in shackl sickle form running from one end to other. This type was gradually superse by the more familiar shape, with a se circular hasp and a flattened lock, in seventeenth century. The first type of padlock had a triangular shape, but later forms were ball or heart-shaped, while the purse shape dates from the early eighteenth century. Padlocks resembling a heart cut down the centre were fashionable in the eighteenth century and are believed to be of French origin, though they were subsequently produced in Britain and Colonial America.

The general shape and styling of keys has remained fairly constant from the earliest times, though the more decorative examples exhibit the prevailing fashions in engraving, inlaying or cast ornament. Furniture keys were generally more ornamental than door keys, the decoration on the latter being restricted by the need to have a circular handle for attachment to a chain or keyring. Nevertheless, many different shapes and sizes of key can be found. Watch keys are a distinctive form, with short square or polygonal shafts and often intricately patterned handles in a wider range of metals (including gold or silver) than that normally used in the manufacture of keys. The pattern of key used with modern cylinder locks invariably has a flattened disc handle, and many examples may be found with makers' trademarks and fancy patterns.

LOVE TOKENS

Objects designed as marks of affection exchanged between lovers are to be found in many different societies and civilizations, the Valentine (q.v.) being the most universal form in use to the present day. Loving cups, despite their name, like their larger derivative, the two-handled bridal chamberpot, do not come within this category since they were seldom (if ever) exchanged between lovers, but were given as betrothal or wedding presents by friends and relatives of the couple. Glass rolling-pins (q.v.), painted or incised with symbols of affection, such as entwined hearts, cupid's bows and love-knots, were a popular form of folk art in Britain, western Europe and America in the eighteenth and nineteenth centuries, and were given by sailors to their wives and sweethearts. They were often hollow, and were

used as containers for sugar or salt. Stay-busks, the long, flattened frontal bones of corsets, were carved and engraved, or decorated with pokerwork (q.v.) in the same genre. Scrimshaw work (q.v.) on walrus tusks and whale teeth, with amorous or sentimental vignettes, was often carried out by seamen as presents for their womenfolk. A high proportion of the decorated artefacts in this category seem to have been fashioned by men deprived of female company for long periods. Whether the work involved helped to assuage the pangs of loneliness, or whether it was believed that the tokens themselves possessed some magical quality which would ensure a wife's fidelity is a matter for conjecture. Certainly the rather stereotyped symbolism found in the decoration of rolling-pins and stay-busks seems to indicate the latter.

Wooden spoons, with elaborate carving, pokerwork, engraving or painting on their shafts and bowls, were given as love tokens in many parts of Europe from the Balkans to Iberia and in some parts of Britain, notably

153

Wales, the last-named having a distinctive 'Siamese twin' form of double spoon. Dates and twin sets of initials on these spoons indicate engagements and wedding anniversaries. The term 'spooning' for courtship is an allusion to this practice.

LOVING CUPS

Originally confined to commemorative cups of pewter or silver produced in England in the eighteenth century, this term is now loosely applied to any large two- or three-handled cup. The earliest examples seem to date from the beginning of the eighteenth century, and were inscribed with dates to signify betrothal or marriage, with the initials (and occasionally the names) of the bridal couple. These cups resembled wide-mouthed vases, with bulging bodies and high rims. The large twin handles were a characteristic feature, derived from earlier ecclesiastical patterns and sporting trophies. They are found in pewter, silver or Sheffield plate. By the middle of the eighteenth century ceramic forms were becoming popular. Brown stoneware loving cups, with incised decoration, were produced in Nottinghamshire in the 1750s and subsequently imitated by the potteries of Staffordshire, Derbyshire and Yorkshire. By the end of the century they were being produced in other types of pottery, from Leeds creamware and pearlware, to the distinctive black basaltes of Wedgwood.

Saltglazed stoneware loving cup; Staffordshire, 1754.

Porcelain loving cups, with lavish rococo gilding and hand-painted vignettes, were a speciality of Minton, Rockingham and other porcelain manufacturers of the early nineteenth century. In more recent years porcelain loving cups have been produced in limited editions to commemorate important national events and anniversaries

LUSTRE WARES

Pottery whose surface is covered with a metallic, often iridescent, glaze to simulate gold or silver. The effect was achieved by painting glazed pottery with a metallic oxide then firing it in a reducing atmosphere to leave a thin deposit of metal. Copper and platinum oxides were used to create gold and silver effects respectively, but other oxides were used to produce a nacreous effect in other colours, purple and pink being the most common. Lustre techniques were employed in Hispano-Mauresque pottery from the late Middle Ages, and by Italian manufacturers of maiolica from the sixteenth century. The earliest English lustre wares were produced by Josiah Wedgwood, using lustre in combination with enamelling on pearlware from about 1820 onwards, mainly on smaller pieces such as cups, saucers, dishes, cream jugs and sugar bowls.

Lustre techniques were used by several potteries at the turn of the century to decorate tiles and hollow wares. Foremost in this field was the Pilkington pottery, which produced decorative lustre wares from 1903 onwards. This distinctive pottery, later known as 'Royal Lancastrian' ware, was produced until the late 1930s. Tiles, plates and bowls with lustre motifs were designed for this company by such artists as Walter Crane, Charles Cundall, Gordon Forsyth, Richard Joyce, William Mycock and C.F.A Voysey. Lustre decoration, with contrasting backgrounds in the so-called 'Persian' colours (blues, greens and turquoises), was a speciality of the De Morgan, Iles and Passenger pottery between 1892 and 1907.

MAPS

Whatever early cartographers may have lacked in the precision and accuracy of their surveying was made up for by the decorative quality and the embellishment of their maps. Although map-making was practised by the Greeks, Romans and Chinese, cartography did not become an exact science until the sixteenth century. While the European cartographers concentrated on maps of the continents, their English counterparts were producing the first county maps, often highly detailed and surprisingly accurate. The first printed county maps of Britain were those produced by Christopher Saxton, deservedly known as 'the father of English cartography', between 1574 and 1579, and eventually published in an atlas of thirty-seven county groups plus a general map of 'Anglia'. Significantly Saxton issued his maps in separate sheets as the plates were completed in order to recoup some of the capital outlay. These maps retailed originally at fourpence each – a far cry from the £60–£70 which even the less popular counties demand these days. Unfortunately for posterity Saxton grouped the four Home Counties of Kent, Surrey, Sussex and Middlesex together on one map and demand for it has now sent the price sky-high.

Saxton was lucky enough to secure a wealthy patron, Thomas Seckford, who underwrote the costs of the project. Not so fortunate, however, was John Norden, whose maps were superior to Saxton's but who lacked the financial backing to make a success of his venture. Consequently Norden's maps are not only comparatively rare but also of greater appeal to the connoisseur.

Saxton and Norden pale into insignificance compared with John Speed, perhaps the best known of all early English map-makers. Under the patronage of Sir Fulke Greville, Speed devoted several years to the compilation of a history and geography of the entire British Isles, which was eventually published in 1611 under the grandiose title of *The Theatre of the Empire of Great Britain*. Its later editions incorporated maps of other countries. Individual maps from Speed's atlases are fairly plentiful but because of their local interest they are in great demand.

Other eminent cartographers of the seventeenth century, whose county maps are not only acceptable from the decorative viewpoint but possess investment potential, include Willem Blaeu, Richard Blome, John Ogilby and Robert Morden.

Nicolas Sanson was Saxton's counterpart in France. His sons, Guillaume and Adrien, produced fine maps of France in the seventeenth century and were succeeded by A.H. Jaillot. The best of the early German map-makers included Braun and Hogenberg, who specialized in elaborate town plans covering the major cities of the world; Matthias Quad, whose *Geographisch Handtbuch* ran into many editions in the early seventeenth century; and Matthäus Merian, whose maps were decorated with attractive scenic vignettes. The Blaeu family of Holland dominated continental cartography in the late sixteenth and seventeenth centuries and their maps, covering most parts of Europe in great detail, are among those most highly prized today. Mercator, Hondius, Ortelius and Jan Jansson are other leading cartographers of the period whose works are eagerly sought after.

The earliest American maps were those published by Matteo Contarini (1506) and Sebastian Münster (1540). Maps of the continent as a whole were included in the works of Mercator, Ortelius and Wytfliet. By the early seventeenth century, maps depicting specific parts of America were being published by Blaeu, Jansson, Visscher and Speed, the last-named showing California as an island, thereby perpetuating an error which was slavishly followed by other map-makers for over a century! Although Hermann Moll (c. 1720) continued this mistake, his maps of North America were otherwise highly detailed, illustrated with views and landmarks and annotated with comments about the inhabitants, their industries, communications and way of life. In the latter part of the Colonial period there were many excellent maps, the most important being Thomas Jefferys's *Americ[an] Atlas* (1776) comprising thirty maps. H[is] successor, William Faden, produced nume[r]ous large-scale maps of the United State[s,] Canada and the West Indies in the la[te] eighteenth century. Indigenous maps [of] America begin with the atlas produced b[y] Carey and Lea (1822). Later maps are st[ill] comparatively plentiful and illustrate th[e] enormous growth of the population be[t]ween 1840 and 1900.

Apart from maps as such, the collector w[ill] find specialized categories such as milita[ry] surveys, street plans, postal communicatio[n] maps (showing the circulation of mail [in] different districts), geological maps, railroa[d] plans and navigational charts, the last-name[d] being a vast subject in itself.

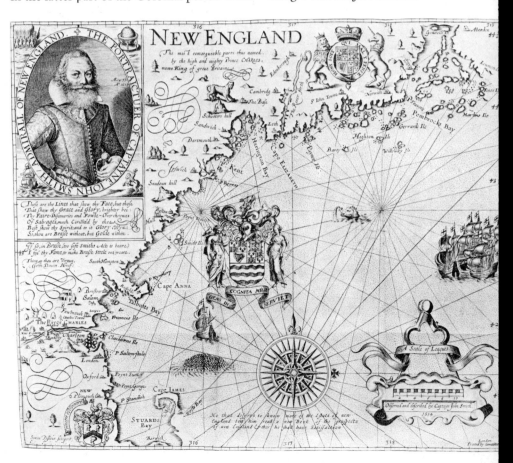

Map of New England by Captain John Smith, London, c. 1630.

MARBLES. See *Beads and Marbles*

MARQUETRY

Form of decoration on the surface of furniture composed of thin veneers of different woods, often stained or scorched, or combined with other materials such as ivory, bone, horn, tortoiseshell and even metals such as brass or silver sheet. A specialized form of marquetry, using alternate pieces of brass sheet and tortoiscshell, is known as boulle (q.v.). Wood veneers were used in marquetry panels on furniture from the late Middle Ages in Italy, and spread to France, Germany and the Netherlands, where they were especially fashionable in the seventeenth and eighteenth centuries. Non-wood marquetry was pioneered in Italy in the sixteenth century and was popular in French furniture of the Louis Quatorze period. Marquetry was widely used in English and American furniturc from the late seventeenth century onwards. Though its popularity declined during the nineteenth century, it never died out and enjoyed a marked revival in the period from 1880 to 1920.

Marquetry was applied to small articles, such as sewing cases, work boxes, trinket boxes and writing cases, but in more recent years marquetry pictures mounted for hanging on walls have become very popular, and fine examples from the beginning of this century are now highly prized.

MARTELÉ

Trade term for a type of American silverware, patented by the Gorham Manufacturing Company of Providence, Rhode Island, in 1900. The word is French for 'hammered' and aptly describes the technique of beating up silver sheet, developed by William Codman, an English craftsman employed by Gorham from 1891 onwards. Since each piece was hand-beaten no two items are quite alike. The term has been used, quite erroneously, to describe sheet metal articles in silver-plate embossed and die-stamped by mechanical methods, but such items bear no similarity to the distinctively soft, fluid surface of genuine *martelé* silver. *Martelé* silver was popular in the period up to World War I and may be found on small decorative articles such as dressing-table sets (q.v.).

MARY GREGORY GLASS

Coloured glassware decorated with white enamel figures and motifs. The glass is named after Mary Gregory, an enameller employed by the Boston and Sandwich Glassworks in Massachusetts in the mid-nineteenth century, though only a very small proportion of the glass thus described could have been her work, and indeed this type of decorative glassware was in existence in Europe long before her time. The true origin of Mary Gregory glass was the translucent coloured glassware produced by the Hahn glassworks in Gablonz (Jablonec) in Bohemia in the early nineteenth century. The glass was predominantly a rich cranberry colour, but red, pink, blue, turquoise, green and amber glass was also produced and decorated in opaque white enamel. The subjects range from flowers and birds to scenery, but children at play formed the most popular subject,

rendered in a somewhat whimsical style. The term is also applied to colourless clear glass with opaque white decoration. Mary Gregory glass consists mainly of jugs, decanters and useful tablewares, rather than more ornamental forms such as vases.
See colour plate page 177

MASKS

In the world of antiques masks exist on two distinct levels. The term is applied to any form of decoration which consists of a human, demonic or animal face, on furniture, silverware, pottery and porcelain. Lion masks were popularly exploited in such diverse objects as door knockers and chair-backs, while satyr masks and Medusa heads were frequently used by makers of grotesquerie (q.v.). Other manifestations in the applied arts of the nineteenth century include Indian feathered head-dress masks, sphinxes, buddhas and cherubs.

Masks worn over the face are of the greatest antiquity and are to be found in every part of the world. Several factors explain the universal significance of masks: a primeval recognition of the fact that the countenance was the most definite symbol of divine intelligence, the almost magical quality of a mask to transform the personality of the wearer or the effect on the onlooker, and a strange mystifying quality which, in unsophisticated societies, conveys an almost supernatural power. For these reasons masks have always played a very important part in ritual and religion, and numerous examples could be cited, from the totemistic paganism of Africa, Polynesia and North America to the comparatively sophisticated carnival ceremonies in Catholic countries. Masks belonging to the field of ethnography include bird, animal and demonic forms, carved in wood or cast in bronze, embodying all the techniques of decorative art indigenous in different parts of the world. Enormous variation may exist in the masks of relatively small areas, as, for example, the tribal masks of Papua and Java, which differ from village to village.

The Egyptians used masks as facial coverings for the mummified bodies of their dead. Funerary masks were modelled with the object of assisting the revivification of the dead in the next world. Canvas masks were employed in Greek drama to convey to the furthest rows of the audience the comic or tragic character of the actors, and this idea was adopted and expanded by the Romans. Numerous examples of dramatic masks in terracotta have been unearthed, as well as funerary masks interred in tombs in order to propitiate the gods of the underworld.

Of the enormous field of Oriental masks the best known are those associated with the Noh drama of Japan. The art of mask making is thought to have been introduced to Japan from China in the seventh century and given great impetus by the development of the Noh drama as an adjunct of Zen Buddhism from the fourteenth century onward. Noh masks conformed to certain traditional patterns, and more than a hundred different major types have been recorded. They were invariably made of wood, coated with plaster and then painted and gilded. Other Japanese masks were semi-ritual in

Dance mask used in
iation ceremonies in
th-west Congo,
900.

ht Aztec stone mask
he god Xipe Totec;
h century.

nature, being sold at various shrines or in connection with different religious festivals. They continue to the present day, although they have become debased into a form of tourist souvenir. Chinese masks were usually made of papier mâché and a rigid colour code enabled the audience to identify the character.

African masks were, and are, mainly of wood construction, painted and elaborately carved, often decorated with long fringes of fibre or feathers. The masks of the American Indians provide many distinctive forms, and range from those which entirely envelop the head and are closed at the top (like a totem pole) to those which merely cover the front of the face. American masks were traditionally made of rawhide (though treated leather is more commonly used nowadays), and embellished with a wide variety of

ry pendant mask,
esenting a king with a
a of miniature heads
Portuguese; Benin,
geria, 16th century.

objects such as corn-cobs, shell-discs, animal bones, deer hair and gourd-stems. Carved wooden masks were favoured by the Indian tribes of the north-eastern United States and Canada, while leather masks pertain mostly to the south-western tribes.

Ritual masks survive in many parts of Europe to this day, particularly in the Slavonic countries, where masks originating in ancient pagan rites have been grafted on to Orthodox Christian festivals connected with Christmas and Easter. Similar masks may have existed in western Europe, though few examples have survived. The banal 'false faces' associated with Hallowe'en bear no more than a shadowy resemblance to the demonic masks of Druidism from which they descended. There are also many instances of masks connected with medieval mystery plays, out of which evolved the pantomime of Italy, now widespread throughout European culture. Italy was also the home of the masquerade or masked ball, which originated in medieval Venice, and reached its height in France, Germany and Britain in the second half of the eighteenth century. Masks produced in connection with these festivities were confined to eye coverings, but were often richly jeweled and embroidered.

Masks for the protection of the wearer in battle were cast in bronze and used extensively

159

by the peoples of the Mediterranean area. For the most part these were naturalistic in appearance, unlike the Japanese battle masks of lacquered iron which were deliberately given a fierce countenance in order to terrify the enemy. Defensive masks disappeared from European warfare with the development of the armoured helmet and visor, but the trench warfare of the present century resulted in masks of chain-mail and leather, iron masks, tank visors and gas masks. Examples of the last-named from World War I, which are now highly prized by collectors of militaria (q.v.), include types with face-pieces of iron (French and Italian), leather (French and German), sheet rubber (Russian) and rubberized canvas (British and American).

MATCHBOXES

The world's first friction matches – 'sulphurata hyperoxygenata' – were invented in 1827 by John Walker, a chemist of Stockton-on-Tees. These matches consisted of splints of wood, three inches in length, tipped with a mixture of antimony sulphide, potassium chlorate, gum arabic and starch. They were drawn through a folded piece of emery paper and ignited with a shower of sparks, releasing such a foul gas that many of early manufacturers printed a health warn on the lids of the boxes. With the substitut of phosphorus for antimony sulphide 1831, matches became safer and less ma dorous. Matches were soon reduced in and special cases, with a serrated or grain edge, were produced by silversmiths manufacturers of objects of vertu from early 1830s onwards. These matchbo were quite small, and held four or matches, which were comparatively pensive, retailing at twopence – or 4 cen each. Early matchboxes were someti made of leather or hardwood mounted v brass or steel strikers, but pewter, white m and silver were the most popular mater A few boxes were circular, but most w slim rectangles, usually having a small hir lid at one end. By the middle of the ninetee century boxes in the form of miniature bo (with simulated binding) were fashion and may be found in engraved silver with enamelled pictorial panels. Some these even had an ingenious spring-loa compartment for gold coins or pos stamps.

The invention of safety matches by Lundstrom of Sweden in 1855 had a found effect on ornamental matchboxes new type was devised which consisted o open-ended box fitting over the ac matchbox, and having an aperture at side to reveal the amorphous phosph

Matchbox (centre), *tablette*, napkin rings, box and miniature letter rack with fern decoration; late 19th century.

safety strip. Such containers, made of silver or electroplate, offered less scope for ornament than the earlier boxes and never attained the same degree of popularity. Decorative matchboxes died out about 1920, by which time matches themselves had dropped sharply in price and were no longer regarded as such a precious commodity. The small wooden or cardboard boxes in which they were retailed provided sufficient protection, and were discarded when the matches were spent.

MAUCHLINE WARE

Distinctive form of decorative treen (q.v.), said to have originated in the Ayrshire town of Mauchline in the late eighteenth or early nineteenth century. Small boxes with painted motifs on their sides were produced in Russia and the Baltic countries even earlier and their import to Scotland may well have been the original influence. The wooden articles now generally known as Mauchline ware were made of Scottish planewood, decorated with small transfer-printed views, portraits and landmarks in black, and varnished over. A large variety of boxes may be found in this material with the characteristic black vignettes, the commonest being snuff boxes, needle cases, pill boxes, trinket boxes, rouge boxes and étuis. Comparatively rare are flat circular boxes, with a transfer print on the base and a tiny replica of a postage stamp stuck to the lid and varnished over; these stamp boxes date from the early 1840s. The views depicted on Mauchline ware cover the whole of the British Isles and they were a popular form of tourist souvenir in the nineteenth century.

Parallel with the transfer-printed wares were small boxes covered with paper in various clan tartans (sometimes with the name of the clan printed in gold lettering). Most of these tartan boxes were used as seal cases, needle cases, pill boxes, tiny pots for eye shadow or rouge and, most of all, stamp boxes, the latter being found with actual Penny Red stamps mounted on the lid or (more rarely) a portrait of the postal reformer, Sir Rowland Hill.

MAZERS

Shallow drinking vessels used in Europe in the period from the thirteenth to the late sixteenth centuries. They were generally made of wood, bird's-eye maple being particularly popular on account of the tiny knots which imparted a spotted appearance to the bowl. The name is thought to come from the German word *Masa*, a spot. The bowl was reinforced with a foot-rim and base, in pewter, silver or gold, and often elaborately chased or engraved. Coins, medallions or embossed roundels were often set in the bottom of the bowl, and the sides of the rim decorated with coats of arms and heraldic symbols. The earlier examples were quite flat, but from the fifteenth century the foot-rim was often raised on a short stem, and a few may be found with matching covers.

MEASURES

Attempts at the standardization of measures date from Roman times, when units for measuring grain were fixed at 24 barleycorns to the ounce. Variability in the size and weight of individual barleycorns, or strains of cereal crops, inevitably led to a wide divergence in the measures which were established in various parts of Europe by the Middle Ages. The situation became even more complex until metrication was gradually introduced in the early nineteenth century. Many of these archaic forms survive

Three wooden measures; English, early 19th century.

to this day (especially in Britain), but the substitution of the cubic centimetre and the litre for the old-style pints, gallons, bushels and pecks will render existing measures obsolete. In the nineteenth century there were numerous differences in the measure of a bushel, for example, depending on whether it measured coal, corn, beer or wine, and this gave rise to a multiplicity of containers for measuring wet or dry goods of different types. These containers, ranging from the diminutive quarter-gill to the bushel (which might hold from eight to twelve gallons), may be found in pewter, copper, brass or even silver. They often bore the royal monogram or civic coat of arms to denote the authority under which they were produced, the size of the measure, the date and the maker's name or mark. The smaller liquid measures were usually balustroid in shape, with or without handles and thumb-pieces and lids. Larger measures, especially those intended for dry goods, were often made of wooden staves bound with copper or brass bands and reinforced with metal lips and bases. Earthenware ale measures were used in England in the seventeenth century, often with faked markings, to cheat the patrons of inns and taverns. The names of these old measures, such as pottle, haystack, noggin, tappit hen, mutchkin and thirden-dale, were inscribed on the sides of the vessels and add considerably to their interest.

MEDALLIONS

Term often used loosely by collectors denote medals of a commemorative artistic nature, not intended to be worn, displayed in a case or cabinet. Very sn examples are often described as medalets. origin of medals can be traced back to 'large brass' of the Roman Empire whi though produced with a fixed monet value, was intended as a commemorat piece and not for general circulation. Ma of the larger medieval coins, such as the g augustale, were really medallions. C medals developed in Renaissance Italy, amc the earliest being the famous medal portr ing the Byzantine emperor John VII Pala logus. This was the work of Pisanello, w developed the portrait medal into an art fo rivalling the portrait miniature (q.v.). Mec lions of this type portrayed a person on obverse and featured his *impresa* (symbol his personal attributes) on the reverse. T were immensely popular in Italy from mid-fifteenth century, and spread to G many, France, Spain and the Low Count in the sixteenth century. Few British mec date from this period, the majority being by European medallists. Engraved d similar to those used for coins, were adap for striking medals in the seventeenth centu and improved techniques such as the scre press made the mass-production of medalli feasible.

wter medallion of
dolph of Burgundy,
Hans Schwarz, 1528.

American medals date from the late
Colonial period and satirized the political
problems leading up to the War of Independence. Numerous medals were produced in
the nineteenth century, the most highly
prized being those commemorating the
world's fairs of 1876 and 1892–93, and the
various presidential inaugurations. Lengthy
sets began with Moritz Fürst's series of 27
medals illustrating battles and personalities
of the War of 1812–14, struck at the Philadelphia Mint by special Act of Congress.

Many of the medals of the seventeenth and
eighteenth centuries were didactic or satirical,
propagating a political viewpoint. Medallions
of this type had a last brief flowering in World
War I, the Germans being particularly adept
at using this propaganda medium. The
majority of medallions dating from the late
eighteenth and nineteenth centuries, however, were purely commemorative, and
covered every aspect of social, political and
economic life in western Europe and North
America, at national, district and even
parochial level. The fact that most of them
were struck in base metals (brass, copper,
pewter, white metal and German silver being
the most popular) ensured their preservation.
Silver medals, often melted down after the
event or person commemorated ceased to be
topical, are therefore comparatively rare.
Sets of medallions illustrating lengthy

subjects such as the kings of England, Shakespearean or biblical characters, were fashionable from the late eighteenth century to the
mid-nineteenth century, and have recently
enjoyed something of a revival. Particularly
sought after are box medals (dating from the
early nineteenth century), whose two halves
unscrew to reveal a hollow interior containing thin discs engraved or even painted with
scenes and portraits connected with the
subject featured on the obverse and reverse
of the medal itself.

MEDICINE BOTTLES AND INSTRUMENTS

Medical and pharmaceutical antiques come
under two main headings – containers and
appliances. The oldest type of container is the
apothecary jar (q.v.), found in maiolica,
faience, delft and other tin-glazed earthenwares, often with elaborate decoration on the
side and including the Latin name of a
medicine. Glass medicine bottles came into
use in the seventeenth century but were not
widespread until the nineteenth. Various
phials and small bottles for tinctures, lotions

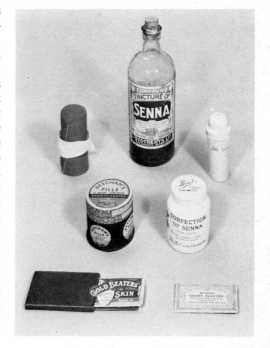

ft Bronze medal of
asmus by Quentin
tsys, 1519.

ght Medicine bottles,
l boxes and patent
edicine packs; English,
th century.

and cordials may be found with the name of the medicine impressed in the glass. Distinctive shapes, patterns and colours of glass were widely used to denote poisons, and numerous examples may be found from different countries. The second half of the nineteenth century was the heyday of the patent medicine, especially in America, where self-medication was often the only available remedy in areas which did not have permanent medical facilities. The labels on these boxes and bottles often bear extravagant claims for the contents and employed all the skills and artistry of contemporary graphics in promoting their virtues. The rise of the pharmaceutical industry and stricter government controls (through the pure food and drug laws and similar legislation) has led to the decline of the old-style patent medicines, though examples of these bottles may still be found. Bottles with glass stoppers of unusual shapes or those with patent droppers and pouring devices are worth looking for.

Early medical appliances also reflect the widespread practice of home medication. Instruments range from the fearsome syringes, with brass cylinders, polished wood handles and bone or ivory nozzles, which served a wide variety of uses (from drenching cattle to administering enemas), to the

elaborate cases in many households, contai ing sets of scalpels, lancets, needles, therm meters and douches. These cases, of polish hardwood with velvet lining, and oft containing the maker's instructions print on ivorine plaques, were fashionable fro about 1840 to 1910, especially in coun districts.

Other interesting medical items inclu invalid feeding bowls (with a spout throu which liquids and gruel could be sucke medicine spoons (sometimes with two si of bowl, one at either end of the stem, or w a hinged lid over the bowl), bleeding bov and cupping dishes, in pewter, silver, potte or porcelain.

MILITARIA

Term denoting any form of collectable ite pertaining to military, naval and air for and sometimes extended to include su uniformed organizations as fire services a police. In recent years the interests collectors have widened beyond the mo traditional forms such as firearms, edg weapons, armour, medals and decoratio and model soldiers. Each of these maj classifications can be sub-divided *ad infinit* depending on the degree of specializatio either by concentrating on one particu item, or material relating to one army branch of the services, or to a particu period or campaign. Thus uniforms ma up one of the largest categories of militar but within that broad field collectors mig concentrate on tunics, or epaulettes, shoul patches, bevo badges or belt buckles w various regimental insignia, German c titles or American collar badges.

As the demand for the more traditio forms of militaria has surpassed the supp collectors have turned to new fields. Th the dearth of daggers and dirks has led attention being focused on bayonets, fro ornamental head-gear to the steel helm and helmet liners of two world wars, fro sabretaches and decorative shoulder pouch to webbing equipment. Map-cases, co passes, binoculars, range-finders, field te

Patent food warmer, poison bottles, pestle and mortar, medicine spoon, and (front) eel-skin garters for alleviating rheumatism.

right Miniature portrait
of the Marquise de
Pompadour, after
Boucher; late 18th
century.

phones and combat radio equipment provide considerable scope for specialization. Offensive and defensive equipment associated with specific types of warfare form another very large category and include helmets, goggles, flying suits and aircraft parts connected with military aviation, gasmasks and protective clothing associated with chemical warfare (including civil defence), and equipment used by signallers, engineers and nursing services.

Two-dimensional material includes all kinds of ephemera from commissions and warrants to pay-books, leave passes and ration cards. Propaganda leaflets dropped on belligerents or neutral civilians are an important branch of militaria known as 'psywar' (psychological warfare). Invasion or occupation money, tokens, vouchers and military payment certificates, and obsidional currency, from the leather coins of the siege of Leyden (1572) to the Filipino guerrilla notes of World War II, are aspects of numismatics of special interest to collectors of militaria. Proclamations, posters, troop orders, training manuals and prints featuring historic uniforms, naval charts, military maps, ordnance inventories and forms designed for innumerable purposes are among the facets of military ephemera.

MINIATURE BOOKS, FURNITURE, GLASS, POTTERY AND PORCELAIN, SILVER
See *Books, Miniature* etc.

MINIATURES

The painting of portrait miniatures developed early in the sixteenth century. At a time when the printed book was replacing the illuminated manuscript, the limners previously engaged in this work turned to a new medium. At the same time the idea of portrait miniatures seems to have spread westward from Persia, where this art form had a long tradition. On the continent of Europe the small portrait, in the form of cast bronze medals, was already well established; out of these developed the Italian *rametti*, or portraits painted in oils on metal, which

became fashionable in the mid-sixteenth century. Miniature painting was introduced to England by the Flemish miniaturist, Gerard Horenbout, but it was Hans Holbein the Younger who established the art in Britain and encouraged indigenous artists to take it up. Between 1532 and his death in 1543 he produced a number of outstanding miniatures, the majority of which are now in museum collections.

Of his successors, Nicholas Hilliard, the Olivers (father and son), John Hoskins and Samuel Cooper produced the finest miniatures, which are now of the greatest rarity. The earliest miniatures were painted in body colours on fine vellum (usually the skin of domestic fowls) mounted on card. R. Carriera popularized the fashion for ivory as a base in the eighteenth century and the great majority of the miniatures produced subsequently used this substance. Miniatures painted in enamels on copper were also fashionable in the later period.

Seventeenth-century miniatures are scarce and correspondingly expensive and, surprisingly, good nineteenth-century pieces are not easily come by. The reason for the dearth of later miniatures is that many of the extant items are still treasured by the families of the original owners and, furthermore, the advent of photography sounded the death-knell of the portrait miniature after 1850. Consequently, the majority of miniatures on

Mrs Fitzherbert by
Richard Cosway
(1740–1821).

the market today date from the eighteenth
century.

Towards the end of the eighteenth century,
it was the custom for officers to have their
portrait painted before going off to the
wars against France. Most of the garrison
towns had at least one miniaturist who would
virtually mass-produce portraits for his
customers. This accounts for the high
incidence of miniatures of uniformed gentlemen. Miniatures in this category are still
relatively plentiful at a reasonable cost.
However, where the identity of either the
sitter or the miniaturist, or both, is established, the price can rise sharply. Acknowledged works by important miniaturists such
as Cosway, Crosse, George Engleheart,
Humphrey, Meyer and Smart in England,
Arlaud, Baudoin, Fragonard, Dumont,
Guerin and Isabey in France, and Füger,
Daffinger and Chodowiecki in Germany,
can fetch up to £1,000 ($2,500) each, and
offer the best investment for the collector who
can afford them. In recent years prices have

hardened considerably for miniatures [by]
lesser artists, such as the members of the Bo[ne]
family, W. Essex, Charles and Andre[w]
Robertson, John Barry and Samuel Shelle[y].
There are many other miniaturists who[se]
work commands little attention at t[he]
moment, but who may some day becom[e]
fashionable, and there are also examples [by]
unknown artists which are of superlati[ve]
draughtsmanship. Since the majority [of]
miniaturists did not sign or initial their wor[k]
identification can be a problem. A go[od]
knowledge of costume is a useful asset [in]
dating or identifying a portrait, while som[e]
acquaintance with the different techniqu[es]
employed in miniature painting at vario[us]
times is an advantage.

Miniature painting was practised [in]
America from the mid-eighteenth centu[ry]
until supplanted by the daguerreotype [a]
hundred years later. The outstanding arti[sts]
in this field were Copley, Inman, Jarv[is,]
Sully, Trumbull and the Peales, all bet[ter]
known for their large-scale portraits. Edwa[rd]
Malbone is regarded as the best Americ[an]
miniaturist, but on account of his short care[er]
(c. 1794 to 1807) his works are scarce.

MIRRORS

It is strange to think that it is only within the past three centuries that people have been able to see themselves as others see them. Prior to the 1670s mirrors were scarce and were comparatively inefficient. Looking-glasses originated in Venice in the mid-sixteenth century, but long before that polished metal discs (usually a copper alloy such as bronze or speculum) were used instead. Glass mirrors were imported from Venice into Germany, France, the Low Countries and England by the beginning of the seventeenth century, but they were extremely expensive and reserved only for the wealthiest classes.

In 1664 the Worshipful Company of Glass-sellers and Looking-glass Manufacturers was incorporated and, in the same year, George Villiers, second Duke of Buckingham, obtained a patent to make glass, gradually extending this to become a virtual monopoly. The duke established a glasshouse at Vauxhall the following year, and by the end of the seventeenth century the manufacture of looking-glasses had expanded enormously. Mirrors continued to be relatively expensive and it was not until the middle of the eighteenth century that they became at all plentiful. From about 1740 onwards mirrors of all shapes and sizes were produced in vast quantities to satisfy the universal demand for them and a large proportion of these eighteenth-century mirrors has survived to this day.

The most important factor in assessing the value of a mirror is the style and decoration of the frame. It is of little importance whether the glass is original or not, since the techniques involved in the manufacture of the glass and the methods of silvering changed very little from 1665 to 1840. The plain cushion style of frame, popular at the beginning of the eighteenth century, gave way to elaborate frames of carved wood and gesso (a substance not unlike plaster of Paris), which could be moulded or carved and lavishly decorated with gilt-work. Walnut frames, with a carved gilt strip between the frame and the glass, were also popular in the early years of the eighteenth century, extending into the 1730s. Mirrors of this period vary enormously in value, depending on the quality of the carving and the decoration of the frames. The earliest mirrors tended to have a rounded top whereas the mirrors from the later years of George I (1714–27) usually had straight tops with rounded corners.

The introduction of mahogany as a substitute for walnut in the frames of mirrors coincided, in the 1740s, with the growing influence of the rococo style of decoration. The ensuing thirty years witnessed a tremendous variety of mirrors. Among the more plentiful examples surviving from this period are small mirrors framed in veneered mahogany with a simple, fretted outline and a narrow gilt slip between the frame and the glass. Additional decoration, such as the inclusion of an eagle at the top (fashionable in the 1750s and particularly popular in Colonial America), or the presence of gilding in the frame, will increase the value considerably.

For their wealthier clients Chippendale, Lock, Copland and their imitators produced extravaganzas in gilt wood, combining the C- and S-scrolls of the rococo, with chinoiserie (q.v.) and Strawberry Hill gothick in great profusion. To the trailing foliage and rock-like incrustations of the rococo they would add eagles, phoenixes, Chinamen and pagodas, flowers and flames, often with more opulence than taste. Apart from the carving of the decoration, a great deal of attention was paid to the gilding, the highlights being burnished to contrast with the matt surface of the background. Where this gilt-work is in fine, original condition the value of these elaborate mirrors could be well in excess of £1,000 ($2,500).

During the last decades of the eighteenth century there was a revival in the so-called classical style, which found expression in mirrors with comparatively plain mounts, decorated with classical motifs – Grecian urns, acanthus leaves and Wedgwood reliefs. At the start of the nineteenth century (c. 1810), mirrors with oval rather than

left Young lady in white, *by* John Smart, 1792.

Art Nouveau silvered
metal mirror; German,
c. 1900.

iron foundries, who produced cast-iron
replicas. Those produced about the time of
the Civil War incorporated flags and trophies
of arms in their decoration.

MODEL SOLDIERS

There are three main categories of model
soldier in which a collector may specialize.
The first consists of models which are of
interest on account of their age or the various
techniques, no matter how crude, by which
they have been produced. The second
consists of predominantly modern pieces
which reproduce in minute and very accurate
detail the uniforms and equipment of
military forces from ancient Greek hoplite
down to Viet Cong guerrillas; their interest
and value lies in the wealth of detail and the
skill with which they have been modelled
and decorated. The third category consists of
models, usually on the small 'double-0'
(20 mm) gauge, used in war-gaming.

Model soldiers were manufactured in
southern Germany from the sixteenth century onwards and were comparatively large
in size, with hollow-cast horses and knights
cast in solid bronze, often gilded and
enamelled. In the seventeenth and eighteenth
centuries model soldiers were produced in
many parts of Europe, using a wide variety of
materials, including carved wood, earthenware, plaster, cardboard and sheet metal
die-stamped and cut out. Cast soldiers had a
two-dimensional appearance and were
known appropriately as 'flats'. They were
cast in moulds made of slate, the two halves
of the impression being carved intaglio on
of the adjoining pieces of slate. Tin, with a
very small amount of lead added to facilitate
casting, was used for the early German flats,
but by the beginning of the nineteenth
century the proportion of lead had been
steadily increased. Nevertheless these pieces
were known as *Zinnfiguren* (tin figures) and
this name is used to the present day. The first
three-dimensional pieces were produced in
France using the *rond bosse* technique of
casting. Nineteenth-century models, and
many produced subsequently, were on the

rectangular plates became increasingly popular, and this fashion was carried through the
Regency into the Victorian period.

A useful, though by no means infallible,
method of dating mirrors is the method of
silvering used. Prior to 1840 this consisted of
an amalgam of mercury and tin, imparting
a soft, dark lustrous appearance. As a result
of the process perfected by Liebig in 1835,
actual silver was used increasingly from then
onwards to give the hard, brilliant appearance
associated with modern mirrors. The latter
process is invariably finished with a protective coating of red lead or brown paint,
absent in pre-1840 mirrors.

American mirrors paralleled European
developments, with one interesting exception. The Gorham company pioneered
mirrors with elaborate silver-plated frames
about the middle of the nineteenth century
and the idea was subsequently taken up by

eld ambulance unit by
illiam Britain, 1906.

so-called Nuremberg scale (54 mm high), and cast in an alloy of antimony and lead. These large models were often cast in several pieces, secured with tiny pins or rivets, so that heads turned and arms and legs could be moved.

The English manufacturer William Britain revolutionized the model-soldier industry in 1893 by inventing a hollow-casting process which required a reduced amount of alloy. This permitted more life-like figures and enabled Britain to undercut his French and German competitors on the world market. At the turn of the century model soldiers with the manufacturer's name 'Britain' impressed on their base were cast in the uniforms of many different armies and exported all over the world. Lead was largely superseded by plastic substances in the soldiers made from 1950 onwards.

MONEY BOXES

Boxes for holding coins date back to Roman times, and many of the coin hoards excavated in the past century have been contained in earthenware crocks and jars fashioned for the purpose. In the Middle Ages elaborate wooden boxes bound in iron were used by merchants and traders for keeping their coins safe. Alms boxes, with a narrow slit in the lid, were kept in churches to collect money for the poor. From the fifteenth century, if not earlier, artisans and apprentices had small wooden money boxes with which they solicited money from their patrons on the day after Christmas – hence the name Boxing Day, which has survived to the present time.

Boxes designed to inculcate habits of thrift developed in the early nineteenth century. Because they were primarily aimed at children they were frequently constructed in a novelty form. The gaily printed earthen-ware pig is a familiar and universal form of money box, but other animals were utilized in this way – sheep, cattle, dogs, cats, fishes and horses – and modelled in earthenware, stoneware or even porcelain. A popular form of bank was shaped like a house, and was analogous to the cottage pastille burners (q.v.) produced by the same potteries. Most of the nineteenth-century money boxes were more decorative than secure, indicating that an attractive appearance was more important than preventing the youthful saver from being able to extract coins.

From the middle of the nineteenth century many banks produced small home-safes and decorative money boxes to encourage the savings habit, and examples with the names and emblems of these early banks are worth looking for. American mechanical banks were very popular in the late nineteenth century. The Sambo money box showed a negro whose eyes rolled when a coin dropped into his mouth, and this type was widely produced for many years. Another favourite, now highly prized by collectors, was the Tammany Bank, showing a prosperous-looking gentleman in an easy chair. This type was produced as a political joke about 1871, following the conviction of William Tweed, the Tammany Hall boss

who gained control of New York City the 1860s and embezzled millions of dolla before he was brought to justice. Many these American mechanical banks were pr duced by the Stevens toy company and included William Tell and his son, the dark and the donkey, the bucking bronco and other popular themes.

See colour plate page 178

MONTEITHS

Deep bowls of oval or circular form d tinguished by their elaborate scalloped rim which the stems and feet of wine glass could be secured while they were suspend in iced water to cool them. The Oxfo diarist Anthony à Wood recorded t introduction of this unusual vessel in 16 and even traced the name to an eccentr

'Uncle Sam' mechanical bank; American, late 19th century.

Scottish gentleman, named Monteith or Monteigh, who wore the hem of his coat looped in scalloped fashion. Monteiths were originally made of silver, silver-gilt or gold, but by the beginning of the eighteenth century they were also being produced in delftware and subsequently appeared in porcelain and glass. Examples in Sheffield plate date from the second half of the eighteenth century. From the early eighteenth century onwards examples were made with a detachable rim, so that they could be used as ordinary punch bowls instead of glass coolers. Monteiths were essentially English vessels, though examples from other parts of western Europe have been recorded.

MOULDS

Flat-surfaced objects with fancy designs or patterns cut intaglio have been used as moulds in the production of cakes and confectionery, and numerous examples of European origin may be found with motifs varying from district to district. The earliest examples were made of wood, but from the sixteenth century onwards stoneware and earthenware were used. Tin-lined brass or copper moulds were used in the making of puddings in Europe from the seventeenth century and the more intricate shapes are highly collectable and look very attractive when polished. Biscuit or cookie cutters were made of metal sheet in star, floral or animal forms for stamping out dough to the required shape. Novelty shapes as well as the standard crimps and cog-wheels were very popular in the nineteenth century. Butter moulds made of wood or pottery resemble pastry moulds but are generally smaller, with such motifs as flowers or a cow's head. Candle moulds resemble groups of small cylinders made of copper, brass, iron sheet or tinware, in clusters of six or a dozen, terminating in a rectangular, spread-collar foot matching a comparable lip at the top. They were commonly used in the seventeenth and eighteenth centuries before the manufacture of tallow candles was mechanized.

MOURNING ITEMS

A high mortality rate prior to the twentieth century meant that death was a more familiar occurrence and inevitably the subject caught the attention of artists and craftsmen in many of the applied arts. The codes of etiquette practised in various European countries dictated a period of formal mourning after the death of a near relative. This ritual manifested itself in particular in personal dress and adornment, and mourning jewelry became increasingly fashionable from the seventeenth to the nineteenth centuries. In England a widespread period of mourning occurred in the aftermath of the execution of King Charles I in 1649, when many Royalists and secret sympathizers wore rings and lockets (q.v.) containing miniature portraits of the dead king. But mourning jewelry reached its height of popularity following the death of Prince Albert, the Prince Consort, in 1861. Queen Victoria went into a prolonged period of deep mourning, which was emulated by her subjects to a lesser extent

when faced with their own bereavements.
Jet jewelry (q.v.) was especially popular at
this time in fashionable society, but at lower
levels in the social scale glass paste in opaque
white and black was very popular, sometimes set with a portrait of the dead, or
embellished with skulls, funerary urns and
other symbols of death.

The custom of mourning permeated
society as a whole in the second half of the
nineteenth century, regulating every detail
and texture of costume and the exact length
of time it was to be worn, dictating the style
of stationery (a black border of varying
width being used on notepaper and envelopes
at different stages in the mourning period),
and, according to the intensity of one's grief,
affecting the furnishings of one's home.
Patchwork-quilted cushion covers in black
and white, and even bedspreads in the same
material were fashionable. Black gloves,
studs and cuff-links, black crosses and even
watches in the form of a skull or *memento mori*
were fashionable. Special mourning cards
were produced in embossed or cut white
card mounted on a black base and were
widely popular in both Europe and the
United States.

MOUSTACHE CUPS

The wearing of moustaches became fashion
able in Europe in the 1850s during th
Crimean War and lasted until the end
World War I. This fashion had certain di
advantages, not the least being the proble
of drinking tea without wetting the whisker
The Staffordshire pottery of Harvey Adar
is credited with having found the solutic
to this problem. From about 1855 the
manufactured tea cups with a small ledg
near the rim on one side. The moustac
nestled on this ledge and remained dr
while the liquid flowed through an openin
between the ledge and the side of the cu
Moustache cups rapidly gained in populari
and remained in fashion until World War
Eventually they were produced by eve
pottery in Britain, and may be found
every ceramic material from coarse earthe
ware to egg-shell porcelain, with the sar
range of decorative treatment as will
found on other examples of late-Victori
ceramics. Judging from the inscriptio
found on them, many of these cups we
given by wives and daughters to paterfamili
as Christmas or birthday presents. They we

also produced in France and Germany, but were never so popular in these countries, and seem to have been destined mainly for export to Britain.

MUGS

Drinking vessels similar to the tankards in use from medieval times, but generally smaller and without any form of lid. Tankards generally had a slightly tapering body, whereas mugs from their inception were straight-sided. Baluster shapes became popular in the eighteenth century and barrel shapes date from the same period. The earliest mugs, from the mid-seventeenth century, were made of earthenware or silver and were relatively plain in form and decoration. More elaborate types, with ornamental designs on their sides and handles, came into fashion at the beginning of the eighteenth century. Pewter mugs came into use in taverns and ale-houses about 1720 and, like contemporary silver mugs, were plain, apart from simple bands of gadrooning and occasional inscriptions giving the name of the inn or innkeeper and the date. In the second half of the eighteenth century shapes became much more varied, the tulip, ribbed or faceted bowl being especially popular, with elaborate handles and in-curving bases set on

a high foot-rim. Pewter tankards with glass bases date from the late eighteenth century, while a rare variant of this had small lithophanes (q.v.) incorporated in the base. Mugs were widely used as a medium for commemorative wares (q.v.) from about 1760 onwards, and many examples may be found with inscriptions, dates and portraits celebrat-

ing coronations, political events, military victories. Christening mugs in silver were very popular in Britain and America from the seventeenth century, and in ensuing generations the idea was extended to other family events, such as coming-of-age, betrothal and marriage. Character mugs, whose bodies were modelled in the form of famous historical or biblical characters, were a late nineteenth-century extension of the Toby jug (q.v.) and have continued to be popular to the present day.

MUSIC COVERS

The application of lithography to the printing of sheet music at the beginning of the nineteenth century raised the music cover to the status of an art form. By 1820 lithography had virtually ousted the traditional and more costly copperplate engraved process. Not only was it possible to print the musical score in this way but greater flexibility enabled the publisher to embellish the cover with an attractive picture, which no doubt helped to sell the music.

It should not be inferred that sheet music was not illustrated before this period, for examples with woodcuts or copperplate engraved illustrations have been recorded from the beginning of the seventeenth century. But there is no doubt that lithography brought the illustration of sheet music within the reach of the cut-price printers and greatly popularized this medium.

The illustrations on early music covers normally occupied only a part of the cover, the opening bars or verses being printed in the lower half. The lettering of the title was usually kept clear of the illustration. It was not until the advent of chromolithography (printing with different coloured inks) about 1840 that the illustration came to assume prime importance. From then onwards the illustration gradually increased in size until it occupied the entire front cover, with the title, inscriptions and imprint (often in a wide variety of ornamental lettering) super-imposed.

It has been estimated that between 18 and 1900 over 100,000 different examples illustrated music covers were produced Britain alone. A comparable number w produced in the United States during t same period, and numerous examples we published all over Europe. The illustrat sheet music of Victorian times was t equivalent of today's pop record. In an before radio, television and motion pictur the music halls and vaudeville shows pr vided live entertainment, and in the hor the ability to sing, play a musical instrume and read music was an accepted soc accomplishment.

Thus songs and ballads were produced every conceivable occasion and in the da before the invention of the phonogra sheet music was the medium by whi popular music was disseminated. The avera piece of music was far from cheap – three four shillings was the usual price, equivale to at least £1 ($2.50) today – and yet t major publishers could produce editic running to 250,000 or more.

The illustrated music cover reached

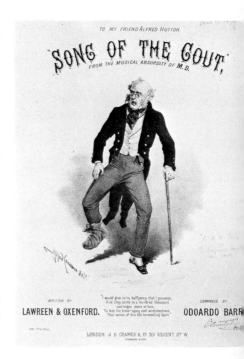

height in popularity in the mid-nineteenth century, between the introduction of colour and the adoption of improved techniques. After 1870, standards of production deteriorated, and from the end of the century until the outbreak of World War I the covers were poorly drawn and often garishly coloured with faulty registration. Gradually lithography was superseded by the use of letterpress and halftone photographic illustration, which unfortunately did little to revive the earlier standards.

With such an enormous range of material available it is possible to specialize in some aspect of music covers, usually according to the theme of the music. Marches, galops and military two-steps, often with a topical title alluding to a popular hero or current campaign, are of interest to collectors of militaria (q.v.) and often have attractive designs featuring the colourful uniforms of the period. Such titles as the *Timbre Poste Polka* and the *Stamp Galop* have long been of interest to philatelists. Patriotic songs, often connected with such conflicts as the Crimean War and the American Civil War, are immensely popular, as are those relating to royalty.

MUSICAL BOXES

Devices containing musical movements operated by clockwork. Musical boxes developed in the mid-eighteenth century as an adjunct of the clock-making industry in France and Switzerland and arose from the technique of incorporating chimes in clocks and watches. The mechanism consisted of tiny bells of various pitches, and hammers activated by a rotating drum. About 1825 the Swiss perfected a rotating brass drum with projecting pins which struck a tuned metal comb to produce a great variety of musical notes. The development of the pin-barrel mechanism led to the production of more compact forms of musical box and permitted greater scope for the manufacturers of automata (q.v.), who frequently incorporated a musical element in their

clockwork toys. At the same time, longer and more complex pieces of music could be reproduced in this manner. Eventually, by the 1860s, it was possible, by using several different pin barrels operating simultaneously, to reproduce the sounds of different musical instruments in an orchestra.

A great deal of attention and skill was lavished on the boxes in which these mechanisms were housed. The earlier cases were in relatively plain polished woods such as elm, cherry or rosewood; after 1830 marquetry (q.v.) was used increasingly. Pictorial panels were inset in lids and sides, the earlier subjects featuring mythological subjects, while landmarks and scenery became fashionable after 1850. Musical boxes with dancing dolls, marching soldiers, circus animals and orchestra groups became popular in the 1850s and reached their peak at the end of the century. Coin-operated musical boxes were usually much larger and offered a choice of tunes. These polyphons and nickelodeons date from the turn of the century and were the forerunners of the modern jukebox.

175

NAPKIN RINGS

Rings for holding table napkins or serviettes first appeared with the introduction of small items of table linen at the beginning of the eighteenth century. Since the custom of using table napkins was confined to the upper classes, the majority of early examples were produced in gold, silver-gilt or silver and these have remained the most popular metals ever since. Every silversmith has included them in his repertoire and they thus offer a relatively inexpensive way of acquiring examples of the work of the great names such as Paul Storr, Paul de Lamerie, Hester Bateman, Paul Revere and the Hennings. In their decoration they reflect the styles and fashions in silversmithing from Queen Anne to Art Deco.

NEFS

Table centrepieces modelled in the form of full-rigged sailing ships, produced in Europe from the thirteenth century onwards. Nefs seem to have been a development of the nautilus shell or beaker, worked in gold, silver and precious stones, and used to contain salt and spices. The famous Burghley Nef in the Victoria and Albert Museum, London, made by Pierre Flamand of Paris in 1482, has a nautilus shell hull with the superstructure of a fifteenth-century galleon and rests on a silver mermaid. The nautical connection continued to be the dominant feature of later nefs, though examples from the sixteenth and seventeenth centuries tended to be less ornamental in appearance, and sought to reproduce in accurate detail the rigging and construction of contemporary

ships, down to the crew members and t[he] cannon in the gun ports. Nefs went out [of] fashion in the seventeenth century, but we[re] re-introduced in the nineteenth century [as] part of the great Gothic Revival.

NEST EGGS

Containers for eggs originated by t[he] Staffordshire potters in the mid-nineteen[th] century. They were modelled in the form [of] nests or baskets surmounted by a hen whi[ch] served as a lid or cover. These objects appe[ar] to have served two distinct purposes, [to] store eggs in the pantry and to house e[gg] cups and spoons on the sideboard in t[he] dining room. The former type was modell[ed] in earthenware, decorated with crude b[ut] vigorous colours, while the latter and mo[re] elegant variety may be found in porcelain [or] electroplate with matching stand and detachable glass liner. Usually a hen w[as] depicted, but other birds, such as swa[ns,] geese or ducks, may occasionally be found[.]

Right Nest-egg tureen in moulded glass from Pittsburgh, Pennsylvania; late 19th century.

Opposite Group of Mary Gregory glass, including mugs, vases, a bowl and a decanter; American, *c.* 1880.

Left margin captions:

ght Bronze netsuke in
~~e~~ shape of a frog; 19th
~~c~~tury.

ove Ivory netsuke of
~~k~~orokoju; late 19th
~~c~~tury.

ht Ivory netsuke of
~~a~~nd Uba.

Mechanical banks and
~~m~~ey boxes; American,
~~h~~ and 20th centuries.

NETSUKE

Small ornaments used in Japan as toggles or dress-fasteners (pronounced 'netsky', and derived from the verb *tsuke* – to fasten). Netsuke probably existed as early as the fifteenth century, when small pieces of wood or tree roots were fashioned in a rudimentary form into toggles to secure a cord to the *obi* (girdle). A variety of objects was suspended from the *obi*, since pockets in the Occidental sense were not a feature of the kimonos worn by both sexes. By the sixteenth century these curious buttons were beginning to take on a more ornamental appearance, though examples which can definitely be attributed to this period are very scarce. The art of netsuke received great stimulus during the Shogunate. Hidetada, the second Tokugawa shogun, passed an edict in 1617 making the display of Buddhist images compulsory for every household and this, indirectly, gave tremendous impetus to the art of wood and ivory carving.

The growth in the popularity of netsuke with all classes of Japanese society encouraged the metal workers and wood carvers to devote their spare time to the production of these delightful toggles. Netsuke probably

reached its zenith during the Genroku Era (1688–1703), a period in Japanese history comparable in many respects to that in France fifty years later. It was characterized by the great luxury and extravagance of the Shogunate, and this was reflected in the arts generally and in netsuke in particular. The craftsmanship of this period was never surpassed, although the general standards in design and technique remained high.

There was a marked revival in the art of netsuke during the Bunsai period (1818–29) which continued until the Meiji Restoration of 1867–68. Prior to this date there had been a growing demand for ready-made netsuke, although the best quality pieces were those commissioned specially from the carvers. After 1868, however, the rapid opening-up of Japan to foreign commerce led to a debasement in artistic standards. The foreign trading companies established throughout the country did brisk business in netsuke. Hitherto the craftsmen who manufactured netsuke had done so merely as a sideline to their main business, but now many of them devoted themselves entirely to turning out more and more netsuke, primarily for export. The real need for netsuke correspondingly declined as the Japanese gradually adopted Western forms of dress. As a result, much of the netsuke manufactured from the late nineteenth century onwards can only be regarded as tourist souvenirs.

Netsuke took a great variety of forms, the commonest being *katabori* or human figures, *junishi*, the twelve signs of the Japanese zodiac, and masks derived from characters in the Noh drama. Animals, figures in mythology and Buddhist saints were other popular

subjects. Wood and ivory are the materials most frequently encountered, but stones such as coral, amber and jade were occasionally used. Of the woods employed, the best was undoubtedly Japanese cypress, prized for its fine texture and aroma. Cypress, unfortunately, does not stand up to a great deal of hard usage, and consequently fine examples of netsuke in this wood are extremely scarce. The most commonly used material, however, was boxwood, a hard, fine-grained timber which takes on a brilliant patina with age and is not so susceptible to wear and damage. Most wood netsuke were merely carved, but one occasionally finds specimens with inlays of ivory or mother-of-pearl, while painted or lacquered netsuke are by no means uncommon.

NIELLO

Italian word meaning 'tiny black' and used to describe a form of inlaid decoration on silver. The surface of the object was first incised with fine lines, a thin coating of borax was applied to the surface and then an amalgam of sulphur, lead, silver, copper and borax, was dusted over in powdered form. The surface was then polished, leaving the amalgam in the grooves and recesses, and

with the application of heat the alloy mel and fused to the incised portions. When silver had cooled, the article was hig polished to provide a sharp contrast to black inlay. The art of inlaying in t manner was practised in Roman Impe times and a few examples dating from first century AD have been preserved. It d out in western Europe during the Dark A but survived in the Byzantine Emp whence it was re-introduced to the West, Venice, in the thirteenth century. There several isolated instances of niello-work having been practised in France and Germa in the tenth and eleventh centuries, but t do not amount to any large-scale indust In its modern form niello was widespread southern Russia from the fifteenth cent if not earlier, and is sometimes known Tula ware, from the name of the dist where it was used extensively. Niello ne gained wide acceptance in the West and usually associated with Russian objects vertu, from snuff boxes to cigarette c manufactured up to the time of the Revo tion. Although mostly associated with sil niello may occasionally be found inlaid gold or bronze objects.

NOTECASES. See *Diaries and Notecases*

Right Ivory okimono
showing five *samurai* in
full armour.

OKIMONO

Japanese word meaning 'place things',
denoting ornaments intended for the alcoves
in houses. Although primarily produced as
religious figures they gradually developed a
secular character. Like netsuke (q.v.) they
mirrored every aspect of Japanese life and
culture, as well as illustrating aspects of
Buddhism and Shinto and alluding to characters and events in folklore. The great majority
of okimono were carved in wood or
fashioned in pottery. Ivory, with which the
finest examples of okimono are associated,
was generally too expensive under the
Shogunate, and it was not until after the
Meiji Restoration in 1867–68 that this
material was used to any great extent. The
decline in netsuke in the latter part of the
nineteenth century prompted the wood and
ivory carvers to turn their attention increasingly to figurines, often no more than an
inch or two in height.

Okimono are often confused with netsuke.
Okimono were never meant to be worn, but
some netsuke were apparently produced
with a dual purpose, either as toggles or as
ornaments. Figures mounted on a flat base
are obviously okimono, but pieces carved
in such a way that they balance on a small
base may well be netsuke which could also be
used as okimono. The presence of the hole to
take the cord which secured the toggle to the
girdle is characteristic of netsuke. Okimono
also frequently exhibit characteristics which
would have been impractical in netsuke –
sharp projections and intricate carving which
would not have withstood the rough usage
to which netsuke were subjected.

In general the subjects found in netsuke

were also interpreted as okimono, animals,
humans and mythological creatures
predominating. Figure groups are not uncommon. The okimono of the late nineteenth
century tended towards excessive intricacy
and detail, demonstrating the skills of the
carvers, and, at the same time, the figures
were imbued with a sense of realism which
often bordered on the macabre or ridiculous.

A vast quantity of ivory okimono was
produced in the last decades of the nineteenth
century, but the quality inevitably suffered.
Much of this material was destined for
export to the United States and Europe. A
revival in the art of ivory and wood carving
began in the 1890s, through the Tokyo Fine
Art School at Ueno, and this led to an
improvement in quality especially since 1920.
Okimono are usually signed by the carvers,
and the works of outstanding artists, such as

181

Ivory okimono of rats, the eyes inlaid with amber; late 19th century.

Ishikawa Mitsuaki, Asahi Meido and Ono Hofu, are now very expensive. Works by lesser artists, however, are often well within the price range of most collectors of average means.

OLLIO POTS

Covered porcelain bowls, also known by the German and French names *Ollientopf* and *pot-à-oille* respectively. Ollio pots were derived from a type of Chinese ritual vessel originally made of bronze. They consisted of deep bowls on high foot-rims, usually with three feet and a matching stand. Twin handles were fitted in the manner of loving cups (q.v.) and a domed and knopped lid fitted into the recessed lip. Ollio pots were used for broth and meat stews and were popular in Europe in the eighteenth and early nineteenth centuries. The idea is thought to have originated with the Viennese porcelain factory under the direction of C.I. du Paquier (1719–44), though his Dutch origin, coupled with the fact that similar pots may be found

in delftware, may point to the Netherland as the birthplace of ollio pots. They wer also made at Meissen and were decorate with the leaf and strapwork motifs chara teristic of late German baroque, often as border to rectangular or oval vignett depicting scenery, chinoiserie or mytho logical groups.

OPTICAL INSTRUMENTS

The invention of the telescope c. 1609 led the development of a vast range of optic instruments connected with surveying, nav gation and astronomy, while the invention the microscope has produced numero variations whose collectability depen largely on their technical features. The mo decorative form of optical instrument w the opera glass, developed in the mi eighteenth century. The earliest exampl took the form of a monocular telescope a were frequently decorated with lacque gilding, inlaid ivory, porcelain or blue a white jasperware. Later examples were bin cular, with a long handle fitted to one si so that they could be raised languidly to t eyes with one hand. Simpler version resembling spectacles with a handle, we known as quizzing glasses, prospect glass or lorgnettes. The handles were made ivory, tortoiseshell or wood, frequent covered with marquetry or boulle (qq.v and often concealing a fan. The twin-le opera glass in its present form originated Paris in 1823, with the rise in popularity the opera and other theatrical entertainmen Numerous examples may be found wi silver, gilt or gold fittings, mother-of-pe or ivory eyepieces, enamelled or inlaid sid and handsome leather cases. They reach the acme of opulence at the end of the nin teenth century, but have since been supe seded by simpler and more functional desig

OPTICAL TOYS

The principle of the persistence of visio known to the ancient Greeks though n scientically proved until 1824, led to t

182

Folding pocket spy-glass; English, late 18th century.

development of a number of toys which created the effect of moving pictures. The same principle, in a highly sophisticated form, underlies the systems employed in motion pictures and television. The idea of moving or rotating a sequence of pictures which varied slightly, in order to convey an impression of movement in the object portrayed, led to the invention of the Thaumatrope in the 1820s. This consisted of a box or drum containing paper discs on which pictures were drawn. Thin cords attached to the discs were wound up, and as they unwound the discs rotated, creating an effect of movement, when viewed through an aperture. An improved form of this peepshow was the Phenakistiscope, patented in 1832. In this, a series of pictures of an object in different stages of a movement was drawn

Zoetrope by Milton Bradley of Springfield, Mass., 1868.

on to a disc. The disc was then rotated swiftly to create a moving effect, and the image was reflected from a mirror to the slit through which the viewer looked. The earliest 'mass-viewing' device was the Zoetrope, a drum with slits on all sides so that several children could peep through simultaneously. In this gadget the pictures were arranged on strips of paper affixed to the inside of the drum, which was rotated rapidly. The Praxinoscope was developed in France in the 1870s, as an improved version of the Zoetrope. In this, a drum containing slides of objects was rotated against a stationary background, the images of both being reflected in a mirror. The Tachyscope was a similar device using real photos instead of hand-drawn pictures.

Various other devices were developed in the late nineteenth century, the most popular being a book of pictures varying slightly from one to the next, so that when the pages were flicked hurriedly the impression of movement was conveyed. This principle was adapted for various mechanical peepshows in which the pictures could be rotated quickly by cranking a handle. Hand versions of this have been manufactured in Europe and America from the early 1900s to the present day.

The stereoscope, based on the principle of overlapping images to create a three-dimensional effect, was developed in the late nineteenth century with the growth of photography (q.v.). The photographs were mounted in almost identical pairs on thin boards and were often sold in sets as tourist souvenirs. A hand-held wooden frame, with a viewing aperture at one end and a slot for the photographs at the other, was used in connection with these stereoscopic pictures.

The principle of the magic lantern, projecting a transparent image on to a screen was known from the sixteenth century, but was not widely exploited till the middle of the nineteenth, when lanterns were produced commercially for home entertainment. Both the lanterns themselves and the massive glass slides are collectable. The latter may be found with verses of songs and nursery rhymes (for community singing), moral

gilding bronze with an amalgam of mercur and gold. The technique known as *dorun d'or moulu* was widely practised in Franc from the sixteenth century, to the grea hazard of the workmen, who suffered mei cury poisoning as a result. It was never use elsewhere to any great extent, althoug various substitutes are often erroneousl referred to as ormolu. Various alloys o copper and zinc, notably that devised b Christopher Pinchbeck, were used i powdered form to simulate gilding an were applied not only to bronze and othe metals but also to plasterwork, pottery an porcelain. Strictly speaking ormolu signifie bronze objects gilded or coated with gol coloured lacquer, mainly of French origi where the technique was fashionable in th eighteenth and early nineteenth centuries.

Above Praxinoscope theatre; French, *c.* 1884.

Right Ormolu jewel casket with Napoleonic motif; French, early 19th century.

tales and precepts, line drawings or photographs of distant lands – illustrating the didactic element in late-Victorian home entertainment.

ORMOLU

Term derived from French *or moulu* (ground gold) and apparently first used by Josiah Wedgwood in 1770 to describe a form of

PAPER KNIVES

Knives specially designed for opening letters were developed in the seventeenth century after daggers (q.v.) had largely gone out of use and the spread of literacy was accompanied by an increase in the volume of mail transmitted in European countries. Prior to the invention of the envelope in the nineteenth century, letters consisted of folded sheets of paper secured with a wax seal or wafer. Considerable skill was required to cut around the seal and slit open the outer wrapping without damaging the letter itself. This required special knives with a long slender blade, a sharp point and an edge which would slit but not cut paper. The earliest paper knives were manufactured in Solingen in Germany and resembled miniature swords, complete with pommels, bowlguards and even scabbards, intricately decorated. Later examples became more purely decorative, with elaborately cast silver or gold handles and blades of horn, wood, ivory or other non-metallic substances. The French and British manufacturers concentrated on these styles, whereas the German and Italian makers clung to traditional forms based on swords and daggers. By the early nineteenth century the design and decoration of paper knives had broadened to include Oriental motifs, novelty shapes and a wide range of ornament from richly enamelled handles to mother-of-pearl and ivory carving. Jet (q.v.), glass, pottery and porcelain handles may be found on mid-Victorian paper knives. There was a revival of pseudo-medieval forms towards the end of the century – all-metal knives with broad blades, in bronze, silver, silver-gilt and electroplate.

Above Silver paper knife designed by Prince Bojidan Karageorgevich; French, *c.* 1900.

Right Baccarat faceted portrait paperweight; mid-19th century.

PAPERWEIGHTS

The manufacture of glass paperweights in the mid-nineteenth century remains one of the greatest technical curiosities of all time. These attractive glass baubles, encapsulating the tiny coloured canes known by the Italian name of *millefiori* (a thousand flowers), were first produced in Venice in or about 1842 and spread to Bohemia and Silesia (at that time, like Venice, parts of the Habsburg Empire). The technique then mysteriously spread to France, where it was perfected by three glass factories in particular, and paperweights were perhaps produced by a handful of other glasshouses. These intricate bibelots, which demanded a very high standard of technical skill, were produced as a sideline to normal output. Production was confined to a few short years. Baccarat is known to have manufactured weights between 1846 and 1849, St Louis from 1845 to 1848 and Clichy during 1849 and 1850.

Considering that the overall period of production was only about five years, the range and versatility of these French paperweights is astonishing. There was no deep-seated tradition of *millefiori* glassmaking in France and yet the quality of workmanship has never been surpassed. Although this distinctive candy-cane style of decoration is the most common, it was by no means the only one and, in general, it is the paperweight decorated in other patterns and techniques which commands higher prices. Among the more popular forms of paperweight is that which incorporates a bouquet or posy of flowers either on a plain opaque or coloured ground, or set on an attractive latticed base. Each of the three main French factories had its own speciality in this field. Bouquet paperweights from Clichy, for example, invariably have a pink or blue ribbon tying the stalks. Both Baccarat and St Louis produced bouquets consisting of upstanding flowers. St Louis also produced a very rare weight showing a bouquet of flowers set in a white spiral basket.

Among the more highly prized types of French weight are those which feature individual flowers, such as bell-flowers, clematis, crocuses, dahlias, pansies, roses, fuchsias and geraniums. Flower weights which also incorporate a bird or an insect are very rare, though the most expensive weights are the great salamander weights, of which no more than a handful are known to exist.

A very small number of the French antique weights were identified by the inclusion of a cane bearing the initial of the factory. Weights which also contained a dated cane are extremely scarce, and the mere presence of either of these features enhances the value considerably. The correct identification of French weights is a complicated matter requiring a great deal of experience and expertise. Moreover, chipped weights have been reground and polished, and star-cut or strawberry-cut decoration added to weights with plain bases. These embellishments, when genuine, are rare and command high premiums. There was a lucrative industry before World War II in fake French weights

manufactured in China, and these might deceive the unwary beginner.

There is a certain snob appeal about the antique French weights, for excellent paperweights were also produced in Belgium, England and the United States at a rather later date. Good *millefiori* weights, and associated items such as door knobs, decanters and inkwells, were produced by the Whitefriars company in London and by Bacchus of Birmingham. Although it is now thought unlikely that English weights were made in Stourbridge, as was formerly believed, the best English weights were comparable to the French, and in recent years their value has been re-assessed.

American paperweight production began much later than in France and has continued more or less without a break up to the present day. Paperweight collectors at one time virtually ignored the home product to concentrate on the French imports. Yet some of the finest weights ever produced were made by the New England Glass Company of Cambridge, Mass. in the late 1850s and 1860s. Both the NEGC and the rival Sandwich Glass Company probably imported many of their *millefiori* canes from France; several of their more prominent employees were European immigrants, who brought their special skills to America. However, it was when the American glasshouses began producing their own designs that they truly excelled. The NEGC produced some competent flower motifs on a lattice ground, and their attractive carpet-ground weights compare favourably with the French, but the company is best remembered for its blown fruit weights. The majority of them consisted of apples or pears, either free standing or mounted on a clear 'cookie' base. Sandwich was renowned for its beautiful flower weights, the speciality of Nicholas Lutz, who also produced some beautiful upright floral bouquet weights.

Gillinder and Sons manufactured their own *millefiori* canes, and the very distinctive types of crimped canes, cogs and ruffle make their weights easy to identify. The later Gillinder weights, popular about the time of the Centennial Exposition (1876)

consisted of clear glass weights containing profiles of Washington, Franklin and Lincoln. The most highly prized examples are those which bear the name of the company and a reference to the Centennial Exposition. Gillinder also produced moulded glass weights in the form of animals, birds and flowers in clear glass or in opaque black or white glass. The Mount Washington Glass Works produced relatively few paperweights, but these are now among the most highly prized. There are two main types for which this company was famous. Flat, rectangular weights incorporating a bouquet or floral arrangement, have chamfered edges and occasionally faceting across the top. The best-known weights are the celebrated Mount Washington Roses, produced mainly between 1869 and 1876.

One of the most widely known names in American paperweights is Millville. A glass-works existed in this New Jersey town since the early nineteenth century, undergoing various changes of name and ownership. Whitall Tatum and Company were prominent in the latter half of the century producing industrial glass, but maintaining a side-line output in paperweights. Traditional style *millefiori* weights were part of the stock in trade of the Dorflinger Glass Works which functioned at White Mills, Pa., from 1865 to 1921. Butterfly, fruit and flower weights

were made by the Union Glass Company of Somerville, Mass., at the turn of the century. Some of the most expensive paperweights are those made by Louis C. Tiffany in his favrile glass in the 1890s. Though paperweights are still produced in the United States today, the best of these are the work of individual craftsmen-artists.

Sulphide paperweights, otherwise known as incrustations, date from the 1820s and were produced in Bohemia, France, Belgium, England and Scotland as well as the United States. Although they declined in the mid-nineteenth century there has been a revival of interest in recent years and several factories, notably Baccarat, are currently producing them. These weights have the same globular or faceted form as *millefiori* weights, but contain a glass-paste cameo (q.v.), usually the profile of some famous person.
See colour plate page 196

PAPIER MÂCHÉ

Term applied loosely to any form of moulded ware, but strictly denoting a near Eastern technique introduced to France in the mid-seventeenth century and subsequently used there in the manufacture of small articles of furniture and objects of vertu. Originally papier mâché was composed of paper pulp stiffened with glue, chalk, plaster, sand, sizing and gum mastic, set hard and varnished over when dry. A subsequent development, pioneered by Henry Clay of Birmingham in 1772, involved sheets of paper glued together, pressed and moulded to shape, then coated with lacquer. Papier mâché was originally used for interior decoration, being cheaper than plaster of Paris and stucco used in ceiling and wall ornament. Subsequently it was applied to picture frames and small ornamental mouldings, usually covered with gilding. Henry Clay gave papier mâché an entirely new application; his process of moulding sheets of paper under great pressure and then lacquering them to a hard glossy finish was widely used in the late eighteenth and early nineteenth century in the production of

Papier mâché paper rack, snuff boxes and work box; English, early 19th century.

japanned furniture. Clay ware, as it was then known, was produced in black, deep green or red lacquered panels, sometimes inlaid with ivory or mother-of-pearl in chinoiserie patterns. Papier mâché was used for screens, trays, panelling and even small tables. Numerous boxes, from trinket and snuff boxes to large writing cases and work boxes, were manufactured in papier mâché. Bronze powders to simulate gilding were applied to black lacquered papier mâché from about 1802 onwards.

Clay's techniques were adopted and greatly expanded by the Birmingham company of Jennens and Betteridge, whose japanned papier mâché ware dominated the world market in this medium during the first half of the nineteenth century. Contemporary artists were commissioned to paint the more elaborate articles with floral and fern motifs, chinoiseries and classical compositions. A great deal of Jennens and Betteridge products were exported to the United States where papier mâché became very popular. In 1850 the Litchfield Manufacturing Company of New York began producing indigenous papier mâché and this continued to be popular until the end of the century. As well as small articles of all kinds, quite large pieces of furniture, including tables, chairs and even bed-heads, were produced.
See colour plate page 195

PARASOLS AND UMBRELLAS

Portable, folding devices for protecti against sun or rain are of great antiquity ar because of their protection against the e ments, were often invested with mysti or ritual importance. Thus umbrellas w symbols of princely or magisterial power ancient Egypt and still perform this functi today in India, Thailand and Malaysia. F this reason many Oriental umbrellas exhi all the skills of craftsmanship and artistry their construction and decoration, especia on the shafts and handles. In Europe u brellas were invested with symbolic i portance in the Byzantine Empire, and t

right Parian ware vase by
Bennington Pottery;
American, mid-19th
century.

later manifested itself in the *baldacchino* or portable canopy used by princes and popes in Renaissance Italy.

The umbrella in its modern form, as a protection against the weather, came into use in the late eighteenth century. The hemispherical silk covering was sewn together in eight to sixteen wedge-shaped sections, often in contrasting colours, and was fitted over collapsible steel ribs. Lighter and more decorative forms were intended for protection against the sun and were of French origin. They gradually replaced the cane or walking-stick used by ladies, and by the mid-nineteenth century the decoration of the handles had become very extravagant. The handles on both ladies' and gentlemen's umbrellas parallel the styles found in cane-handles (q.v.) of the same period.

The umbrella stand was developed in the early nineteenth century. They range in size from ornate standing frames of wood and wrought iron, to the more convenient cylindrical pottery type, often decorated in Chinese blue and white. Other common types include those in bronze or brass sheet with pierced decoration, and the style so redolent of the British Raj, an elephant's foot with a hollow centre.

PARIAN WARE

Objects such as small figures and tableware, manufactured in a fine-grained, hard-paste porcelain, usually unglazed and resembling marble in texture and appearance. The name is derived from the Parian marble widely used in the eighteenth and nineteenth centuries for small sculptures. The process of firing hard-paste porcelain of this type at a lower temperature made it particularly suitable for casting small figures. It was adopted about 1844 by the Stoke-on-Trent pottery of Copeland and Garrett and received great impetus from the decision of the Art Union of London to commission reductions of statuary. Copeland and Garrett were soon followed by Minton, and by the early 1850s parian ware was widely manufactured all over England. Much of it was exported to

America, but in 1852 the United States Pottery Company at Bennington, Vermont, began producing parian ware figures. These items, bearing the name of the pottery in a ribbon, are relatively scarce since the company had gone out of business by 1858. American parian was noted for its beautifully modelled flowers and foliage, intricately modelled grapes and vine leaves being a characteristic feature. Unfortunately for the Bennington pottery, both retailers and their customers continued to prefer English parian; by 1855 one American importer was listing over 400 varieties in his advertisement. Allegorical compositions, mythological groups, biblical figures and quasi-symbolic 'conversation pieces' were the principal favourites. Nevertheless, American parian was subsequently made in many other potteries, from Carolina to Ohio.

Numerous English firms made parian ware

left Black lace and chiffon
parasol, *c.* 1885.

189

in the latter half of the nineteenth century as a sideline to their other products, but Robinson and Leadbetter specialized in this ware alone. It was also widely produced in Europe, mainly in the German potteries of Saxony and Thuringia, which undercut the prices for the British wares and gradually forced the traditional manufacturers to turn to more profitable lines. Tinted or coloured parian was popular from about 1870, and gilding was also applied, mainly to small portrait busts.

PASTILLE BURNERS

Small containers made of pottery, porcelain or silver were used from the sixteenth century onwards to sweeten the atmosphere. They derive their name from the small pastilles of aromatic substances which gave off a pleasant scent when burned. The earliest form was a simple lidded bowl, with two handles like a porringer, a high foot-rim or feet. More elaborate examples came into use at the end of the seventeenth century,

Mennecy-Villeroy pastille burner; French, first half of 18th century.

with elaborate perforated lids and side[s]. Thomas Whieldon is thought to have be[en] the first English potter to manufactu[re] pastille burners in the form of Tudor cottag[es] or medieval castles. He modelled them [in] slipware from about 1755 onwards, a[nd] subsequently cottage pastille burners b[e]came immensely popular until the mi[d] nineteenth century, when the need for the[m] gradually died out. Later examples we[re] modelled in porcelain by Coalport, Minto[n] Rockingham and Spode, but to the end th[ey] continued to be widely produced in Staffor[d] shire pottery as cottage ornaments.

Pastille burners in vase shapes were know[n] as cassolettes (q.v.) and were usually pr[o] duced as matched pairs for the mantelpiec[e.] Vase-shaped pastille or perfume burne[rs] were a speciality of the Derby porcela[in] works in the mid-eighteenth century. Eur[o] pean pastille burners may be found in ma[ny] different forms. The German style, emanati[ng] mostly from Meissen and Ludwigsbur[g] favoured cherubs and rococo floral orn[a] ment, while the Italian factory of Le No[ve] produced cylindrical burners with coni[cal] lids and detachable bases.
See also *Cassolettes*

PATCH BOXES

The prevalence of smallpox in Euro[pe] resulted in a curious form of cosmetic; ti[ny] silk or taffeta patches were applied to the fa[ce] to cover unsightly pock-marks. Special box[es] to contain the patches were produced [in] circular, oval or oblong shapes, simi[lar] to snuff boxes (q.v.) but generally shallow[er.] They were elaborately decorated in t[he] prevailing styles of objects of vertu. Silv[er] and gold boxes encrusted with preci[ous] stones are not unknown, but the majori[ty] were produced in enamels, ivory, pap[ier] mâché (qq.v.), hardwood with marquet[ry] or boulle (qq.v.) decoration, leather a[nd] even porcelain. Late eighteenth-centu[ry] examples were intricately fitted with ti[ny] compartments for different types of pat[ch,] a small pot of gum and the special bru[sh] with which to apply the patch, and so[me]

examples may be found with a mirror set into the lid. The advent of vaccination caused a marked decline in the disease, and the wearing of patches and 'beauty-spots' by both sexes went out of fashion by the beginning of the nineteenth century.

PEWTER

Alloy of tin with lead or copper, often with small amounts of antimony, bismuth, silver or zinc to improve its appearance and durability. Thus an alloy of tin with 25 per cent lead was used for hollow-ware, while a similar proportion of copper was substituted for lead in dishes and platters. From the seventeenth century onwards, however, the composition of pewter alloys varied con-

siderably. Britannia metal, containing copper and antimony, was used in the nineteenth century to produce a harder and more silvery appearance. Cock metal, an alloy of copper and lead, resembles pewter but is much softer and lacks the attractive patination of pewter.

Pewter was used extensively in metalwork from Roman times, but was largely confined to useful wares and domestic plumbing. In the Middle Ages it became more and more acceptable as a substitute for silver in tableware, and the emergence of pewterers' guilds in many European countries testifies to its growing importance. A Pewterers' Company was established in London in 1348 and rigidly controlled the manufacture and composition of pewter from then on. The introduction of compulsory touchmarks in 1503 means that pewter articles after that date can be identified and dated reasonably accurately. Pewter was widely used in domestic and ecclesiastical wares and may be found in a wide range of articles, such as candlesticks, bowls, porringers, tankards, plates and serving dishes, boxes and canisters, inkpots and flasks. Objects such as dishes and flatware (forks and spoons) were often fashioned out of pewter sheet. Hollow-ware (mainly tankards, mugs and bowls) was usually cast in moulds. Decoration on pewter was either cast or embossed, but engraving and cutting were also practised, mainly on the European continent. Pewter was occasionally used in the casting of small figures, pipe stoppers (q.v.) and the panels of small boxes. It was

also used for die-struck medallions (q.v.), especially in the nineteenth century, as a substitute for silver.

In Colonial America pewter was used extensively for domestic purposes from the mid-seventeenth century onwards, reaching the peak of production in the period from 1750 to 1850. Although pewter was widely manufactured throughout the country the centre of the industry was Boston, which produced some of the finest examples of domestic wares and ecclesiastical plate. The appearance of pewter in America at a time when it was waning in Europe, and its continuing popularity long after other materials were readily available, indicate the enormous influence of pewter on American taste. This alloy may be found in every kind of domestic utensil as well as candlesticks, trinket boxes and ornaments.

PHOTOGRAPHY

The development of photography took place over a period of centuries, following the observations of scientists who noted the change in the appearance of certain chemicals by the action of light. Experiments by J.H. Schulze (1727), W. Lewis (1763), K.W. Scheele (1777) and T. Wedgwood (1802) with compounds such as silver nitrate or silver chloride on paper and leather established the principles of photography long before they could be given any practical application. Parallel with these experiments were developments in the camera, the principles of which were known to Arab scientists in the twelfth century. The camera obscura was described by Leonardo da Vinci, though it was Giovanni della Porta who produced the first practical example in 1523. Developments in the science of optics led to smaller and improved versions of the camera obscura, and by the eighteenth century small boxes of this type were widely used by artists to obtain an accurate image of landmarks and scenery. The invention of lithography in 1795, later to revolutionize prints, posters and book illustration, led the Frenchman Nicéphore Niepce to experiment

with light-sensitive compounds on sto[ne] metal and glass plates. In 1816 he produc[ed] a positive image on paper using silv[er] chloride, and six years later developed t[he] first fixing agent to produce a permane[nt] photograph. Etched metal plates using [a] process known as heliography were in use [by] 1826, and shortly afterwards Niepce form[ed] a partnership with the painter L.J.[M.] Daguerre, who had previously experiment[ed] with silver salts. They spent ten years perfe[ct]ing their process using iodized silver pla[tes] and fulminate of mercury, and by 1839 t[he] daguerreotype process was fully developed [on] a commercial basis. In England the astr[o]nomer, Sir John Herschel, experimented w[ith] photography in 1819 and subsequently F[ox] Talbot and the Rev. J.B. Reade experiment[ed] independently with the process which su[b]sequently became known as calotype, usi[ng] specially prepared paper to obtain a phot[o]graphic negative. Fox Talbot's experimen[ts] were completed in 1841. Other early pr[o]cesses which were widely employed in t[he] mid-nineteenth century included the niepce[o]type (using silver chloride on glass plat[es]) and the wet collodion process developed [by] the architect Scott Archer in 1851. T[he] collodion process superseded both caloty[pe] and daguerreotype by 1860, and was its[elf] displaced by the gelatine-emulsion proc[ess] patented in 1871. Dry-plate photograp[hy] was developed by 1877; George Eastman pioneered roll film in 1884 and marketed his first Kodak camera in 1888. Since then the principles of photography have not altered much, though there have been numerous technical improvements both in the films and plates used and in the mechanism of cameras.

Early photographs have become eminently collectable in recent years, to the point that virtually any nineteenth-century photograph, irrespective of subject, now has a market value. Later photographs depend to a large extent on the interest of the subject. Photographs dating before 1851 are regarded as the *incunabula* of photography, and prized accordingly, but examples from the second half of the century, especially portraits and groups, are worth looking for.

Photographic equipment is a wide field in itself, from the very large and cumbersome cameras of the 1840s, with ornate, polished wooden cases and brass mountings, to the early bellows cameras of the 1890s. Later cameras have little antiquarian interest at present, though examples with unusual technical features command a fair premium.

As photography ousted the portrait miniature (q.v.) the demand arose for small picture frames with decoration in keeping with the sentimental nature of family photographs. Ornamental frames, with a small back-rest or stand, became very popular in the late nineteenth century and early 1900s. All kinds of materials were used in their production, from gilt plaster to plush and velvet. Hardwood frames were the most common in the 1870s and 1880s, either polished plain, or carved and veneered with marquetry motifs. By 1890, however, the vogue for metal frames was well established and an enormous range of silver, pewter, electroplate, copper and brass frames was available, with cast or die-struck decoration, engraving, *martelé* or repoussé work. Ornament ranged from the extravagant encrustations of the neo-baroque to the flowing lines of Art Nouveau and the more geometric forms favoured by central European designers from 1910 onwards. Photo frames were sometimes inlaid with semi-precious stones and pearls, but were more frequently decorated with enamelling. In the Edwardian period there was a return to cloth-covered or leather frames, ornamented with gilt foliage. Ivory and glass mosiac frames were also fashionable in the period before World War I.

PICTURE POSTCARDS

Postcards, transmitted through the post at a lower rate than letters, had their origins in Austria in 1869 and spread to many other countries in the ensuing decade. At first only

*Stereoscopic
daguerreotype of a street
scene in Paddington,
London, 1852.*

Opposite Papier mâché
sewing cabinet, painted
and inlaid with
mother-of-pearl floral
bouquets; English,
c. 1840.

Below Picture postcards,
1895–1911, including an
early aviation card from
Paris, 'A Yankee Goddess'
by Charles Gibson, and a
card celebrating the 90th
birthday of Prince
Luitpold of Bavaria.

Post Office cards were permitted, with embossed or imprinted stamps as part of their design, and regulations prevented any pictorial element, since the address had to appear on one side and the message on the other. As early as 1871, however, a pictorial element began to appear on certain European cards, when stationers and other businessmen were allowed to print their own advertising matter on the reverse side of the cards. As the regulations were gradually relaxed the pictorial element increased in size, and by the late 1880s the custom was firmly established in Europe of producing cards with tiny vignettes of scenery and landmarks occupying a portion of the side intended for the message. These cards are often known t collectors as *Grüss Aus* cards, from th German greetings line with which they we captioned. The majority bore halfton illustrations, but chromolithographs becam increasingly fashionable in the 1890s. Car of this sort were also produced by post administrations in several countries (notabl New Zealand) with impressed stamps, b the majority of European examples wer private productions. The Columbian Expos tion of 1893 greatly stimulated the use picture postcards in the United States, but i Britain postal regulations banned pictur cards until 1894. Subsequently, pictures wer permitted, but their dimensions were severel restricted. The regulations were furthe relaxed in 1897 when the Post Office per mitted the back of cards to be partitioned, s that the message appeared on the left sid and the address on the right. Thus the fron of the card was left entirely free for th picture. Cards were increased in size in 189 to conform to existing European standard and this further stimulated the developmen of picture cards, including multiples, i which as many as six different views ap peared on one card. Early novelty cards o British origin are comparatively rare, sinc the Post Office regarded them as 'embarras ing', and charged double postal rates if the bore tinsel, cloth scraps or had concertir pull-out pictures.

The heyday of the picture postcard wa the period from 1900 to World War Increases in postal rates and the costs c production thereafter led to a marked declin in their popularity, though they have cor tinued to be a universal medium for vacation greetings. As the cheapest form of touri memento they have always had a wide appe and countless examples have been preserve in mint, unposted condition in special album

The revival of deltiology as a separat collecting hobby in recent years has cor siderably hardened the market in early pos cards. Examples by such artists as Lou Wain (famous for his humanized cats) an Raphael Kirchner (an early exponent of th 'pin-up') are now highly prized, as are carc

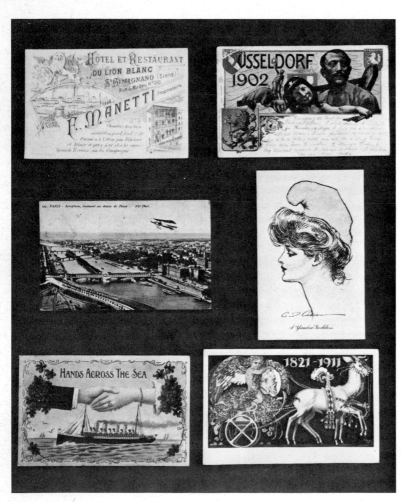

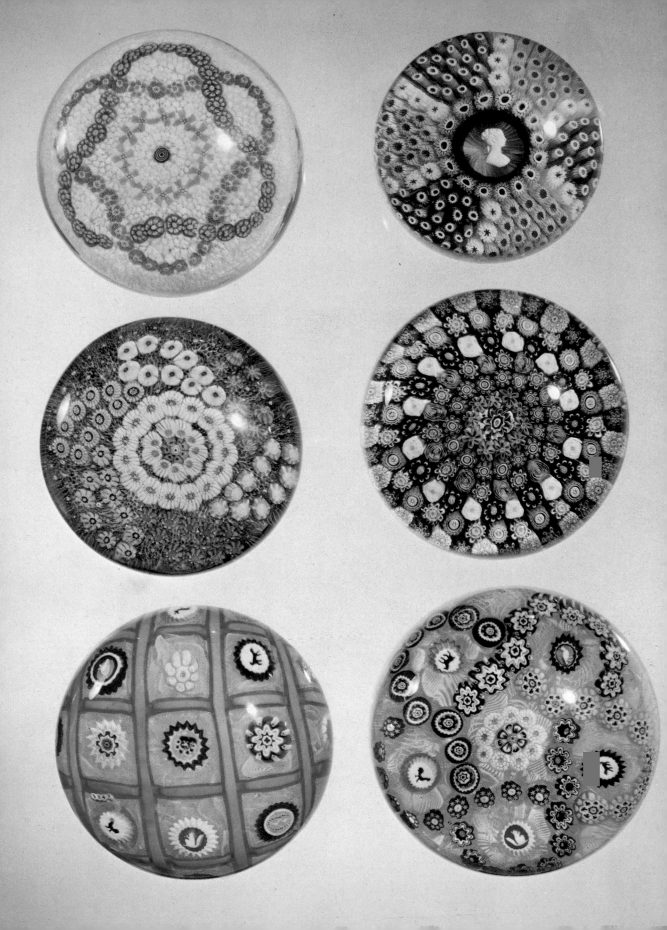

ft French paperweights:
p) Baccarat white star-
t colour ground weight,
d St Louis carpet-
ound weight with
*l*phide portrait of
*u*een Victoria; (middle)
o Clichy *millefiori*
*e*ights; (bottom)
*.*ccarat blue chequer
*e*ight date 1849, and
*.*ccarat *millefiori* weight.

featuring vintage airplanes, exhibitions and other topical events. Postcards portraying stage and screen actresses and society beauties were immensely popular in the Edwardian era and form a separate collectable group. Woven silk and embroidered postcards, similar to stevengraphs (q.v.), patriotic cards from the Boer War and World War I, and cards bearing firms' advertisements up to about 1920 may also be considered.

Cards may be collected in mint condition or used, but the presence of stamps and postmarks can affect their value considerably. Since the postcard rate was prepaid by the lowest denomination stamps of the period (also used on printed matter), the stamps themselves are seldom of any real value; but there are numerous examples of postmarks which can boost the value of a card enormously. These include the special postmarks of fairs and exhibitions, those used in connection with advanced Christmas posting experiments, early slogan-machine cancellations, and village hand-stamps from remote or sparsely populated areas. Many tourist postcards of the turn of the century bore a cachet or rubber stamp, to signify that they were posted at the top of the Eiffel Tower, Land's End, John o' Groats or the summit of Ben Nevis, and many of the Alpine resorts and hotels bear similar marks.

PICTURES IN UNUSUAL MATERIALS

The nineteenth century witnessed an extraordinary vogue for pictures composed of unusual materials, including some which, at first glance, seem totally unsuited to this medium. Pictures in materials other than canvas and oils or paper and watercolours became popular about 1830 and continued until World War I. Cork pictures were a popular form of tourist souvenir from the countries of the Middle East, North Africa, China and Japan, using the bark of the Abemaki tree or the evergreen oak, which could be carved and cut in thin strips, often in layers to create a three-dimensional effect. The majority of these pictures had Oriental or Moorish subjects, figure groups and

landscapes. Such pictures are rare in fine condition on account of their fragile nature. Pictures of birds made up of actual feathers became fashionable in the late eighteenth century, originally in combination with oil-painting. In many cases such pictures appear as a cross between oil-painting and taxidermy and the resulting effect was often quite grotesque. In the mid-nineteenth century the subject matter of feather pictures was extended. Goose feathers in particular lent themselves admirably to cutting and shaping to form flower petals and leaves, dyed or painted and curled. This type of feather art was particularly popular in the United States from about 1850 onwards.

Vegetable matter other than cork was widely used in the creation of pictures. Spatter-work panels and pictures were composed of dried leaves, especially ferns. The scales of pine cones could also be arranged ingeniously on a cardboard base. Straw marquetry was widely practised in Europe, not only for the decorative panels of small boxes but also for wall pictures. Marquetry (q.v.) was adapted in the late nineteenth century for pictures, mostly of scenery but occasionally of portraits. Pictures composed of various coloured sands were a speciality of

ght Tinsel portrait of
*l*liam IV, *c.* 1831.

Butterfly-wing picture of
a Dutch scene, c. 1925.

Bottles or flasks with flattened circular bodi
and long, slender necks have been record
from Roman times, though they are popular
associated with the religious pilgrimages
the Middle Ages. They were characteriz
by their elaborate stoppers and tiny tw
handles or rings set at the base of the nec
through which passed a chain or leath
thong by which they were suspended fro
the belt, saddle or shoulder of the travell
The earliest medieval examples were ma
of leather, earthenware, stoneware or pewt
and were relatively plain. The shape w
adapted in the seventeenth century as a for
of sideboard ornament, and larger, mo
elaborate examples resulted. Decorative flas
proliferated in the eighteenth century, bei

the Isle of Wight, where the multicoloured
sands of Alum Bay provided the raw
materials, but sand pictures of this type were
originally produced in Germany in the
eighteenth century and introduced to Britain
by Benjamin Zobel. Pictures composed of
tinsel and various colours of metal foil were
popular from 1850 to 1930, often portraying
famous persons or commemorating important events, the motif usually being surrounded by a plain black area to provide
maximum contrast. Theatrical prints from
Hoxton, London, were often similarly decorated with coloured tinsel.

Other materials in which pictures were
produced in the nineteenth and early twentieth centuries include pieces of leather,
scraps of cloth and wool arranged as a
montage, shells, the iridescent wings of
butterflies, and mosaics composed of pieces
of postage stamps.

produced in faience, porcelain or silver, with polychrome glazes, enamelling and engraving or embossed ornament. Glass flasks emulating medieval pilgrim bottles were also produced in the eighteenth and nineteenth centuries for ornamental purposes.

PILL BOXES

Small circular or oblong boxes for pills and breath-sweeteners were a popular form of object of vertu in the eighteenth and nineteenth centuries and may be found in gold, silver or enamels (q.v.), in leather, carved ivory, hardwoods, bone, horn or porcelain. Lids may be completely detachable (in the circular types) or hinged in the oblong version. Pill boxes were a common subject for the manufacturers of Mauchline and Tunbridge wares (qq.v.) supplying the lower end of the market. Pocket pill boxes went out of fashion in the late nineteenth century, but there has been some revival in recent years with the advent of saccharin and other artificial sweeteners.

PILL SLABS

Small, flat slabs of delftware in various shapes, usually pierced with one or two holes at one end for hanging from a wall when not in use. They may be found in square or oblong shape, or less frequently in octagons, ovals, shields or heart shapes. Their decoration follows the style of tin-enamelled earthenware of the second half of the seventeenth century, often incorporating the arms of the Apothecaries' Company or civic emblems. It is thought that the more decorative examples were not intended for use, but were displayed as shop signs. Plain earthenware pill slabs, on which apothecaries mixed and rolled the ingredients of pills, continued in use until the nineteenth century. Eighteenth- and nineteenth-century examples were covered with velvet and often with black transfer-printed pictures. Many of these, with suitable American motifs, were exported from 1790 to 1860 by Wedgwood and other English potteries.

PIN CUSHIONS

Holders for pins and needles were a common object on dressing and work tables in the nineteenth century, and were frequently decorated in the sentimental fashions of the period. Heart-shaped pin cushions were covered with silk or taffeta and lavishly embroidered with mottoes and decorated with beads and sequins. Less-decorative examples were covered with velvet and filled with straw, horsehair or similar materials. Though the surface did not permit the same degree of ornament as silk, the velvet cushions were often shaped like animals. Many pin cushions of the nineteenth century had ceramic or metal bases with a plush-covered cushion set in the top. A popular form was a silver slipper or boot stuffed with cushioning material, but animals, such as elephants, pigs, cats, dogs and cows, were also modelled in silver or white metal with pin-cushion backs. Small work boxes and ornamental caskets, in silver, brass or pewter, had pin cushions mounted in their lids. Allied to pin cushions were pin holders, resembling yoyos with strips of felt or padding between two discs, into which the pins were stuck. These holders were usually made of wood and decorated with marquetry, lacquer or Tunbridge ware (qq.v.), but examples in pottery, porcelain, ivory or glass are also known.

199

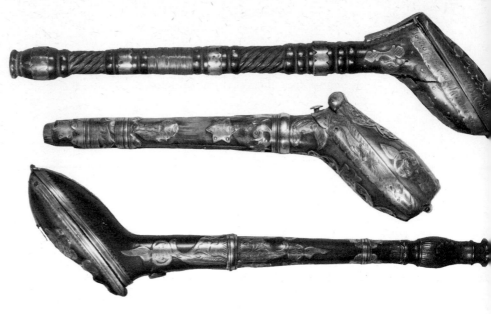

Carved wooden pipe cases; Dutch, 17th and 18th centuries.

PIN TRAYS, CUPS AND BOXES

As an alternative to the pin cushions and holders, there were many forms of small container in which pins, needles and paper clips were kept loose. Circular pin cups were produced in silver, brass or electroplate, occasionally with glass liners, either individually or as part of inkstands (q.v.). A novelty form, in glass with a metal top, concealed a magnet which attracted steel pins and needles to the central receptacle. Pin trays may be found with several open compartments to house different types of pins, clips, fasteners, staples and thumb-tacks. Boxes range from small simple wooden or metal boxes with hinged or sliding lids, to elaborate examples, resembling miniature chests of drawers, with multiple drawers for different sizes of pin. Circular boxes with segmented compartments and sliding glass covers were developed in the early years of this century.

PIPES

The smoking habit was well established in many parts of Europe long before the introduction of tobacco from the Americas in the late sixteenth century. It was a barba custom, confined largely to the Celtic a Teutonic tribes of northern Europe. Vari aromatic herbs were smoked through in wooden or clay pipes, fragments of wh have been found in archaeological exca tion. The earliest tobacco pipes were th used by the American Indians and numer different types of pipe have been fou varying from one tribal area to anoth though as a rule the earlier examples shallow bowls and straight stems, 'like a li ladell', as one English observer of the 15 described them. The earliest Colonial pi emulated Indian examples but were fashio from coloured clays rather than wood had very short stems. They were decora with incised or embossed ornament. C pipes spread to Europe in the seventee century as smoking increased in popular The earlier pipes had short stems and v small bowls, reflecting the high cost of i ported tobacco. Bowls became progressiv larger in size and diameter throughout seventeenth and early eighteenth centur and, at the same time, the angle of the b to the stem changed from obtuse to act The short-stemmed 'Gambier' pipe was u versal in the eighteenth century, but in 1 the long, slender 'Churchwarden' came into fashion. Clay pipes were frequently decorated with cartouches (embossed roundels) on the bowls, but gadrooning, spiral effects and fluted motifs were also fashionable. Coats of arms, human or animal masks and unusual shapes became popular from 1770 onwards. Pipes may be found with regimental insignia stamped on the bowl and these were commonly used in the nineteenth century.

Wooden pipes were introduced to Europe from South America in the early nineteenth century, rosewood being a popular timber for this purpose. Cherrywood pipes were favoured in south-eastern Europe and were introduced to France, Italy and Britain at the time of the Crimean War. Turkish or Indian pipes also came to western Europe in the mid-nineteenth century. Porcelain pipe bowls were fashionable in Germany from the late eighteenth century and many fine examples were manufactured by the Meissen, Nymphenburg and Berlin factories, with delicately painted scenes on their elongated sides. They reached the height of their popularity in the late nineteenth century, by which time they were produced all over Germany and Austria, depicting classical, mythological,

hunting and patriotic motifs in great profusion. Meerschaum pipes were another German speciality, developed in the early nineteenth century and consisting originally of ornately carved bowls from blocks of magnesia silicate, though a cheaper substitute was developed in Austria and used for the majority of the intricately carved pipe bowls now in existence.

PIPE STOPPERS

Otherwise known as tobacco tampers, these objects resemble seals with small heads and usually ornate handles manufactured in brass or some other base metal, and rarely in silver or gold. The pipe stopper was used to keep the tobacco reasonably tightly packed in order to produce the correct amount of 'draw'. The techniques of pipe-smoking have not altered since the middle of the nineteenth century and thus it is something of a mystery that the pipe stopper should have gone out of use by about 1850. It is presumed that some form of tamper was in use from the early seventeenth century onwards, though the majority of examples seem to belong to the eighteenth and early nineteenth centuries.

Many of the earlier stoppers were carved from wood or bone, but the use of these materials is not a sure indication of age since they continued to be popular among the poorer classes until the 1840s. Better-quality stoppers were elaborately carved in ivory and these are among the kind most highly prized. Numerous examples have been recorded of stoppers carved from pieces of wood with a special association or historical interest. Examples of stoppers carved from pieces of the Boscobel Oak which sheltered King Charles II are in the British and London Museums. Whalebone, mother-of-pearl and various kinds of shell were also used, though such materials are relatively scarce. Among the other non-metallic substances sometimes encountered are glass, earthenware and porcelain, the latter occasionally intricately painted and glazed.

The favourite medium was brass, and the majority of the ornamental stoppers found

Clay pipes from St Omer, France, and a Staffordshire serpentine pipe; 19th century.

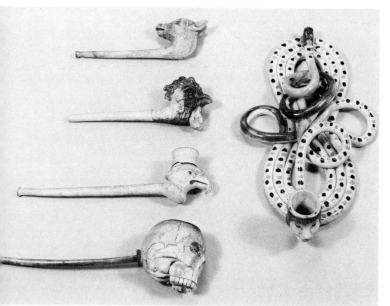

Pipe stopper caricaturing the Duke of Wellington; 19th century.

in antique shops today were produced in this alloy. In ascending order of scarcity one will find stoppers in copper, bronze, latten, lead, iron, silver and gold. Many of the brass stoppers now in circulation are somewhat spurious in that they were produced at the end of the nineteenth century for sale to collectors, long after they had gone out of fashion with pipe-smokers.

The principal attraction of pipe stoppers lies in their decoration. A popular device was the stopper in the shape of a human leg in various forms, either unclothed or booted. Small figures, representing popular heroes, Dickensian characters, mythological or allegorical personages (such as Britannia and St George), cherubs and ladies were also popular. A not uncommon figure on pipe stoppers was the Duke of Wellington, an allusion to the fact that, as Commander-in-Chief, he had forbidden smoking in army barracks. Resentment against this arbitrary edict by a non-smoker found expression in the numerous stoppers portraying the Iron Duke.

Many stoppers incorporated medallions of a religious or political nature, often inscribed with satirical slogans. Some stoppers of the early eighteenth century took the form of a ring which could be worn on the finger. Few stoppers are dated, though an approximate date can be attributed on stylistic grounds, or because of the subject depicted. Generally, those stoppers with a small diameter are the earliest ones, from the seventeenth century when pipe bowls were narrow. As tobacco became cheaper the bowls became more capacious and the diameter of pipe stoppers progressively increased.

PIQUÉ

Technique of inlaying gold or silver in bone, horn or ivory, either in strips (*piqué posé*) or dots (*piqué point*), to form elaborate patterns. It was practised almost exclusively in France in the seventeenth century, but Huguenot craftsmen brought the art to the Low Countries and England after they were forced out of their homeland in 1685 by the Revocation of the Edict of Nantes. The

finest English *piqué* belongs to the perio from about 1700 to 1750, but thereafter declined in quality. *Piqué* was confined t articles of jewelry and objects of vertu. It ma be found on snuff boxes, étuis, bonbonnière perfume bottles, watch cases, needle cases an similar small items.

PISTOLS

Hand-guns whose name was derived eithe from the Italian town of Pistoia where the may have originated in the early fifteent century, or from the word *pistallo*, the sadd pommel where cavalrymen kept their sma arms. Improved techniques in the construc tion of firearms led to a reduction in the size and made it possible to produce a weapo which could be discharged with one han only. The earliest pistols had a matchloc form of ignition and were relatively cumbe some. An improvement was the snaphaunc or 'pecking fowl' action developed in th sixteenth century, but gradually supersede by the wheel-lock in the mid-seventeent century. Flintlock pistols first appeared abou 1600 and survived well into the nineteent century, though percussion-lock pistols cam into use about 1820. The invention of th percussion cap and the metal cartridge in th 1860s revolutionized hand-guns and stimu lated the growth first of revolvers and, at th turn of the century, automatic weapons i which the recoil or gases from the discharg of a shot re-cocked the mechanism.

The earliest types of pistol, the matchlock

wheel-locks and snaphaunces, are now very expensive and rarely seen, while percussion-cap weapons are subject to strict controls in many countries. The majority of collectors concentrate therefore on flintlock and early percussion-lock weapons from 1600 to 1850. This subject can be divided into countries noted for the manufacture of pistols, such as Italy, France, Spain, Germany, Britain, the United States, Belgium, Austria or Bohemia (Czechoslovakia); into types such as duelling pistols, target pistols, Highland all-steel pistols, Birmingham pocket pistols, and Derringer miniatures, pepper-box and other multi-barrelled pistols; early revolvers and firearms curiosa (q.v.). Pistols issued to soldiers, sailors, mail-guards and policemen, and stamped with the appropriate insignia, are important categories which have their own specialist literature.

PLAQUES

Decorative, uniface tablets made in many different materials as ornaments for walls and furniture. They range in form from square tiles with low-relief or underglaze decoration to large circular carved wooden roundels or small circular or rectangular metal bosses

in high relief. Many bronze medallions (q.v.) of the late Renaissance period were produced in Italy and France as plaquettes, to be mounted in the lids of caskets or the panelling in furniture. Similar plaques were later produced in earthenware, stoneware or porcelain and inset in furniture, the practice being especially popular in the late eighteenth century. Many of the distinctive blue-and-white jasperware plaques made by Josiah Wedgwood were produced for this purpose. Moulded or pressed plaques in delftware or faience evolved out of the late medieval hafner ware (q.v.) and were designed for mounting on walls either individually or in composite groups.

Metal plaques were die-struck or engraved in silver, copper, brass or pewter sheet, or cast in precious metals and bronze, usually in circular, oval or rectangular form, but frequently with scrolled and chamfered borders. Enamel plaques were fashionable from the mid-eighteenth century onwards, either purely for decoration or for some utilitarian purpose. In the latter category come fire insurance marks (denoting those buildings insured with certain companies who maintained their own fire brigades) and boundary marks, affixed to the exterior walls of buildings to denote the boundaries of wards and parishes. Enamelled iron plaques as trade signs came into use in the late nineteenth century, and although many of them are still *in situ* they are now being collected.

Decorative wall plaques in maiolica, Staffordshire earthenware, black basaltes, jasperware, porcelain and creamware have been widely produced since the early nineteenth century, with a vast range of subjects – biblical, historical, religious, patriotic or frankly sentimental – and range from relatively crude 'folk art' to the exquisite productions for which such firms as Minton and the King's Porcelain Works in Berlin were renowned.

See also *Hafner ware, Tiles*

PLATES

Far right Glazed earthenware plate by Theodore Deck, shown at the Paris Exhibition, 1878.

Any form of flat tableware encompassing saucers (in their original sense), meat plates, pudding and pie-dishes, platters, serving plates, chargers and trenchers. The more functional examples of plates may be found in wood, pewter, tinned copper or brass, silver, silver-gilt or gold, the more expensive examples being embellished with coats of arms on the rim, and with decorative features such as beaded rims, wavy or scalloped edges and reeding. Metal plates varied little over a period of four centuries (from the fifteenth to the nineteenth), the differences being

Right Lambeth delftware plate portraying Queen Anne; early 18th century.

mainly in the depth of the plate and th width of the rim.

Ceramic plates gradually displaced woode platters and pewter dishes in the sixteent century, though these types survived i everyday use at different levels of societ until the early 1800s. Since then pottery an porcelain plates have been virtually universa The more collectable varieties include fir examples of delftware (dating from th seventeenth century), maiolica and faienc from the same period, red stoneware fror the early eighteenth century and porcelai from about 1730 onwards. The comparativel

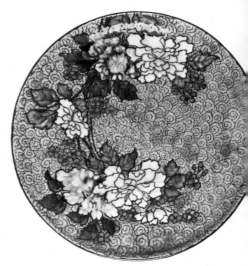

large flat surface of plates made them a obvious favourite for commemorative war (q.v.) and countless examples of rack-plat have been produced since the fifteentl century Italian *istoriato* pieces, down to tl Wedgwood jasperware commemorativ plates of the present day. Electioneerin plates, recording candidates, their co stituencies and the dates of the electio were a speciality of Bristol and other We Country potteries in the early eighteen century. Christmas plates originated in Ge many and Scandinavia in the late nineteen century and have spread to other countri in more recent years, with a different mot for each year. Alphabet plates, for teachir

right Card from 'The
~~Geography Game~~, an
~~Educational~~ card game
~~Commissioned~~ from
~~Stefano~~ della Bella by
~~Cardinal~~ Mazarin for the
~~boy~~ king Louis XIV,
~~1~~645.

young children their letters, have been recorded from the seventeenth century, but there are many other plates designed for children which feature nursery rhymes and fairy-tale characters.
See also *Dishes*

PLAYBILLS. See *Posters and Playbills*

PLAYING CARDS

Card games are probably the most universal form of indoor entertainment and their origin goes back to the Middle Ages, if not earlier. They were certainly popular in Europe by the end of the fourteenth century, though historians are uncertain of the country of origin. The earliest cards are believed to be the *tarocchini*, or tarot cards, which appeared in Italy in packs varying in number from 78 to 97. One feature which was constant, however, was the arrangement of the cards in four suits, each containing four picture cards, the King, Queen, Knight and Valet. There were also ten number cards and a number of atouts or trump cards, together with an unnumbered extra card known as Le Fou (the fool or joker).

The trump cards, with their macabre symbolism representing life, death, justice and fortune, embody motifs whose allusions have been lost over the centuries, but though tarot as a game has never been popular in Britain or the United States the cards are part of the indispensable equipment of fortune tellers. Fine examples of tarot cards were richly decorated and gilded in the manner of the medieval limners of manuscripts and, as a branch of minuscule art, are highly regarded by connoisseurs of the Italian Renaissance. They are exceedingly rare and individual hand-painted cards of the fifteenth century now fetch four figures on the few occasions when they appear in the salerooms.

It was about 1488 that card-playing was introduced to England, by Elizabeth of York, wife of Henry VII. It is significant that even today the costume on the face cards in British and American playing cards is that of the late fifteenth century. Card-playing

became extremely popular in England in the ensuing century and various statutes and bylaws were enacted to control the pastime. At the same time attempts were made to restrict the import of foreign cards in order to protect the English card industry, though it was not until 1628 that the Worshipful Company of Makers of Playing Cards emerged. A seven-years' apprenticeship was necessary before a manufacturer could become a Freeman and register his mark at the King's Receiver's Office and with the Clerk of the Company. This mark was printed on the ace of spades.

Between 1744 and 1860 there was a government duty on playing cards and this was levied ingeniously by the insistence that all ace of spades cards had to be printed at the Stamp Office, Somerset House, from plates supplied by the manufacturers and then sold back to them so that they could complete their packs. The comparatively ornate

205

Playing card
incorporating a moral
precept; English, early
18th century.

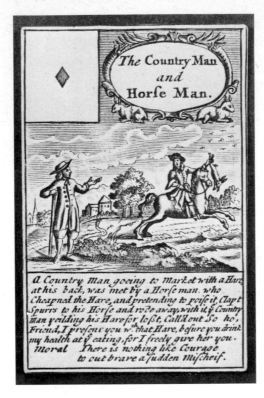

The Country Man
and
Horse Man.

A Country Man goeing to market with a Hare at his back, was met by a Horse man. who Cheapned the Hare, and pretending to poise it, Clap t Spurrs to his Horse and rode away, with it y Country Man yeilding his Hare for loast, Call'd out So ho, Friend, I present you w:h that Hare, before you drink my health at y eating, for I freely give her you. Moral There is nothing like Courage to out brave a sudden Mischeif.

Playing card
incorporating a moral
precept; English, early
18th century.

appearance of ace of spades cards is a relic of this procedure. The extension of this tax to the American Colonies in 1765 (though quickly repealed) was one of the causes of the War of Independence.

The first cards in both France and England were hand-drawn and painted, but by the end of the fifteenth century rather crude but charming cards were being block-printed in Germany and examples are now the highly prized *incunabula* of ephemeral printing. Gradually copperplate printing was later developed and was extensively used in the eighteenth century. The playing-card industry was revolutionized in 1832 by Thomas De La Rue, who was granted Letters Patent in that year to produce both the back and front of cards by letterpress and lithography. Thenceforward the backs of playing cards became increasingly decorative and, at the same time, the concept of playing cards was widened infinitely to include all manner of games, many of which had an educational

bias. This idea was not, in itself, new sinc many sets of eighteenth-century cards, wit conventional hearts, diamonds, clubs ar spades symbols, had the major portion their face taken up with an illustration teach heraldry, warfare, botany, history geography, to depict current events, or amuse and entertain with doggerel verses ar caricatures. By contrast, the late nineteent century examples often abandoned the trad tional suits altogether – an indication Victorian moral antipathy towards gamblir – although games of chance were retained f their educational value. The American 'I Bushby' and English 'Happy Families' we the earliest examples in this genre, but the were many other, more ephemeral game often linked to contemporary events such the American Civil War or the Women Suffrage movement.

POKAL

German term for a distinctive type of ve large wine goblet on a tall balustroid ster with a domed cover. Large vessels of th sort, modelled on the medieval chalice us in religious ceremonies, were made in silv or silver-gilt from the fourteenth centur onwards and were noted for the richness ar extravagance of their decoration. About t same time, however, they were also bei fashioned from rock crystal, usually wi gold or silver stems, bases and mounting, ar were richly engraved and faceted. T Venetians produced similar vessels in fi soda-glass from the fifteenth centur Examples from this period were relative plain, with *craquelé* surfacing in colour glass, decorated to some extent with col painting and gilding and confining orn mental features to the balusters and knops stem and cover. A few examples have be recorded of seventeenth-century Veneti covered goblets of this type with stems in t shape of animals in dark blue or red gl contrasting with the pale or colourless gl of the bowl. The most lavish examples fro the Venetian glasshouses had numerc prunts (projections) on the stem, *lattici*

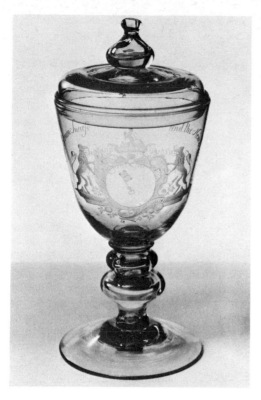

have been recorded in America, where they were introduced by Frederick Amelung and produced at the New Bremen Glass Manufactory in Frederick, Maryland, in the late eighteenth century.

POMANDERS

Containers for aromatic substances and perfumes to ward off contagious diseases and sweeten the atmosphere. They were made in Europe from the Middle Ages to the mid-seventeenth century. Thereafter they went into disuse, although the idea was revived a century later in the guise of the vinaigrette (q.v.). The name is thought to be derived from the French *pomme d'ambre*, apple of ambergris (a substance used widely as a prophylactic and now employed as a base in perfumes). Pomanders were generally apple-shaped and consisted of simple spheres or elaborate segmented devices, each compartment holding various spices and perfumes. A ring at the top was provided for suspension from a chain round the neck. The sides were pierced in ornamental patterns to allow the perfumes to escape and they were frequently decorated with enamelling, inlays and precious stones. They were usually made of silver or gold, though examples in copper or brass are known. Occasionally shapes other than a sphere were used, such as ovals, ellipses and hearts. Seventeenth-century pomanders were significantly smaller, some examples being less than an inch in diameter,

and *millefiori* decoration in the stem and base respectively, and ornate covers in the form of dolphins, crowns and human figures. Some examples are known with an all-over *latticinio* effect.

Undoubtedly, however, the finest examples of pokal came from the German and Austrian glasshouses in the seventeenth and eighteenth centuries. The comparatively large surface of the bowl afforded considerable scope to engravers and enamellers and many splendid examples of these large goblets may be found with portraits, historic scenes, landscapes and armorial bearings. The majority of pokal glasses had long stems and relatively short bowls, either globular or tapering outwards and upwards, but some early seventeenth-century examples have almost perpendicular, cylindrical sides and very short stems, being more beaker- than goblet-shaped. This type of covered goblet never won acceptance in France or England to any extent, but some interesting examples

ht English pomander,
y 17th century, and
aigrette, 18th century.

indicating that by this time they were regarded rather as jewelry than as protective devices.

In more recent years there have been attempts to revive the pomander, not so much for personal adornment but as a small decorative object. Many of these latter-day pomanders, of British or European origin, may be found in hardwood or porcelain and are invariably globular in shape, with floral patterns on their sides and perforations on the top.

See also *Vinaigrettes*

Hand-painted Pontypool tray; 19th century.

PONTYPOOL WARE

Name given to a distinctive type of japanned metal ware originating in the Welsh town of Pontypool in the late seventeenth century. John Allgood, previously employed in japanning furniture, invented a new form of lacquer which could be applied to sheet metal. He mixed raw linseed oil, asphalt and thinning substances to form a durable, heat-resistant varnish with a high gloss which imitated Japanese lacquer. The process was perfected by Edward Allgood (1681–1763) and turned into a commercial proposition, as a result of which he established a factory known as the Pontypool Japan Works some time between 1725 and 1730. At first only black was used as a base colour, chinoiserie decoration being applied in gold, but by 1740 other colours, such as crimson and brown, were coming into use. The earliest wares were laboriously worked by hand, using hammering, chasing and fretting techniques, but after 1760 much of the work was mechanized and patterns were die-struck. A split in the Allgood family led to the estab-

lishment of a rival factory at the nearby tow of Usk. If anything, the competition mere served to improve the standards of product tion and the best japanned metal wares we produced in the ensuing period. The decor tion became more ambitious, with a mu wider range of colours, and subjects depart from the original chinoiserie to inclu landscapes, pastoral and sporting scen Improvements in the process enabled manufacturers to apply their japanning kettles, saucepans, urns and other domes utensils which were subject to considera heat. The use of cast-metal handles, kno and finials also extended the range of goo produced in Pontypool and Usk during latter part of the eighteenth century. U fortunately cheaper, mass-produced wa from the English Midlands (but ingeniou known as Pontipool ware with the na slightly mispelled to distinguish it from original) forced the Welsh factories out business. The Pontypool Japan Works clo in 1820 though the Usk factory lingered for another forty years.

Japanned tin-plate and toleware (q.v.) produced in Bilston and Wolverhampt from about 1760 onwards. The earl examples were poor in quality and decora in garish colours, but the defection o Pontypool craftsman named Jones led t vast improvement in the Midland wares. formed a partnership with Taylor of Wolv hampton using the name 'Pontipool' a built up an enormous export trade, mos with America, where Pontipool trays beca immensely popular. The use of bro powder after 1812 gave this Pontipool w its distinctively lavish gilt decoration. E after the establishment of an Ameri factory in 1890 to produce Pontipool wa the Wolverhampton products continued flood the United States market.

Similar japanned metal wares were p duced in France, the Low Countries a Germany, but, with the exception of Stobwasser company in Brunswick (fr about 1770 to 1830), European japan wares were generally inferior to the Wel See also *Toleware*

PORCELAIN

Distinctive form of ceramics originating in China in the eighth century AD, introduced to Europe in the sixteenth century and now widely manufactured in Europe and America as well as Asia. The term porcelain embraces three quite distinctive substances. True, or hard-paste porcelain consists of ceramic material manufactured from clay and fusible stone. Chinese porcelain used china clay (kaolin) and feldspathic rock (petuntse). The latter (literally meaning 'white stone') was powdered and mixed with the clay to form a paste which was fired at about 1450° Centigrade. Petuntse was also used as a glaze, being powdered and dusted over the surface of the vessel, fusing as a thin layer of natural glass when fired. The high cost of imported Chinese porcelain stimulated experiment in Europe to produce a passable substitute. Johann Friedrich Böttger, working for the Elector of Saxony in Meissen, discovered the nature of true porcelain in the early 1700s and began the manufacture of hard-paste porcelain about 1703. The technique spread to Vienna in 1718 and to France and England about fifty years later. Hard-paste porcelain is exceedingly hard and cannot be marked with a file. It has a thin, glittering glaze and enamel colours do not penetrate the surface but lie in ridges which can be felt with the fingertips.

Soft-paste, or artificial porcelain describes a vast range of European substitutes for Chinese wares, produced from about 1575 onwards. So-called Medici porcelain was formed from a mixture of clay and silicates. It was manufactured in Urbino under the patronage of Francesco de' Medici, Grand Duke of Tuscany. French attempts to simulate Chinese porcelain date from 1673 when Claude Révérend and Louis Poterat independently began producing hard white ceramic materials at Paris and Saint-Cloud respectively. Saint-Cloud eventually produced a distinctive form of artificial porcelain known as *blanc-de-Chine* (Chinese white). Soft-paste porcelain experiments were conducted at Vincennes from 1738 to 1745 and resulted in a passable substitute. The factory, under royal patronage, subsequently moved to Sèvres in 1756. Other factories developed in the late eighteenth century and continued to make soft-paste porcelain till the 1770s, when the formula for hard-paste porcelain was acquired from Meissen. The production of porcelain revived after the Revolution and continues to this day, notably at Sèvres and Limoges. Soft-paste porcelain was known as *Porcelaine de France* or *pâte tendre*, while hard-paste was known as *Porcelaine royale* or *pâte dure*.

The production of soft-paste porcelain in England started in the early 1740s at Chelsea and Bow in London. A form of hard-paste porcelain was manufactured at Bristol from 1748 (transferred to Worcester in 1752), using china clay and steatite or soap-rock. This soap-rock porcelain was subsequently made at Liverpool from 1756 and at Caughley from 1772. The artificial porcelain of Chelsea used ground glass in the Italian manner; this technique was subsequently used at Derby and Longton Hall. A third type of porcelain, using bone-ash, was developed at Bow in 1749 and subsequently used at Chelsea from 1755, and Derby in 1770. True porcelain, using feldspathic stone, was made at Plymouth from 1768 onwards and subsequently at New Hall in Staffordshire. Josiah Spode adapted the earlier bone-ash technique to the production of true porcelain about 1800, evolving the distinctive English substance known as bone china, which continues to be the principal medium for English porcelain to this day.

209

Lowestoft porcelain jugs
with underglaze-blue
decoration; 18th century.

Bone china is also made to some extent in the United States, although most factories in America, like those on the continent of Europe, prefer true hard-paste porcelain using the Chinese formula. Soft-paste porcelain can be easily marked with a file, the glaze is glassy and sometimes uneven, and the enamel colours often sink into the surface slightly, giving a more rounded feeling.

In Germany, the Meissen factory entered the period of its finest products in 1720, following the appointment of Johann Gregor Heroldt as director. There followed the sumptuous tablewares known generally by the types of flowers with which they were decorated: Japanese and Chinese (*indianische Blumen*) and the more naturalistic European forms (*deutsche Blumen*); but chinoiserie (q.v.) was also very popular. Meissen was renowned for its ornamental figures, mainly produced after the appointment of J.J. Kaendler as *Modellmeister* in 1731, but he was also responsible for porcelain interpretations of many large and ornate tablewares previously fashioned in silver. Despite the vicissitudes of the Seven Years' War and the Napoleonic Campaigns (not to mention the devastation of World War II) the Meissen factory has continued to flourish to this day.

Other German princes were quick to emulate Augustus the Strong, founder of

Meissen, and established their own porcelai[n] factories. The more important factories [of] the eighteenth century included those [of] Berlin, Höchst, Fürstenberg, Frankenth[al] and Nymphenburg. Claude du Paqui[er] established a factory at Vienna in 1718 an[d] this came under royal control in 1744; i[ts] tablewares were famous for their exquisi[te] decoration by freelance enamellers (*Hau[s maler]*). In the Low Countries porcela[in] manufacture was carried on at Weesp (after[wards] transferred to Oude Loosdrecht) an[d] at The Hague. In Scandinavia, Copenhag[en] has long been the main centre of porcela[in] manufacture, though some fine soft-pas[te] porcelain was also made at Marieberg, ne[ar] Stockholm in the late eighteenth centur[y.] Although Meissen-style porcelain was bei[ng] made in Russia as early as 1745, the industr[y] was greatly expanded under the patronage [of] Catherine the Great, and the St Petersbur[g] factory produced some excellent figures [in] traditional Russian costume. The best-know[n] Russian porcelain was produced in the nine[e]teenth century by the Gardner factory [at] Verbilki. This porcelain works was found[ed] by an Englishman, Francis Gardner, in 17[60] and it continued in production until the 19[17] Revolution. Like the St Petersburg facto[ry] its speciality was Russian peasant figures.

Christoph Konrad Hunger, a defect[or] from Meissen who assisted du Paquier

right Pair of Meissen
figures of gardeners; late
18th century.

Vienna, subsequently helped to establish the
first Italian porcelain factory in Venice in
1720 under the Vezzi brothers. Its porcelain
closely resembled that of Meissen. The best-
known Italian factory was founded at Doccia
in 1735 by the Ginori family, under whose
name it trades to this day. A factory was run
at Capodimonte from 1743 to 1759 under
the patronage of the King of Naples. When
King Charles of Naples succeeded to the
Spanish throne he transferred the works to
Buen Retiro, where 'Capodimonte' porcelain
has been produced to the present time,
specializing in figure groups whose realism
has never been surpassed.

Attempts to manufacture soft-paste porcelain in America began in 1769, when Gouse
Bonnin and George Morris established a
pottery in Philadelphia. Very few examples
of their ware – mainly fruit bowls and
trinket boxes in the manner of Derby and
Bow – have survived, the factory having
ceased operations in 1772. Blue-and-white
porcelain of indigenous manufacture was
revived about 1850 by C.W. Fenton's
pottery in Bennington, Vermont. Its successor, the United States Pottery, produced fine
quality porcelain between 1852 and 1858.

PORRINGERS

European bowls used for eating or drinking
from the fourteenth to the seventeenth
centuries, sometimes known as earred dishes
on account of the large flat 'ears' on either
side as handles. The earliest examples were
relatively shallow, with or without a lid,
and having either one or two handles. Later
examples were generally larger and deeper,
and were fitted with a lid and twin handles.
They were first produced in pewter but by
the sixteenth century were widely manufactured in silver, silver-gilt or even gold.
Considerable variety occurs in their decoration, armorial bearings and allegorical subjects being engraved on their sides. The lids
and ears were often lavishly decorated with
engraved, hammered or cast ornament. Prior
to about 1650 the shape of porringers was
usually straight-sided, tapering slightly upwards from a flat base. Later examples had
perpendicular sides with a rounded bottom
on a high foot-rim or feet (particularly those
made in Germany). English porringers tended
to be shallower than Continental versions;
Dutch porringers often had a characteristic
rose motif on their sides and lids, though this
was copied elsewhere. American porringers
often had the owner's or maker's name cast

Pair of silver porringers
and bowl by William
Calder; American, first
half of 19th century.

restrictions continued until the latter half
the seventeenth century when they we
gradually relaxed. This encouraged the fi
illustrated posters, relatively crude woodcu
used by packmen, traders and showmen,
advertise quack medicines or fairgrou
booths where plays and other spectacles we
presented. Thus, at a comparatively ea
stage, the poster and the playbill were close
interrelated.

The majority of early trade posters fo
lowed the pattern of official proclamatio
and consisted entirely of letterpress, oft
using contrasting sizes and styles of typefa
to create maximum impact. More elabora
two- or three-colour posters began to appe
in the late eighteenth century, but these we
rare. It was the advent of lithography in 17
that revolutionized the poster, and allow
the designer greater freedom. A grea
number of pictorial posters emerged in t
second half of the nineteenth century, large
as a result of the pioneering work of Ju
Chéret. His first theatrical colour post
appeared in 1867 and immediately esta
lished the name of a young actress – Sar
Bernhardt. In the ensuing thirty years Ché

or impressed in the handle. Handles were
often solid, with a simple ring for suspension
from a hook, but some examples of American
origin have elaborately pierced handles.

POSSET POTS. See *Caudle Cups and Posset Pots*

POSTCARDS. See *Picture Postcards*

POSTERS AND PLAYBILLS

Printed, written or illustrated announce-
ments, publicly displayed, date back over
5,000 years to the wall paintings of Egypt and
Assyria. Tablets of wood, papyrus and parchment were also used for this purpose in pre-
Christian times and, indeed, it is the style of
lettering found on Roman stone columns
which has served as a model for graphic
designers in more modern times. Wooden
sign-boards were used in Europe in the
Middle Ages, but the earliest printed paper
posters appeared in Germany in the second
half of the fifteenth century and made their
début in England as early as 1476. At first
this medium was largely confined to royal or
official proclamations and there were regulations in many countries restricting their
usage and imposing heavy penalties on those
guilty of removing or defacing them. These

ght Poster for *Harper's*
zar Thanksgiving
mber, 1894.

designed over a thousand different posters advertising stage performances, music halls, charity fêtes, carnivals, newspapers and an astonishingly wide range of domestic consumer goods, from chocolate and cigarettes to corsetry. More than any other designer Chéret raised the poster to an important art form and inspired artists such as Toulouse-Lautrec, Steinlen, Mucha and Willette to produce posters which are now considered as works of art in their own right. The chromolithographed poster spread to Germany, the Low Countries, Britain and the United States in the late nineteenth century. The earliest English poster in this genre was Frederick Walker's advertisement for *The Woman in White* (1871), but in the ensuing decades fine theatrical posters were produced by Walter Crane, Aubrey Beardsley, Will Owen, Gordon Craig and the Beggarstaff Brothers. The best German posters in the period prior to World War I were produced by Otto Fischer, Max Klinger, T.T. Heine, Sattler, Hoffmann and Kolo Moser; in Holland Thorn-Prikker and Toorop established international reputations. Outstanding poster artists of the early twentieth century included Léon Bakst (Russia), H. Cassiers (Belgium) and Toyokuni (Japan).

Apart from the delightful circus posters of Matt Morgan, American theatrical posters in the modern genre did not exist before 1889. The earliest illustrated posters, advertising magazines published by Scribner's and Harper's, were designed by Will Bradley, Louis Rhead and Maxfield Parrish and departed from the European style of dreamy girls by injecting a greater element of realism into the figural compositions. Poster art developed enormously in the United States in the early 1900s, and such artists as Charles Dana Gibson, Ethel Reed and Will Carqueville established distinctive styles imitated by many others.

World War I gave the poster new impetus. Considerable ingenuity and originality were shown in the patriotic and recruiting posters produced by many countries. The best known include the British poster portraying Lord Kitchener ('Your Country Needs You')

Wells Fargo reward
ter, 1875.

and, in the same vein, James Montgomery Flagg's portrait of Uncle Sam. The poster as an effective propaganda medium was developed particularly in central Europe, and used by Italy, Germany, Hungary and Russia for political purposes in the 1920s.

In more recent years posters have been used extensively to advertise goods and services of all kinds, to promote tourism and transportation, and to project a country's image or a political viewpoint. Many posters from the late nineteenth century onwards have been reproduced in recent years, but such reproductions are invariably marked as such and should present little difficulty to the collector seeking only originals. Techniques such as multicolour offset and photogravure have improved the production of posters and greater attention to graphic design in recent years has improved artistic standards.

POSY HOLDERS

Tiny vase-shaped objects for keeping posies or individual flowers fresh. They exist in two distinct forms – for interior decoration or personal adornment. The larger version, intended for the mantelshelf, often took the form of a cornucopia which contained sufficient water to keep the flowers fresh. Others consisted of slender vases on footed stems or human hands holding a narrow cup. Flat-backed specimens were fitted with a ring for suspension from walls. They were made in pottery, porcelain, glass, silver, electroplate, or bronze, often encrusted with pearls and semi-precious stones or inlaid with other metals and enamels. The smaller version, intended for wear on the person, often had a brooch fitment so that they could be pinned to the costume. Ornate examples in gold or silver were used by ladies to keep their corsage fresh in the heated atmosphere of the ballroom. Smaller and plainer examples were used by gentlemen to keep buttonhole flowers fresh. Some larger posy holders were fitted with a chain (for attachment to the girdle or belt) or terminated in a handle so that they could be held; this type was favoured by brides and bridesmaids for nosegays and bouquets and was usually finely wrought in silver.

POT LIDS

Decorative earthenware lids for the flat, shallow jars in which cosmetics, and later fish paste were sold. The earliest of these jars were produced at the beginning of the nineteenth century to contain bear's grease, which, in a refined form, was the ancestor of modern hair creams. The use of bear's grease as a hair dressing seems to have been borrowed from the North American Indians and came into fashion in Europe after the French Revolution, when powdered wigs declined in popularity. Bear's grease, pomatum or pomade, as it was variously known, went out of vogue by 1850, only a few years after the pictorial lids had been introduced.

The pomade tops were invariably decorated in black and white and usually bore some allusion to bears in their pictures. Among the earliest and most valuable are the lids simply inscribed 'Bears Grease Manufacturer' or

showing the Prowling Bear motif. Lat[er] bear designs were rather whimsical, depictin[g] humanized bears at work and play. Apa[rt] from bear's grease, jars with decorative li[ds] were produced for various cosmetic prepar[a]tions and ointments such as Royal Circassia[n] Cream or Cherry Toothpaste. The beau[ti]cians of the period did not scruple at usin[g] the profile of Queen Victoria on their li[ds] and some inscriptions even included [an] endorsement from the Queen herself.

The greatest impetus to the production [of] pictorial pot lids, however, came from t[he] rapidly expanding fish-paste industry centr[ed] on the Kent coast. Pegwell Bay shrimps w[ere] esteemed as a delicacy in the mid-ninetee[nth] century and have been immortalized in t[he] decorative pot lids with their enchanti[ng] views of seaside resorts and nautical subje[cts]. The vast majority of pictorial pot lids w[ere] produced by four Staffordshire potteri[es:] Mayer Brothers and Elliott, Ridgeway [&] Cauldon, Ridgeway of Shelton and F. & [J.] Pratt of Fenton.

Of these, the pot lids produced by the la[st] named are the most highly prized by c[ol]lectors. The success of this firm was large[ly] due to the inventive genius of Felix Pra[tt] who patented in 1847 'improvements in t[he] manufacture of cylindrical articles compos[ed] of earthenware', and to the technical br[il]liance of Jesse Austin, who developed t[he] process for four-colour transfer printing. Pratts were commissioned by the two leading fish-paste manufacturers – Tatnell and Sons and S. Banger – to produce pictorial pot lids for them. This venture was apparently a huge success, demonstrated by the large number of Pegwell Bay pot lids still in existence.

Pictorial pot lids might never have risen above the mundane nature of the goods they enclosed were it not for the Great Exhibition of 1851, at which the pot-lid manufacturers displayed their wares. They broke away from the nautical genre on this occasion by producing pot lids showing the Grand International Building and other views of the Exhibition. The International Exhibition of 1862, L'Exposition Universelle of 1867 and the Columbian Exposition of 1893 were also commemorated in this way. Exhibition pot lids are now among the most expensive. The Great Exhibition also encouraged the production of pot lids with purely artistic motifs, and some of these, such as the Strawberry Girl and the Hop Queen, framed in a gold border, are also highly prized nowadays.

These attractive designs paved the way for the wide variety of pot lids portraying contemporary personalities (from the Duke of Wellington to Jenny Lind), topical events such as the battles of the Crimean War, animals, scenery and Shakespearian subjects. Reproductions of popular masterpieces, such as Gainsborough's *Blue Boy*, and paintings by contemporary artists such as Landseer, Mulready and Wilkie, were also popular.

The production of pictorial pot lids ended abruptly following the death of Jesse Austin in 1879. Although Pratts ceased manufacturing them in 1880 a large quantity of remainders came on the market shortly after F. Pratt Jr.'s death in 1894, and it is from that date that the collecting of pot lids really commenced. Although there was little manufacture of decorative pot lids in America in the same period, the English potteries exported large quantities to the United States. Significantly the last flowering of pot lids came in the 1890s when the life and times of Christopher Columbus provided the subjects for many lids produced in connec-

tion with the Columbian Exposition. In a similar fashion the Centennial Exposition at Philadelphia in 1876 was the occasion of pot lids decorated with scenes from American history, such as Washington crossing the Delaware and the Signing of the Declaration of Independence.

POTS

Term used to denote kitchen utensils of many different shapes and sizes. Small pots for cooking or drinking were fashioned in sun-dried pottery or oven-fired earthenware from prehistoric times. Bronze pots were widely used from the first millennium BC, and many decorative examples have been recorded from China, India, the Near East and the Mediterranean countries. Iron pots are also of great antiquity though they have seldom survived in comparable condition and were never decorated to the same extent. In the Middle Ages brass or bronze cooking-pots ranged from small, long-handled skillets and posnets to large cauldrons. Pewter was fashionable for pots manufactured from the fifteenth to the late seventeenth centuries, and tinned copper or brassware was favoured after that period. Pots may be found in matching sets of different shapes and sizes for soups, stews, fish, puddings and preserves. Tin-plated iron pots became popular in the 1730s and tinned steel came into use in the early nineteenth century. Enamelled iron pots have also been widely used since about 1850.

Tiny pots, often highly ornamental in style, were used from the seventeenth century

for cosmetics. Commercially produced earthenware pots, for pomade and bear's grease, often had decorative sides, though it is their pot lids (q.v.) which are mainly collected. Glass, pottery and porcelain pots have also been manufactured as packaging for butter, cheese, honey, preserves and confectionery and many of these have decorative sides and lids.

See also *Chamberpots, Pounce Boxes, Salts and Peppers*

POTTERY

In its widest sense this term embraces all forms of ceramics, though it is usually restricted to categories other than porcelain (q.v.). Pottery depends on two important qualities possessed by clay: its plasticity and its convertibility, through the action of heat, into a hard and durable substance. The earliest pottery was sun-baked and fashioned entirely by hand. This form has survived in the more primitive parts of the world down to the present century. Fire-baked pottery, however, was being produced in China and Egypt in the second millennium BC. The techniques of the potter's wheel, glazing and firing in kilns were highly developed in both areas long before the Christian era. Following the collapse of the Roman Empire the art of pottery was lost to western Europe, though it was nurtured in the East and was gradually re-introduced to Europe via the Islamic potters of western Asia and North Africa. Moorish potters brought their skills to Burgundy, Spain, France and Italy in the thirteenth century. Their earthenware was distinguished by its colourful tin glazes and came to be known by different names, as it spread from different centres. Thus Majorca, Faenza and Delft gave their names to maiolica, faience and delftware (sometimes rendered in English as delf or delph). Tin-glazed earthenware was highly popular in western Europe in the sixteenth and seventeenth centuries, giving rise to such forms as the Italian *istoriato* wares, with their themes drawn from historical or biblical subjects, and the famous 'blue dash' favoured in

Holland and England. Faience wares we brought from Faenza to France in the mi sixteenth century and Lyons and Neve became the centres of its production. As we as everyday tablewares (*faience blanche*), the factories produced figures (*faiences parlant* and commemorative wares with patrio slogans, especially during the French Revol tionary period (*faiences patriotiques*). T maiolica of Spain was brought to Antwe (then part of the Spanish Netherlands) ear in the sixteenth century, and Protesta refugees from that city during the wars of t 1560s brought their skills to Holland a England. Delft itself did not become important centre of manufacture until abo

left and right Four
Lambeth delftware
dishes, late 17th–early
18th centuries.

right Stoneware crock
with blue cobalt
decoration by Norton of
Bennington; American,
19th century.

the influences being Dutch delftware and Italian maiolica, the latter spreading through Austria to Bavaria. Faience on the French model was a speciality of Strasbourg in the eighteenth century, and enamel-painted wares of this type were introduced to Scandinavia when the Marieberg factory near Stockholm began production in 1758. Similar wares were produced at Holitsch (Holics) in Hungary from 1743.

Glazed pottery with decoration moulded or impressed in relief was produced in many parts of northern Europe from the thirteenth century. It is best associated with the German stove tiles known as Hafner ware (q.v.), but it was also used in the manufacture of jugs and jars. Hard-fired, semi-vitrified pottery with a distinctive glaze caused by throwing handfuls of salt into the kiln during firing, developed in Germany in the fourteenth century. This was the forerunner of the salt-glazed stoneware which was subsequently produced all over Europe and spread to America in the seventeenth century. Though mainly employed on household wares it has also been applied to decorative wares and figures in more recent years.

1605, but during the ensuing century its numerous factories (known confusingly by the prefix *De Porceleyne*, followed by their house-symbol) exported delftware all over the civilized world. Delft declined as a ceramics centre in the late eighteenth century, though earthenware of this type continued to be made in Friesland until recent years.

Delftware was introduced to England by Flemish refugees in 1567 and was produced at Norwich and subsequently at Lambeth in London. In the seventeenth century delftware was produced at factories at Liverpool, Bristol, Wincanton, Dublin and at Delftfield near Glasgow. Tin-enamelled earthenware was made in Germany from 1620 onwards,

Bernard Palissy experimented with lead glazes in France in the late sixteenth century and used them on earthenware decorated with small cast reliefs based on animals, birds and flowers of his native region, Saintes. Palissy laid the foundations for the lead-glazed earthenwares produced all over western Europe, often as a cottage industry. Both stoneware and lead-glazed earthenware were introduced to England from Germany in the seventeenth century and inspired local potters to emulate them. John Dwight of Oxford established a pottery at Fulham, London, in 1670 and began producing stoneware bottles, mugs and figures (the last-named being attributed to the sculptor, Grinling Gibbons). Subsequently stoneware was manufactured in Nottingham, York, Chesterfield and Swinton. A somewhat similar ware with a red body was produced in the late seventeenth century by the Elers brothers, Dutch refugee silversmiths who manufactured teapots in this medium.

The Elers developed the traditional English surface decoration known as slip (diluted clay) and applied shallow relief decoration to their hollow-wares. This, in turn, was taken up by John Astbury in the early 1700s and tea services with white relief decoration on a red ground were produced. Subsequent experiments with clays of different colou[r] resulted in marbled wares and tortoisesh[ell] ware (with a characteristic mottled glaz[e]. Much of this mid-eighteenth-century potte[ry] is attributed to Thomas Whieldon, who to[ok] Josiah Wedgwood into partnership in 17[..]. Wedgwood later revolutionized the ceram[ic] industry by introducing several entirely n[ew] forms, including black basaltes and jasp[er] ware, with its coloured matt surface decora[ted] with albino cameos. During the second h[alf] of the eighteenth century Wedgwo[od's] competitors vied with him in produci[ng] stoneware and earthenware of high qual[ity] and developing other lines, such as pearlw[are] and creamware, thus named on account [of] their characteristic coloration.

Earthenware figures emulating those [of] the porcelain factories were made at Bursl[em] from about 1765 onwards by Ralph W[ood] and subsequently by many other Staffo[rd]-shire potteries. These Staffordshire potte[ry] figures (q.v.) were immensely popu[lar] throughout the nineteenth century and c[on]-tinued well into the twentieth. Lead-gla[zed] earthenware of excellent quality was a[lso] produced in the late eighteenth century [at] Newcastle, Liverpool, Sunderland, Swan[sea] and at Portobello near Edinburgh.

Although Colonial America relied heav[ily] on imported pottery, mostly from Engla[nd,] sheer necessity forced the early settlers [to] produce their own pottery wherever possi[ble.] The resulting 'pioneer' pottery is n[ow] exceedingly scarce. Both glazes and bo[dies] depended on local materials, so a fairly w[ide] variety of types may be encountered. [The] decoration, usually incised or scratched on [the] surface before glazing, or emulating [the] contemporary English slipware, inclu[ded] quaint designs, mottoes and patriotic sloga[ns] and ranks among the more naïve expressi[ons] of early American folk art. Several potte[ries] were established in Massachusetts and Virg[inia] before 1650. The German colonists in east[ern] Pennsylvania in the early eighteenth cent[ury,] however, put the American ceramic indu[stry] on a proper commercial footing. It has b[een] estimated that by 1735 no fewer than [...] potteries were operating in that area al[one]

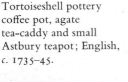

Tortoiseshell pottery coffee pot, agate tea-caddy and small Astbury teapot; English, *c.* 1735–45.

making competent hollow-wares decorated with both slip and *sgraffito* (scratched) techniques. Many of these small potteries continued to operate until the end of the nineteenth century, when increased mechanization by their larger competitors forced them out of business. Important centres of ceramic production were established in the mid-eighteenth century in New York and Cincinnati. Connecticut was the origin of a distinctive American pottery form, the bean-pot, later manufactured all over the country. Fine stoneware was produced at Bennington, Vermont, from 1793 until the end of the nineteenth century. Philadelphia became the centre for the industry specializing in china-ware, fine quality white-bodied pottery using Cherokee unaker (china clay). Alexander Trotter began as a manufacturer of Queens-ware (fine earthenware) in 1808, but had graduated to porcelain by 1824. Hard, unglazed white ware, resembling European parian ware (q.v.) was produced in the second half of the nineteenth century and known as Belleek, though it had no connection with or resemblance to the Irish porcelain of this name.

In the late nineteenth century pottery in America was elevated to become an important art form. Pottery-working and decoration became a domestic pastime for middle-class ladies, and clubs and associations of amateur potters sprang up all over the country, leading to the formation of the National Ceramic Association in 1891. Enthusiasm for pottery as an amateur pastime led to the vogue for art or studio pottery and contributed to the success of several important commercial potteries in this field, including Rookwood, Lonhuda and Louwelsa, whose distinctive glazes and decorative wares were fashionable in the period from 1890 to 1920.

See also *Cow Creamers, Cups and Saucers, Dishes, Fairings, Figures, Jugs, Lustre Wares, Mugs, Ollio Pots, Parian Ware, Pastille Burners, Pill Slabs, Plates, Prattware, Puzzle Jugs, Rogers Groups, Shaving Dishes and Mugs, Tea Bowls, Terracottas, Tiles, Toby Jugs, Transfer Wares, Trembleuses*

Miniaturized versions of utensils and table-ware in pottery and porcelain were produced from the sixteenth century in China and western Europe, originally as elegant toys for the display cabinets of the wealthier classes but also, from about 1830 onwards, as part of the furnishings of dolls' houses. From the mid-sixteenth century, the potters of Nuremberg in particular were renowned for their miniature platters, bowls, vases, dinner services and kitchen wares in earthenware decorated in bright colours. Tiny pottery items decorated in blue and white were manufactured in the Netherlands in the seventeenth century for the same purpose and were introduced to England in the 1690s. Subsequently 'baby house' wares were part of the stock in trade of the Staffordshire potteries, which even produced miniaturized versions of their famous flatback figures as chimney ornaments for dolls' houses. Many of these tiny figures featured the young children of Queen Victoria, including some as tiny infants in cots or cradles. Miniature creamware, stoneware and porcelain dishes were widely manufactured in the nineteenth century and marked examples by such well-known firms as Minton, Spode, Coalport and Worcester are now avidly sought after. Much of this tiny porcelain, however, was unmarked, particularly the dolls' tea services imported from China and Japan at the turn of the century. German dolls' china was usually rather larger than the Oriental kind and less finely decorated. Miniature table-wares were also produced in France and Denmark and exported to Britain and the United States.

Small bibelots in white porcelain richly gilded and enamelled were (and still are) a speciality of Limoges. These items include miniature chairs, tables, pianos, caskets and animals, as well as hollow-ware, and were intended as occasional ornaments and trinkets. Somewhat similar, though aimed at a humbler market, were the miniature vases, bowls, lamps and novelty ornaments produced in Goss china (q.v.). Small pottery ornaments

known as 'dabbities' were produced by the Scottish potteries of Portobello and Bo'ness in the late nineteenth century. They derive their name from the distinctive underglaze blues, browns, yellows and purples which appear to have been dabbed on. The majority of these tiny ornaments consisted of animals and birds. Miniature candlesticks and candle-snuffers were produced in porcelain by the Derby and Worcester potteries in the early nineteenth century.

See also *Cow Creamers*, *Fairings*

POUNCE BOXES

Sometimes referred to as pouncet-boxes or pounce pots, these containers were designed to hold aromatic substances to sweeten the atmosphere and ward off plagues and pestilence. Boxes intended for this purpose were usually small, flat and oblong or square with a pierced lid to release the perfume from a sponge soaked in aromatic oils or vinegar. This usage therefore comes midway between the medieval pomander and the eighteenth-century vinaigrette (qq.v.).

The name is also applied to boxes and casters with domed, pierced tops, which contained a fine sand or material, composed of powdered pumice or resin, which was sprinkled on vellum or writing paper, not so

much to dry the ink as to prevent it fro spreading all over the surface. Boxes of tl type, often confused with pepper pots, we made of pewter, brass, silver, Sheffield pla or electroplate from the mid-eighteen century until about 1870. They were oft made as part of a set for inkstands (q.v.), b individual items were sometimes fashion in novelty shapes, such as animals, hous windmills or birds. Pounce boxes may recognized by the perforated top, and threaded cap which could be unscrewed replenish the contents. Improved types writing paper and the advent of the blot in the late nineteenth century led to t decline of pounce boxes.

POWDER FLASKS AND HORNS

Between the discovery of gunpowder Europe in the thirteenth century and t appearance of smokeless powder late in t nineteenth century, the composition a appearance of this explosive material vari little. Gunpowder consisted of three essent ingredients – charcoal, sulphur and saltpe – which were ground up and mixed t gether in varying proportions. The resulti black, dusty powder may have been explosi but it was unstable. It tended to attr moisture when stored in a damp place even when exposed to the atmosphere for any length of time. Damp gunpowder had a distressing habit of forming into lumps which would fizzle slowly but would not explode. Apart from refusing to ignite with any force, lumpy gunpowder had a tendency to clog the barrel of the gun, thus rendering it more dangerous to the user than the enemy at whom it was aimed.

Although gunpowder itself hardly changed over the centuries, the methods of carrying it, dispensing it and using it altered considerably, from loose to semi-fixed and fixed ammunition. In the earliest type of ammunition the gunpowder was kept entirely separate from the bullet until the weapon had to be loaded; in the second type, the cartridge evolved gradually from a bullet with a measure of powder individually packaged in a more convenient form; and finally the modern metal-cased cartridge, which contained the bullet, powder and percussion cap.

Cartridges of the second category were certainly in existence by the end of the sixteenth century, but for long after that time the practice of carrying gunpowder in loose form continued and, in fact, did not die out until the early nineteenth century. The well-equipped soldier of the late Middle Ages, therefore, had to carry a bullet-bag and some form of receptacle for his gun-powder. The earliest type consisted of a wooden flask, covered with leather and bound with iron. It had a tiny nozzle closed by a simple stopper, but by the middle of the sixteenth century several varieties of spring closure had been devised and remained equally popular throughout the rest of the period in which loose gunpowder was used.

From the collector's viewpoint it is more or less impossible to date a powder flask by the method of closure, though the intricacy and efficiency of the spring closure are factors which may affect the value of the item. Powder flasks were also manufactured in a wide variety of materials other than wood. Flasks made entirely of leather are known, but because this material is difficult to preserve such examples are comparatively rare and usually in poor condition. Various metals, ranging from brass to silver inlaid with gold, were popular, and lent themselves admirably to decorative treatment at the hands of the metalworker and the silversmith.

The value of such items naturally varies considerably. The cheapest examples are the ordinary brass or steel flasks of the eighteenth century, rating a premium if engraved with military insignia, while the most expensive examples include those in gold or parcel-gilt associated perhaps with some royal or famous personage. This is an enormous subject whose scope may be tailored to suit the individual purse.

During the entire period in which loose powder was favoured, the poorer classes made do with homemade flasks produced from a cow horn, with the large end closed and a simple stopper inserted at the point. Powder horns were particularly popular in America in the Colonial period, and many survived as late as the early nineteenth century, when they were gradually superseded by cheap, mass-produced powder flasks. The decoration on these primitive powder horns is an important branch of American folk art, and the more intricate the carving the more

istol and powder flask; .merican, early 18th entury.

221

desirable the horn. Animals and hunting scenes were a relatively common subject for the engraving of powder horns; less common, and therefore more valuable to the collector, are those horns which depict scenery and landmarks. Identifiable portraits are rarely found engraved on powder horns, though they were a popular motif in other forms of scrimshaw (q.v.).

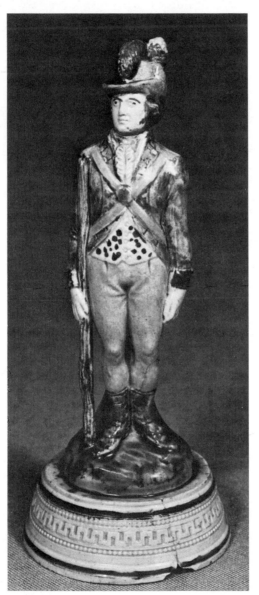

Pratt earthenware figure of a trooper, c. 1790.

PRATTWARE

British earthenware with distinctive orang. blue, and green glazes and bright underglaz colours applied by stippling or sponging often over moulded relief decoration. It take its name from Felix Pratt (1780–1859) wh established the pottery of F. & R. Pratt Fenton, Staffordshire, in 1812. Though th Pratts made large quantities of this type pottery, it is unlikely that they were th originators, for much Prattware was in fa produced elsewhere. Earthenware of th type was produced in great quantities b the Yorkshire potteries and also those situate in the east central Lowlands of Scotlanc Prattware is mainly associated with mug tankards, vases and jugs, often of a com memorative nature (Lord Nelson and oth naval heroes were popular subjects). Oth examples featured members of the roy; family or marked the opening of the earlie railways. This type of earthenware was als applied to Toby jugs and plaques (qq.v. small figures and rack-plates. The majority pieces were produced in the first half of th nineteenth century. The Pratt company itse subsequently concentrated on transfer printed pot lids (q.v.), and traditional Pratt ware declined as public taste became mor sophisticated.

PRIMITIVE ART

Term often used quite arbitrarily to denot material of ethnographical interest. Wherea antiquities (q.v.) are regarded as emanatin from the principal civilizations of ancien times – Greek, Roman, Minoan, Egyptia1 Assyrian, Indian, Chinese and Japanese – th art and artefacts of Africa generally, pr. Columbian America and the Pacific are come into the category of primitive art. Th dividing line is often tenuous, and is furthe confused by the standard practice in sal rooms of grouping primitive art with a forms of antiquities other than those of Chin and Japan, which are invariably treate separately. Moreover, it is difficult to unde1 stand why such technically and artisticall

accomplished works as the bronzes of Ife and Benin should be regarded as primitive art. Perhaps the age of Benin bronzes (dating from the fourteenth to the late nineteenth centuries) has some bearing, since primitive art, by and large, is of more recent origin than the antiquities of the classical world.

Primitive art is an enormous subject which can be sub-divided by areas and districts or by media. Thus masks (q.v.) form a very important group of primitive art in themselves. Wood-carving is the largest single medium of primitive art and may be found in such diverse objects as the elaborately decorated canoe-prows of Polynesia and Melanesia, the totems of North America and tribal reliquary figures of West Africa. Wood was also widely used in musical instruments, from the *marimba* and *amadinda* of East Africa to the carved rhythm pounders of the Ivory Coast and the *Yaqona* drums of Fiji. Wooden utensils are universal, and many reserved for ceremonial purposes were embellished with carved figures, handles, stands and ornate rims. Carved ivory cup-stands and drum-rests have long been a speciality of western Central Africa, the traditional patterns varying from one tribal area to another.

Relatively few examples of early primitive pottery have survived, on account of the fragile nature of the materials used, but terracotta (q.v.) figures from pre-conquest Mexico and Peru are not uncommon. Carved stone panels, heads, axes and bowls, with human and animal representation or stylised patterns range from the onyx bowls of Mixtec origin to the greenstone *patu* (war-clubs) of the Maoris. Textiles range from the ponchos woven from the brightly dyed wool of the llama in Peru to the geometrically patterned *tapa* of Samoa, woven from the bark of certain trees.

PRISONER-OF-WAR WORK

Prior to the Napoleonic Wars prisoners taken in battle were usually ransomed or exchanged soon after the event. The lengthy series of campaigns which began with the French Revolutionary War in 1792 and ended with Napoleon's Hundred Days in 1815 resulted in thousands of French prisoners spending years in British prisons, camps and hulks. Each of the prisons had a market within its gates, where the prisoners could sell or barter their handicrafts to visitors, tradesmen or farmers. Since the majority of the French prisoners were seamen it is hardly surprising that they should turn to ship modelling as a pastime. Oddly enough, wood does not seem to have been widely used for this purpose. Instead the prisoners utilized the bones obtained from the camp kitchens. Apart from a sharp knife and a small amount of dye, little was required except skill and patience. The rigging was made of thread or hair while the metal parts were produced from wire, or even silver and gold (the raw materials being the coins or earrings worn by seamen).

Judging by the care lavished on these models it has been surmised that for the

223

Straw marquetry writing box made by a prisoner of war; early 19th century.

most part they were specially commissioned by wealthy patrons and prison visitors. It is known, for example, that over £40 was paid for the bone model of a warship, made by two prisoners at Forton near Portsmouth, and that the prisoners spent upwards of six months making it.

Although models of warships were the most popular product, the prisoners also made trinket boxes, cribbage sets and dominoes. Straw, dyed in different colours, was used as a form of marquetry or mosaic to decorate the lids and sides of boxes.

Although the work produced by the French prisoners is that most highly prized nowadays, the relics of subsequent wars and campaigns should also be considered. Prisoners in both World Wars produced a wide range of arts and crafts, utilizing scraps of wood, metal or bone and employing such techniques as pyrography and scrimshaw (qq.v.). There is no hard and fast market for these later items, though they have a large following among collectors of militaria (q.v.). Unfortunately, increased interest in prisoner-of-war work, particularly the traditionally French items, has encouraged the manufacture of reproductions in recent years.

See also *Straw work*

PURSES

Leather pouches or bags attached to t[he] waist-belt were used in Europe from Rom[an] times by both sexes. As a male dress accessor[y] however, they went into decline after pock[ets] were incorporated in coats, tunics, breech[es] and trousers from the sixteenth centu[ry] onwards, though examples small enough [to] fit into the pocket have been fairly commo[n] place over the past two centuries. Ladi[es] purses or handbags have varied enormous[ly] in size, shape and material and afford gre[at] scope for the collector. Evening purses a[nd] small vanity cases were fashionable from t[he] early eighteenth century, and may be foun[d] in silks with lace trimming and decorate[d] with pearls, glass-paste jewelry or sequin[s]. Iron jewelry was popular in Germany an[d] France in the early nineteenth century, an[d] purses may be found in iron filigree wor[k] decorated with steel sequins. Small net bag[s] known as reticules, were carried by ladies f[or] everyday purposes and many of them we[re] ornamented with beadwork (q.v.). Sma[ll] cylindrical purses, known as rouleaux, we[re] designed specifically for coins, and had a[n] ingenious ring device which prevented coi[ns] from accidentally escaping. In more rece[nt] years small leather purses in embossed leath[er] have been very popular as tourist souveni[rs] embellished with scenery, landmarks a[nd] coats of arms. The sporran worn with Hig[h]land dress is a distinctive male purse whi[ch] had its origins in the medieval pouch slu[ng] from the waist belt of the tunic. Scotti[sh] sporrans are made basically of leather but a[re] frequently covered with horsehair, otte[r] skin or fox fur and decorated with silv[er] mounts worked in characteristically Celt[ic] motifs. Plainer leather sporrans for everyd[ay] wear often bear clan crests in silver, whi[le] many highly decorative types are still use[d] by Highland regiments.

PUZZLE JUGS AND CUPS

Numerous different kinds of trick drinki[ng] vessels were produced from the sixteen[th] century onwards, their chief aim being [to]

drench the unwary or uninitiated with beer, for the entertainment of onlookers. In their most common form these puzzle jugs are vessels with a multiplicity of spouts connected to the inner bowl by tubes placed at different angles, so that no matter which way the drinker tilted the jug he was almost bound to spill a copious quantity over himself. More ingenious examples have hollow handles with apertures through which one must blow to prevent the beer escaping through holes at various levels. A popular form in Germany and France from the seventeenth century was a type of double cup, one bowl forming the inverted base of the other, which swivelled between brackets or upstretched arms. The secret of drinking from these double cups was to empty the larger vessel first then carefully invert it and drink from the other. The German cups were known as *Jungfraubecher* (virgin beakers) since the larger vessel resembled a girl with billowing skirts, holding the smaller cup aloft. Another type, popular in the Low Countries, was known as a Jack-in-the-

cellar, from the figure contained in a central column inside the bowl, which shot up and hit the drinker as the liquid rose rapidly inside the column.

The majority of puzzle jugs were fashioned in folk pottery, slipware and scratch-blue stoneware being the most popular forms in England and Holland. Fuddling cups were another type which were guaranteed to make the party go with a swing. They consisted of two or three mugs whose bodies were joined together and their handles interlinked, so that they had to be emptied simultaneously to prevent spillage. The triple-bodied variety was sometimes known as Three-merry-boys. German wager cups were generally of a much higher quality, both in material (gold or silver) and intricacy of decoration. Upper-class versions of the simple tavern puzzle jug were also made in porcelain in the eighteenth century, and a few examples have been recorded in pewter or silver, though these are exceptional.

See also *Yard-of-Ale*

225

PYROGRAPHY

Literally 'fire-writing', this technique of working on wood surfaces with fire, pokers or heated points has been practised in Europe and America from the seventeenth century as a form of folk art. Simple geometric patterns and line drawings were applied to the lids of caskets and boxes of all kinds using needles heated until red hot. More subtle effects were achieved in the nineteenth century by using fine blow-pipes to produce toned areas and gradations of charring. The best effects were obtained from close-grained hardwoods, but a great deal of inferior pyrography was produced for the tourist trade, using pine, deal and planewood. Though widely practised as a cottage craft in the nineteenth and early twentieth centuries, pyrography occasionally rose to the status of an art, in the hands of such craftsmen as Ralph Marshall, active in the 1840s.

QALIANS

Oriental tobacco pipes in which the smoke is cooled by being inhaled through a long flexible tube in a vessel containing water. These pipes originated in the Middle East and were produced in Islamic pottery and coloured glass. The bowls may also be found in brass or silver, frequently decorated with inlays and enamelling. Persian examples used decorated and silver-mounted coco[co] shells and were known as *narghiles*. Chin[ese] qalians were produced in characteristic b[lue] and-white ware during the Ming Dyna[sty] primarily for export to western Asia. M[ost] of them have unusual shapes, the bowls be[ing] modelled in the form of elephants or fro[gs.]

QUAICHS

Scottish drinking vessels whose name[s] derived from the Gaelic *cuach*, the depress[ion] in the centre of a bird's nest. The earl[y] quaichs, from the Middle Ages till ab[out] 1600, were carved out of a block of wo[od.] This was superseded by turned woodw[ork] and by 1650 other materials such as horn [and] bone were being widely used. Quaichs w[ere] characterized by their shallow bowls [and] horizontal twin handles projecting from [the] lip. These were usually flat but varied fr[om] simple rectangular shapes to elabora[te] carved and fretted designs. Short woo[den] staves on a circular wooden rim, bound w[ith] metal hoops, were also used for the bo[dy] of quaichs. In the eighteenth and ninetee[nth] centuries most quaichs were of metal c[on] struction, silver (and less commonly pew[ter]) being employed. These later examples w[ere] frequently decorated with extravagant n[eo] Celtic tracery and ornament, embodying [the] Highland Romanticism engendered by Walter Scott.

RAIL RELICS

The largest and most prolific branch of industrial archaeology is concerned with railroads and tramways, which spread to every corner of the globe in the nineteenth century and the years leading up to World War I. The later replacement of steam by electric or diesel locomotives was accompanied by the drastic pruning of uneconomic services and the rationalization of the multitude of small private companies into huge state-run combines. Paradoxically, as railways disappeared almost totally, interest in them has developed. Railway workshops and scrapyards have become a happy hunting-ground for enthusiasts as steam engines became redundant, and latterly even railway companies have exploited this lucrative market. There are now over fifty preservation societies in the United Kingdom alone.

Name-plates and crests form the most expensive class of rail relic, the value depending on the importance of the original locomotive. In a humbler class are coach destination boards and head-boards, number plates from cab-sides and smoke-boxes, builders' and works' plates formerly mounted on locomotives, wagons and carriages, and even obsolete station signs. There are also lamps, engine whistles and smaller items of equipment. The furniture and fittings of carriages should not be overlooked; cast iron or enamelled signs and notices, wooden

painted crests with the rich panoply of railroad-company heraldry, and even the crested cutlery and crockery used in the dining-cars, are all highly collectable.

Railwaymen's hats, uniforms and watches, office rubber-stamps and ticket machines, tickets, way-bills, timetables, badges and insignia – all are legitimate objects for study. Collectors of ephemera will also find much to interest them in posters, postcards, railway letter stamps, prints of early locomotives, car cards advertising the scenic attractions of the route, company maps and regulations, railroad share certificates and brochures.

Silver baby rattle with coral handle; American, late 19th century.

RATTLES AND TEETHERS

Objects for pacifying babies are of the greatest antiquity, examples having been found in Egyptian, Greek and Roman archaeological sites. The earliest examples from the Mediterranean area were fashioned of bronze or terracotta with animal or human heads containing a solid ball to provide the rattling noise which distracted the fretful infant. Small bells were a feature of Roman baby rattles and have remained in evidence ever since. Teethers incorporated a strip or ring, usually of bone, on which the infant could cut his teeth. Again, the basic design has remained in use till the present, though other materials have been employed. Seventeenth- and eighteenth-century European examples may be found in gold or silver; electroplate was common in the nineteenth and bakelite in the early twentieth century. Often rattles and teethers were combined in the same object, the hollow metal ring containing tiny balls being common from about 1760 onwards. Highly decorative examples in sterling silver, die-stamped from sheet metal, became popular in the United States and western Europe in the late nineteenth century, and were a fashionable christening gift. Most of the rattles in novelty shapes date from the beginning of this century, often featuring fairy-tale, story-book, nursery-rhyme or strip-cartoon characters.

REICHSADLERHUMPEN

German term meaning 'Imperial eagle glass', denoting tall cylindrical glasses or beakers decorated in enamel with the Imperial motif. The technique of enamelled glass (q.v was brought to southern Germany fro Italy at the beginning of the sixteenth ce tury. It was fashionable for the nobility a gentry of Germany to have dishes, beake jugs and other vessels decorated with th coats of arms. This fashion soon extended glassware and the resulting enamelled gl was of such a high quality that much of is as fresh today as it was four centuries ag

About 1570 the decoration on enamell glass became more elaborate and the heralc theme was expanded beyond the simp embellishment of the owner's coat of ar to cover the armorial emblems of the Ho Roman Empire. A popular motif was t double-headed Imperial eagle (*Reichsadl* with its talons bared and its beaks gaping the traditional heraldic fashion. On its brea was either a crucifix, symbolizing the divi protection, or the orb of imperial power.

The most striking feature of the *Reichsad* motif, however, was the wings, decorat with the fifty-six shields representing t various divisions of the Empire. The to row of shields was emblazoned with t heraldic emblems of the seven Electors a sometimes the arms of the Apostolic S were included. The remaining shields we arranged below in vertical columns of fo each column containing four representativ of the principalities, margravates, free citi bishoprics, knights, landed gentry and pr fessional classes within the structure of t Empire – an interesting expression of t political ideal which, in theory at lea inspired the continued existence of t ramshackle edifice.

The inscriptions on these glasses are great interest and inconsistencies of spelli

are often useful in dating examples, the orthography of the German language being in a transitional state during the sixteenth and seventeenth centuries. Some of these glasses had verbose quotations from the Bible, a favourite being from Deuteronomy 32: 'As an eagle stirreth up her nest, fluttereth over her young . . .' Among the later *Reichsadlerhumpen* the portraits of the seven Electors and representatives of the nobility were substituted for their coats of arms. The bulk of glassware featuring the Imperial eagle consisted of large beakers, but a few rare examples of this motif are known on vases or bottles. Enamelled *Reichsadler* glassware was popular for more than 150 years and dated examples as late as 1743 have been recorded, though the majority of those still extant date from the seventeenth century.

See also *Enamelled Glass, Glasses, Kurfürsten Glasses*

RIBBONS

Narrow bands of silk woven in continuous strips were a speciality of the French and Italian textile industry from the Middle Ages and such 'ribbands' were widely exported to other parts of Europe as dress accessories. Improved techniques of silk weaving in the eighteenth century produced a much wider variety of patterns including intricate scenery and even portraits as repeating motifs. Woven silk ribbons continued to be popular until threatened, first by the advent of artificial silks at the turn of the century, and later by the arrival of nylon in the 1940s. Printed ribbon patterns were introduced in the mid-nineteenth century and often applied to cottons and other cheaper substitutes, but these never attained the popularity of woven silk. Patterned ribbons were used extensively for hatbands, while narrow plain ribbons were employed to trim costume and underwear. Lettered ribbons have been used for sailors' hatbands since the mid-nineteenth century, and similar ribbons, with the names of regiments and military formations, have been used as cuff-bands by the German and

other Central European armies since the late nineteenth century. Medal ribbons of particoloured or watered silk were derived from the medieval neck ribbons used for the suspension of lockets, pendants and medallions. They became universal in the nineteenth century and have evolved a distinctive heraldry of their own. Embroidered or woven silk ribbons were employed as book markers (q.v.) from the early nineteenth century onwards.

See also *Stevengraphs*

RING TREES

Devices for the storage of rings when not being worn. The most basic form consists of a tapering rod of metal or wood on which rings of various diameters may be impaled. More elaborate examples resemble miniature trees with several branches on which individual rings can be hung. In the late eighteenth century numerous fancy designs were fashionable, some resembling an outstretched human hand or a stag's antlers. They were manufactured in wood, pottery, porcelain, brass, silver or even gold and mounted on heavy bases of alabaster, bronze, cast iron, earthenware or wood. A late nineteenth-century type consisted of a sphere suspended by a chain and hook from an ornamental stand; the sphere had a number of tiny projections on which the rings could be threaded. Some examples from the early 1900s had branches curving round a central oval containing either a mirror or a photograph.

ROGERS GROUPS

Small cream- or dun-coloured figure groups which enjoyed enormous popularity in the United States in the second half of the nineteenth century and became, for America, what Staffordshire pottery figures (q.v.) were for Britain. The groups were named after the sculptor, John Rogers (1829–1904), who originally designed them. Rogers was born at Salem, Mass., in October 1829 and trained as a draughtsman. He wanted to become a sculptor and to this end he spent about a year in Europe, studying in Rome and Paris. His brand of realism was not in keeping with the stereotyped traditionalism of European sculpture and his work was rejected. Discouraged, he returned to the United States in 1859 and became a draughtsman in the office of the Chicago city surveyor. He continued to sculpt small figure groups in his leisure time and won acclaim with his group entitled *The Checker Players.* Following this success he took up full-time sculpting, becoming a National Academician in 1863. His figures attained the height of their popularity after they were displayed at the Centennial Exposition in Philadelphia, 1876.

Rogers never pretended to produce sculpture in the traditions of classical art. His subjects were invariably folksy, the familiar and often humorous situations of everyday American life, but he had tremendous flair in conveying the message with absolute clarity. In the aftermath of the Civil War many of his groups struck a high patriotic note, but later examples concentrated on homely sentiment and emotions expressed naturally. Rogers never descended to the Rabelaisian humour which characterized the contemporary china fairing, preferring 'situation' comedy. One group depicting an awkward young couple entitled *Coming to the Parson* was virtually a standard wedding present in the 1870s and 1880s. These pottery figures were extensively reproduced and became a symbol of working-class gentility. It has been estimated that at one time almost 100,000 of them held places of honour in the parlours and bay-windows of the East and Middle West – the

lace curtains pulled crisply apart so that th accepted witnesses to one's good standing the community might be glimpsed in all th putty-coloured glory.

Marietta Holley's fictional charac Samantha Allen, describing her visit to Centennial Exposition, expressed Ameri middle-class approval of the Rogers grou 'I stood a lookin' at some beautiful li statues . . . They was perfectly beauti though middlin' small sized, and they all clothes on, which was a surprise to me, indeed a treat . . . Oh what beautiful li white stun children there was before in every beautiful posture that children got into – a laughin' and a cryin', an feedin' birds, and a pickin' thorns out of th feet and a hidin' and a seekin' . . .'

ROLLING-PINS

The collectable examples of rolling-pins those which were made of pottery or gl rather than the more functional woo

ones, which seldom possess any decorative qualities. Pottery rolling-pins were widely manufactured in western Europe from the late Middle Ages and were frequently covered with underglaze decoration. Seventeenth-century examples were produced in delft-ware and decorated with mottoes, dates and names and were a popular memento of christenings, betrothals and weddings. From the early eighteenth century onwards glass rolling-pins gradually superseded pottery ones as a form of love token (q.v.). They were especially popular with sailors, who gave them to their wives or sweethearts, and this explains the high incidence of nautical subjects found on them, ranging from general views of the sea and shipping to portraits of admirals and naval heroes. Glass pins were also used to contain sugar or salt, and were hung over the fireplace to keep the contents dry. Rolling-pins in dark blue or green, decorated with gilding, were a speciality of the Bristol and Nailsea glass-houses. Other colours included red or pale blue loops on an opaque white ground. Between about 1830 and 1860 opaque white pins, with coloured decoration incised, were fashionable mementoes of seaside resorts. Many of them may be found with the names of vacation resorts as, for example, 'A Gift from Pwllheli' or, more specifically, 'A Brother's Gift from West Hartlepool'. These attractive and useful souvenirs declined in the second half of the nineteenth century, despite periodic attempts to revive them. Decorative glass pins were primarily English, though a few American and French examples have been noted.

ROSARIES

Strings of beads for counting prayers, traditionally used in the Catholic Church. The normal rosary consists of a chaplet of five decades (groups of ten) each composed of one Pater Noster (Our Father) bead and ten Ave Maria (Hail Mary) beads, though the full rosary consists of fifteen decades.

The number of beads has varied from medieval times to the present day, and also

differs from one country to another. Rosaries seem to have come into use about the late tenth century and did not become widespread until the thirteenth century. The chief interest of rosaries lies in the type and quality of the beads. Many different materials have been used, ranging from semi-precious stones, such as chalcedony, lapis lazuli and crystal, to jet, coral, amber, ivory, glass, maplewood and enamelled gold or silver. Rosaries often incorporated a pendant gemstone and could be worn as a necklace, combining Christian practice with a much older pagan form of amulet or good-luck charm. More modern forms also combine a crucifix.

RUGS AND CARPETS

Though these terms are largely synonymous and mean any form of woven or knotted floor covering they have been distinguished in different ways at different times. Thus the word 'carpet' was used widely until the

231

nineteenth century to denote a textile covering for walls and furniture as well as floors, while nowadays the laymen differentiates rugs from carpets mainly by size. Rugs are of surprising antiquity; apart from numerous biblical references, it has now been proved that knotted rugs (of a type still produced in Western Asia) were in existence in the fifth century BC, judging by well-preserved examples excavated in Siberia in 1949. The Scythians and the ancient Persians were noted for their carpets in the pre-Christian era, and the traditions of hand-knotted rugs come down, through the Seleucids and the Seljuks, to the Turks and Persians of the Islamic period.

The carpets of the Middle East owe their astonishing durability to the techniques of knotting the yarn to every pair of warp threads (extending from one end of the carpet to the other). Two kinds of knot were employed – the Ghiordes or 'full' knot, and

Kashan silk rug with a vase pattern.

the Senneh or 'half' knot. In general, latter was the type of knot favoured in r and carpets manufactured in Persia from fourteenth century onwards, whereas former was employed in Turkey and Afgha stan. The Turkish carpets were woven i continuous pattern, cut off abruptly by border strips and with awkwardly finisl corners. By the beginning of the sixtee century, however, the Persians, under SI Ismail, the first of the Safavid dynasty, broken away from this custom and develoy a style based on a central motif with corners carefully planned to achieve a p fectly symmetrical effect.

The earliest of the medallion carpets played a decorative scheme which v exclusively floral. Pieces of this sort w characterized by clever layout of the patt and tasteful formalization of the leaf-ar blossom motif borne on delicate vines, w carefully balanced colour contrasts. Beca of the Islamic ban on animal or hun representation, Turkish carpets concentra on floral or geometric compositions. F tunately the Arabic script was highly deco tive and this encouraged the ornamentat of borders with verses woven in pleas patterns. The Persians, belonging mai to the Shia sect, were not so rigorous in tl observance of the taboo on figural work a as a result their carpets were often embellisl with hunting scenes, mythical beasts allegorical composition.

Great attention was paid to the bord which were usually woven in bright colo contrasting vividly with the field of carpet. The Afghan weavers of Herat beg the fashion for a floral border consisting blossom surrounded by four elongated lea curving symmetrically about the centre.

Turkish and Persian carpets declined quality during the eighteenth and early ni teenth centuries, paralleling the decline the power and prosperity of these countr Paradoxically, this decline stimulated inte in Europe. In 1683, when the Ottoman Tu were forced to abandon the siege of Vie and retreat, their tents and furnishings into the hands of the Austrians and Po

Spotted leopard on a fringed, hooked rug; New England, early 19th century.

Successive campaigns by the European powers against Turkey in the eighteenth and nineteenth centuries resulted in great quantities of rugs and carpets finding their way to western Europe as part of the spoils of war. Eventually, it was French, German and British entrepreneurs that revived the dying industry in Turkey and Persia. Persian carpets won high acclaim at the Vienna World's Fair in 1873 and subsequently European traders established emporia in Tabriz, Sultanabad and other cities, for the export of rugs and carpets to the West. From Kirman came the so-called American patterns, designed specifically for the United States market in the late nineteenth century.

Associated with this subject are khilims (often referred to as kelims), a kind of rug produced in Turkey and Persia without any pile. The pattern is identical on both sides, hence the term 'double-faced' which is often used to describe them. The majority of khilims were produced as prayer rugs, and may be identified by the presence of the *mihrab*, the curved and pointed arch which is a characteristic feature of mosque architecture.

Hooked rugs, otherwise known as rag rugs, were a popular domestic pastime in many parts of Europe and America, and the practice survives in some areas to this day.

They were made by hooking lengths of wool (thrums) or strips of rag through a canvas backing. Traditional motifs varied from district to district, but the more ambitious examples bore biblical scenes and pious inscriptions. These small rugs, usually intended for hearth or bedside, form a somewhat neglected aspect of folk art.

Although rugs and carpets are known to have been woven in Europe from the tenth century, they were produced in Spain during the Moorish period and are thus virtually indistinguishable from the carpets made in the Near East at that time. The earliest distinctive carpets were produced in France at the beginning of the seventeenth century, the necessary equipment having been installed in the Louvre under the personal supervision of King Henri IV though subsequently moved to La Savonnerie. The Gobelins factory was established in 1607 and taken under state control in 1662, combined with the original royal carpet manufacturing to form the *Manufacture Royale des Meubles de la Couronne* five years later. The premises at La Savonnerie closed in 1825 and the looms and personnel were absorbed into the Gobelins factory.

Rivals to the factory at La Savonnerie were established at Aubusson and Beauvais in the second half of the eighteenth century, concentrating on tapestry-woven carpets on high-warp looms. The Beauvais factory ceased production in 1819 following its amalgamation with La Savonnerie but Aubusson continued to manufacture carpets in the manner of the khilims of the Near East, reaching the height of their popularity in the early nineteenth century. Knotted and tapestry carpets were also produced at Felletin in the late eighteenth century, based on the styles of Aubusson and Gobelins.

English carpets with hand-knotted pile were produced at Kidderminster from 1749, though excellent knotted carpets were subsequently made by Thomas Moore (Moorfields) and Thomas Whitty (Axminster). Ingrain carpets without pile and woven like tapestry were produced at Wilton from the end of the seventeenth century. Moquette carpets, woven on narrow looms like velvet, originated in Belgium in the sixteenth century and were extensively manufactured in Antwerp, Brussels and Tournai. Carpets of this type were subsequently produced in Bradford, Kidderminster, Norwich and Wilton. Eighteenth-century European carpets were relatively expensive to produce and are of the greatest rarity today.

RUMMERS

Large wine glasses, otherwise known as *Römer* or *roemer*, originating in the Rhineland and the Netherlands in the fifteenth century. The earliest examples were fashioned in dark, coloured *Waldglas*, usually green, but occasionally amber or brown. These vessels had distinctive deep, cup-shaped or ovoid bowls mounted on high thick stems and heavy bases. The stems were elaborately decorated with prunts and the bowls often finely engraved. A leading exponent of this work was the Dutch artist, Anna Roemers Visscher (1585–1681). This type of wine glass became the standard form in the Low Countries and northern Germany and survived into the late eighteenth century, before being superseded by smaller and lighter glasses. *Roemers* were introduced to England in the

reign of William of Orange and were produced by George Ravenscroft in lead glass. Examples in the more traditional soda-glass have also survived from this period but are comparatively rare. The name changed to rummer in the eighteenth century, and the form likewise changed. By 1760 the large ovoid bowl was set on a relatively short plain stem with a thick, circular foot. The distinctive bucket bowl was popular about 1800, and rummers of the early nineteenth century were often elaborately engraved. Knopped stems and square feet were also popular in this later period. Round, funnel-shaped, ogee and double-ogee bowls were used successively in the first half of the nineteenth century, but rummers became unfashionable after 1850. The shape has been revived in recent years for commemorative engraved drinking glasses produced in limited editions.

See also *Firing Glasses*

SALTS AND PEPPERS

Salers or salts were originally made in medieval times, often in the form of elaborate table centrepieces as befitted a commodity which was relatively scarce and highly prized. The standing salt was regarded as the principal article of tableware and was placed before the master of the household (hence the alternative name of master salt). Other salts were positioned strategically on the board, and the expression 'below the salt' indicated a person of inferior social standing whose position at table was beyond the salt. Inevitably medieval salts are of great rarity and represent some of the finest examples of the gold- or silversmiths' art. As salt became cheaper and more plentiful the containers in everyday use became more functional, and pewter was often substituted for gold. Pewter salts of the sixteenth and seventeenth centuries were sometimes known as chapnets or chopnuts. They were made in much smaller dimensions and consisted of shallow, open pots, usually with a cup depression in the middle and fluted, circular or octagonal bases. A few examples are known with high-domed lids. Bell and bobbin shapes were also fashionable in the seventeenth century. Trencher salts were larger, bowl-shaped containers and were made in glass from the late seventeenth century onwards. This material was especially popular in America during the Colonial period, and some fine examples have been recorded in pressed lacy glass in the period from 1830 to 1870.

Salt-cellars were elaborate silver, silver-gilt, gold or Sheffield-plate containers which came into fashion in the eighteenth century, ranging from small, relatively plain bowls to extravagantly decorated footed cauldron shapes replete with rococo ornament. Examples from the 1780s onward were usually fitted with a glass liner. Small salts in dark blue glass were mounted in circular silver mounts, usually decorated with piercing and fretting to provide an attractive contrast to the glass. They were made in sets, and provided with matching stands and tiny salt-spoons.

The earliest pepper pots were produced in

Right Silver-gilt mounted nautilus shell in the form of a gamecock used as a salt; English, *c.* 1580.

235

the sixteenth century in the form of tiny perforated balls attached to the large bell-shaped salts of that period. From the mid-seventeenth century, however, they were manufactured in the familiar caster shape in a wide range of materials, from precious metals to pewter, glass, pottery or porcelain. By 1730 they were being produced *en suite* with small table salts and this practice has continued to the present day. From the late nineteenth century onwards salts and peppers in an infinite range of novelty shapes have been produced all over the world, often as tourist mementoes.

SALVERS

Small trays or plates, generally of silver, Sheffield plate or electroplate, used for serving food or drink. The earliest salvers date from the mid-seventeenth century and were usually circular, with a squat, fluted stem and a circular trumpet foot. Later examples were fitted with three or four ball feet. By the middle of the eighteenth centu[ry] oval and polygonal forms had becor[ne] fashionable. The early plain rims were super[r]seded by elaborate cast, pierced, chased hammered ornament, the centres often bei[ng] engraved with coats of arms. From the ea[rly] nineteenth century, however, more decor[a]tive examples became fashionable, and t[he] centres were frequently decorated in an ove[r] all pattern or engraved with pastoral hunting scenes. Rims also became mo[re] prominent and a raised gallery with frett[ed] decoration became fashionable. Salvers we[re] produced in Sheffield plate from about 17[ ] and in electroplate from 1840 onwar[ds] Silver salvers were a popular form presentation piece and numerous examp[les] have survived from the mid-nineteer[th] century with testimonial inscriptions [en]graved on them.

SAMPLERS

Pieces of linen with embroidered desig[ns] produced widely in both Europe and Amer[ica] from the early seventeenth century. Earl[y] samplers are very rare since the practice w[as] confined to ladies of the upper classes, and t[he] passage of time has taken its toll of su[ch] fragile materials. By the mid-seventeen[th] century sampler-working was descendi[ng] the social scale, though still fairly restricte[d] Samplers consisted of two types, instru[c]tional and ornamental. The former we[re] worked by girls learning needlework a[nd] exhibit a wide range of stitches in pract[ice] rows, the letters of the alphabet and t[he] numerals in cross-stitch, and usually the na[me] of the youthful seamstress and the date [on] which the sampler was completed. [An] examination of the stitching on such sampl[es] shows that they were worked over a lengt[hy] period, often of years, and many examp[les] may be found in an incomplete sta[te] Ornamental samplers, with quite ambitio[us] pictures of well-known landmarks or scene[s] or with composite motifs, are rare up to t[he] end of the eighteenth century, since on[ly] ladies of the wealthier classes had the time [to] devote to this pastime. After 1800, howev[er]

Whitman sampler; American, 1805.

236

ornamental samplers become more commonplace, reflecting the growing amount of
leisure time available to the new middle
classes. The craze reached its height in the
period from 1830 to 1870, and was stimulated
by the publication of elaborate sampler
patterns in Germany, Britain and the United
States.
See also *Berlin Woolwork*

SAUCEBOATS

Otherwise known as gravy boats, these boat-
shaped containers for sauces were originally
made of pewter or silver in the late seventeenth century, and in Sheffield plate from
about 1750. Earthenware, stoneware and
porcelain were used for sauceboats from
1720 onwards and the majority of nineteenth-
and twentieth-century examples are found
in various ceramic materials. The earliest
sauceboats had elliptical bodies terminating
in spouts at both ends and an arched handle
across the middle. The modern form, with a
spout or pouring lip at one end and a handle
at the other, dates from the 1720s. Sauceboats
were made with matching saucers or dishes,
and may also be found with knopped lids
having an aperture cut at the spout end to
accommodate a sauce-spoon or ladle. At the
same time the foot-rim was raised and in a
few cases takes the form of a short pedestal.
Three or four feet on an ornamental base
were also fashionable from the mid-
eighteenth century. Various devices are
known from the late eighteenth century
incorporating hot-water containers placed
under or around the sauceboat to prevent the
contents from congealing. An elaborate
metal gravy warmer of this period is known
as an argyle, allegedly after the fourth Duke
of Argyll, who is credited with its invention.

SCALES. See *Balances and Scales*

SCENT BOTTLES

Small glass bottles for containing perfumes
were being produced by the Venetians from
the thirteenth century. The glass simulated
semi-precious stones, such as aventurine or
chalcedony, but very few examples have
survived. Scent bottles were part of the
repertoire of glass manufacturers in Bohemia,
Silesia, France and England in the sixteenth
and seventeenth centuries, but it was only in
the eighteenth century that the scent bottle
was elevated to the status of an object of
vertu. During this period there developed a
close liaison between perfumiers and such
fashionable craftsmen as jewelers and goldsmiths in the production of vessels worthy of
the precious liquid.

Many different materials have been used
in the production of scent bottles, but glass is
perhaps the most common. The glassblowers
of Murano produced their finest scent bottles
in coloured glass with *millefiori* or *latticinio*
decoration in the seventeenth century. The
Germans specialized in the use of *milchglas*,
an opaque-white glass which was frequently
decorated with flowers or figures in coloured
enamels and gilding. Italian glassworkers
took their art to France in the seventeenth
century and produced beautiful scent bottles
in coloured or opaline glass, often formed
into fancy shapes. Although the great glass
factory of Baccarat is best known for its
paperweights (q.v.), it should be remembered
that it produced many exquisite scent bottles
with heavy bases incorporating *millefiori*
patterns.

In England the manufacture of glass scent
bottles is usually associated with Bristol,
whose merchants, by securing a monopoly
of cobalt oxide exported from Silesia, gave
the town the lead in the production of
brilliant blue Bristol glass (q.v.). The Bristol
glass-makers also produced scent bottles in
emerald, amethyst and opaque-white glass in
the latter part of the eighteenth century. The
scent bottles in clear glass were often
exquisitely cut and engraved. Those in
opaque glass were usually decorated with
enamel painting and embellished with gold
or silver mounts.

Clear glass scent bottles can be dated to
some extent by the style of cutting. Prior to
about 1790 the glass was suitable only for
cutting in shallow relief, but after that date,

237

especially in the Regency period, deep cutting was immensely popular. Glass-paste cameos (q.v.) were set within the fabric of scent bottles, and set off by deeply cut faceting. This process, invented by Apsley Pellatt, was fashionable in the mid-nineteenth century. Where gold or silver mounts were used it may be possible to date scent bottles from their hallmarks, but many of them were unmarked if the mount was below a certain weight.

From the middle of the eighteenth century onwards porcelain was increasingly used in the manufacture of scent bottles. Among the stock sold by the Chelsea factory in 1754 was listed 'Smelling Bottles'. These elegant toys were modelled as humans or animals whose heads opened to reveal the stopper. In the later examples stoppers were often disguised as flowers, perched birds or bunches of fruit. The earliest Chelsea scent bottles had a comparatively deep hollow base, this being intended as a container for patches. Derby also produced a large number of early scent bottles, but very few emanated from Bow or Worcester at this time. Wedgwood produced many attractive scent bottles in his distinctive jasperware, decorated with tiny cameo portraits or classical figures.

Enamel scent bottles undoubtedly formed part of the stock in trade of the Battersea factory, but it seems certain that the majority of those in existence came from Bilston or Wednesbury. The Bilston enamellers included artists such as Dovey Hawksford and the Homer brothers, while the best of the Wednesbury products were decorated by William Beilby and his sister Margaret, whose work is now very highly regarded. The decoration on Staffordshire enamel scent bottles is fairly uniform in character, being copied from contemporary porcelain. Portrait miniatures in enamel are occasionally found but, in general, landscapes and flowers predominate.

Among more modern scent bottles it should be noted that the leading French perfumiers commissioned Gallé, Lalique and Daum Frères to produce bottles which are now highly collectable. The majority of them

date from the late nineteenth century up World War II and exhibit all the contem porary styles and techniques in glass man facture, including pressed and mould glass, acid-etched and engraved cameo gla plated fancy glass and lustre effects.

SCIENTIFIC INSTRUMENTS

In the sixteenth and seventeenth centuri mathematicians and astronomers were oft attached to a royal household and we accustomed to use instruments befitting th high office. Craftsmen of the first ra lavished a great deal of skill in the producti of scientific instruments and it was not u common for these to be made of silver gilt-metal, elaborately chased and engrave The elaborate ornament on early math matical and scientific instruments is deceptiv What may appear to the layman as attracti though useless decoration may, in fact, fu a particular function. The mysterious curv on a medieval astrolabe, for example, we actually devices for calculating the altitude sun and stars, from which time and latitu could be deduced. A study of the traditio ornament on such instruments can oft provide an insight into the development scientific knowledge in different parts of t world in different eras.

Drawing instruments form the larg group of scientific instruments, ranging value from nineteenth-century cased sets the more elaborate types of the seventeen and eighteenth centuries. Of all the instr ments used by the draughtsman the ruler probably the most important and interestin The graduations engraved on rulers and t units of measure employed usually enal the expert to date a ruler and assign it to correct locality, even if the maker's name its historical provenance are unknown. Wh it is considered that the metric syste devised in 1804, has yet to be adopted in so highly sophisticated countries, it is easy imagine the bewildering variety of weigl and measures which were current in Euro in the eighteenth century. Apart from t simple rules, parallel rules, consisting of tv

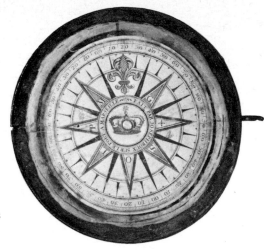

Charles Boyle, Earl of Orrery, for whom the first planetarium was constructed). Telescopes date from the beginning of the seventeenth century, when Galileo conducted his famous experiments in optics. By the middle of the century telescopes were widely produced, notably in France, the Netherlands and England. The earliest examples have cardboard tubes covered with leather, but wooden tubes were prevalent in the late seventeenth century, and brass from the early eighteenth century onwards.

arms joined by pivoted connection bars, were popular in Germany from the mid-sixteenth century onward. Others made in two or more pieces and hinged in the middle or at equal intervals seem to have originated in France, where they were known as *pieds de roy*, since they usually made up one foot when extended. A more elaborate development of the joint-rule was hinged in such a manner that it formed a right angle when opened out, thus making a set-square.

In 1606 Galileo developed this idea further, and invented the sector, which he described as 'a geometric and military compass'. From the early seventeenth century date elaborate compendia containing a range of drawing instruments, hexagonal pillars engraved with calendars, lunar volvelle, miniature computer, sundial (q.v.), magnetic compasses and other paraphernalia indispensable to the mathematician, astronomer, surveyor or military engineer of the period. More elaborate surveying instruments included the theodolite, which originated in the late sixteenth and developed in the seventeenth century; navigational instruments such as the octant, quadrant or sextant, often elaborately constructed of brass, ivory and ebony; and the waywiser, or surveyor's wheel, devised in the seventeenth century for measuring distances. Astronomical instruments include clockwork or hand-driven planetaria and orreries (the latter name being derived from

At the other end of the optical scale, the microscope developed simultaneously. The earliest examples were monocular, though compound lenses were in use in Italy by 1615. The greater complexity of microscopes offered more opportunities to the maker to combine craftsmanship with artistry, and the heavy metal bases were frequently cast in the forms of animals or mythological groups.

The principle of magnetism was known in the Middle Ages, having come to Europe from China, but the modern magnetic compass did not develop until the late sixteenth century. Like pocket sundials (q.v.), with which they were often combined, compasses were produced in brass or silver and were elaborately engraved. Barometers developed in the 1660s, the name having been coined by Robert Boyle in 1663, though the principle of measuring atmospheric pressure with a column of mercury had been proposed by Torricelli twenty years earlier. The earliest barometers had a simple scale mounted alongside the mercury column, but the arrangement of dial and pointer was in use by the end of the seventeenth century. From the mid-eighteenth century onwards many barometers were designed as attractive pieces of furniture and may be regarded among the finest examples of the cabinet-maker's art.

Dental, surgical and pharmaceutical instruments are now avidly collected, mainly by members of these professions. Whatever their aesthetic shortcomings, these relics of a more primitive and brutal approach to medicine compensate in human interest.
See also *Optical Instruments*

SCRAPS

Decalcomania, or the craze for collecting scraps of paper and ephemera (q.v.), dates from the early nineteenth century when it became fashionable for young ladies to keep albums into which they pasted pictures cut out of magazines and newspapers. Illustrations in periodicals being comparatively rare at that time the decalcomaniac used many other sources. The vignettes from trade cards

(and latterly the cards themselves), trade men's letter and billheads, decorative not paper and Valentines (q.v.) provided the ra material for these early scraps. After t advent of envelopes in the 1840s and t fashion for embossed crests and monogra on the flap (a relic of the wax seals of earl generations), these embellishments were lik wise cut out and pasted into scrapbooks. Tl gave rise to a minor industry in the seco half of the nineteenth century. Stamp deal and stationers published sets of crests a even produced special albums for them.

At the same time printers began to pand to the craze for small pictures. It was longer necessary to cut them out of magazin for lithographers and die-stampers produc sheets of coloured pictures ready cut, usi rouletting or die-struck processes, and by t end of the century these scraps were provid with mucilage on the back so that no paste gum was required. With the rise of t printed scrap the hobby of decalcoman declined. By the early 1900s it was no long the elegant pursuit of young ladies but mer a child's pastime. The better examples scrapbook, with their scraps tastefully a thematically presented, belong to the peri from 1840 to 1890 when it was still an ad hobby. The earlier scraps themselves h artistic and literary pretensions, whereas t majority of the post-1900 scraps w distinctly juvenile in appeal. Scraps of t late nineteenth century were published sheets arranged according to subjects, su as flowers, wild animals, birds, and there w usually a strong didactic element in the Their very cheapness (often as low as a pen a sheet) led to their downfall as a serio subject for collecting. Nevertheless, th have continued to be popular with you children (especially girls) to the present d and are produced all over the world with infinite range of subjects. Individual scra were also widely used as decoration Christmas crackers, Easter eggs and simi seasonal novelties, and in more recent ye have vied with trade cards as giveaways packages of confectionery and foodstuffs.
See colour plate page 245

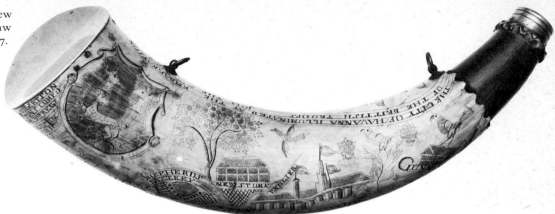

owder horn with view
f Havana in scrimshaw
vork; American, 1767.

SCRIMSHAW

Form of folk art peculiar to the United States
and developed originally by the whalers and
sealers of New England on their long sea
voyages from the North Atlantic to the South
Pacific. Otherwise known as scrim-shouting
or skrim-shander, this art consisted of engraving or carving on whalebone, whale's teeth,
walrus or narwhal tusks. The only tools
required were knives and marlin spikes, and
with these primitive implements the seamen
produced elaborate and often beautiful
works. Scrimshaw was essentially two-
dimensional. Although low relief is occasionally found, the pattern or images were
usually created on a fairly flat surface by
engraving, etching or incising the material.
Ships and whaling scenes were the most
popular subjects, but intricate examples of
scenery and portraiture have also been
recorded. Scrimshaw was often applied to
whalebone stay-busks, intended as love
tokens (q.v.) and in many such cases the
subjects were of a more sentimental nature.
Small domestic articles of whalebone or
whale teeth, such as napkin rings and the ends
of rolling-pins (qq.v.) were decorated with
scrimshaw work.

The art of engraving on bone spread
inland and became popular in the frontier
lands of the Middle and Far West. Animal
horns, often made into powder flasks (q.v.),
were frequently decorated with hunting and
pastoral scenes, views of such landmarks as

the early forts and frontier posts, or portraits
of heroes of the old Wild West. This form of
'inland' scrimshaw work reached its apogee
in the late nineteenth century. Patriotic
motifs from the Civil War and the Spanish-
American War, presidential portraits and
references to the Centennial and Columbian
Expositions are among the topical and more
desirable examples of this later scrimshaw
work.

SEALED GLASSWARE

Glass, usually bottles but also including jugs,
mugs and tankards, with a circular or oval
cartouche in moulded or pressed glass on the
side of the vessel. These glass seals bore
initials and sometimes dates or coats of arms
and served to identify the owners. This
practice developed in England in the middle
of the seventeenth century. The earliest dated
seal was made for John Jefferson and is
marked with his initials and the date 1652.
Sir Kenelm Digby, however, is said to have
invented these glass seals some twenty years
earlier when glass bottles first began to
replace the leather jacks and costrels previously used. Undated seals have been
confidently attributed to gentlemen who are
known to have died prior to 1652, and
examples of this type have been excavated in
sites ranging from London to Williamsburg
and Jamestown (Virginia), indicating their
widespread usage. The earliest seals seem to
have been made either for private individuals

or for inns and taverns, though examples have been recorded with the arms of trade guilds and the colleges of Oxford and Cambridge. Initials usually refer to a man or a married couple, three-letter combinations indicating the latter. Occasionally initials refer not to the owners but the contents, especially mineral waters of English or European manufacture in the eighteenth century. Sealed bottles were used in France for both wine and olive oil and continued to bear the initials of the growers until the late nineteenth century. Other seals bore royal ciphers and such devices as a broad arrow, a crown or an anchor, indicating bottles provided for the public services or armed forces. Examples with GR, WR and VR monograms (for George III or IV, William IV

Green glass bottle bearing the seal of William Savery; American, 1752.

and Victoria) have been found as far afield as Canada and Australia.

The practice of impressing seals on glassware declined in the nineteenth century, but has been revived in recent years by certain manufacturers or bottlers of wines and spirits and these modern seals bear the firms' trademarks. Commemorative glassware, with decorative seals featuring symbols alluding to the event or person thus honoured, has been revived in Britain and the United States since 1970.

SEALS AND FOBS

Small engraved stamps for making impressions on sealing-wax, or with ink on paper, date back over 3,000 years, and examples of them, cut in gem-stones or metal such as gold, silver or bronze, are known to have been used in China, Assyria and Egypt. The practice of making an impression from a seal with ink is peculiarly Oriental and such 'chops', as they are termed, are used in China and Japan to this day. They were often carved in bone, ivory or hardwood and the device and characters appear in colourless silhouette against a solid background.

European seals prior to the seventeenth century are of considerable rarity. They range from the small personal seals and signet rings used for sealing letter sheets and wrappers to the very large and ornately engraved seals of state, bearing enthroned or equestrian portraits of the reigning sovereign or the national coat of arms. State seals were always carefully guarded and often defaced or broken up at the end of the reign, and thus examples of the actual matrices are rare, though impressions are more plentiful.

The majority of collectable seals date from the beginning of the eighteenth century, when the practice of wearing jeweled fobs became fashionable. Seals were mounted on gold bases and attached to fobs or chatelaines (q.v.), jeweled and enamelled to match other dress accessories. Jade or other hardstones, glass, brass or steel were used for the matrix of seals. Gentlemen's personal seals became increasingly ornate at the beginning of the

right Combined scent bottle and seal in English porcelain, 1753–54; and al in the form of a shepherd with a lamb in Chelsea-Derby porcelain, 1775–80.

far right Serinette with marquetry casing and ormolu mounts; French, 1765.

when not in use. Such interchangeable seals had fancy designs, mottoes like 'Forget me not' or 'Thank Rowland Hill for this' – the latter being an allusion to the man who instigated cheap postage in the 1840s. Late nineteenth-century seals often had novelty shapes for the handles – horses' hooves and ladies' befrilled legs being especially popular. See colour plate page 246

nineteenth century, as the principal object of personal adornment. Such fob-seals went out of fashion in the 1830s and larger, heavier desk seals were used instead. When seals were no longer worn their mounts became more ornamental and handles were fitted to them. These range from tiny, slim shafts of mother-of-pearl or ivory to massive bronze or iron pieces, cast in the form of statuettes or animal heads, and richly gilded. Some desk seals of the mid-nineteenth century had glass handles, incorporating *millefiori* or *latticinio* decoration. Porcelain handles enjoyed a brief vogue on desk seals of the late eighteenth century.

Small seals were often made in sets which could be screwed into a standard shaft. These sets were mounted on a circular base of steel

SERINETTES

Miniature barrel organs used from the seventeenth century onwards for teaching birds to sing. The name is derived from the French word *serin* (canary). The mechanism consisted of one or more rows of organ pipes in a bank above a pair of bellows; the sound was produced by cranking a handle which rotated a pinned cylinder against the ends of the pipes and which also worked the bellows. Being much smaller and less complex than the standard barrel-organs and hurdy-gurdies of the period, serinettes did not produce tunes in any recognizable sense but imitated bird notes.

243

SERVING IMPLEMENTS

Individual knives, forks and spoons were produced in silver, Sheffield plate or electroplate for the purpose of serving different kinds of food. The majority of these implements date from the early eighteenth century and may be found with contemporary styles of engraving on blades and bowls, or cast ornament and finials on both hafts and handles.

Large serving spoons with ovoid bowls and plain stems became fashionable about 1690. The bowls were often engraved with coats of arms. By 1730 large serving spoons were produced in styles matching the other pieces in a cutlery service. Individual ladles ranged from small examples with fluted bowls, for sauces and gravy, to long-handled, deep-bowled varieties with ornamental rims, used for serving punch and toddy. In between were soup ladles and tureen spoons of various sizes and shapes. Large spoons were known in England as basting spoons, but in Ireland and Scotland as hash spoons, and the latter term was also adopted in Colonial American usage.

Broad-bladed serving implements were used for cutting and serving cakes and sweetmeats. Large, broad knives with scimitar blades were used extensively from the mid-eighteenth century as fish servers; later examples were known as fish slices and had elongated trowel blades. Scoops with long handles and deep, elongated bowls were used in the cutting of cheese. Examples from the early nineteenth century often incorporated a device for removing the cheese from the scoop. Smaller and slimmer scoops, often double-ended, were used for extricating the marrow from bones. Pickle forks, with trident tines and ornamental handles, were fashionable from the early nineteenth century onwards.

Salad servers, in wood, bone, ivory, silver or stainless steel, were produced in matched pairs of spoon and fork, the latter generally provided with some sort of rudimentary prongs.

See also *Cutlery*

SHAGREEN

Type of leather made from the untann skin of the shark and similar large fish usually polished and dyed black or gre Shagreen was widely used in the manufa ture of small cases for objects of ver medallions, watches, snuff boxes, étuis a similar articles in the eighteenth and nir teenth centuries.

SHAVING DISHES AND MUGS

The barber's bowl is a late-medieval relic the days when barbers were also surgeo Circular dishes or shallow bowls, with small semi-circular piece cut out of the r on one side, were used by barber-surgeo in blood-letting. They were made in ma parts of Europe in pewter, silver or brass, well as delftware, earthenware, stoneware porcelain in the late seventeenth and eig teenth centuries. They were latterly ma *en suite* with jug and soap dishes, oft decorated with coats of arms or the emble of the barber's profession.

From the barber's shaving basin and bo evolved a much smaller and neater uter resembling a mug with two bowls, smaller one set within or jutting out of t larger bowl. The smaller bowl contained t soap or shaving brush while the larger o held the shaving water. Such mugs w

produced in Britain from the early eighteenth century when beards became unfashionable, and they continued to appear sporadically throughout the nineteenth century. These mugs were produced in stoneware or earthenware, often elaborately decorated and even fashioned in human form, emulating the contemporary Toby jugs (q.v.). Shaving mugs in silver or electroplate were fashionable in the mid-nineteenth century. The Utility shaving cup, patented about 1850 and manufactured in Boston, Mass., incorporated a razor holder, brush compartment, hot-water bowl and a sliding drawer underneath for the soap. Numerous other patent devices were produced, mainly in the United States from 1860 to 1930, with such names as the Champion, the Toilet, or the Requisite.

In the 1870s a vogue was established in the United States for barber shop individual shaving mugs, each customer having his own distinctive mug which was kept in a special rack in the shop, and a specialized branch of the American ceramics industry was created to cater for the demand. The more important manufacturers of these pottery or porcelain mugs included the Koken Barbers' Supply Company of St Louis, Kraut & Dohnal of Chicago, Herold Brothers of Cleveland and the Boston Barbers' Supply Company. These mugs were produced in an infinite variety of designs, embellished with owners' names or signatures, with vignettes representing trades and professions, floral, bird or nautical patterns or plain numerals gilded on a white ground. Self-shaving, brushless creams and the electric razor led to the decline of these barber-shop mugs in the decade after World War I.

SHEFFIELD PLATE

Process of coating articles of copper with silver by means of fusion, named after the English town where Thomas Boulsover first manufactured it *c.* 1742. It is said that Boulsover discovered the process accidentally when a silver sixpence was fused to the copper haft of a knife which he was repairing.

The two metals were fused by the action of heat and Boulsover found that the resulting metal could be treated as a single entity when subjected to hammering. As a result of experiments Boulsover began producing small copper boxes and buttons with a thin silver sheet fused to their surface. Articles in Sheffield plate resembled the much more expensive objects in solid silver at a fraction of their cost. Joseph Hancock, who served his apprenticeship with a relation of the inventor, was quick to appreciate the commercial possibilities of the process and was the first manufacturer to apply Sheffield plate to larger articles such as candlesticks, hollow-ware and tablewares.

The nascent industry was revolutionized about 1760 when Henry Tudor formed a partnership with the London silversmith, Thomas Leader. Subsequently Tudor and Leader produced a wide range of articles which equalled anything produced in silver at that period and raised the artistic and technical standards of Sheffield plate to a new level. Leader established a factory in Sheffield itself, to rival Hancock and Boulsover, and soon evolved new and highly distinctive styles of decoration, employing artists such as John Flaxman and the Adam brothers to design dishes, candelabra, salvers, tureens and other useful and decorative wares hitherto made in silver. Furthermore the makers of Sheffield plate began marking their wares in such a way that they were easily mistaken for silver assay marks. This practice was stopped in 1773 when the London silversmiths obtained an injunction restraining the Sheffield manufacturers. Eleven years later, however, the Sheffield plate makers succeeded in overturning this court ruling, but only on condition that henceforward they had to put the maker's name on the piece, together with a device which could readily be distinguished from the silver hallmarks.

By the end of the eighteenth century fused silver plate of this type was being manufactured not only in Sheffield but also in Birmingham, Matthew Boulton's Soho works being prominent in this field. Though Sheffield plate was largely confined to

Inkstand and argyles in
Sheffield plate, 1790.

Sheffield and Birmingham in England it was
also widely manufactured in other parts of
Europe in the early nineteenth century,
principally in Russia, France, Germany and
Austria, but this Continental fused plate was
generally inferior to the English wares in
quality and craftsmanship. The advent of
electroplate (q.v.) in 1840 rapidly ousted
Sheffield plate; by 1865 it was no longer
manufactured except for fused-plate silver
buttons.

SHELLWORK

Interest in sea-shells as decorative items arose
in the late seventeenth century with the
exploration of the Pacific and Indian Oceans
and the growing expansion of European
trade. Merchants and traders imported vast
quantities of exotic shells into western
Europe and shell-collecting became a serious
hobby in France by the 1690s. By the early
eighteenth century large shells were frequently mounted in gold or silver and the natural
shapes of shells were widely used in nefs (q.v.)
and nautilus beakers. Shells exerted an
enormous influence on the rococo movement
and in the craze for grotesquerie (q.v.).
Small shells were arranged in patterns and
glued to the surfaces of boxes and vases, but
few authentic examples of this type of
decoration can be dated before 1800. In the

nineteenth century shellwork became a ve
popular pastime in Europe and Americ
Only latterly, when out-workers in certa
parts of Europe were organized into
cottage industry, did shellwork become
commercial proposition. The great bulk
nineteenth-century shell-decorated artic
were amateur products, but this does n
imply shoddy workmanship. Shell mosa
were often remarkably intricate, great ca
being taken to match the colours and shad
of shells to achieve the most pleasing
accurate effects. Shells were also used
cover the borders of photographic fram
small West Indian rice shells were ev
applied to napkin rings; and elaborate she
work panels were designed as Valentin
(q.v.).

The most common form of shellwo
occurred as a decorative pattern on the li
and sides of boxes. Glove boxes, trinket box
work boxes and musical boxes were frequen
ly covered with shells. The plain boxes we
sold individually, and the shellwork patter
could be worked at home. Those who we
unable to scour the seashores for their she
could purchase them from craft sho
haberdashers and even street pedlars. She
work declined in popularity towards the e
of the nineteenth century though it has nev
quite died out as a home pastime, and
more recent years shellwork has been reviv

for the tourist trade. Apart from their application to the surfaces of boxes, shells were glued together to form statuettes, flower bouquets and other elaborate confections, many of which were mounted in domed glass cases as mantlepiece ornaments. The most highly prized shellwork objects are those which incorporate an inscription of a commemorative nature, the lettering worked in small shells of contrasting colours.

SHIPS IN BOTTLES

Models of sailing ships mounted inside bottles were produced as a form of nautical 'folk art' by seamen in the period from about 1840 to 1914. A few examples of this type of object have been recorded from the late eighteenth century, including some very fine miniatures carved from bone by French prisoners of war, but the great majority of extant examples belong to the second half of the nineteenth century. Bottles of every size and shape have been used, but the type most favoured was a bottle with a globular or oblong body and a relatively slender neck.

The tricky part consisted of laying the base for the sea and the shore, modelled in plaster of Paris and painting this as well as the inside back and foot of the bottle to simulate the horizon, sky and coastline. The ship was carved and built up quite independently and the masts and rigging folded ingeniously to permit insertion through the neck of the bottle. Once the ship was glued into position, fine draw-lines were used to pull the masts erect and unfold sails and rigging. This art was widely practised by sailors during the long and monotonous voyages in the days of sail. The advent of steam radically changed the seamen's way of life and left less time for modelling and other pastimes such as scrimshaw (q.v.).

SHOE HORNS

Implements for easing the foot into boots and shoes, recorded in Europe from the late Middle Ages onwards. The earliest examples were made of sections of cow horn, curved to fit the back of the ankle and generally flattened at the end to facilitate the insertion of the heel. By the seventeenth century, however, metal shoe horns, in brass or pewter, formed a more robust and reliable substitute, and by the mid–eighteenth century elaborate examples mounted in ivory, silver or polished hardwood were becoming fashionable. The handles were frequently carved and inlaid, compensating for the purely functional nature of the horn itself. Novelty horns, with handles of brass cast in animal or human form, were popular in the late nineteenth century. Like button hooks (q.v.) shoe horns were frequently given away by cobblers and shoemakers and may be found with the names, addresses and advertisements of manufacturers and retailers, particularly in the period from 1880 to 1920.

SILHOUETTES

Otherwise known as profiles or shades, these portraits date from the seventeenth century, although they attained their greatest popularity in the late eighteenth century. Their

Illustration for 'Noon'
from Karl Frölich's
*Frolicks with scissars and
pen*, 1860.

common name was derived from Etienne de Silhouette, who was not only an enthusiastic exponent of this art, but a finance minister to Louis XV with an unenviable reputation for economic stringency. There was therefore an element of conscious irony in applying the name 'silhouette' to these cut-paper portraits, though the older name of 'shades' survived in Britain well into the nineteenth century.

The older and more accurate name – shades – came from the process by which the shadow of the sitter was thrown by candlelight on to a sheet of oiled paper and the outline drawn in pencil. This outline was then transferred to black paper which could either be cut out, or applied to white paper which was then shaded with black ink. Silhouettes of British or American origin were either cut from black paper and mounted on white board, or painted in black ink on white card, with little ornament applied to the profile. Continental silhouettes, however, adopted a more subtle approach, using gold or silver metallic inks to achieve highlights and attain a three-dimensional result. French silhouettes were often touched up with inks of different colours.

Various mechanical techniques were employed to secure an accurate likeness, from the special chair and frame devised by Lavater and Goethe, to the camera obscura

Right Silhouette of
Mrs John Probyn by
Auguste Edouart
(1789–1861).

and the pantograph. The last-named, adopted early in the nineteenth century, gave to the silhouette an almost photographic quality at the expense of artistic standards. The majority of silhouettes are unsigned, but some bear the advertisement of the profilist on the back of the frame. Silhouettes by the leading profilists are in great demand and include the work of Auguste Edouart (who also published a noteworthy treatise on the subject in 1835 and introduced the term 'silhouette' to the English language). Edouart and Sarah Harrington specialized in cut-paper silhouettes, John Miers and A. Charles were prolific silhouettists in pen and ink, while Francis Torond was versatile in both media. The art spread to the United States in the late eighteenth century and enjoyed enormous popularity before the advent of photography (q.v.), William King and Charles Polk being the leading exponents. Edouart himself worked in America for a decade (1839–49) and cut profiles of Presidents Tyler, Polk and Taylor, the poet Longfellow and many other personalities of that period.

Silhouettes were reproduced in other media. A French speciality involved painting silhouettes on the reverse side of glass in a style reminiscent of *verre églomisé*, but black profiles on white plaster plaques may also be encountered. Silhouettes of celebrities were sometimes used to decorate commemorative pottery and porcelain, a notable example being the Jubilee mugs in honour of King George III in 1809. Silhouette figure groups in black on a white ground may also be found on dinner services and tablewares of the early nineteenth century. Like the portrait miniature (q.v.) the silhouette went into decline as a portrait medium about 1850, but as a decorative art (especially in cut paper) it has survived fitfully and enjoyed periodic revivals in Germany and elsewhere.

SILVER

A brilliant white metal, resistant to oxidation and widely used from earliest times in both useful and decorative forms, in utensils, as mounting for glass and pottery vessels and containers, in the shape of buckles and buttons (qq.v.) and especially in jewelry and costume accessories (qq.v.). Like gold, silver is too soft on its own and is therefore alloyed with other metals, mainly copper, to produce a durable substance. Silver alloyed to gold formed electrum or white gold, the earliest of precious metals used for coinage from the seventh century BC in Asia Minor and Greece. Silver has been used by both civilized and primitive races for religious figures, jewelry and coinage, and in these forms has been recorded from Scandinavia to South-East Asia. Early examples of silverware from Europe are comparatively rare and its ready convertibility in times of economic or political upheaval means that the bulk of silver belonging to earlier periods in many countries, such as Britain, France and Germany, has been melted down for use as coinage and subsequently recalled and melted down for industrial use. Industrial requirements, for plating and photography, now account for the bulk of the world's production; jewelry and the applied arts account for a relatively small proportion.

Silver has been widely used in Asia in conjunction with other metals, such as copper or brass, in filigree or inlay work and in damascening to create a 'watered silk' effect. High-grade silver was mined in central Europe from the tenth century and in parts of the British Isles (notably North Wales and southern Scotland) from the fifteenth century. Silver became increasingly fashionable in the seventeenth century for domestic plate as a more expensive medium than pewter (q.v.). Silver was occasionally gilded to simulate solid gold, and produced a more pleasing result than gold itself. The standard of fineness (or degree of precious metal content) was jealously guarded by the guilds of silversmiths in most European countries. In England, for example, the Goldsmiths' Company could trace their origins back to Anglo-Saxon times and had established the Sterling standard by the end of the thirteenth century. This standard, of 925 parts of silver to 1,000 parts of metal, was guaranteed by the impression of a Sterling mark showing a lion

Norwich silver wine cup;
English, c. 1600.

date or place of manufacture. Hallmarking was widely employed in Europe from the fourteenth century though never as rigidly as in England; the numerous different systems used by even the larger and better organized countries (such as Spain and France) make the attribution and dating of Continental silver a complex subject. On the eve of the French Revolution, for example, almost 200 towns had assay offices applying their own distinctive marks and, in addition, charge and discharge marks applied by the tax farmer.

English silver dating before the Restoration of the monarchy in 1660 is scarce, much of the plate belonging to the preceding period having been melted down or cut up for coinage during the Civil Wars of 1642–5. After the Restoration in Britain and the greatly increased level of prosperity there was an inordinate demand for silverware, which was partially met by the illegal melting of coins. To combat this menace the authorities instituted the Britannia Standard in 1697.

passant. This mark was instituted in 1544 and is still used in England and Wales. The Scottish equivalent, a thistle, was instituted in 1759. Additional marks appearing on a piece of silver include the assay mark, denoting the provincial assay office at which the article was tested, the year letter and the silversmith's own personal device or initial. These marks on a piece of silver are often known as hallmarks. The American colonies adapted this system to suit themselves, but never applied it rigidly. Thus American silver may be found with no more than the maker's name or initials and no indication of

(·928 fine). Articles manufactured in this quality of silver were marked with a seated figure of Britannia and a lion profile erased. The Act establishing this standard was repealed in 1719 and the Britannia and lion's head erased marks ceased in 1720. Between 1784 and 1890 silverware bore a fifth mark, a small profile of the reigning monarch (from George III to Victoria). This mark was added to show the payment of a duty on silver. Impressions similar to hallmarks are found on pewter and are known as touchmarks, but their quite different appearance, together with the nature of the metal, should present no problems of identification. More dangerous and misleading are the marks often found on Sheffield plate and electroplate (qq.v.) applied by the manufacturers in the hope of passing off their wares as silver. Legislation at various times, however, either abolished such marks or regulated their appearance. The very severe penalties imposed for forging hallmarks deterred the makers of Sheffield plate from producing identical marks, and often their own marks bear no more than a superficial resemblance to the genuine assay marks. Nevertheless, it is surprising how often the layman is deceived by the presence of 'hallmarks' which, on closer scrutiny, turn out to be the letters EPNS (electroplated nickel silver) in fancy ovals or shields.

In the eighteenth century silver was extensively used in table and ornamental wares. Sheffield plate (from 1750 to 1860) and electroplate (since 1840), together with increased industrial requirements, have greatly lessened its application to larger articles, such as centrepieces, salvers, tureens, dinner services or tea equipages, though it continued to be immensely popular as a medium for decorative wares of all kinds, small boxes, jewelry, photograph frames and objects of vertu.

SILVER, MINIATURE

Miniaturized versions of tableware, hollow-ware and ornaments were made in silver from the sixteenth century onwards. The earliest (and now extremely rare) forms were probably made as presents for royal children. By the early eighteenth century the fashion for elegant display cabinets and 'baby houses' created a specialized branch of silversmithing. English silver toys, invariably in the form of hollow-wares, were produced in the early eighteenth century by such craftsmen as David Clayton, Jonah Clifton, Matthew Madden, Edward Medleycott and George Middleton. The predilection for useful wares seems to indicate that miniature silver pieces were used by silversmiths and their retailers as trade samples which could more easily be transported around the country and would not be so tempting to highwaymen as the real thing.

The finest silver toys, however, came from the continent of Europe, especially the Netherlands where the craftsmen excelled in modelling tiny human and animal figures, mechanical contrivances such as windmills, coaches, artillery and ships. Many of these elegant silver toys pandered to the craze for chinoiseries (q.v.), featuring Chinese mandarins and coolies, pagodas, sampans, dragons and ritual vessels. The Dutch and German silversmiths also turned out vast quantities of tiny chairs, tables, chests and other pieces of furniture, exquisitely modelled in every detail. Candlesticks, buckets, beer-barrels, garden implements and wheelbarrows are

Miniature silver tankard
by Charles Le Roux;
American, c. 1716.

but a few of the utilitarian objects modelled in silver on a small scale, often no more than an inch in height. The earliest cow creamers (q.v.) were of Dutch origin and modelled in silver in the mid-eighteenth century. The majority of nineteenth-century silver miniatures were Dutch, French or German; examples from Britain or the United States are comparatively scarce.

SMOKING EQUIPMENT

Many of the implements and containers connected with tobacco are dealt with under separate headings. Among the miscellaneous collectable items connected with smoking may be mentioned patent cigarette-rolling machines, which became popular in the 1890s and survive to this day in many different forms. Pocket and table lighters date from the mid-nineteenth century and include devices fuelled by oil, kerosene, benzine, petrol, or gasoline, electric batteries and butane gas cartridges. Pocket lighters are invariably constructed in metal, usually steel, though brass, bronze and silver have also been used, and numerous decorative techniques, from engraving to enamelling and inlaying, are involved. Table lighters are

generally much larger and more elabora with mounts in pottery or porcelain, c bronze, carved wood and even opaque m glass, though the lighter element itself follo the usual metal construction. The majority such lighters date from the 1860s wh smoking became more socially acceptable See also *Ashtrays, Cigar and Cigarette Ca Cigar and Tobacco Cutters, Matchboxes, Pip Pipe Stoppers, Qalians, Tobacco Boxes and J Union Cases*

SNUFF BOTTLES

Whereas Europeans, whose clothes h pockets, preferred to keep their snuff in sm flat boxes, the Chinese found it more co venient to use little bottles which were of carried in the folds of their large sleeves. first existing bottles were utilized or adap for the purpose. Some of the earliest sn bottles consist of miniature vases to whic stopper has been added. These little vas standing barely two or three inches in heig may usually be recognized by their bevel lips, whereas proper snuff bottles have a rim in order that the stopper should tightly.

Although various makeshifts of this natu were used at first, it was not long befc craftsmen were beginning to produce sm bottles tailored to the exact requirements the snuff-taker. By 1644 small bottles w tight-fitting stoppers and small spoc attached were being manufactured. T Oriental method of snuff-taking was vo elegant and fastidious by comparison w Western manners. The tiny spoon was us to extract the required grains which w then placed delicately on the nail of the fo finger and conveyed discreetly to the nost

A great deal of care was lavished on manufacture of these bottles and many them were decorated with that astonishing minuscule art in which the Chinese excell No other small antique from the Far E exhibits such a wealth of material and sty of ornament for the collector than the sn bottle. Perhaps the most common mater was glass, used extensively from about 1(

Art Deco table lighter
and cigarette holder by
Ronson, 1930.

stone but are, in fact, glass is to mark them with a crystal point (on the foot-rim or on the lip where it would normally be covered by the stopper). True hardstone cannot be scratched in this way.

Although many of the glass bottles were relatively free of decoration, enamelling or painting was sometimes applied to the surface. Particularly attractive are those bottles which have been painted, with infinite patience, on the inside, the artist working in a confined space with a very fine pen, or a brush of one or two bristles. Even rarer, and now extremely expensive, are those bottles which have been painted on the inside and subsequently lined with a layer of milk glass which provides an attractive contrast to the painting. Apart from painting, several types of enamelling may be found, including repoussé, painted, cloisonné (q.v.) or champlevé, often featuring subjects which are suspiciously Occidental in appearance. French craftsmen, who were recruited by the Manchus in the eighteenth century, were responsible for the techniques and style of decoration in these enamelled bottles.

Not surprisingly, porcelain figured high on the list of materials used in the manufacture of snuff bottles. This could be left in the white but was more usually given some form of applied decoration, the familiar Chinese blue being the most favoured medium. As well as underglaze colours, overglaze enamel and lacquer were used, while incised, pierced or carved porcelain is not uncommon. Amber of various qualities was employed and was carved intricately, painted on the inside or left plain. Metals ranging from iron and brass to silver and gold, sometimes with contrasting inlays of other metals, were used for snuff bottles.

Ivory, either carved or painted, was another popular material, while horn of various kinds was also utilized. A rare variant of this was the ivory-like substance known as *ho-ting*, taken from the crest of the Helmeted Hornbill. This bird is not native to China and quantities of this substance had to be imported from Malaya, hence its comparative rarity. Undoubtedly the best-

onwards. The craftsmen who produced these bottles were pastmasters in the art of glass-blowing and in the creation of subtle shades of glass, both translucent and opaque. They were often able to produce very good imitations of jade and other semi-precious stones, which were reserved for the better class of snuff bottle. Examples of carved cameo glass simulating that most precious of all Chinese hardstones, Imperial jade, have been recorded and the glass has been weighted in some mysterious fashion in order to achieve the right feeling of density. Imperial jade snuff bottles are also known; for almost a century the making of snuff bottles was an Imperial art for which no expense was spared. A sure test for snuff bottles which appear to be hard-

Right Snuff box with
enamel portrait of
Madame de Maintenon;
French, 18th century.

known, though rather expensive, snuff bottles
are those made from jade, agate, tourmaline,
aquamarine, lapis lazuli, beryl, amethyst and
other semi-precious stones.
See colour plate page 263

SNUFF BOXES

The habit of sniffing tobacco in powder form
is as old as smoking. Romano Pane, who
accompanied Columbus on his first voyage
to the New World in 1492, recorded the
strange custom of the Indians who ground a
golden leaf and sniffed the resulting powder.
Snuff-taking was thus established in Europe
by the mid-sixteenth century, though it was
often regarded as a disgusting practice and
Tsar Michael even went as far as decreeing
that persons convicted of snuff-taking should
have their noses cut off for the second offence.

Despite opposition of this sort, snuff increased in popularity and eventually became
acceptable in the best circles, where an
elaborate ritual evolved for taking it. The
art of the miniaturist and the skill of the
jeweler and the goldsmith combined to
produce some of the finest objects of vertu,
and these delightful bibelots reached the
peak of their perfection in the third quarter

Snuff box with
marquetry lid
incorporating a coin of
Queen Anne, *c.* 1710.

of the eighteenth century. However, like
many other expressions of that golden
decadent period, snuff boxes suffered eclipse
in the French Revolution. They returned to
favour in the Napoleonic era, but by this
time it had become fashionable for gold
snuff boxes to be elaborately and extravagantly ornamented; these later examples
somehow lack the tactile satisfaction which
is characteristic of the best eighteenth-century
boxes.

Snuff-taking diminished in popularity as
the nineteenth century progressed, so that
fine modern boxes are relatively rare and
cannot be compared aesthetically with earlier
examples. The finest boxes of the eighteenth
century were produced in France, and
ranged from the costly jeweled and gold
boxes to those with delicate enamel painting
on the lids and sides. Pure gold, being too
soft for the purpose, was seldom employed,
but various alloys with copper or silver were
used to produce the effects of different
shades of gold, thin layers of which were
chased in relief and carefully inlaid to form a
contrasting pattern. During the latter part of
the eighteenth century painted enamels were

Soap-making spread from Italy to France and Germany in the thirteenth century and came to England a hundred years later. Soap was usually made in the home, and there were few attempts at commercial production until the late eighteenth century. The earliest forms of milled toilet soap were developed in France. Previously soap was manufactured in gigantic blocks, sometimes weighing as much as 1,000 lb, and cut into cakes and bars. Special containers for soap originated in the mid-eighteenth century and were designed to keep the soap as dry as possible. Soap boxes were often spherical on high foot-rims, and made of silver with elaborate piercing all over to allow moisture to drain and evaporate more easily. Such silver globes were often made in matched pairs as part of a toilet set, the other globe containing a sponge.

The advent of the French milled cake led to the development of a new type of soap box, in the form of a flat, chamfered rectangle with a close-fitting lid. The earliest examples were made of silver but Sheffield plate and electroplate were used increasingly in the nineteenth century. Brass soap boxes proved unsatisfactory, since they tended to tarnish very rapidly, but by the mid-nineteenth century brass and copper soap boxes with silver or glass linings were popular. Later nineteenth-century examples may be found in nickel-faced brass or steel. Pottery and porcelain boxes were preferred for permanent use on toilet tables and washstands, the more compact metal boxes being used for travelling. A wide variety of ceramic soap boxes was developed in the nineteenth century, as well as porcelain dishes with perforated trays and shallow stands which caught the excess moisture. These designs have remained in use to the present day, though increasingly various forms of plastic have been employed. Nineteenth- and early twentieth-century soap stands, dishes and trays were highly decorative with moulded relief or underglaze ornament. Similar devices were also made in moulded or pressed glass, especially in the United States.

popular and the lids, both inside and out, were decorated with miniature portraits, pastoral scenes or mythological groups. One of the most intricate techniques of enamelling was *basse taille*, in which the gold or silver ground was elaborately carved out and then filled with transparent enamel which gave the appearance of an intaglio gem.

Snuff-taking became widespread in all classes of society, and boxes were produced in a wide variety of materials to suit even the humblest walk of life. Silver snuff boxes are still reasonably plentiful, while those in brass or pinchbeck are relatively cheap. Polished wood, mother-of-pearl, ivory, japanned papier mâché and even leather were used in the manufacture of snuff boxes in the eighteenth and nineteenth centuries. Horn and bone were also popular, particularly in Scotland, where such boxes were often mounted with cairngorms or other semi-precious stones.

SOAP BOXES AND TRAYS

Soap has been widely used since Roman times, the earliest reference to its manufacture being in the works of Pliny, who stated that soap could be made by boiling goat's tallow and causticized wood ashes.

Lowestoft porcelain inkwell and creamware mug attributed to Robert Allen, *c.* 1795 – typical late 18th-century seaside souvenirs.

SOUVENIRS

Term now widely used to denote any form of tourist memento, derived from the French inscription '*Souvenir de . . .*' followed by the name of a place. This formula was used to decorate small boxes and trifles of all kinds from the middle of the eighteenth century when tourism on a large scale first developed. The inscription may also be found on pottery and porcelain mugs and plates, small enamel boxes and the cheaper range of objects of vertu. Nineteenth- and early twentieth-century examples include stamp boxes, *carnets de bal* and picture postcards (qq.v.). The English counterpart was inscribed 'A Trifle from . . .', and may be found in the same styles and materials from the 1760s onwards. These 'trifles' gradually died out in the second half of the nineteenth century, other words, such as 'present', 'gift' or 'souvenir' becoming more common.

SPITTOONS

Relics of one of the less salubrious and hygienic habits of yester-year, particularly necessary in the period from 1790 to 1920 when tobacco-chewing was fashionable. The majority of spittoons resembled large, glo-bular jugs, with a wide funnel-shaped mou or a broad-rimmed lip. Single or tw handles were optional. These vessels, som times known in polite society as cuspido were made in sheet pewter, brass or coppe though silver is not unknown. Earthenwa or stoneware spittoons of the seventeen and eighteenth centuries followed the gene pattern of metal examples. In the second ha of the nineteenth century more elega spittoons were produced, with smaller bow mounted on tall stands. The addition of a ashtray device marked the change fro pipe-smoking and tobacco-chewing to ciga and cigarettes. Many of the late nineteent and early twentieth-century spittoons we more ornamental than functional and m be found with cast-relief ornament hammered and die-stamped decoration.

SPOONS

The oldest form of table implement, datin from neolithic times, was a rudimenta spoon roughly fashioned from elongate sea-shells or wood splinters. The Egyptia had spoons carved from slate, flint, wood ivory, whereas both Greeks and Roma used metal spoons, in silver or silver bronze. In medieval Europe horn, bone a wood were carved into spoons, though t wealthier classes used silver or even go spoons as early as the fourteenth centur Metal spoons, in pewter or latten (a form brass), became widespread in the seventeen century. Silver continued to be the pri cipal metal used until the advent of electr plating in the mid-nineteenth century. Nickel and chromium-plate and stainless steel have been used extensively in more recent years, the last-named having been pioneered in Germany and Scandinavia.

The earliest metal spoons had a fig-shaped bowl, the tapering end being attached to a hexagonal stem with a knop at the end of the handle. The bowl and stem were made from a single piece of metal, drawn out and hammered to shape, while the knop was soldered on. The knop was the only part of the spoon which permitted any scope for variety or decorative treatment, and successive fashions favoured knops in the shape of a plain ball, pineapple, diamond-point, acorn or spiral-fluted globe. By the mid-seventeenth century

seal-topped spoons were in vogue. More decorative types were Apostle (q.v.) and Maidenhead spoons. In the second half of the seventeenth century knops were replaced by broader, flatter stems with spatulate ends. So-called Puritan spoons had square ends, but by the late seventeenth century the familiar rounded end was well established. The broader surface permitted the development of more ornamental styles. Trifid and wavy-end spoons were popular in the eighteenth century. From about 1760 onwards successive styles included the slightly ribbed stem known as Hanoverian, the fiddlehead, the shell and anthemion motif (King's pattern), the stem ending turned downwards (Old English), fluted ribbing (Onslow pat-

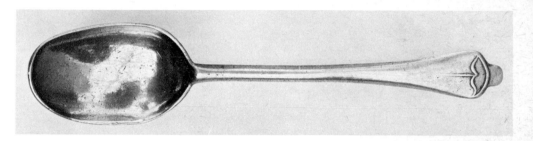

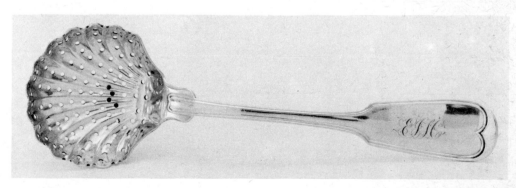

American spoons: Pewter serving spoon, 18th century; silver spoon with mark NB (probably Nicholas Burdock), *c.* 1800; silver strainer by J. and W. Moir of New York, *c.* 1845.

259

tern) and bright-cut engraving. Spoons made of latten were popular in the American style. Latten gave way to pewter about 1700, and numerous examples have been recorded of pewter spoons cast in homemade moulds.

By the mid-eighteenth century the bowls were becoming longer and narrower, tapering towards the point. The rat-tail reinforcement between bowl and stem was popular from about 1660 to 1730, being superseded by a single or double overlapping scale-like ornament. Spoons became more specialized in the early eighteenth century, with the emergence of distinctive types for use with mustard, salt, coffee, tea, sugar, puddings, desserts, and so on up the scale of size to the tablespoon and serving spoon. Porcelain handles were a speciality of the German potteries in the late eighteenth century, while handles of wood, ivory or mother-of-pearl have appeared fleetingly since the early nineteenth century. Spoons with enamelled metal crests mounted on the stem ends have been a popular form of tourist souvenir since the 1880s.

See also *Apostle Spoons, Cutlery, Serving Implements*

SPUN GLASS

Technique of drawing out molten glass rods into very fine threads, developed by the ancient Egyptians and subsequently employed by the Romans and the Islamic glass-makers of the Middle Ages. The art of spun glass spread to Venice in the sixteenth century and from thence came to France, Italy and Holland in the seventeenth century. It was widely used for decorative work, especially such virtuoso pieces as friggers and whimseys – the rigging of ships, the feathers of birds and the petals and foliage of flowers – which were enclosed in glass domes. Spun-glass ornaments were popular in Britain in the nineteenth century. Ornamental table-ware was also decorated with spun-glass threads of different colours. The production of glass threads fine enough for weaving was perfected in the mid-nineteenth century. The resulting silk-like cloth was displayed as a technological curiosity at the Great Exhibition of 1851. It never attained much popularity as an ornamental medium, though it was the forerunner of the modern fibreglass industry.

STAFFORDSHIRE POTTERY FIGURES

Although pottery ornaments of a homely nature had been produced as a cottage industry for well over a century, the best known examples, and those most in demand today, were the flatback figures of the middle- and late-Victorian period. These hollow moulded earthenware pieces, with their simple oval bases and distinctive flat backs, suddenly became very popular in the 1840s, having evolved out of the flower vase and spill-holders made from the late eighteenth century onward. Public demand for simple ornaments to decorate the chimney pieces in Victorian cottages combined with attempts on the part of the manufacturers to streamline production techniques and thus cut costs, led to the appearance of the flat-back figure group. Kilted highlanders, wide-eyed milkmaids and naïve spaniels formed the bulk of the figures throughout the latter half of the nineteenth century when the

taffordshire pottery
gures; mid-19th
entury.

ft Allegorical
affordshire flatback
gure celebrating the
sh Peace Treaty, 1882.

vogue for chimney ornaments was at its peak.

The marriage of Queen Victoria and Prince Albert in 1840, however, also inspired the production of pottery portrait figures of famous people and these, on account of their historical allusions, are now eagerly sought after. Figures of the Queen and the Prince Consort were turned out in their thousands to satisfy patriotic sentiment. In due course they were followed by similar figures inscribed 'Prince and Princess', featuring the young Prince of Wales and his sister, Princess Victoria Louise. The success of these groups induced the Staffordshire potters to extend the range of royal figures. The dowager Queen Adelaide (who died in 1849) was the subject of flatback groups, while foreign royalty, such as Tsar Alexander I of Russia, Kaiser Franz Josef II of Austria and the Empress Eugénie of France, were also immortalized in these robust pottery figures.

The perennial favourites, however, were the British Royal Family. The numerous progeny of Queen Victoria, from infancy to middle age, provided the potters with a never-ending source of material for which there was always a ready sale. Considering the countless figures which must have been manufactured for shillings or pence in Victorian times it is surprising that relatively few have survived to compete for the attention of collectors of Victoriana. Although the Royal Family furnished the enduring favourites, many celebrities of a more ephemeral nature were also portrayed in this manner and they include many of the more expensive items today. They can be divided into various classes according to subject or profession and many collectors tend to specialize in one or other of these categories.

Religious subjects form an important group, ranging from biblical characters to the exploits of popular saints and the martyrdom of Latimer and Ridley. Contemporary religious figures, from John Wesley to the American revivalists, Sankey and Moody,

Opposite Chinese snuff
bottles: (top) jadeite,
carved in relief with a
fabulous animal under a
pomegranate tree,
1750–1860; snowflake
glass, with a single
overlay of blue, red and
green carved in relief,
1750–1860; (bottom)
enamel painted on glass,
early 20th century;
lacque burgaute, inlaid with
silver, gold foil and
mother-of-pearl,
1780–1860.

were reproduced in earthenware. Almost as popular were figures connected with crime, and these now rank among the major rarities. Highwaymen turned folk heroes, such as Dick Turpin and Tom King, are relatively plentiful, but much scarcer are figures of James Rush and Emily Sandford, connected with the notorious Stanfield Hall murder of 1849, or William Corder and his victim Maria Martin of the Polstead murder of 1828.

Popular heroes and politicians, prize-fighters and lion-tamers provide numerous examples of these Staffordshire portrait groups. Military heroes ranged from the generals of the Crimean War to the brass-hats of the Boer War, but the minor campaigns of the intervening half-century were also duly commemorated in this manner. Female figures are comparatively rare, among the notable examples being Jenny Lind the singer, Florence Nightingale and Amelia Bloomer, the American feminist.

The best-known manufacturer of these figures was Sampson Smith of Longton (whose wares often bore the mark SS). There were many others whose work, usually unmarked, is actually superior in quality. William Kent of Burslem began making them in 1885 and production of similar, though inferior, figures continued until fairly recent times.

STEVENGRAPHS

Trade name given to woven silk pictures manufactured by Thomas Stevens (1828–88) and emulated by his rivals. For centuries the Midland city of Coventry was renowned for the weaving of silk ribbons (q.v.). The industry reached its peak during the first half of the nineteenth century, but by 1860 a slump had set in and unemployment in Coventry was acute. Thousands of silk-weavers left the town to seek work elsewhere. It was at this time that Stevens began experimenting with his looms, trying to produce small decorative items, such as book markers (q.v.). From this humble beginning there developed a great industry in its own right.

Right Stevengraph portraying the jockey Fred Archer; late 19th century.

As business expanded Stevens establish his Stevengraph Factory, specializing in t manufacture of small silk articles, such embroidered hat ribbons, badges, sc sachets and Valentines, but it is for t Stevengraph itself that he is best remember This consisted of a woven silk pictu usually about two by six inches, which w then mounted on a background of green fawn-coloured mat and framed. The brea through came at the York Industrial Exhibi tion of 1879 when Stevens gave demonstr tions of Stevengraph production and t attractive coloured silk pictures becam immensely popular with the late Victoria

Famous sportsmen of the nineteenth ce tury shown on Stevengraphs include t jockey Fred Archer, the boxers John Sullivan and Jem Smith, while a full-leng portrait of Dr W.G. Grace, woven on t occasion of his century of centuries, is nc one of the most highly prized of all si pictures. Others dealt with sporting subje in general, such as the set of three concern

WOVEN IN PURE SILK BY T, STEVENS, COVENTRY.

THE LATE

FRED. ARCHER.

WOVEN IN PURE SILK
AT THE
COLUMBIAN EXPOSITION, CHICAGO 1893
BY THE
STEVENGRAPH WORKS, COVENTRY, ENG.

with fox-hunting or those featuring cricket matches and regattas. Not surprisingly many of the best-known Stevengraphs have a local connection, perennial favourites being 'Ye Ladye Godiva' and 'Ye Peeping Tom of Coventre', of which several versions are known. Landmarks and historic scenes, portraits of royalty, statesmen and contemporary personalities were also popular, especially those with a topical flavour. Stevengraphs were widely exported, particularly to the United States, and this explains the relatively high incidence of pictures with an American slant, including portraits of Presidents Harrison and Cleveland, Sergeant Bates and Buffalo Bill Cody. In this context a surprisingly rare Stevengraph was that portraying George Washington. British politicians, especially Gladstone and Disraeli, were favourites of long standing and many different versions of them may be found. Popular heroes, from the Boer War and the minor campaigns of the late nineteenth century, were perennial favourites. Ships and early locomotives are among the more highly prized Stevengraphs today, but the most expensive are those featuring the exploits of Columbus and other events in American history, prepared by the Stevengraph Company in connection with the Columbian Exposition of 1893.

In recent years a great deal of research into Stevengraphs has been conducted in the United States and Britain and the comparative rarity of the different issues has been largely established. Considerable significance is attached to the type of mount and the precise wording of the manufacturer's label found on the back of the picture. Periodic changes in the wording enable the various editions to be accurately dated.

STRAINERS

Utensils with shallow circular or oval pierced bowl used for straining tea, coffee, fruit juice and other liquids to remove leaves, grounds and extraneous particles. Strainers may be found with one or two handles and the more elaborate types have a matching stand or dish, sometimes attached by swivel brackets. Strainers came into use in the second half of the seventeenth century, mainly in connection with fruit punch and similar alcoholic beverages. The majority of the more decorative types belong to the eighteenth century when tea became popular. They were made in silver, silver-gilt, silvered bronze or brass, pewter or Sheffield plate, and in electroplate from about 1840 onwards. Strainer spoons with elaborately pierced bowls were used for various purposes in the

Silver tea or punch strainer; American, 18th century.

same period. Those with ecclesiastical motifs were used in churches for straining Communion wine. Spoons with pointed ends were used to strain coffee or tea, the point being employed to clear blockages in the spouts of tea- and coffee-pots. Larger versions of the strainer spoon were mote skimmers, for removing foreign bodies and scum from the surface of soups and stews. They were made in pewter, tinned copper or brass and often had ornament on their handles.

STRAW-WORK

Form of marquetry (q.v.) using pieces of straw instead of wood veneers. The straw was used either in its natural state or dyed in

Straw marquetry box; English, early 19th century.

266

various colours. Strips and small pieces straw were applied to wood, metal, silk papier mâché bases, usually to decorate t lids and sides of boxes, but also the frames pictures and mirrors and even the panels furniture. The art developed in Italy in t sixteenth century and spread to Franc Germany, Holland and England in t seventeenth. The art was revived during t Napoleonic Wars being a popular mediu for prisoner-of-war work (q.v.). Straw ma quetry has survived fitfully to the pres day, being found on small boxes and oth tourist mementoes of European origin.

STUMPWORK

Name given to a form of raised needlewo and thought to derive from the 'stump' wool used to fill out the figures. This d tinctive style of needlework was wid practised in Europe in the fifteenth and si teenth centuries and came to England in t reign of Queen Elizabeth. The technique w originally used for the elaborate ecclesiasti embroidery which enriched the vestme of the clergy, but in England it was adapt for heraldic canopies and rich court dre Raised embroidery was worked on a sa base, and was decorated with gold or sil wire, small pearls and semi-precious ston Examples of this type of court embroide have survived from the sixteenth century heralds' coats, bags for the seals of State a the covers of rare books. The decorati was initially heraldic, but gradually a mo naturalistic approach was adopted and land-scapes, animals and human figures were featured.

By the beginning of the seventeenth century, however, raised embroidery was becoming popular with young ladies of the highest classes of society. This was the sort of needlework to which girls would aspire, once they had shown their basic proficiency with a sampler (q.v.). The feature which distinguished stumpwork from the raised embroidery of an earlier generation was the inclusion of tiny figures of people and animals worked separately, like little dolls, and then sewn into place on the background. These figures were made of old pieces of material sewn together and stuffed with wool or horsehair. The three-dimensional effect was heightened by the use of wooden limbs and wax faces. Flowers and the branches of trees were often worked separately and attached to the stem or trunk by means of thin wires.

The aim of the youthful seamstress appears to have been to crowd as much as possible into the picture. While the main figures might tell a story – biblical or popular historical subjects were the favourites – the background would be crammed with incidental detail, such as flowers, animals and birds, all worked separately and then stitched into position. The background might also include patches of real moss, pieces of fur, feathers or straw, all neatly sewn into place in what would now be termed a collage.

In view of the high ratio of labour required to the area embroidered, most examples of stumpwork are comparatively small. As a rule stumpwork was carried out on a piece of satin less than a foot square. These small pieces of embroidery could then be used as panels on articles of furniture (often set under glass to protect the surface of the needlework) or on the covers of books or small boxes. Occasionally stumpwork was used for the covers of cushions, but in such cases the work was in relatively low relief and less elaborate in composition, for the sake of comfort as much as anything else.

Dressing cases and toilet boxes were very often decorated with stumpwork. Boxes for lace collars and cuffs, glove boxes, needlework caskets and the backs of looking-glasses are other articles on which stumpwork panels may sometimes be found.

Stumpwork, being a far more tedious process than straightforward needlework, was never as popular. Although it survived fitfully into the nineteenth century the craze for stumpwork did not really outlive the Stuart era. By the end of the seventeenth century it had been superseded by other pastimes, such as marquetry (q.v.) and japanning. Embroidered samplers continued to be produced, as part of the basic training for girls in needlework. As a result, fine examples of stumpwork are relatively rare. Many of the surviving examples are panels dismounted from boxes and covers preserved in glazed mounts.

SUNDIALS

Primitive sundials were in existence by 300 BC. In the latitudes of the Mediterranean the altitude of the sun, and thus the length of the shadow cast, was the significant factor in the measurement of time. In northern Europe, however, the change in direction of the sun, and thus the direction of the shadow,

Stumpwork panel;
English, 17th century.

was of greater importance. These factors led to the development of the two principal types of sundials: altitude sundials and azimuth (directional) sundials.

For centuries, time was reckoned in temporary hours, the period of sunlight being divided into twelve equal parts which, of course, differed in length from one day to the next. Many simple sundials engraved on, or set into, the walls of buildings to this day give only an approximation of time since no allowance is made for the varying length of time between sunrise and sunset. It was the Arab astronomer and mathematician, Abdul Hassan, who devised the system of equal, or equinoctial hours. Hassan also invented a great variety of sundials traced on cylindrical and conical surfaces as well as on horizontal or vertical planes. From the mid-thirteenth century onwards his system of equal hours gradually came to be accepted, the introduction of mechanical clocks in the fourteenth century greatly accelerating its adoption.

The measurement of time in hours of equal length was based on the fact that, throughout the year, the direction of the shadow cast by the sun is invariable at only one moment during the day, namely at midday. At other times the direction varies from day to day, on account of the apparent movement of the sun which takes place on an oblique axis directed towards the pole star. The direction in which the shadow is cast can be made constant for the same time on different days by orientating the gnomon, or pointer, towards this celestial pole. It is then possible to draw hour lines which remain correct all the year round. This practice was admirably suited to sundials which were fixed in a particular place and had the hour lines engraved specifically for that locality. It was not long, however, before astronomers were devising pocket or portable sundials which, in theory at least, could be used in any part of the world. In grappling with this problem the astronomers and their instrument-makers produced some weird and wonderful devices, which, on account of their small size, form an interesting subject for collection.

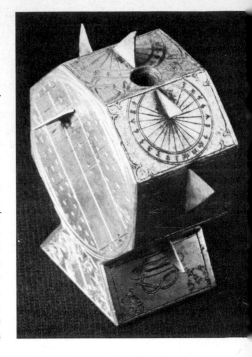

In an age before clockmakers had mastered the intricacies of the mechanical measurement of time, the only reliable time-keepers were sundials. It was important, therefore, that these dials should be as accurate as possible and great care and skilled workmanship were lavished on their construction. As befitted instruments of such importance, they were often made of gold, silver or ivory. Ornamentation was generally related to the function of the sundial, but the harmony of its proportions, the technical excellence of its construction and the choice of materials used all combined to make an instrument which was seldom inelegant and usually a thing of great beauty.

The seventeenth century was the heyday of the pocket dial and an enormous range of different types has survived from this period. Portable dials range from the tiny instruments in the form of finger-rings to the pedestal dials which could be placed on a table. Columnar dials are sometimes found with lines registering both Jewish and Italian hours – the two systems employed at the time. The Nuremberg dial-makers produced

eft Gilt-brass polyhedral
undial; probably by
Nicholas Kratzer,
tronomer and horologer
» Henry VIII, *c.* 1518–30.

the distinctive diptych dial, consisting of two leaves (usually of ivory) which opened out like a book. After the Revocation of the Edict of Nantes in 1685, many Huguenot instrument-makers settled in Augsburg, where they specialized in equinoctial dials consisting of an octagonal base inset with a magnetic compass and surmounted by an adjustable gnomon and hour-scale.

The traffic in craftsmen was not all in one direction. Towards the end of the seventeenth century the English craftsman, Michael Butterfield, settled in Paris and eventually became instrument-maker to Louis XIV. His sundials were made of silver and were octagonal in shape. As a rule, four hour-scales, for 43, 46, 49 and 52 degrees of latitude, were engraved on the plate. Further adjustment could be made by means of the movable gnomon (often in the shape of a bird) which was calibrated from 40 to 60 degrees. Pocket sundials survived into the eighteenth century, but the advent of cheaper and more accurate mechanical timepieces led to their demise. Circular or polygonal dials are those most frequently encountered. Diptychs, and unusual shapes such as columns, polyhedrals and crucifixes are comparatively rare.

SYLLABUB GLASSES

Large drinking glasses of English origin, popular in the late seventeenth and eighteenth centuries for the consumption of syllabub and other milk-based beverages and desserts composed of whipped cream, wines and spices. The earliest glasses resembled caudle cups (q.v.) and were fitted with twin handles, a spout and a domed cover. Later examples were taller, with a wide lip and bell-shaped bowl, and sometimes have a single handle. More ornamental types had scalloped decoration on the lip and foot-rim, and cut or moulded ornament on the handles. Eighteenth-century syllabub glasses had squat, knopped stems and occasionally the stem was entirely omitted. Glasses with plain conical bowls on short stems were used for syllabub, jelly and ices, and this style, with variations, has remained in use in Europe and America to this day. These conical glasses were likewise fitted with twin handles originally, but later examples had either a single handle or none. The bowls were relatively plain, sometimes fluted or faceted. A few have been recorded with engraved motifs.

TANKARDS

Drinking vessels for cider, ale or beer, usually having a hinged lid which is raised by an elaborate thumb-piece. They may be found in a wide variety of shapes and sizes, with tall or short cylindrical bodies, globular shapes or slightly tapering sides. Considerable regional variations exist in the style of handle, foot, lid and thumb-piece. Wood staves bound with metal hoops, leather, glass, pewter, brass, silver and pottery have all been used in the construction of tankards. Glass tankards enclosed in a shell of filigree silver were a German speciality in the sixteenth and seventeenth centuries. Later German tankards were of coloured or enamelled glass, and elaborate stoneware or earthenware tankards with relief decoration in contrasting colours were also very popular. European earthenware and faience tankards were often given silver rims, lips and thumb-pieces. Silver tankards with engraved all-over pattern became fashionable in England in the late seventeenth century and spread to America, where this form remained popular until the mid-nineteenth century. Many tankards made from the late eighteenth century dispensed with the hinged lid. After the rococo extravagance of the eighteenth-century tankards, the majority of nineteenth-century examples were relatively plain. Tankards with glass bottoms are fairly plentiful, but those incorporating lithophanes (q.v.) their base are worth looking for.

See also *Mugs*

TAPE MEASURES

Measuring devices developed in the nineteenth century, containing a reel of tape with divisions marked in inches or centimetres and their fractions. Designed primarily for the use of milliners and seamstresses, the

Group of pewter tankards; English, late 17th–early 18th centuries.

Tunbridge ware tape
measures and pin holders;
late 19th century.

measures were produced in decorative form from the outset, and even the tapes themselves were frequently printed on coloured linen or silk, sometimes with a patterned reverse. The majority of nineteenth-century tape measures were comparatively tall and cylindrical, sometimes rectangular and very occasionally flat and disc-shaped like their modern counterparts. They were produced in silver, brass, pewter, bronze, pottery and porcelain of various kinds, in carved wood, Mauchline and Tunbridge wares (qq.v.). Tape measures were ideally suited to presentation in novelty form, and numerous examples of mid-Victorian measures may be found in the shape of windmills or lighthouses, with revolving sails and lights which worked when the tape was pulled out. Other popular shapes were barrels and tall silver tankards, complete with handle, thumb-piece and lid, the sides decorated with embossed or repoussé

ornament. Novelty tape measures were often embellished with tiny vignettes and sold as tourist souvenirs. After the turn of the century, tape measures disguised as motor cars and airplanes kept pace with the times. The novelty tape measure declined in popularity after World War I, and the construction became more compact with the advent of metal or spring-loaded tapes. Nevertheless, many handsome tape measures with transfer-printed enamel decoration in neo-classical motifs were produced in the 1920s.

TEA BOWLS

The earliest utensils for tea-drinking were small porcelain bowls imported from China by the Honourable East India Company and its French, Dutch and Portuguese equivalents in the early seventeenth century. An examination of contemporary prints and paintings

271

reveals that handle-less bowls of a comparatively small diameter continued to be used for tea-drinking until the second half of the eighteenth century. European tea bowls, emulating Chinese and Japanese originals, were produced in stoneware and porcelain from the early eighteenth century onward and were often decorated with chinoiserie (q.v.) motifs. The saucers which matched the tea bowls were comparatively large and deep, reflecting the fact that drinking tea from the saucer was an acceptable alternative. By the late eighteenth century, however, handles were fitted to the bowl to form the now familiar tcacup, and saucers gradually shrank in size as cups became larger.
See colour plate page 264

TEA-CADDIES

Containers for storing tea, the name being derived from *kati*, a Malay unit of weight of about half a kilogram. The name did not become common in the English language until the end of the eighteenth century, earlier examples being known as canisters.

Curled paperwork tea-caddy; English, *c.* 1800.

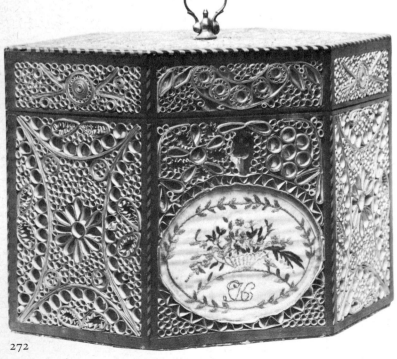

The earliest caddies were made of silver an often fitted with locks, reflecting the relativel high cost of tea in the seventeenth century when the beverage was confined to th wealthier classes. Caddies without individu locks were made in sets of two or three, an housed in a small chest with a lock on the li and compartments within for the caddies an mixing bowl. The earliest caddies wer usually oblong or octagonal with straigh sides, a relatively small opening and a stoppe or domed lid. Many caddies of this type wer fitted with a sliding bottom to facilitat refilling. In the 1720s vase-shaped caddie became fashionable and these were ofte made in sets, decorated with engravin chasing and embossing in Chinese motif Sheffield plate (q.v.) was also used extensivel in the manufacture of caddies from abou 1780, while early nineteenth-centur examples were made in Pontypool war (q.v.). Both opaque white glass and porcelai were used in the production of oblong o circular caddies in the late eighteenth century the former being decorated with enamelle chinoiserie (q.v.). Caddies of this period ma be found with names of different types of te (Green, Congou, Souchong, Pekoe, Bohea Black, etc.), and separate labels, similar t wine labels (q.v.), were also fashionable.

The earliest teapots used in Europe were Chinese hot-water pots which, in turn, were derived from ritual wine vessels fashioned in bronze. The Chinese hot-water pots were modelled in Yi-hsing red stoneware and were closely imitated by Johann Friedrich Böttger in the red stoneware produced at Meissen in the early eighteenth century. The earliest European teapots, however, were made of silver from the middle of the seventeenth century, while ceramic examples began with the Dutch delftware teapots of the 1670s. Curiously enough, it was the style of the Dutch delftware pots, with their characteristic short spouts, which influenced the later Chinese export porcelain teapots of the mid-eighteenth century. In general, ceramic teapots of both Oriental and European manufacture followed the styles established in metal teapots.

European metal teapots were constructed on the same lines as chocolate and coffee pots (q.v.), with a tall cylindrical body, high-domed lid and handle set at right angles to the spout. The Chinese pioneered the style, universally adopted since, of a low bulbous body with the spout and handle on opposite sides. The majority of metal teapots of the seventeenth and eighteenth centuries were made of silver, though Sheffield plate (q.v.) was used from the 1760s until it was superseded by electroplate in the 1840s. Base-metal pots, in brass or pewter, date from the end of the eighteenth century, when tea-drinking extended down to all social classes, though examples which may be dated before about 1850 are rare.

The shape of teapots is often a good guide to approximate date. Apart from the type modelled on chocolate pots, the earliest examples on Chinese lines had egg-shaped bodies. By the beginning of the eighteenth century circular, polygonal or pear-shaped bodies, all with high-domed lids, were coming into fashion. In the second half of the century the flat-bottomed, drum-shaped teapot was popular and lids were lower, eventually becoming quite flat. Elliptical or

boat-shaped teapots were fashionable in the late eighteenth century. An unusual type, peculiar to Scotland, was the bullet teapot, with its distinctive spherical shape and high foot-rim. Decoration on metal teapots is also a useful guide to date, the simple lines of the early eighteenth century giving way to lavish rococo ornament which, in turn, was superseded by the gadrooning and acanthus motifs of the neo-classical period at the beginning of the nineteenth century. Both shapes and decorative styles became eclectic in the second half of the nineteenth century, often combining forms and patterns from different periods. Ceramic teapots of the nineteenth century varied enormously in shape and underglaze ornament, with many novelty forms – cabbage, cauliflower, cottage, animal or human shapes and relief decoration. Enormous brown earthenware teapots were

produced in the English Midlands and Wales in the second half of the nineteenth century until World War I, and are known as barge teapots, from their association with the 'water gipsies' of the canals. These pots had a capacity of up to four gallons and usually had a miniature teapot mounted in their domed lid. They were lavishly decorated with floral patterns and often incorporated inscriptions and dates commemorating family events such as christenings, weddings and wedding anniversaries.

There was a revival in pewter teapots at the end of the nineteenth century, allied to the curving motifs of Art Nouveau. More severe, geometrical styles were pioneered in Germany, the Low Countries and Scandinavia before World War I and spread to other parts of Europe in the 1920s. These forms were imitated in ceramic teapots of the same period, with gaudy geometric motifs in the prevailing Art Deco style.

TEETHERS. See *Rattles and Teethers*

TERRACOTTAS

Objects, usually small animal or human figures, modelled in ferruginous clay and then fired without glazing, to produce a characteristic red or buff biscuit appearance. The name is Italian, meaning literally 'baked earth'. Terracottas are of great antiquity and have been found throughout the Mediterranean area. The finest are those from classical Greece, particularly the figurines from Tanagra (Boeotia) which date from 330–200 BC. The art of terracotta was already well established in China before the Han Dynasty and reached its pre-eminence during the T'ang period, when greyish figures, often painted in different colours, were produced. Terracottas from pre-Columbian times have been discovered in many parts of Latin America, especially in Mexico, Guatemala and Peru, both in the form of statuettes and in vases, jugs and jars in animal or human shape.

After the fall of the Western Roman Empire in the fifth century the art of working in terracotta continued sporadically in many parts of Italy, France and Germany, but enjoyed a marked revival in the fifteenth century when it was used extensively in the mouldings and tracery of church decoration. The sculptors of the Renaissance turned to this medium for the production of relief, busts and even life-sized groups, and Florence became an important centre for this art. Oil colours and enamels were used in the sixteenth century. Italianate terracottas were introduced to England in the reign of Henry VII by Torrigiano. Terracotta declined in face of the competition, first from marble and then from stoneware and porcelain, but was revived fitfully at Sèvres in the late eighteenth and early nineteenth centuries when excellent terracottas were produced by such artists as Clodion, Falconet and Boizot.

THEOREM PAINTINGS

Paintings on cloth, usually cotton velvet, using stencils or 'theorems' to produce the outlines which were then coloured in. This technique was developed in the United States in the early nineteenth century. The practice of theorem painting grew out of the craze for ladies' art classes and enabled

Boeotian terracotta figure of a woman cooking, *c.* 500 BC.

French terracotta group of nymphs and Bacchante by Clodion (1738–1814).

part of the user, and rather hackneyed motifs were employed. The pictures were composed in black ink on white or yellow velvets and the colour filled in, using special liquid pigments. The technique of painting on velvet, for cushion covers, fire screens and even purses, was originally known as Oriental tinting, but this term was subsequently transferred to pictures painted on glass (see *Glass Pictures*). The term theorem painting is applied loosely to any American velvet painting of the early nineteenth century, though those painted entirely in freehand are generally superior to those which required the use of stencils.

See colour plate page 281

THIMBLES

These small protective devices used in needlework date back to Roman times and were originally carved from wood or bone. Medieval thimbles were produced in brass, silver and even gold. Thimbles in enamels (q.v.) and porcelain were fashionable in the eighteenth century. Those made of precious metals often had a broad ring round the rim inlaid with other metals or precious stones paralleling fashions in finger-rings. Even copper and brass thimbles frequently had engraved decoration round the rim. Enamel thimbles were a speciality of the Midlands and had finely painted scenes on their sides and rims. Comparatively few thimbles were made of other materials, but ivory, jade, horn and mother-of-pearl have been recorded. The invention of the 'nose' machine in the mid-eighteenth century mechanized the production of thimbles and henceforward the characteristic indentations became regularly spaced. Souvenir and commemorative thimbles were very popular in Victorian times, and examples celebrating jubilees, coronations and other royal events were produced up to 1914.

Base-metal thimbles may be found in bronze or pewter as well as brass. Iron thimbles were produced in the nineteenth century, not so much for use in needlework, but as a cruel instrument of school discipline.

those whose natural talents for freehand drawing were scanty to keep up with their more accomplished sisters. Cards with various cut-out shapes were sold by stationers and fancy goods shops in the period from 1830 to 1860 for this express purpose. These stencils included circles of various diameters, curved lines, ellipses and the shapes of leaves and flower petals. Such cards, known popularly as 'theorems' or 'formulas' from their geometrical appearance, were used to build up quite complex patterns or compositions, flowers, fruit and vegetables being the most popular subjects. Some of the later stencils featured entire flowers, and this technical perfection undoubtedly contributed to the downfall of theorem painting, since it removed the necessity for any skill on the

Popularly known as dames' thimbles, they were used by the mistresses in schools for 'thimble pie-making', or drumming vigorously on the heads of unruly pupils.

Thimble cases may be found in many different forms and materials. The most common form was a small barrel which unscrewed to reveal the thimble inside. Other types included an egg or an acorn. These cases were usually carved in ivory or made of turned wood, decorated with painting or engraving. Nineteenth-century thimble cases may also be found in Mauchline ware (q.v.), covered in tartan, or banded with Tunbridge ware (q.v.) mosaic. Shagreen (q.v.) thimble cases were popular in the late eighteenth century.

See also *Étuis*, *Work Boxes*

TILES

Thin slabs of ceramic material, usually earthenware, used extensively for the surfacing of floors, walls, ceilings, fireplaces and roofs from the first millennium BC, if not earlier. Surviving examples of roof tiles from Greek temples are so highly developed technically as to point to a much earlier usage in the Mediterranean area. Japanese and Chinese tiles date from before the Christian era and, though similar in composition, differ radically in shape and especially in the degree of ornamentation applied to even the most functional examples. Floor tiles date from the Roman Empire, but died out in Europe during the Dark Ages. Roof tiles were revived in the ninth century and floor tiles in the twelfth. The earliest medieval floor tiles were usually square with decoration in two contrasting colours, generally dark brown-red and a pale orange or brownish yellow. These tiles were cast in two operations, the darker colour forming the base, with recessed portions filled in with lighter clay, though examples may be encountered in which the pattern is reversed. Tiles cast in a single colour were decorated with incised motifs. Geometrical, floral, ecclesiastical and heraldic designs were applied to individual tiles, but more frequently each

tile bore only a part of a design which w. composed when the tiles were laid togethe in mosaic fashion. Unglazed baked earther ware tiles died out in the sixteenth centur being superseded by the more colourf maiolica or faience tiles with polychron decoration.

Maiolica tiles were of Islamic origin an spread from the Middle East to Turke North Africa and thence to Italy and Spa respectively. Italian and Spanish tiles we subsequently exported to France and Englan Relatively few examples of Hispan Mauresque floor tiles have survived, since t glaze was too soft. The Moorish potter however, developed techniques for makin decorative wall tiles, the distinctive blu *Azulejos* which may still be seen in t Alhambra at Granada. A surprisingly hig proportion of these fourteenth-centur Moorish tiles bear Christian heraldic device indicating a thriving export market fro Granada and Seville to Castile and Arago and later to France. Three types of tile ma be distinguished. The oldest technique w. known as *cuerda seca* (dry cord) in which t various enamel colours were kept apart b raised fillets (like the leading in stained-gla windows). *Cuenca* (depression) was the nam given to tiles decorated in the norther European manner, with the areas to be fille with enamel colours depressed below th surface. *Pisano* was the name of the Italia maiolica tile introduced to Spain from Pisa i the sixteenth century. Both *cuenca* an *pisano* tiles have been widely manufacture in Spain from the early 1500s to the preser day.

During the late medieval period there wer important developments in northern Europ In Germany tiles with decoration impresse or moulded in relief were developed primaril for stoves but later applied to interic decoration in general and formed the bas of the Hafner-ware (q.v.) industry. The mos significant development, however, too place in Holland where the distinctive delf ware tiles were produced from the end of th sixteenth century. These plain, square til with a bluish-white ground were originall

States. Decorative wall tiles in the traditional unglazed Gothic fashion, as well as glazed Hafner ware, Spanish *cuenca* and *pisano* techniques and delftware, were among the products of the late nineteenth-century studio potters. Minton pioneered glazed earthenware maiolica tiles with relief decoration in the 1850s and these continued to be fashionable until World War I. Earthenware and delftware tiles, based on Dutch or English styles, were manufactured in Philadelphia and New Jersey in Colonial times. The best-known American manufacturer of the nineteenth century was the Grueby Faience Company of East Boston, which produced excellent maiolica architectural tiles until 1912, in addition to its renowned art pottery wares with a matt finish.

TIMEPIECES

Apart from sundials (q.v.) the non-mechanical forms of timepiece include water-clocks and hour-glasses. The water-clock or clepsydra was widely used in classical times and took a variety of forms, all of which depended on the leakage or gravitational feed of water for their operation, depending on the volume of water and the fineness of the aperture for their duration and accuracy. The principle of the clepsydra was revived in the seventeenth century in western Europe, and over the ensuing 200 years many distinctive and often elaborate clocks were constructed, the flow of water operating rotating drums and pointers. The collector should be wary, however, of fake water-clocks, which enjoyed a temporary popularity in the 1920s and were of English origin.

The hour-glass or sand-glass is said to have been invented by a Carthusian monk in the eighth century, and timepieces of this sort were widely used in churches and monasteries until the eighteenth century. They consisted of two glass bulbs united at their apices and containing a certain quantity of fine sand which would fall from the upper to the lower bulb in a given space of time. The hour-glass was then turned over and the process reversed. The development of the

decorated with freehand sketches in blue, but later in manganese purple or red. These tiles enjoyed enormous popularity, not only in the Low Countries but also in Germany and Britain. Vast quantities of Dutch tiles were imported into England in the first half of the seventeenth century. The rift with the Netherlands, which culminated in the Dutch Wars of the 1660s and 1670s, led to the development of an indigenous delftware industry and English tiles soon diverged from their Dutch models, incorporating a wider range of floral motifs, pastoral and hunting scenes, landscapes, biblical subjects and portraits of contemporary celebrities. Delftware tiles have continued to be popular down to the present time, but from about 1750 onwards hand-painting has been replaced by transfer-printing from copper plates.

The medieval baked earthenware tile reappeared with the Gothic Revival of the mid-nineteenth century, but new processes were used. Powdered clay compressed in steel dies resulted in the encaustic tile, pioneered in the potteries of Stoke-on-Trent but subsequently widely manufactured elsewhere, notably in Germany and the United

hour-glass kept pace with the improvements in the techniques of glass-blowing. The earliest examples had twin bulbs blown separately and joined by a metal collar, but from the middle of the eighteenth century the twin globes were blown as one piece. Apart from the quality of the glass, hour-glasses may be dated by the type of frame, the earliest being of iron, though later turned wood, carved bone, ivory or even silver were used. The nautical version, known as log-glasses, consisted of several hour-glasses mounted in one frame and set for different times. While the use of sand-glasses as time-pieces declined, smaller versions for use as timers in cooking became popular and these may be found with capacities ranging from one to ten minutes.

TINS

The application of tinware (q.v.) to small boxes and containers for the packaging of foodstuffs and other consumer goods dates from the middle of the nineteenth century. Prior to the 1870s tins were handmade and were a relatively expensive substitute for wood. The invention in 1872 of tin-making machines as well as presses for printing on tin revolutionized the English packaging industry, and the methods quickly spread to Europe and America. By 1890 wood had virtually gone out of use in the packaging of small articles. A curious exception was the match. Bryant & May originally turned from wooden to tinplate boxes but by the turn of the century had reverted to wood which, with various forms of card, has been used for this purpose ever since.

The most important application of tin-plate to packaging concerned perishable goods such as foodstuffs. Cookies and biscuits in particular have long been packaged in this way, the English firm of Huntley & Palmer of Reading having pioneered the method. Thomas Huntley sold boxes of biscuits to passengers on the coaches between London and the West Country, using metal boxes constructed by his brother Joseph, who had an ironmongering business. Early Huntley &

Palmer biscuit tins are among the m͏ collectable items. Biscuits, chocolates a͏ other luxury goods were among the first be attractively packaged, and great attenti͏ was paid to devising artistic motifs for t͏ lids, and subsequently to producing bo͏ and tins in novelty shapes. Chocolate t͏ disguised as books were a popular device, b͏ many other forms may be found, includi͏ blacksmith's anvils, mail coaches, hea͏ guitars, bells and clock shapes. Tea mercha͏ at the turn of the century frequently present͏ their wares in tins, decorated with Chinese Japanese motifs, which could subsequent͏ be used as caddies (q.v.).

By the beginning of the twentieth centu͏ tins of all shapes and sizes were being used f͏ a vast range of branded goods, and even t͏ most utilitarian examples illustrate the tre͏ in graphic design at different periods over t͏ past hundred years. Apart from the m͏ pictorial and decorative biscuit, confectione͏ and branded goods tins, there are co͏ memorative tins, produced in connecti͏ with coronations and jubilees and given schoolchildren. An important category co͏ sists of tins containing tobacco, chocola͏ sweets or biscuits, prepared as 'troop co͏ forts'. Examples produced by the belligere͏ on both sides exist from the Boer War, t͏ Spanish-American War and both Wo͏ Wars, with patriotic motifs, portraits a͏ military insignia, and these are much sought after by collectors of militaria (q.v.).

TINWARE

Though tin by itself is a brittle and unstable metal, its qualities – resistance to corrosion and low melting-point – have made it invaluable as an alloying metal (in bronze and pewter) and as a wash or plating applied to copper or brass. The object of tinning copper vessels was to prevent food and drink being contaminated by poisonous copper oxides. In the late eighteenth century, however, tinning was also being applied to iron sheeting as an anti-corrosion measure. Iron sheets were dipped in one or more baths of molten tin and then rolled in a press to obtain an even, consistent surface. Mild-steel sheets were substituted for iron in the early nineteenth century and this process, with modifications, has continued to this day.

The most important use of tinware has been in the commercial manufacture of packaging, and tins (q.v.) from the 1870s onward are now highly collectable. Die-stamped and embossed tinware was widely used in the production of small boxes, combining decorative and useful qualities, as well as numerous types of kitchen utensils from jelly moulds to cookie cutters. Tinware buckets and spades, with brightly coloured transfer-printed patterns, became popular at seaside resorts in the 1890s. Tinware was also applied to cheap toys, whistles and mechanical banks, originally of German manufacture but subsequently produced widely in Britain, France, the United States and Japan. Since the 1950s tinware has largely been superseded by plastics and this has heightened the antiquarian interest in even the most mundane tinware articles of the early twentieth century.

TIPSTAVES AND TRUNCHEONS

Weapons primarily associated with the maintenance of law and order. Tipstaves were wooden or metal rods formerly carried by village constables, sheriffs and other law officers as a badge of authority. They were usually decorated with cast metal heads or painted shafts, bearing civic or royal emblems. Though originally provided as a defensive weapon, like the night-stick still carried by personnel in many police forces, they soon became purely ceremonial and their decorative qualities increased accordingly. They were also carried by civic dignitaries and minor functionaries, such as workhouse overseers and town clerks, and may be found with the name of the office and town or district inscribed on them. Tipstaves were carried by inspectors of the Metropolitan Police as late as the 1870s.

Truncheons or batons were used by the majority of police forces in Britain, Europe and America. Leather cases and holsters were in use until the current practice of inserting them in special trouser pockets was adopted. Like tipstaves they were often embellished with badges and monograms, but since about 1860 plainer and more functional truncheons have been used.

TOBACCO CUTTERS. See *Cigar and Tobacco Cutters*

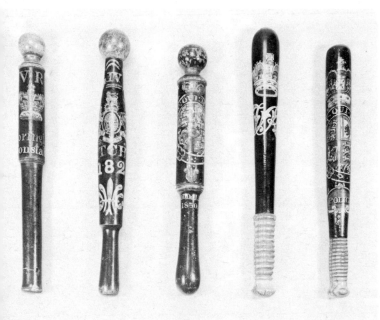

Containers for tobacco began to appear in
the early seventeenth century, the boxes
being intended for carrying tobacco on the
person while the jars were destined for a
more permanent situation on desk or table.
Tobacco boxes were pioneered by the Dutch,
who made small oblong, oval or circular
boxes with close-fitting lids in brass or copper,
often with inlays of one on the other. From
their inception these boxes were lavishly
decorated with engraved or embossed scenes
and figure groups. Biblical and classical
subjects, military and sporting themes,
allegories of tobacco and smoking, and
general landscapes were popular, but the
most desirable forms are those which incorporate a perpetual calendar. Profiles of
famous men, from Roman emperors to
medieval popes, may also be found on these
Dutch boxes. Brass or copper boxes were
made in England and America from the late
seventeenth century, but the best examples
were produced in silver, with comparatively
little ornament other than scrolled borders
and engraved monograms or coats of arms.
This style remained fashionable in Britain

until the mid-nineteenth century, though
later examples were often made of steel,
Sheffield plate, Bath metal and sometimes
pewter. The advent of tobacco in ready-cut
form popularized the leather tobacco pouch
and led to the decline of the tobacco box.
The *coup de grâce* was administered by the
tins (q.v.) in which tobacconists sold their
wares.

Jars for storing larger quantities of tobacco
were invariably of metal construction. Lead
was the usual material, though examples may
also be found in pewter, silver, cast iron or
brass. The earliest type, dating from the
1620s, was tall and cylindrical with a domed
lid and ornamental knop, usually incorporating a lead weight to keep the tobacco firmly
pressed down and ensure that the lid would
not be easily dislodged. Eighteenth-century
jars were often rectangular and are sometimes
confused with tea caddies (q.v.), though
their decoration is often a clue to their
identity. Engraved or embossed motifs
generally featured smoking, sporting or
military subjects, unlike the chinoiserie (q.v.)
favoured on tea caddies. Since many of these
jars were used by clubs, inns and taverns they
frequently bore the emblems of masonic or
political societies or alluded to the name of
the inn in their pictorial treatment. Tobacco
jars of the early nineteenth century frequently
had pseudo-medieval motifs in keeping with
the fashions of the Gothic Revival. They
declined in popularity in the second half of
the nineteenth century.

TOBY JUGS

Character jugs produced by the English potteries from the mid-eighteenth century down to the present day. Their origins illustrate the curious connections between the literary and artistic world of that period. In 1761 the Rev. Francis Hawkes published his *Original Poems and Translations* and included a translation of the 'Metamorphosis' by the Italian poet Geronimo Amalteo. The

translation was sub-titled 'Toby Reduced' and told of the life and death of a hearty tippler named Toby Fillpot. The last verse ran:

'His body, when long in the Ground it had
    lain,
And time into Clay had resolv'd it again,
A Potter found out in its Covert so snug
And with part of fat Toby he form'd this
    brown Jug.'

This poem was extremely popular and inspired an engraving of Toby Fillpot, published by Carrington Bowles, after a design by Robert Dighton. The corpulent character of Toby Fillpot, with his brimming tankard in one hand and his clay pipe in the other, was popularized through the Bowles print and, in turn, inspired the elder Ralph Wood of Burslem to manufacture jugs in Toby's image. Though it seems fairly certain that the origins of the Toby jug can be traced back to Amalteo through Hawkes, cases have been made out in favour of Shakespeare (Sir Toby Belch in *Twelfth Night*) and Laurence Sterne (Uncle Toby in *Tristram Shandy*).

Several claimants have also been put forward as the toper on whom Toby Fillpot was modelled. Some maintain that he was none other than Harry Elwes, who is credited with having sunk during his life 2,000 gallons of beer from a plain silver tankard; others claim that the Yorkshire farmer Paul Parnell (who downed £9,000 worth of liquor in his lifetime) was Toby's original. Toby's antecedents may be wrapped in mystery but those of his female counterpart are well documented. Martha Gunn was a famous bathing attendant at Brighton who died in 1815 at the ripe old age of 88. She is usually depicted with feathers in her hat, an allusion to her connection with the Prince of Wales.

A variation on the Martha Gunn jug was the gin woman, distinguished by her coarse features and luxuriant moustache. The Prince of Wales himself has left his mark in the comparatively rare type of Toby known as Prince Hal or Bluff King Hal. This figure in Tudor costume is allegedly based on the

figure, Admiral Vernon; was commemorat[ed] in this way, probably not so much on accou[nt] of his capture of Portobello in 1739 as for [the] institution of the naval rum. John Wes[ley] was also rendered in the form of a Toby ju[g].

Most Tobies are shown in a seated positio[n] but several standing types may be foun[d] the Hearty Good Fellow and the Snuff Tak[er] are well-known examples. In the nineteen[th] century, as their popularity grew, ne[w] subjects were added to the Toby family. Pa[ul] Pry, for example, dates from the publica[a-] tion of John Poole's play of that name [in] 1825. Later additions included Punch a[nd] Judy, while the Woodman Toby is genera[lly] believed to be modelled on Gladstone, t[he] British Prime Minister who took his exerc[ise] by chopping down trees. The Winst[on] Churchill Tobies of more recent years are [a] late flowering of this folk art, though most [of] the modern manufacturers seem to [be] content to produce imitations of t[he] eighteenth-century types. Most of t[he] modern Tobies lack the artistic quali[ty,] potting technique and vigorous colouring [of] the originals. A notable exception is t[he] series by Carruthers Gould featuring Alli[ed] war leaders, produced during World War [I.]

Although Ralph Wood senior is credit[ed] with inventing the Toby jug about 17[60] other potters were quick to imitate. Many [of] the earliest Tobies were unmarked and it [is] very difficult to assign them to the corre[ct] potter. Conversely, marked jugs exist whi[ch] prove that Neale, Pratt and Spode amo[ng] others made Toby jugs before the end of t[he] eighteenth century. There is considerab[le] variation in the size, style and colouring [of] these popular pieces of earthenware an[d] apart from the type of Toby jug itself, the[se] factors have an important bearing on t[he] value of the piece. The quality and colouri[ng] of the glaze can also affect the value, wh[ile] examples in silver lustre are of the great[est] rarity.

An interesting attempt by a mode[rn] manufacturer to break away from tradition[al] forms is provided by the Colonial William[s-] burg and Character jugs currently produc[ed] by Royal Doulton.

fancy dress worn on one occasion by the Prince at a Brighton masquerade. There are many other Toby characters, such as the Thin Man, the Parson, the Sailor, the Night Watchman and the Convict. The Unfrocked Parson, distinguished by his coloured coat, is sometimes, though erroneously, known as Doctor Johnson of dictionary fame.

Direct attribution of a Toby to a contemporary celebrity is unusual, though several naval heroes of the eighteenth century were thus honoured. Lord Howe, hero of the 'Glorious First of June', formed the subject of Toby jugs current in the 1780s. An earlier

TODDY GLASSES AND LIFTERS

The popularity of toddy (a hot beverage made from spirits, sugar, lemon juice, spices and water) in the second half of the eighteenth century led to the production of special glasses and servers. To overcome the problems of pouring hot liquid into glass vessels toddy glasses were made in comparatively thick and heavy glass, and resembled firing glasses (q.v.) but without stems. Larger glasses were known as toddy rummers and had a bucket-bowl with a short stem. The feet were usually circular, though rectangular bases are sometimes encountered. On account of the convivial nature of toddy the glasses in which it was served were frequently engraved with sporting scenes or the emblems of clubs and societies.

Toddy lifters were long-necked vessels with squat, bulbous bodies, similar to but smaller than the decanters of the same period (late eighteenth and early nineteenth centuries). They were ingeniously constructed with a hole in their flat base, and were plunged into the punch-bowl until full, the air being released through the hole at the top of the neck. This was then covered with the thumb to create a vacuum and the vessel was then lifted out of the bowl. The toddy poured into the glass when the thumb was released from the neck. Most English lifters had round bodies with a flat base, whereas Scottish examples were club-shaped with elongated bodies and rounded bases. Like toddy glasses they were often elaborately engraved, although Regency examples (*c.* 1810–30) were elaborately cut with an all-over diamond pattern.

TOILET SETS

Matched sets of pottery or porcelain utensils and containers, dating mainly from the early nineteenth century when standards of personal hygiene were improving. These sets comprised anything up to a dozen separate items, including a single or matched pair of chamberpots, ewer (qq.v.), washbasin, toothbrush stand, tooth-glass holder, soap boxes, dishes and stands (q.v.), shaving mug (q.v.) and toilet jars for powders and ointments. They were manufactured in Europe and America by most potteries and may be found with a wide range of decorative styles.
See colour plate page 291
See also *Dressing-Table Sets*

TOLEWARE

Articles of sheet iron, originating in France about 1740 and subsequently manufactured in other parts of Europe, Britain and America. This medium became popular for decorative objects of all sizes after the development of a heat-resistant varnish which was applied to the metal to prevent rust. A factory for the commercial production of *tôle peinte* (painted iron wares) was established by Clement in 1768, and thereafter this form of decoration became very popular. In its original form toleware relied on a special paint, several coats of which were applied to the surface, which was then blackened with smoke from a resinous torch. Ornamental patterns and motifs were executed in coloured varnishes on this surface, often with gilt borders. The style of decoration imitated the chinoiserie (q.v.) found on Sèvres porcelain of the same period. The technique was used extensively on the Continent for iron articles exposed to the weather, such as jardinières, planters and window-boxes. It was also used to decorate wine coolers, ice buckets, cassolettes (q.v.) and table lamps. Toleware was the French equivalent of the japanned metalwares produced at Pontypool (q.v.) and Usk.

Tole was also produced extensively in Holland in the early nineteenth century and was introduced to the United States by the Pennsylvania German settlers. In America tole was applied to small iron chests and boxes of all kinds, to pails, molasses jugs, tankards and canisters and remained popular as a form of decoration for much of the nineteenth century. The term is often loosely applied to painted tinware (q.v.) manufactured in Birmingham and other English industrial centres in the same period or later.
See colour plate page 292

Tortoiseshell and *piqué* box; French, 18th century.

TORTOISESHELL

Horny, translucent and mottled substance obtained from the back plates of certain species of sea turtle, especially the Hawksbill of the Cayman Islands, though it was formerly extracted from the sea turtles of Celebes and New Guinea. The plates of the carapace are removed from the skeleton and flattened under pressure and heat. The substance is noted for its rich mottled colours ranging from warm yellow to sepia tints, and for the high polish and durability. This material has been highly prized since Roman times as an inlay for small decorative objects and as a veneer in the panelling of furniture. Objects prior to the mid-eighteenth century are comparatively rare, but thenceforward it was widely used as an inlay on furniture using the boulle (q.v.) technique, and, with silver, as an inlay on the frames of portraits and mirrors as well as toilet articles of all kinds. Tortoiseshell was used in the lids of snuff boxes and other small objects of vertu and cut into combs or the narrow panels for knife handles. Collectors should beware of modern imitations in celluloid.

TOYS

In general parlance this term denotes children's playthings, but in the strict sense it is applied to an enormous variety of what have been defined as 'trifles, worthless petty ornaments, gew-gaws and baubles'.

Children's toys are as old as mankind itself and examples have survived from the most remote periods. The majority of these primitive playthings consist of dolls (q.v.) cast in bronze, baked earthenware or terracotta (q.v.) or made of wood and decorated with glass or pottery beads. Examples of non-human figures are also known, ranging from tiny bronze or pottery figures of cats, dogs, birds and more exotic animals to the elegant carved ivory or silver beasts of India and the Far East. Medieval European toys were made of carved and painted wood, or leather stuffed with hair or chopped straw. Given the fragile nature of the materials and the hard wear and tear to which they were subjected it is not surprising that early children's toys are now exceedingly rare.

Commercially produced toys date from the late-medieval productions of south Germany, Nuremberg having long been a centre of this industry. In the nineteenth century the Bavarian toymakers turned increasingly to mechanical toys, producing some of the earliest working models of locomotives. Early toy trains, complete with rolling-stock, manufactured by such firms as Märklin and Bing, are now very expensive. At the lower end of the scale, however, Bavaria and Saxony were centres of an industry supplying the world with cheap tinware (q.v.) playthings from penny whistles to hollow, die-stamped pop-guns and pistols, clowns and performing monkeys. These cheap toys were sold from about 1850 till the outbreak of World War I. So-called Bristol toys were cheaper still, being made from wood in back-street sweat-shops and cottages.

Toys very often reflect the age in which they were produced; changes in fashion, inventions such as the steam locomotive and the airplane, wars and outstanding international events have all had marked influences on the designs of toys. At the present day each season produces novelties often based on pop idols or the heroes of motion pictures and television series.

Trifles and trinkets intended as objects of curiosity for adults became popular in the late seventeenth century and reached their heyday in the eighteenth and early nineteenth centuries. These elegant playthings of the upper classes were usually manufactured in expensive materials such as silver or porcelain, though similar objects in brass or pottery may also be found. The dividing line between objects of vertu and toys is shadowy but the former are more usually regarded as small decorative items which have some useful function, whereas toys were merely decorative. This classification, however, is somewhat arbitrary, and toys often include such small useful objects as thimbles, snuff boxes, bonbonnières, needle cases and étuis. A large part of the Meissen production in the late eighteenth century consisted of *Galanterien* ('gallantries') or porcelain trinkets consisting

not only in Bristol (where they may have originated) but also in Birmingham, London and many other industrial cities. Toymaking as a major industry in its own right developed in the late nineteenth century and the range of products is enormous. Although stamped tinware survived World War II, it was gradually superseded by toys composed of metal castings of the highest precision, a technique applied especially to accurate miniature versions of motor cars from the 1930s onward. Cast-metal toys are still widespread, despite the increasing use of plastics.

of miniature figure groups or tiny ornaments which could be mounted in cane-handles (q.v.). Small porcelain boxes, for pills and patches, were made at Meissen, Chelsea, Sèvres and Limoges, while their enamelled copper or silver counterparts were made in the English Midlands and Switzerland. Toy furniture was made in silver, inlaid with tortoiseshell, and set out in glass-fronted display cabinets. Glass toys date from the early eighteenth century and are produced to this day in many parts of Europe, Asia and America. Tiny glass canes, top hats and slippers are among the most popular items, but animal and human figures in blown, pressed or moulded glass have long been a popular sideline of the Venetian, Scandinavian and American glasshouses in particular. See colour plate page 293

See also *Dolls, Enamels, Furniture – Miniature, Glass – Miniature, Model Soldiers, Optical Toys, Pipe Stoppers, Rattles and Teethers, Silver – Miniature*

TRANSFER WARES

Pottery, porcelain, enamelled metal or wood wares decorated by various mechanical processes known as transfer-printing. The design was first etched or engraved on a copper plate and enamel colours squeezed into the grooves and recesses. The pigment was then transferred under great pressure on to paper sheets, producing ridges of colour on the sheets themselves. While the enamel was still wet the sheet would be placed face down on the object to be decorated and the colour transferred under pressure. There were several variations of this. In both ceramic and metal wares the transfer paper was laid on the surface of the object which was then placed in a muffle kiln and baked. The heat burned off the paper and fused the enamel to the surface. This variant was used initially, during the second half of the eighteenth century, but by the 1820s special transfer papers had been patented and enabled the mass-production of mugs and plates decorated in this manner. The use of transfer papers which did not require heat extended transfer wares to wood, small objects with black-printed vignettes being a speciality of Mauchline ware (q.v.).

John Brooks, an Irish engraver working in Birmingham, is credited with having applied the technique of copper engravings to ceramics in 1751, but his early attempts seem to have met with little success. John Sadler and Guy Green, working in Liverpool, developed transfer-printing into a commercial proposition from about 1760 onwards and the process was quickly copied elsewhere. The earliest transfers were usually printed in black to provide an outline which could then be filled in with other colours by hand, or in blue on a white ground for the chinoiserie (q.v.) patterns then popular. Other colours became fashionable after 1820, while metallic transfers in gold or silver date from about 1810. Polychrome transfers were developed in the 1840s and were exploited by the New Jersey potteries. Prattware pot lids (q.v.) were decorated with polychrome transfer pictures, using a stippled technique.

Lithographic transfers made their début at the Great Exhibition of 1851 and rapidly superseded copperplate-engraved transfers thereafter. Stippled transfers on thin films of soft glue known as 'bats' were also used on porcelain from the late eighteenth century, this technique being known as bat-printing.

TRAYS

Small flat objects used for serving food and drink, developed in Europe in the sixteenth century and introduced to Britain from Holland in the late seventeenth century. From their inception trays were either functional or decorative, being made in wood, brass or silver according to their purpose. Wooden trays were decorated with carved or poker-work borders, often painted or lacquered. Paper mâché (q.v.) trays were fashionable in the early nineteenth century, their surfaces inlaid with ivory and mother-of-pearl. Oblong or rectangular wooden trays with marquetry (q.v.) decoration were originally known as butler's trays and were fashionable in the late eighteenth and early nineteenth centuries and were meant to rest on a tray table or voider stand, an X-shaped folding support. The style and decoration of silver trays generally followed that of salvers (q.v.),

though they were larger and often more elaborately decorated on the handles. Numerous small trays were produced for specific purposes, ranging from the silver or porcelain circular spoon tray which formed part of the tea equipage, to the small, narrow trays, in embossed silver, Sheffield plate, copper, brass or even pewter, used on dressing tables and writing desks for combs and pens respectively.

The earlier trays had a raised gallery or rail round the edges and fitted handles. Later trays, especially the metal examples, merely had a raised edge, and pierced handholds were often substituted for handles. Trays became increasingly popular from 1850 onwards. The rise of the great breweries, soft drinks manufacturers and tobacco companies led to the production of tin trays decorated with the advertisements of these firms and their products. Trays of this type are still being produced and a large collection can be formed showing different trademarks, slogans and miniature forms of poster art. From the turn of the century many manufacturers have sponsored trays reproducing famous paintings and latterly colour photographs of scenery and landmarks to promote their wares. Pictorial trays of this type are also universally popular as tourist souvenirs, and the same medium has been used in recent years to publicize or commemorate important events and personalities.

Ring holder and
magnifying glass in
treen; English, 19th
century.

Ring holder and
magnifying glass in
treen; English, 19th
century.

TREEN

Old English term for wooden articles (derived
from the word 'tree'), which has been
revived in recent years as a convenient
generic term for small, collectable wooden
objects. Although treen signifies anything
made of wood, it is usually restricted to
simple, domestic articles which cannot be
classified according to their decorative styles,
such as Mauchline or Tunbridge wares
(qq.v.). Basically it comprises spoons, bowls,
cups, trenchers, platters and utensils, usually
in oak, elm, sycamore or lignum vitae, both
turned and jointed. Such articles were in use
particularly in Britain and Colonial America
by the common people who could not afford
pewter or pottery tableware. As earthenware
became more commonplace at the end of the
seventeenth century, treen gradually declined.

The term is often applied to a wide variety
of small wooden objects which can also be
classified as love tokens (q.v.). These include
wooden stay-busks, needle or bodkin cases,
butter moulds or mangle boards.

TREMBLEUSES

Distinctive type of large saucer with a pronounced ring or rail in the middle to hold the
rim of the cup securely. The French name
implies that such saucers were a boon to those
with trembling or shaky hands. Examples
may be found in which the central ring is
elaborately pierced, so that any liquid slopped
over the side of the cup could drain away
into the bottom of the saucer. Trembleuses
originated in the French potteries (especially
St Cloud) in the early eighteenth century and
were widely imitated by the porcelain manufacturers in Austria, southern Germany and
England. Maiolica trembleuses were made at

Right Standing cup and
nest of goblets in turned
pearwood with silver
mounts; English, 17th
century.

Opposite Toilet or
dressing-table set,
including pots,
candlesticks, ring tree and
flower vase, in Noritake
porcelain; Japanese,
c. 1925.

Overleaf
Left Group of
Pennsylvania German
toleware; early 19th
century.

Right Selection of penny
toys; English, early 20th
century.

Castelli in the Abruzzi region of Italy. Similar objects, known as teacup stands, were made in silver or Sheffield plate, the central ring often being detachable. Porcelain trembleuses may be found with matching cups, often fitted with twin handles.

TRUNCHEONS. See *Tipstaves and Truncheons*

TUMBLERS

Small, cylindrical drinking cups with heavy rounded bases which prevent them from tipping over. The earliest tumblers were made in silver, often in sets as part of a travelling canteen used by sportsmen, hence the predilection for engravings of hunting scenes and other sporting subjects found on them. Tumblers of this type were popular in the seventeenth and eighteenth centuries and examples may be found from every part of Europe as well as Britain and North America. Glass tumblers became fashionable in the eighteenth century and have continued to this day, though the term is now used to denote any drinking glass with a thick heavy base and straight or slightly tapered sides.

TUNBRIDGE WARE

left Tunbridge ware desk
t with matching inkpot
d paper knife; English,
id-19th century.

Small wooden objects decorated with a distinctive wood mosaic, named after the Kentish town of Tunbridge Wells where the bulk of it is thought to have been produced as a form of tourist souvenir. Thin rods of wood, dyed in different colours or left in the natural state, were combined into a solid block which was then sawn into thin cross-sections which were applied like veneers to the surfaces of boxes and picture frames. This form of decoration, which seems to have been peculiar to the Tonbridge and Tunbridge Wells area, was well established by the end of the seventeenth century. Celia Fiennes recorded in her diary (1697) that the shops of Tunbridge Wells were 'full of all sorts of curious wooden ware which this place is noted for . . .' The earliest examples of Tunbridge ware consisted of platters and small picture frames, decorated with relatively simple geometric mosaic patterns, but by the middle of the eighteenth century the makers were becoming much more ambitious and applying tiny bands of mosaic to the lids and sides of snuff boxes, patch boxes, trinket boxes, napkin rings and even the beading on egg cups. The art reached its acme in the mid-nineteenth century when elaborate pictures composed entirely of tiny *tesserae* were worked on the lids of boxes or even produced as pictures. Profiles of Queen Victoria were a popular subject on small stamp boxes, the portrait being based on Wyon's medallic profile on the contemporary British stamps. Larger pictures were worked in small sections

Silver tureen with elk finial on cover and elk's head handles; American, 1859.

Otherwise known as terrines, these larg serving dishes date from the early eighteen century. The early form was oval, wit handles at either end, four cast feet, and domed cover with a central handle knopped finial. Tureens were made in silve though pewter or tinned brass have also bee noted. Sheffield plate and electroplate wei used for tureens from 1760 and 1840 re spectively. Late eighteenth-century exampl were produced with a large oval matchin stand or tray, often with a raised centr area which helped to steady the feet of tl tureen. Sauce tureens, modelled on the larg soup tureens but much smaller, were fashion able from about 1760 to 1840 and were als made in silver or Sheffield plate. Porcela tureens were produced as part of dinn services from the mid-eighteenth century Pottery tureens, with circular bowls an relatively steep, straight sides, twin handle domed cover and stand, have been made many parts of Europe since the early 180 and are still being produced in earthenwar stoneware and other ceramic materials. The may be found with pottery soup ladles matching glazes and decoration.

(about an inch square) and assembled skilfully into larger compositions up to a foot square. The versatility of the makers was enhanced by the import of exotic and colourful foreign timbers, and the best work was produced in the 1850s and 1860s. Perhaps the market was satiated, because Tunbridge ware declined sharply in popularity in the 1870s, and by 1890 it was no longer made. An attempt to revive the craft in the 1920s was a failure and Tunbridge ware of this period is readily identifiable by its poor quality and the relatively few types of wood employed.

UMBRELLAS. See *Parasols and Umbrellas*

UNION CASES

Small decorative cases popular in the United States during and after the Civil War, and thus named on account of the patriotic scenes and allegories with which they were decorated. They consisted of a shallow box with a hinged joint down one side and a clasp or lock on the other. They were carved in wood or ivory, but the introduction of a substance called *bois durci* accelerated their popularity. This wood-based compound was patented in France by F.C. Lepage and consisted of a mixture of sawdust, blood and water combined by heat treatment and then moulded into decorative shapes to simulate ebony carving. Other wood substitutes – the forerunners of bakelite and modern plastics – were also used in the manufacture of union cases in the latter part of the nineteenth century. Although union cases could be used to hold cigars or cigarettes they were primarily intended to house daguerreotypes and other early portrait photographs, echoing the *boîte à portrait* (portrait box) fashionable in Europe from the sixteenth to the eighteenth centuries – snuff boxes (q.v.) in which the portrait of the donor or owner was mounted inside the lid. Significantly many of the later nineteenth-century union cases had motifs consciously derived from carved wooden European originals.

Two union cases, one depicting the Washington Monument in *bois durci*, the other of leather; American, 1855–60.

VALENTINES

Christmas and Easter excepted, there is no festival in the Christian calendar which has been so commercialized as St Valentine's Day. The manner in which this obscure third-century priest, renowned for his chastity, became the patron saint of lovers was purely accidental. He was beheaded on 14 February in the year 270, the date of his execution coinciding with the eve of Lupercalia, an ancient pagan festival involving fertility rites and traditionally celebrated in connection with the return of spring.

For many centuries St Valentine's Day has been celebrated by lovers exchanging gifts and tokens of their affection. In times past there were many customs attached to the memory of this saint. The custom of drawing lots for one's Valentine, once prevalent in Britain, survives to this day in certain rural districts of the United States. From about 1760 onwards the giving of expensive presents to one's Valentine became the exception; instead it was customary to give a love token (q.v.) or a prettily written letter. To assist the lover in his romantic composition there were numerous volumes of suitable verses and manuals of complimentary phrases.

Gradually these *billets-doux* came to be lavishly decorated with lovers' knots, cupid's bows, hearts and other symbols of affection. Early examples of these Valentines, with hand-drawn or painted pictures, intricate pin-prick and cut-out work, or collages of lace, silk and thread, are now greatly prized by collectors. Printed Valentines appeared soon after pictorial writing paper, which was introduced in the closing decade of the eighteenth century. Some of these early printed Valentines were engraved by Francesco Bartolozzi and have long been in demand by collectors of Bartolozzi prints.

By 1803 H. Dobbs and Company were established as fancy paper manufacturers and had begun the production of Valentines on commercial scale. Dobbs' Valentines were renowned for their superb decoration and intricate embossing; many of them can be dated by the subtle changes in the firm's imprint. The production of embossed and die-stamped Valentines had been raised to fine art by the mid-nineteenth century. 1834 Joseph Addenbrook devised a method of simulating a lace effect in paper, and Valentines produced in the ensuing decade are notable for the intricacy of their decoration, often consisting of several fine layers of paper lace.

Even before the advent of cheap postage in 1840 the sending of Valentines by post had reached formidable proportions, some 60,000 being handled in London in 18— alone. At this time the method of computing postage was according to the number of sheets, and the use of an envelope doubled the charge. Thus Valentines, complete with ornate lacy envelopes, dated before 18— (Britain) or 1847 (United States) are exceedingly rare. The use of special Valentine envelopes increased in popularity after the introduction of uniform postal rates. Nevertheless, Valentines up to about 1870, complete with matching envelope, are worth a considerable premium. The custom was also widespread in Europe.

Comic Valentines, often of a malicious nature, became increasingly popular in the latter half of the nineteenth century. The advent of the picture postcard in the 18—

Sailor's shellwork valentine; English, c. 1880.

popularized and cheapened the Valentine even further. This, in a sense, was its undoing, for the cheap, joke Valentines of the early twentieth century put an end to the serious and sentimental nature of St Valentine's Day customs. The custom of sending Valentines in Britain died out during World War I, but it survived in America and it was probably from there that the custom was re-introduced by Raphael Tuck in 1926.

Although the prettiest Valentines sent in America were those of English origin, a home industry soon became established. Valentines, with mottoes embroidered on perforated card, were fashionable in the mid-nineteenth century. A form popular in New England consisted of Valentines with cut-paper motifs, usually of birds and flowers, mounted on card and framed. Valentines produced in shellwork (q.v.) were also fashionable. Simple heart and floral motifs were composed of shell mosaic, with simple mottoes such as 'Truly Thine', and glued to wooden bases for framing.

Valentine in the form of a banknote; English, mid-19th century.

VASES

Vessels of ornamental form, with a height greater in proportion to width. The term is usually confined to vessels without a lid or cover. Stems are either very short or non-existent, with heavy foot-rims or pedestal bases. Shapes vary enormously, from slender bases and wide, bell-shaped lips, or cylindrical with perpendicular sides, to comparatively wide, bowl-shaped bodies. Vases have been recorded in bronze from China in the Han Dynasty; in terracotta from the Mediterranean area in the pre-Christian era; and in glass from Roman Imperial times. The vase was a form popular with the medieval Venetian glassblowers, and distinctive styles were subsequently wrought in Bohemia, Silesia, Germany, France and Britain from the sixteenth century onwards, the relatively large surfaces being admirably suited to such decorative techniques as engraving, etching, enamelling and cutting.

The vase was also associated closely with the development of porcelain. The tall, cylindrical forms of China and Japan influenced early European porcelain designs, but by the early eighteenth century the

Two Mettlach earthenware vases, *c.* 1900–6.

classical urn shape had become more popular. In more recent years both classical and Oriental styles have been equally fashionable, though naturalistic forms with cast decoration were popular in the late nineteenth century and gave way to more angular shapes in the early 1900s. The vase was one of the most popular forms, particularly in art and fancy glass and studio pottery, in the United States in the second half of the nineteenth century. Other notable examples of ceramic vases include the Hispano-Mauresque wares of the sixteenth and seventeenth centuries, the Italian *istoriato* vases of Urbino and the Art Nouveau vases produced by French and Dutch potteries in the 1890s.

Wooden vases, usually in matched pairs, were fashionable in late eighteenth-century England as cutlery containers. Sumptuous and floridly decorated silver vases (subsequently copied in Sheffield plate) were fashionable in Regency England, modelled on classical Greek amphorae and *krateres*, their sides embossed with classical friezes. Similar vases, in blue and white jasperware, were produced by Wedgwood from the late eighteenth century onwards. Carved ivory vases with delicate relief decoration on their sides, were a Japanese speciality of the early nineteenth century, while vases in semi-precious stones such as malachite were produced in Russia prior to the Revolution, often with gilt mountings.

VINAIGRETTES

Small silver boxes containing aromatic vinegar intended as a prophylactic against disease and pestilence. Despite their French name they were an English invention and were alternatively (though less commonly) known as vinegarettes. The French refer to them as *boîtes de parfum* (perfume boxes) which gives a better description of their function. Although containers for aromatic spices had existed for centuries – Cardinal Wolsey's spiced orange and the late medieval pomanders (q.v.) are examples – the vinaigrette did not come into existence until the eighteenth century. Isolated examples have

been recorded as early as 1720, but the great majority of vinaigrettes date from the end of the century and were common during the period from *c.* 1780 to 1880. They were manufactured chiefly in London and Birmingham.

The inner part of the vinaigrette was heavily gilded to prevent corrosion of the box by its contents. A piece of sponge soaked in aromatic vinegar was placed inside and held in position by the perforated grill. Vinaigrettes were carried by persons of both sexes and sniffed at constantly when in public places as an antidote to possible infection or, more probably, to kill the unpleasant odours of the eighteenth-century street. Great impetus to the popularity of the vinaigrette was given by Dr William Henry, who lectured in the 1780s on the subject of prophylaxis and advocated the use of an aromatic liquid which became known as Dr Henry's Vinegar.

The function of the vinaigrette altered somewhat in its later years. By the middle of the nineteenth century the aromatic vinegar was giving way to a blend of smelling salts and the vinaigrette was being used by ladies to ward off 'attacks of the vapours'. Vinaigrettes reached their height of popularity in the 1820s, when they were often exchanged as tokens of affection or as keepsakes. As their utilitarian purpose diminished in importance they became more and more decorative. The grills, originally perforated quite simply, became increasingly ornate and the intricate patterns display considerable ingenuity on the part of the silversmith. The boxes were delicately engraved, often with scenery or allegorical subjects, in such techniques as repoussé, engine-turning and bright cutting.

Many vinaigrettes will be found unmarked, often being too small to require hallmarking, so that dating them and ascribing them to the correct manufacturer can be difficult. The makers of vinaigrettes were greatly influenced by styles in furniture, architecture and decoration, and it is sometimes possible to date them from ornament echoing the chinoiserie or rococo of contemporary fashions. Some vinaigrettes allude to outstanding events, the Battle of Trafalgar being

Above Silver-gilt vinaigrette in the shape of a pink; English, 1867.

Right Vinaigrette in the shape of a keg, with compartments for pills, scent and aromatic vinegar; English, 1871.

a well-known example, or can be identified by commemorative or personal inscriptions.

Vinaigrettes may sometimes be encountered in pinchbeck, gold, glass, porcelain or semi-precious stones such as cornelian or agate, but most of them were produced in silver. Examples featuring landmarks and identifiable scenery, or portraits (King George III and Lord Nelson were favourite subjects) are among those most highly prized.

VISITING CARDS

Otherwise known as calling cards, *cartes de visite* or *billets de visite*, these small pasteboard cards became fashionable in France in the reign of Louis XIII (1610–43). The earliest cards bore only the name and address, and etiquette demanded that the inscription be engraved by copperplate and not printed in letterpress. By the late seventeenth century

decorated with flowers, birds and fanc
flourishes. The ritual of presenting or leavin
cards was always a very formal one. Th
French also originated the custom of exchang
ing visiting cards as a form of New Year
greetings. During the brief life of the cele
brated Parisian Petite Poste in the mid
eighteenth century, the engraver Demaiso
instituted the practice of sending visitin
cards through the post – an all but forgotte
ancestor of the picture postcard (q.v.).

Visiting cards were adopted throughou
western Europe and the idea spread, vi
Britain, to North America where such card
reached the height of their popularity i
Victorian times. The more expensive card
were beautifully engraved in the Frenc
manner but plain cards could be purchase
and people took great delight in exercisin
their skills in penmanship. Homemade card
of this type were often embellished wit
small scraps (q.v.) or transfers.

The visiting card was given a new direc
tion in the 1860s with the increasing popu
larity of photography (q.v.). Many of th
early photographs were in the dimensions c
$2\frac{1}{2} \times 4$ inches; the collecting of such *carte
de visite* (the term applied to this typ
of photograph) reached enormous pro
portions in the 1880s and 1890s and specia
albums, with heavily padded binding an
thick leaves, were produced in large quantitie
to house these cards. Photographic *cartes a
visite* declined after the turn of the centur
and had died out completely before Worl
War I. In more recent years visiting card
have reverted to their original seventeenth
century style, and personal cards, as well a
those used by business and professional men
are engraved quite simply without an
ornamentation. Modern visiting cards ar
substantially smaller than those of the nine
teenth and earlier centuries.

See also *Card Cases*

Above Four *cartes de visite*
showing photographs
and the photographer's
trademark.

these cards were embellished with fine
engravings of landscapes, architectural or
classical compositions. At first confined to
gentlemen, they were soon adopted by
ladies also, and their cards were frequently

Opposite Pair of witch
balls and vases in red,
white and blue striped
glass, made by the New
England Glass Company;
American, *c.* 1840.

WALKING-STICKS. See *Canes and Walking-sticks*

WARMING PANS

Brass or copper pans containing hot charcoal and used to warm beds. The pan had a hinged lid with perforations to allow the heat to escape. Considerable variety may be found in the piercing and fretting of the lid, with the addition of embossed or cast ornament at the junction of the handle. The earliest warming pans, widely used in Europe from the fifteenth century, were made of iron, with iron handles. Later examples had brass or copper pans and by the middle of the seventeenth century wooden handles, usually of beech, oak or ash, were in use, the latter being carved or turned and ornamented with balusters and knops. Such an important domestic implement was a popular wedding present, hence the existence of so many examples from the early seventeenth century

onwards bearing dates and sets of initials. The earliest pans were straight-sided with flat lids, but towards the end of the eighteenth century curved sides and slightly domed lids became fashionable. Long-handled pans without pierced ornament on the top, and fitted with a screw stopper and aperture, were used from about 1770 to hold hot water instead of hot embers. Detachable handles came into use at the beginning of the nineteenth century and by 1820 pan-shaped hot-water bottles in copper or brass had ousted the long-handled variety. These metal hot-water bottles remained in use until the early twentieth century, being superseded by the earthenware 'pig' bottle. By 1890 the hot-water bag in various forms of sheet or moulded rubber was beginning to appear, though the earthenware hot-water bottle continued in use until recently and may still be found in certain parts of northern Europe.

The decorative qualities of the long-handled warming pan have led to its popularity as a wall ornament in recent years, and as a result there has been a considerable industry in the manufacture of reproduction pans. These are usually of inferior and thinner metal and lack the elaborate piercing and hammered ornament of the genuine article.

WATCHES

Small timepieces carried on the person evolved out of late medieval techniques in clock-making. Peter Henlein of Nuremberg is credited with inventing the first practical watch about 1510. The so-called Nuremberg Eggs were massive, spherical timepieces, superseded later in the sixteenth century by

ight Two pierced and engraved brass warming pans; English, 17th century.

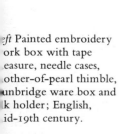

eft Painted embroidery work box with tape measure, needle cases, mother-of-pearl thimble, Tunbridge ware box and k holder; English, mid-19th century.

the neater drum-shaped clock-watch. The form then progressed via the globular and elliptical watches of the seventeenth century to the flat, circular shapes of the eighteenth and subsequent centuries. Watch-making spread from southern Germany to France about 1550; Blois became the centre of the French watch-making industry. English watches followed French and German models in the early seventeenth century but soon evolved the distinctive Puritan style.

European watches, with gilt-metal mounts and cases, were manufactured in oval or octagonal shapes in the seventeenth century, and even now are not too difficult to obtain. More elaborate items, such as the naturalistic forms in the shape of animals or birds, were developed in France and Switzerland in the eighteenth century and have always fetched high prices. The early watches had a single hand and the watch-face was unglazed. The face and hand were protected by pierced lids, later superseded by rock crystal mounted over the dial, but glazing did not become general until the latter half of the seventeenth century. Enamelling, originally confined to the dial, extended to the inner and outer sides of the case at the end of the century, and exquisite examples of polychrome pictures found on these watches are keenly regarded by collectors, boosting the value of such items considerably.

The technical advances of the late seventeenth century, which included the balance spring *c.* 1675, led to a decrease in the importance of the watch case and interior decoration. At the beginning of the eighteenth century the fashion for ornately enamelled watches waned and comparatively plain watches became popular. As the century wore on, however, enamelling returned to favour, culminating in the interesting pictorial types which were so fashionable in the last years of the French monarchy. Watch cases of the late eighteenth century were often decorated with transparent enamel over an engine-turned background. Pictorial enamelled watches remain the most keenly sought after, while technical variations and refinements, such as musical quarter repeaters with

or without automata, can greatly enhance the value of a watch. Where pictorial enamelled watches are concerned the value will depend not only on the artistic quality but on the subject depicted, and subsequent research can greatly raise the value of a piece.

Watch cases are collectable items in their own right; pastoral scenes are not particularly highly rated, but mid-nineteenth century examples depicting balloons, locomotives and maritime subjects are extremely popular. Conversely, the movement itself can be of value, particularly if it exhibits some interesting technical feature.

The earliest watches were too cumbersome to be carried in the pocket and were usually hung from the girdle by a chain. From this there gradually developed the elaborate chatelaines (q.v.) which attained their peak of perfection in the eighteenth century. Watch and chatelaine combinations can be very expensive, especially if they are richly jewelled. Great care should be exercised in the purchase of such items since the watch and chatelaine may not have originally belonged together and obviously they will tend to fetch more together than as individual items. Points to note are the materials used and the style of

ft 'Columbus' dollar
atch by Ingersoll, for
e Columbian
xposition, 1893.

decoration employed. Conversely, genuine though unusual combinations of watch and chatelaine have been recorded; where this can be authenticated the value of the combination is greatly enhanced. Richly ornamented fobs became fashionable at the beginning of the nineteenth century as part of the personal jewelry (q.v.) worn by gentlemen.

The earliest watches were wound by turning a miniature windlass but by the mid-sixteenth century keys fitting a square winding spindle had appeared. Later keys were attached direct to the winding mechanism, or took the form of crank keys, often folding into the case. As watches became more decorative in the eighteenth century, ornamentation was also lavished on the keys, which are collectable in their own right (see *Locks and Keys*). Watch chains offer little scope in themselves, but the ornaments often attached to them are of interest, ranging from enamelled coins and masonic jewels to talismanic devices and good-luck charms. From the middle of the eighteenth century onwards small collapsible stands were used to hold the watch upright when not worn, and thus formed a useful bedside timepiece. These stands may be identified by the circular (often padded) recess designed to hold the watch, or the hook and frame arrangement for the suspension of the watch.

WINDOW DISPLAY PIECES

Brightly coloured boards, cards and figures used by shopkeepers to catch the eye of passers-by date from the late eighteenth century. The earliest examples, carved from wood and hand-painted, were crude by modern standards of display technique, but their style of lettering and direct approach to the would-be customer have a naïve charm. The advent of branded goods and patent medicines in the nineteenth century led to the decline of the homemade display pieces and resulted in the enamelled metal plaques and stout pasteboard placards of the 1890s. Three-dimensional display pieces include miniature versions of a wide range of durable

goods, from furniture to motor cars. Miniature dummy figures with clothing and underwear scaled down to match form a specialized aspect of interest to collectors of costume. Replicas of foodstuffs in painted plaster or chalkware (q.v.) have been widely used since the mid-nineteenth century. Conversely, many small articles such as ink bottles and mustard pots may be found in the form of outsize stand-up cardboard dummies.

Mechanical display pieces, operated by clockwork, developed in the 1840s, and by the turn of the century the more complex types consisted of a number of moving figures capable of working for several hours at a single winding of the mechanism. Illuminated signs and winking lights were developed in the early 1900s. Display ornaments may be classified according to the type of goods advertised: liquor, tobacco, foodstuffs, consumer goods and miscellaneous services.

WINE COOLERS

Large vessels used to contain ice for cooling wine bottles. In size they range from the small and relatively simple ice pail or bucket, made in silver, Sheffield plate or electro-

ght Terracotta wine
oler portraying Lord
elson; Davenport,
1805.

plate, in the form of urns, tubs or buckets, to the large wine cisterns of the seventeenth to nineteenth centuries. The larger vessels were often made in base metal such as copper, brass, pewter or white metal, while many of them were made of wood with liners of tinned copper or lead. The wooden coolers were sometimes mounted on a pedestal with castors and had a hinged lid, which made them ideal as small occasional tables when not actually being used as wine coolers. The side panels and lids were often decorated with marquetry (q.v.) and were particularly fashionable in the Regency period.

WINE GLASSES

Prior to the seventeenth century the vast majority of European wine glasses were either made in Venice or followed the Venetian styles and materials. These early glasses were made in a light soda-glass with elaborately moulded stems, often vertically

English 18th-century wine glasses featuring an unusual incised twist, cylindrical tear stem, and balustroid stem.

or horizontally ribbed and embellished wi[th] excrescences known as prunts. The bow[ls] were either funnel- or bell-shaped and the[ir] exterior surfaces were often elaborately e[n]graved with a diamond point. In the sixteen[th] century Italian *cristallo* spread northwar[d] to Silesia and Bohemia and westward [to] France and the Low Countries. Italia[n] glasses were introduced to England b[y] Giacomo Verzelini in 1571. Subsequent English glasses followed Continental patter[n] the popular seventeenth-century form bei[ng] tall and elongated with inverted balust[er] stems known as cigar stems. Stems frequent[ly] had spiral or entwined motifs in contrasti[ng] colours, imitating contemporary glasses fro[m] Venice and Flanders.

George Ravenscroft revolutionized t[he] English wine glass in the late seventeen[th] century by inventing a much heavier ty[pe] of glass containing lead oxide. This 'lea[d]' or 'flint' glass with its attractive lustre, is ve[ry] rare and fewer than a dozen wine glass[es] attributed to Ravenscroft have been recorde[d]. It was unsuited to the light ornament pr[e]ferred by the Continental craftsmen; instea[d] English craftsmen concentrated on devisi[ng] more massive shapes which exploited t[he] dark beauty of flint glass. The wine glasses [of] the period from 1690 to 1730 are very lar[ge] and thick by modern standards, and identic[al] styles were quickly established in the Amer[i]can colonies where they generally remaine[d] popular for a decade or two after they ha[d] ceased to be fashionable in the moth[er] country.

After 1730 the style of wine glasses becam[e] much more varied, the hitherto simp[le] baluster stem being decorated by one [or] more rings or knops. Elongated bubbles [or] 'tears' were incorporated in the balust[er] stems and these gradually evolved int[o] complex patterns and spirals of fine air line[s]. Different types of wine glass were produce[d] for specific purposes and these are discusse[d] in detail under the appropriate heading. T[he] chronology of the shapes in bowls and sten[s] is discussed under Glasses (q.v.).
See also *Firing Glasses, Rummers, Syllab[ub] Glasses, Toddy Glasses*

Group of silver wine
labels; English, late 18th
and early 19th centuries.

Sometimes known as bottle tickets, these tags, which were hung round the necks of wine bottles and decanters, became fashionable in the mid-eighteenth century and have continued in use to this day. It has never been ascertained precisely when wine labels were introduced, but their origins probably coincided with the change in the practice of labelling decanters. The earliest decanters, dating from *c.* 1710, had parchment labels affixed to their necks identifying the wine, and from this the modern printed paper label gradually evolved. Something more substantial, however, in keeping with the elegance of the dining table, was required. At first decanters were manufactured with the names of wines engraved on their sides, but the fashion for cutting glass in an all-over pattern precluded this and hastened the development of the wine label. The metal label, in silver or Sheffield plate, slightly curved to fit the side of the decanter, and hung around its neck by a fine chain, was the result. Most authorities seem to agree that two of the earliest manufacturers were Isaac Duke, who registered his hallmark in 1743, and Sandylands Drinkwater, who produced labels between 1735 and 1750; but in view of the fact that the hallmarking of such small articles did not become compulsory until 1790 it is possible that wine labels were in existence at least a decade earlier.

Wine labels vary greatly in design and the style of lettering. Plain rectangles with chamfered corners are the most plentiful. Popular motifs were the vine-leaf or bunch of grapes, which are found in many different forms with the name of the wine inscribed across the centre. Scallop shells and scrolls, sometimes incorporating heraldic devices, were also fashionable, while wine labels in the shape of animals, such as bulls or pigs, are comparatively rare. The earliest silver labels were wrought by hand. About 1800 Linwood of Birmingham devised a method of die-stamping which resulted in lighter, more intricate patterns; but a decade later cast-metal labels came into vogue. The wine-label industry declined during the nineteenth century, the *coup de grâce* being the law of 1860 making paper labels on wine bottles compulsory. Nevertheless, there has been something of a revival in more recent years to supply decanters, but the range of names has shrunk considerably, embracing only the fortified wines such as sherry, port and madeira.

Wine labels are found in a wide range of materials. While silver or silver-gilt was the most popular, enamels (q.v.) enjoyed a brief vogue in the 1750s and labels in this material are now highly prized. As a substitute for silver, close-plating was very seldom used and examples of wine labels with a thin foil of silver soldered on to a steel base are extremely rare. Not quite so rare, but still uncommon, are wine labels in Sheffield plate (not to be confused with electroplate, which can be worth very little). Porcelain, ivory and mother-of-pearl and even humble pewter have been recorded. An incredible variety of names may be found on wine labels, including countless wines which have disappeared into oblivion. Unusual and obsolete wines found on these labels include shrub, raspberry brandy, Teneriffe, Lisbon and mountain. Also worth looking for are such mis-spellings as maderia (madeira) and noyeo (noyeau). The names are found in English and French, the latter indicating that wine labels, which were very much an English custom, were also exported in large quantities to the continent of Europe.

WINE TASTERS

Small metal cups originally used by wine tasters and vintners to sample wines. They were made of pewter, silver or silver-gilt with plain, fluted or embossed bowls and a variety of handles or no handles at all. They may be found with twin handles or single handles, in swan's neck form or lugs at right angles to the bowl, or even elongated like the handles of a spoon. A similar form, with plain lugs at right angles and a very shallow bowl, was used for Scottish quaichs (q.v.). These small metal cups are thought to have been made in

Europe from medieval times, though examples dating before the seventeenth century are very rare. The majority of them date from the late seventeenth and eighteenth centuries. A popular device was to insert a silver coin, of florin, half-crown or half dollar size, in the inside of the base. European tasters of the seventeenth and eighteenth centuries were often elaborately engraved with scrolled thumb-pieces instead of handles.

WITCH BALLS

Small hollow glass spheres made in England from the mid-eighteenth century and in America from the early nineteenth century. They were produced as a kind of talisman, to ward off evil spirits or bring good luck to a house, and were often hung up over windows and doorways. They were made of coloured glass but the nineteenth-century examples also include balls with silvered interiors or fancy patterns in the glass in contrasting colours. They had an excrescence at one end bored with a hole to take a cord for suspension. Genuine witch balls are comparatively scarce and should not be confused with larger glass balls, in green, blue or brown glass, widely used until recent years as floats on fishing nets and lines. These balls, especially when fitted with net covers and cords, are attractive cottage ornaments.

See colour plate page 303

WORK BOXES

Boxes used by seamstresses and needleworkers to house their tools and materials. They seem to have originated in Europe in the late seventeenth century though the majority of extant examples belong to the nineteenth and early twentieth centuries. The more elaborate examples, sometimes known as *tricoteuses*, were fitted to tripod stands and thus served as work tables, with a drawer or drawers and a satin work-bag suspended beneath. The best work boxes were made of mahogany, walnut, lingwood, pearwood or satinwood and their lids and backs were often decorated with marquetry

panels or borders. The earlier examples had two or more compartments arranged one above the other like a tiny chest of drawers. Later examples had banks of drawers or trays which opened on brackets attached to their sides to reveal the contents. Work boxes of Oriental manufacture were frequently inlaid with ivory or mother-of-pearl. Papier mâché (q.v.) work boxes were fashionable in the nineteenth century, with black lacquered lids decorated with chinoiserie (q.v.). Oval work boxes were popular in America from the late eighteenth century, with semicircular compartments at either end and tiny drawers underneath. Like their European counterparts these boxes were often mounted on legs and were known as Martha Washington tables.

See colour plate page 304

WRITING CASES

Boxes or cases containing writing materials date from the seventeenth century and were usually made of wood, though examples in copper, pewter or brass have been recorded, while papier mâché and leather were popular in the nineteenth century. There are three basic forms with numerous variations. The earliest type consisted of an oblong box with a hinged or sliding lid, containing ferrules, pens, pencils and crayons in the centre and having small inkpots at either end. This style is still favoured for children's writing cases and many examples may be encountered with the lids and sides decorated with characters from fairy tales and nursery rhymes. This style is also a perennial favourite in Far Eastern countries and has been noted in silver filigree, inlaid brassware and wood decorated with ivory. The most popular Occidental form consists of an upright box whose front drops to reveal a series of small drawers and vertical compartments, to hold notepaper, envelopes, sealing materials, pens, ink, scissors, rulers and erasers. The third type, often referred to as a compendium, consists basically of a blotter and writing pad, with side flaps and pockets containing writing implements and materials.

See also *Inkstands and Inkpots*

YARD-OF-ALE

Trick form of drinking glass, of English origin. It consists of a vessel with a slender neck, about a yard in length, attached to a globular bowl. The mouth flares to a trumpet-shaped lip. The capacity of yards-of-ale is usually about one pint. Shorter vessels known as half-yards are also fairly plentiful. These vessels, similar in appearance to the coaching horns of the period, were popular in English taverns and ale-houses in the seventeenth and eighteenth centuries, though genuine examples of that era are scarce. The majority of yards-of-ale now in existence date from the second half of the nineteenth century and they have been frequently reproduced in recent years. The secret of draining a yard-of-ale was to take it very slowly; any sudden access of air to the bulbous bowl would result in the drinker's face being liberally splashed.

See also *Puzzle Jugs and Cups*

ZARFS

Small holders for the handle-less cups used in drinking Turkish coffee. They resemble egg-cups with a rather wider and shorter bowl and, generally, a taller pedestal. Traditional zarfs were fashioned in silver or brass and frequently chased, pierced or inlaid with gold and other metals. They were popular throughout the lands of the former Ottoman Empire from Morocco to Arabia and the Balkans, and are made to this day in many of these countries as tourist souvenirs. Curiously enough some of the finest zarfs, intended for genuine usage, were of European manu-facture, being produced in France and Switzerland in the mid-nineteenth century for export to the Levant. These zarfs were fashioned in gold or silver and decorated with semi-precious stones, glass paste inlay and richly enamelled.

ZELLENMOSAIK

Name given to a distinctive type of decorate hardstone box, produced in Dresden in th second half of the eighteenth century. Th decoration consists of mosaic patterns o hardstones set in gold cells. The techniqu was developed by Heinrich Dattel or Tadde a goldsmith who also held an appointmen at the Saxon Court as Inspector of th Repository of Royal Treasures. Small boxe such as snuff boxes, tobacco boxes an bonbonnières (qq.v.) were originally com posed of a quartzite core covered with piece of different hardstones such as jasper, cor nelian, bloodstone and agate. In the majorit of the boxes produced by Dattel the quartzit core was dispensed with and the base, side and lid built up using a process borrowe from cloisonné enamelling (q.v.).

Dattel's pupil, Johann Christian Neube

Two zarfs with matching cups; Bosnian, late 19th century.

who became Saxon Court jeweler in 1775 and established a factory making objects of vertu, developed the *Zellenmosaik* technique and exploited the contemporary craze for geology. Young men on the Grand Tour visited Dresden to secure specimens of the hardstones for which Saxony was famous. Neuber neatly supplied this demand with boxes composed of many different hardstones. The base of these boxes had a secret compartment in which was concealed an explanatory booklet identifying the various hardstones. Each box was numbered individually and the serial number printed on the booklet. Similar *Zellenmosaik* boxes were made by Christian Gottlieb Stiehl, both with a hardstone backing and in the *pliqué à jour* technique (again borrowed from enamelling), in which the gold cells had no backing and created a stained-glass window effect. *Zellenmosaik* boxes were in vogue until the 1830s but the art declined after that time.

ZINC

A metallic chemical element, so unstable that it is never found in its pure form, but usually in oxide compounds such as calamine. Zinc was widely used to form the alloy with copper known as brass (q.v.). Zinc in its pure form was not isolated in England until about 1730 and the earliest European zinc-works was not established at Liège in Belgium until 1807. Until 1833 the bulk of the world's supplies of zinc came from Germany, but other sources were developed thereafter, first Russia, then Belgium, Britain and latterly the United States (1873), which now produces a third of the world total. Not surprisingly, the Germans were the first to make use of zinc in the field of the applied arts. An alloy containing pure zinc and a small quantity of lead, known as *Spiauter* or spelter, was used in the second half of the nineteenth century to produce small casts of sculpture, similar to, but usually much cheaper than, the bronze figures which were so popular at that time. Several foundries in the Berlin area specialized in zinc figures, varying considerably in quality and craftsmanship. A

technician named Geiss devised a process for bronzing the surface of these figures. Many late nineteenth-century cast-metal clock-cases, in the French style, were produced in Germany using bronzed spelter. The use of spelter declined after 1900 and pure zinc is now used in various brass alloys such as Muntzmetal, tombac brass and pinchbeck.

ZWISCHENGOLDGLÄSER

Literally 'gold sandwich glasses', they consist of double-walled glasses with engraved gold leaf between the two walls. This technique was developed in Hellenistic times, Greek goblets with gold-leaf inserts being recorded from the second century BC. Very few of these Greek double-walled glasses have survived and their sporadic appearance in archaeological sites all over the eastern Mediterranean area, from Antioch to Alexandria, is too scant for positive attribution.

The art was revived mysteriously in Bohemia in the early eighteenth century. Engraved leaves of gold or silver foil were inserted into large beakers, and subsequently goblets and wine glasses. This type of decoration was sometimes combined with coloured glass or cold-painting. The earliest motifs were invariably of a religious nature, which seems to support the theory that the art was revived in the monasteries, and it is not improbable that it was inspired by an early Christian goblet of Alexandrian origin. *Zwischengoldgläser* were produced commercially by Johann Jacob Mildner of Gutenbrunn in Lower Austria from 1787 onwards, using medallions and cartouches of gold or silver leaf in the walls of tumblers, which were also decorated with wheel or diamond-point engraving. Glasses of this type have been produced infrequently in more recent times in Bohemia, Silesia and Austria but examples are scarce. The late eighteenth- and nineteenth-century glasses depicted hunting scenes, allegorical subjects and compositions derived from classical mythology. A few examples have been recorded which are decorated with silhouette (q.v.) motifs.

Bibliography

GENERAL

Amaya, Mario *Art Nouveau*, 1966
Angus, Ian *Collecting Antiques*, 1972
Battersby, Martin *The World of Art Nouveau*, 1968
　Art Nouveau, 1969
　The Decorative Twenties, 1969
　The Decorative Thirties, 1971
Boger, Louise Ade and H.B. *The Dictionary of Antiques and the Decorative Arts*, 1969
Bridgeman, Harriet (ed) *Discovering Antiques*, 1970
Butler, Joseph T. *American Antiques, 1800–1900*, 1965
Cameron, Ian and Kingsley-Rowe, Elizabeth (eds) *Collins Encyclopedia of Antiques*, 1973
　The Collector's Encyclopedia, 1974
Chu, Arthur and Grace *Oriental Antiques and Collectibles*, 1973
Comstock, H. *The Concise Encyclopedia of American Antiques*, 1958
Coysh, A.W. and King, J. *The Buying Antiques General Guide*, 1970
　The Buying Antiques Reference Book, 1974
Davidson, Marshall B. *The American Heritage History of Antiques*, 1969
Dorfles, Gillo *Kitsch*, 1969
Field, June *Collecting Georgian and Victorian Crafts*, 1974
Garner, Phillippe *The World of Edwardiana*, 1974
Gohm, Douglas *Small Antiques for the Collector*, 1969
Hayward, Charles *Antique or Fake?*, 1970
Hillier, Bevis *Art Deco*, 1968
　The World of Art Deco, 1971
Honour, Hugh *Chinoiserie*, 1961
Hughes, G. Bernard *The Country Life Collector's Pocket Book*, 1963
Hughes, Therle *Small Antiques for the Collector*, 1964
　Cottage Antiques, 1967
Hume, Ivor Noël *A Guide to the Artifacts of Colonial America*, 1969
Jefferson, Louise, E. *The Decorative Arts of Africa*, 1974
Klein, Dan *All Colour Book of Art Deco*, 1974
Latham, Jean *Miniature Antiques*, 1972
Laver, James *Victoriana*, 1966
Lichten, Frances *Decorative Art of Victoria's Era*, 1960
McClinton, Katharine M. *Art Deco: A Guide for Collectors*, 1972
Macdonald-Taylor, Margaret *A Dictionary of Marks*, 1962
Mackay, James A. *An Introduction to Small Antiques*, 1970

Mackay, James A. *Antiques of the Future*, 1970
　Dictionary of Turn of the Century Antiques, 1974
Madsen, S. Tschudi *Sources of Art Nouveau*, 1956
　Art Nouveau, 1967
Mebane, John *New Horizons in Collecting*, 1967
　The Coming Collecting Boom, 1968
Peter, M. *Collecting Victoriana*, 1965
Ramsay, L.G.C. (ed) *The Concise Encyclopaedia of Antiques* (5 vols), 1955–60
　The Complete Encyclopedia of Antiques, 1975 (revised ed.)
Reade, B. *Regency Antiques*, 1953
Rheims, Maurice *The Antique Collector's Handbook*, 1959
　The Age of Art Nouveau, 1966
Savage, George *Dictionary of Antiques*, 1970
Schmutzler, Robert *Art Nouveau*, 1964
Speck, G.E. and Sutherland, Euan *English Antiques*, 1969
Toller, Jane *Regency and Victorian Crafts*, 1969
Whittington, Peter *Undiscovered Antiques*, 1972
Wilson, Peter (ed.) *Antiques International*, 1966
Wood, Violet *Victoriana: A Collector's Guide*, 1968

ANTIQUITIES AND ORIENTAL ART

Anderson, L.J. *Japanese Armour*, 1969
Bedford, John *Chinese and Japanese Lacquer*, 1969
Boyer, M. *Japanese Export Lacquer (1600–1800)*, 1959
Chesterman, James *Classical Terracotta Figures*, 1974
Cosgrove, Maynard G. *The Enamels of China and Japan*, 1974
Davey, Neil *Netsuke*, 1974
Ede, Charles *Antiquities for the Small Collector*, 1975
Garner, Sir Harry *Chinese and Japanese Cloisonné Enamels*, 1962
Herberts, K. *Oriental Lacquer*, 1962
Jonas, F.M. *Netsuke*, 1969
Newman, A.R. *Japanese Art*, 1965
O'Brien, M.L. *Netsuke: A Guide for Collectors*, 1965
Perry, L.S. *Chinese Snuff Bottles*, 1960
Reitichi, U. *The Netsuke Handbook*, 1964
Robinson, Basil W. *Arts of the Japanese Sword*, 1961
Robinson, H. Russell *Oriental Armour*, 1967
　Japanese Arms and Armour, 1969
Ryerson, E. *The Netsuke of Japan*, 1968
Watson, W. *Ancient Chinese Bronzes*, 1962
Willetts, W. *Chinese Art*, 1958

CLOCKS, WATCHES AND SCIENTIFIC
INSTRUMENTS

Baillie, G.H. *Watches*, 1929
Bell, G.H. and E.F. *Old English Barometers*, 1970
Bruton, Eric *Clocks and Watches, 1400–1900*, 1967
　　Clocks and Watches, 1968
Camerer Cuss, T.P. *The Country Life Book of
　　Watches*, 1967
Chamberlain, Paul *It's About Time*, 1964 (new ed.)
Chapuis, Alfred and Droz, E. *Automata*, 1960
Chapuis, Alfred and Jaquet, Eugène *The Swiss
　　Watch*, 1970 (new ed.)
Clarke, J.E.T. *Musical Boxes: A History and
　　Appreciation*, 1961
Clutton, C. and Daniels, George *Watches*, 1965
Coole, Philip and Neumann, S. *The Orpheus Clock*,
　　1972
Cousins, F.W. *Sundials*, 1969
Daniels, George *English and American Watches*, 1967
Daumas, M. *Scientific Instruments of the 17th and 18th
　　Centuries and Their Makers*, 1972
Edey, Winthrop *French Clocks*, 1967
Goaman, Muriel *English Clocks*, 1967
Goodison, N. *English Barometers, 1680–1860*, 1969
Hayward, John F. *English Watches*, 1969
Joy, Edward T. *The Country Life Book of Clocks*,
　　1967
Lloyd, H. Alan *The Collector's Dictionary of Clocks*,
　　1969
　　Old Clocks, 1970
Michel, H. *Scientific Instruments in Art and History*,
　　1967
Morpurgo, E. *Precious Watches*, 1966
Ord-Hume, Arthur W.J. *Collecting Musical Boxes*,
　　1967
Palmer, Brook *A Treasury of American Clocks*, 1967
Tait, Hugh *Clocks in the British Museum*, 1968
Thomson, Richard *Antique American Clocks and
　　Watches*, 1968
Tyler, E.J. *European Clocks*, 1968
Ulyett, Kenneth *In Quest of Clocks*, 1969
Wenham, Edward *Old Clocks*, 1965

GLASS

Amaya, Mario *Tiffany Glass*, 1967
Barrington-Haynes, E. *Glass through the Ages*, 1959
Beard, Geoffrey W. *Nineteenth Century Cameo
　　Glass*, 1956
Bedford, John *Bristol and Other Coloured Glass*, 1964
Belknap, E. McC. *Milk Glass*, 1949
Blount, B. and H. *French Cameo Glass*, 1968
Charleston, R.J. *English Opaque White Glass*, 1962
Cloak, Evelyn C. *Glass Paperweights*, 1969
Crompton, Sidney (ed.) *English Glass*, 1967
Davis, Derek C. *English and Irish Antique Glass*,
　　1965
　　English Bottles and Decanters, 1972
Davis, Derek C. and Middlemas, Keith *Coloured
　　Glass*, 1968
Davis, Frank *The Country Life Book of Glass*, 1966
Elville, E.M. *English and Irish Cut Glass*, 1953
　　Paperweights and other Glass Curiosities, 1954
　　Collector's Dictionary of Glass, 1961

Fleming, J.A. *Scottish and Jacobite Glass*, 1938
Fletcher, Edward *Bottle Collecting*, 1972
Gros-Galliner, Gabriella *Glass: A Guide for
　　Collectors*, 1970
Grover, Ray and Lee *Art Glass Nouveau*, 1967
　　Carved and Decorated European Art Glass, 1970
Hollister, Paul Jr *The Encyclopedia of Glass
　　Paperweights*, 1969
Hughes, G. Bernard, *English Glass for the Collector*,
　　1967
Jokelson, Paul *Glass Paperweights and Cameo Heads*,
　　1968
Koch, Robert *Tiffany Coloured Glass*, 1964
Lee, Ruth W. *Early American Pressed Glass*, 1952
Lindsay, Bessie M. *American Historical Glass*, 1967
Lloyd, Ward *Investing in Georgian Glass*, 1969
Mackay, James A. *Glass Paperweights*, 1973
McKearin, G.S. and H. *200 Years of American
　　Blown Glass*, 1966
Middlemas, Keith *Continental Coloured Glass*, 1971
Revi, Albert C. *American Pressed Glass and Figure
　　Bottles*, 1964
Robertson, R.A. *Chats on Old Glass*, 1969
Ruggles-Brise, Sheelah *Sealed Bottles*, 1949
Savage, George *Glass and Glassware*, 1973
Thorpe, W.A. *English Glass*, 1961
Vavrá, J.R. *5,000 Years of Glassmaking*, 1954
Warren, P. *Irish Glass*, 1970
Watkins, Lura W. *American Glass and
　　Glassmaking*, 1950
Webber, Norman *Collecting Glass*, 1972
Weiss, Gustav *The Book of Glass*, 1971
Wilkinson, R. *The Hallmarks of Antique Glass*, 1968
Wills, Geoffrey *English Looking-Glasses*, 1965
　　English and Irish Glass, 1968
　　Antique Glass, 1971

METALWORK

Bury, Shirley *Victorian Electroplate*, 1971
Cooper, Jeremy *Nineteenth-Century Romantic
　　Bronzes*, 1974
Eras, Vincent M. *Locks and Keys Throughout the
　　Ages*, 1957
Frost, T.W. *Price Guide to Old Sheffield Plate*, 1971
Haedeke, Hanns-Ulrich *Metalwork*, 1970
Hartfield, G. *Horse Brasses*, 1965
Hayward, John F. *English Cutlery*, 1956
Hughes, G. Bernard *Antique Sheffield Plate*, 1970
John, W.D. *Pontypool and Usk Japanned Wares*, 1953
Kauffman, H.J. *American Copper and Brass*, 1968
Kisch, Bruno *Scales and Weights*, 1965
Lindsay, J. Seymour *Iron and Brass Implements of
　　the English and American Home*, 1964 (new ed.)
Mackay, James A. *Commemorative Medals*, 1970
　　The Animaliers, 1973
Michaelis, R. *British Pewter*, 1969
Montgomery, Charles F. *A History of American
　　Pewter*, 1974
Peal, C.A. *British Pewter and Britannia Metal*, 1971
Perry, Evan *Collecting Antique Metalware*, 1974
Savage, George *A Concise History of Bronzes*, 1968
Underwood, L. *Bronzes of West Africa*, 1967

Whiting, J.R.S. *Commemorative Medals*, 1972
Wills, Geoffrey *Collecting Copper and Brass*, 1962
    The Book of Copper and Brass, 1969
    Candlesticks, 1974
Wyler, Seymour B. *The Book of Sheffield Plate*, 1949

MILITARIA

Abels, Richard *Classic Bowie Knives*, 1967
Akehurst, Richard *The World of Guns*, 1973
Albaugh, W. *Confederate Hand-guns*, 1963
Atkinson, J. *Duelling Pistols*, 1964
Blackmore, H.L. *British Military Firearms*, 1965
Blair, Claude *Pistols of the World*, 1968
Clark, E.F. *Truncheons, Their Romance and Reality*, 1935
Coggins, J. *Arms and Equipment of the Civil War*, 1962
Dicken, E.R.H. *Truncheons, Their History*, 1952
Edwards, T.J. *Regimental Badges*, 1966
Hayward, John F. *Swords and Daggers*, 1951
Martin, P. *European Military Uniforms*, 1968
Riling, R. *The Powder Flask Book*, 1953
Taylorson, A. *Revolving Arms*, 1967
Wilkinson, Frederick *Swords and Daggers*, 1967
    Militaria, 1969
    Battle Dress, 1970
    Antique Arms and Armour, 1972
Winant, L. *Firearms Curiosa*, 1956

MODELS, TOYS, DOLLS AND GAMES

Bell, R.C. *Board and Table Games*, (2 vols.), 1960–9
Blum, Peter *Model Soldiers*, 1971
Bullard, Helen *The American Doll Artist*, 1965
Coleman, D.S., E.A. and E.J. *The Collector's Encyclopedia of Dolls*, 1968
Cook, Olive *Movement in Two Dimensions*, 1963
Daiken, Leslie *Children's Toys Throughout the Ages*, 1953
Fraser, Lady Antonia *A History of Toys*, 1966
Garratt, John *Model Soldiers: A Collector's Guide*, 1961
Greene, V. *English Dolls' Houses*, 1967
Harbeson, J.F. *Nine Centuries of Chessmen*, 1964
Harris, H. *How to Go Collecting Model Soldiers*, 1969
Hart, Luella *Directories of British, French and German Dolls*, 1964–5
Hillier, Mary *A Pageant of Toys*, 1965
    Dolls and Dollmakers, 1968
Johnson, A. *Dressing Dolls*, 1969
Latham, Jean *Dolls' Houses.* 1969
Mackett-Beeson, A.E.J. *Chessmen*, 1968
McClintock, Inez and Marshall, *Toys in America*, 1961
Nicollier, J. *Collecting Toy Soldiers*, 1967
Speaight, George *A History of the English Toy Theatre*, 1969
Yamada, Tokubei *Japanese Dolls*, 1955

OBJECTS OF VERTU, JEWELRY AND COSTUME ACCESSORIES

Armstrong, Nancy *A Collector's History of Fans*, 1974
Barsali, Isa Belli *European Enamels*, 1969

Berry-Hill, H. and S. *Antique Gold Boxes*, 1953
Bradford, Ernle *English Victorian Jewellery*, 1967
    Four Centuries of European Jewellery, 1967
Buck, A. *Victorian Costume and Costume Accessories*, 1961
Clifford, Anne *Cut Steel and Berlin Iron Jewellery*, 1971
Cooper, Diana and Battershill, Norman *Victorian Sentimental Jewellery*, 1972
Delieb, Eric *Silver Boxes,* 1968
Ellenbogen, Eileen *English Vinaigrettes*, 1956
Epstein, Diana *Buttons*, 1968
Evans, Joan *A History of Jewellery, 1100–1870*, 1970 (2nd ed.)
Falkiner, Richard *Investing in Antique Jewellery*, 1968
Flower, Margaret *Victorian Jewellery*, 1967
    Jewellery, 1837–1901, 1968
Foskett, Daphne *British Portrait Miniatures*, 1969
Foster, Kate *Scent Bottles*, 1966
Gere, Charlotte *Victorian Jewellery Design*, 1972
Hickman, P. *Silhouettes*, 1968
Hinks, Peter *Jewellery*, 1969
Hughes, G. Bernard *English Snuff-boxes*, 1971
Hughes, G. Bernard and Thirle *English Painted Enamels*, 1951
Hughes, Graham *Jewelry*, 1966
    The Art of Jewelry, 1972
Launert, Edmund *Scent and Scent Bottles*, 1974
Le Corbeiller, Clare *European and American Snuff-boxes*, 1966
Lewis, M.D.S. *Antique Paste Jewellery*, 1970
Long, B.S. *British Miniaturists, 1520–1860*, 1967
Luscomb, Sally C. *The Collector's Encyclopedia of Buttons*, 1967
Mayne, Arthur *British Profile Miniaturists*, 1970
Mew, E. *Battersea Enamels*, 1926
Peacock, Primrose *Buttons for the Collector*, 1974
Peter, M. *Collecting Victorian Jewellery*, 1970
Ricketts, Howard *Objects of Vertu*, 1971
Schidlof, L. *The Miniature in Europe*, 1965
Snowman, Kenneth *Eighteenth Century Gold Boxes of Europe*, 1966
Woodiwiss, John *British Silhouettes*, 1966

POTTERY AND PORCELAIN

Aldridge, Eileen *Porcelain*, 1969
Bacci, Mina *European Porcelain*, 1969
Ball, A. *The Price Guide to Pot Lids*, 1970
Barnard, Julian *Victorian Ceramic Tiles*, 1972
Barret, Richard C. *Bennington Pottery and Porcelain*, 1958
Bedford, John *Toby Jugs*, 1968
Bemrose, Geoffrey *19th Century English Pottery and Porcelain*, 1952
Beurdeley, M. *Porcelain of the East India Companies*, 1962
Boger, Louise *The Dictionary of World Pottery*, 1971
Boulay, Anthony du *Chinese Porcelain*, 1967
Bristowe, W.S. *Victorian China Fairings*, 1971 (2nd ed.)
Butterworth, A. *Pottery and Porcelain*, 1964
Caiger-Smith, Alan *Tin Glaze Pottery in Europe and the Islamic World*, 1974

Charles, Rollo *Continental Porcelain of the Eighteenth Century*, 1964
Charleston, R.J. (ed.) *English Porcelain (1745–1850)*, 1965
    World Ceramics, 1968
Clark, Harold *The Pictorial Pot Lid Book*, 1955
Cooper, Ronald G. *English Slipware Dishes, 1650–1850*, 1968
Coysh, A.W. *Blue and White Transfer Ware, 1780–1840*, 1970
Cushion, John P. *English China Collecting for Amateurs*, 1967
    Continental China Collecting for Amateurs, 1970
    Pottery and Porcelain, 1972
Cushion, John P. and Honey, W.B. *Handbook of Pottery and Porcelain marks*, 1965 (new ed.)
Fisher, Stanley *British Pottery and Porcelain*, 1962
Garner, F.H. *English Ceramics*, 1966
    English Delftware, 1972
Garner, Sir Harry *Oriental Blue and White*, 1964
Godden, Geoffrey A. *Encyclopedia of British Pottery and Porcelain Marks*, 1965 (new ed.)
    An Illustrated Encyclopedia of British Pottery and Porcelain, 1966
    Jewitt's Ceramic Art of Great Britain, 1972
    British Porcelain: an Illustrated Guide, 1974
    British Pottery: an Illustrated Guide, 1974
Grant, M.H. *The Makers of Black Basaltes*, 1967
Guillard, Harold *Early American Folk Pottery*, 1971
Haggar, Reginald *Concise Encyclopedia of Continental Pottery and Porcelain*, 1960
Henzke, Lucille *American Art Pottery*, 1970
Hillier, Bevis *Pottery and Porcelain 1700–1914*, 1968
Hodges, Henry *Pottery*, 1972
Honey, W.B. *German Porcelain*, 1947
    European Ceramic Art, 1949–52
    French Porcelain of the 18th Century, 1950
    English Pottery and Porcelain, 1964
Hughes, G.B. and T. *English Porcelain and Bone China*, 1955
Imber, Diana *Collecting Delft*, 1968
Jenyns, Soame *Later Chinese Porcelain*, 1965
    Japanese Porcelain, 1965
    Japanese Pottery, 1971
John, W.D. and Baker, Warren *Old English Lustre Pottery*, 1951
Jonge, C.H. de *Delft Ceramics*, 1970
    Dutch Tiles, 1970
Landais, Hubert *French Porcelain*, 1961
Lane, Arthur *French Faience*, 1948
    Italian Porcelain, 1954
    English Porcelain Figures of the Eighteenth Century, 1961
Lewis, Griselda *A Collector's History of English Pottery*, 1969
Mackay, James A. *Commemorative Pottery and Porcelain*, 1971
Mankowitz, Wolf and Haggar, Reginald *Concise Encyclopedia of English Pottery and Porcelain*, 1957
Mountford, Arnold R. *Staffordshire Salt-glazed Stoneware*, 1971
Oliver, Anthony, *The Victorian Staffordshire Figures, a Guide for Collectors*, 1971

Peck, Herbert *Book of Rookwood Pottery*, 1968
Penkala, Maria *European Pottery*, 1968
Pugh, P.D. Gordon *Staffordshire Portrait Figures and Allied Subjects of the Victorian Era*, 1971
Rackham, Bernard *Medieval English Pottery*, 1947
    Islamic Pottery and Italian Maiolica, 1959
    Italian Maiolica, 1964
Ramsay, John *American Potters and Pottery*, 1939
Rhodes, Daniel *Porcelain and Stoneware*, 1960
Rosenthal, E. *Pottery and Ceramics*, 1949
Ross, Marvin D. *Russian Porcelains*, 1968
Rust, Gordon A. *Collector's Guide to Antique Pottery*, 1973
Savage, George *Pottery through the Ages*, 1958
    Seventeenth and Eighteenth Century French Porcelain, 1960
    Porcelain through the Ages, 1961
    Eighteenth Century German Porcelain, 1968
Savage, George and Newman, Harold *An Illustrated Dictionary of Ceramics*, 1974
Scavizzi, Giuseppe *Maiolica, Delft and Faience;* 1970
Shinn, Charles and Dorrie, *Victorian Parian China*, 1971
Spargo, John *Early American Pottery and China*, 1926
Tait, Hugh *Porcelain*, 1962
Tilley, Frank *Teapots and Tea*, 1957
Towner, Donald *English Cream-coloured Earthenware*, 1957
Wakefield, Hugh *Victorian Pottery*, 1962
Ware, George *German and Austrian Porcelain*, 1963
Watkins, Lura W. *Early New England Potters and their Wares*, 1950
Williams-Wood, Cyril *Staffordshire Pot Lids and their Potters*, 1972

PRINTED MATTER

Abdy, Lady Jane *The French Poster from Chéret to Capiello*, 1969
Barnicoat, John *A Concise History of Posters*, 1972
Baynton-Williams, Roger *Investing in Maps*, 1969
Buday, G. *The History of the Christmas Card*, 1965
Crone, G.R. *Maps and their Makers*, 1962
Gentleman, David *Design in Miniature*, 1971
Hillier, Bevis *Posters*, 1968
Holland, Vyvyan *Hand Coloured Fashion Plates*, 1955
Holt, Toni and Valmai *Picture Postcards of the Golden Age*, 1971
Howarth Loomes, Bernard *Victorian Photography*, 1975
Klamkin, Marian *Picture Postcards*, 1974
Langley Moore, Doris *Fashion Through Fashion Plates*, 1971
Lee, Ruth W. *A History of Valentines*, 1953
Lewis, John *Printed Ephemera*, 1962
Lister, Raymond *Antique Maps and their Cartographers*, 1970
Mann, S. *Collecting Playing Cards*, 1967
Rendall, Joan *Matchbox Labels*, 1968
Rickards, Maurice *Posters of the First World War*, 1968
    Posters of the Nineteen-Twenties, 1968
    Posters of the Turn of the Century, 1968

Skelton, R.A. *Decorative Printed Maps of the 15th to 18th Centuries*, 1966

Spellman, D. and S. *Victorian Music Covers*, 1969

Staff, Frank *The Picture Postcard and Its Origins*, 1966
The Valentine and its Origins, 1969

Steinberg, S.H. *Five Hundred Years of Printing*, 1955

Tilley, Roger *History of Playing Cards*, 1974

SILVER

Ash, Douglas *Dutch Silver*, 1965

Banister, Judith *English Silver*, 1969
Late Georgian and Regency Silver, 1971
Collecting Antique Silver, 1972

Bennett, Douglas *Irish Georgian Silver*, 1972

Bigelow, Frank *Historic Silver of the Colonies and its Makers*, 1950

Bradbury, Frederick *Guide to Marks of Origin on British and Irish Silver*, 1968

Brunner, Herbert *Old Table Silver*, 1967

Came, Richard *Silver*, 1972 (new ed.)

Carré, Louis *A Guide to Old French Plate*, 1971

Chaffers, W. *Handbook to Hallmarks on Gold and Silver Plate*, 1971

Clayton, Michael *The Collector's Dictionary of the Silver and Gold of Great Britain and North America*, 1971

Davis, Frank *French Silver, 1450–1825*, 1969

Delieb, Eric *Investing in Silver*, 1967
The Great Silver Manufactory, 1971

Dennis, Faith *Three Centuries of French Domestic Silver; its Makers and Marks*, 1960

Dennis, Jessie M. *English Silver*, 1970

Dixon, S.C. *Antique English Silver Trays and Tazze*, 1964

Finlay, Ian *Scottish Gold and Silver Work*, 1956

Grimwade, Arthur *Rococo Silver, 1727–1765*, 1974

Hayward, John F. *Huguenot Silver in England*, 1964

Holland, Margaret *Old Country Silver*, 1972

Hood, Graham *American Silver*, 1971

How, G.E.P. and J.P. *English and Scottish Silver Spoons*, 1952

Hughes, G. Bernard *Small Antique Silverware*, 1957

Hughes, G. Bernard and Therle *Three Centuries of English Domestic Silver, 1500–1820*, 1968

Jackson, Sir Charles *English Goldsmiths and their Marks*, 1965

Kovel, R. and T. *A Directory of American Silver, Pewter and Silver Plate*, 1961

Langdon, J.E. *Canadian Silversmiths, 1700–1900*, 1967

Miles, E.B. *Antique English Pocket Nutmeg Graters*, 1967

Oman, Charles C. *English Domestic Silver*, 1959
English Silversmiths' Work, 1965

Penzer, N.M. *The Book of the Wine Label*, 1947

Phillips, John M. *American Silver*, 1949

Ramsay, L.G.C. (ed.) *Antique English Silver and Plate*, 1962

Rupert, C.G. *Apostle Spoons*, 1929

Taylor, Gerald *Silver*, 1965
Continental Gold and Silver, 1967

Thorn, C. Jordan *Handbook of American Silver and Pewter Marks*, 1949

Ticher, Kurt *Irish Silver in the Rococo Period*, 1972

Turner, Noel D. *American Silver Flatware 1837–1910*, 1972

Wardle, Patricia, *Victorian Silver and Silver-plate*, 1963

Whitworth, R.W. *Wine Labels*, 1966

Wills, Geoffrey *Silver for Pleasure and Investment*, 1970

TEXTILES

Bode, Wilhelm von and Kühnel, Ernst *Antique Rugs from the Near East*, 1970

Campana, Michele *Oriental Carpets*, 1969

Churchill Bath, Virginia *Lace*, 1974

Con, J.M. *Carpets from the Orient*, 1966

Dilley, A.U. *Oriental Rugs and Carpets*, 1960

Erdmann, Kurt *Seven Hundred Years of Oriental Carpets*, 1970

Formenton, Fabio *Oriental Rugs and Carpets*, 1972

Godden, G.A. *An Illustrated Guide to Stevengraphs*, 1970

Hubel, Reinhard *The Book of Carpets*, 1971

Kendrick, A.F. *English Needlework*, 1967

Kent, William Winthrop *The Hooked Rug*, 1930

King, D. *Samplers*, 1960

Morris, B. *History of English Embroidery*, 1954
Victorian Embroidery, 1962

Pond, Gabrielle *An Introduction to Lace*, 1968

Reed, Stanley *Oriental Rugs and Carpets*, 1968

Ries, Estelle H. *American Rugs*, 1950

Turkhan, Kudret *Islamic Rugs*, 1968

Wardle, Patricia *Victorian Lace*, 1968

WOOD AND OTHER MATERIALS

Beigbeder, O. *Ivory*, 1965

Boothroyd, A.E. *Fascinating Walking Sticks*, 1973

Buist, J.S. *Mauchline Ware*, 1974

DeVoe, Shirley Spaulding *English Paper Mâché of the Georgian and Victorian Periods*, 1971

Frere-Cook, G. *The Decorative Arts of the Mariner*, 1966

Freeston, Ewart C. *Prisoner of War Ship Models*, 1974

Gould, M.E. *American Wooden Ware*, 1942
Household Life in America 1620–1850, 1965

Pinto, Edward H. *Encyclopedia and Social History of Treen and other Wooden Bygones*, 1969
Tunbridge and Scottish Souvenir Woodware, 1970

Scott, Amoret and Christopher *Tobacco and the Collector*, 1966

Thomas, Alan G. *Great Books and Book Collectors*, 1975

Thomas, O.E. *Domestic Utensils in Wood*, 1932

Toller, Jane *Antique Papier Mâché in Great Britain and America*, 1962
Prisoners of War Work 1756–1815, 1965

Waterer, J.W. *Leather Craftsmanship*, 1968

Wills, Geoffrey *Ivory*, 1968

Acknowledgments

The publishers would like to thank Angelo Hornak for taking many of the colour and black-and-white photographs, and Mrs Rosemary L. Klein for undertaking the picture research in the United States. They would also like to thank the following for permission to reproduce illustrations:

American Clock and Watch Museum Inc., Bristol, Conn., 64*t*, 306

American Museum in Great Britain, 21*t*, 22*b*, 68, 78*b*, 115, 148, 176, 199*r*, 212*t*, 213, 221, 266*t*

Antique Hypermarket, London, 33 (courtesy Lee-Davis), **97**, **246**

Associated Biscuits Ltd, Reading, 278

Author's collection, 17*l*, 30*r*, 123*t*

Anita Besson, 160*b*

Bihler & Coger Antiques, 11*b* (photo: Helga Photo Studios Inc.)

Blair Museum of Lithophanes, Toledo, Ohio, 151

British Museum, 36, 58*b*, 158, 159, 179*b* and 181 (photos: Cooper-Bridgeman), 223, 234 (photo: Octopus Books Ltd)

Campbell Museum, USA, 296

Alison Cathie, **291**

Christie, Manson & Woods, London, 94*l*, 101, 191*b*, 232 (photo: Cooper-Bridgeman), 308

Cincinnati Art Museum, **98**

City of Birmingham Museum and Art Gallery, 123*b*, 126*r*, 146, 286*b*

City Museum and Art Gallery, Hanley, Stoke-on-Trent, 14, 38, 53, 89, 154, 188*b*, 203*r*, 214, 218, 222, 225*r*, 261, 273*b*, 280*b*, 283, 284, 307

City of Norwich Museums, 20, 22*t*, 49*b*, 95, 163*b*, 171, 201, 202, 206, 210, 211*b*, 252*l*, 256*b*, 257, 258*l*, 267, 279

Coca-Cola Company, Atlanta, Georgia, 29*t*

Gary C. Cole, 78*t*, 217*r* (photos: Helga Photo Studios Inc.)

Cooper-Bridgeman Library, 41, **127**, 180

Fitzwilliam Museum, Cambridge, 12, 132

Werner Forman, 124

Free Library of Philadelphia, **100**

Geoffrey Godden, 262, 265

John Hall, London, **69**, **99**, **245**

Frank Herrmann, 216, 217*l*, 290*t*

Howarth-Loomes Collection, 184, 192, 193

International Geological Survey, 136*t* (photo: Octopus Books Ltd)

Jellinek & Sampson, London, **52**

London Museum, 13, 23, 66, 105*l*, 197, 299*b*

Mr and Mrs George Scheide Mantel, 150*b*

Martins-Forrest Collection, 62*b*

Metropolitan Museum of Art, 26*r*, 119*b*, 207*t* (Rogers Fund); 30*l* (Gift of Mrs Robert W. de Forest); 44*b* (Bequest of Charles Allen Munn); 45, 73, 119*t* (Gifts of Mrs Emily Winthrop Miles); 61, 85*t*, 259*t* (Gifts of Mrs J. Insley Blair); 81*b*, 189 (Gifts of Dr and Mrs Charles W. Green); 81*t* (Bequest of Mrs Mary Mandeville Johnston); 125*r* (Gift of Susan Dwight Bliss); 241 (Gift of Mrs J.H. Grenville); 252*b*, 259 (Bequest of A.T. Clearwater); 259*b* (Gift of Mrs Arthur C. Steinbach); **303** (Edgar J. Kaufmann Charitable Foundation Fund)

Milton Bradley Company, USA, 183*b*

Hugh Moss Limited, London, **263**

Museum of Childhood, Menai Bridge, 54, 172*tr*, 173*b*, **177**, **178**, 299*t*

Museum of the City of New York, 84*t*, 102, 228, 254, 287

National Museum of Wales, 85*r*, 116, 121, 152, 153

National Trust, London, 275

Newark Museum, N.J., 131 (Gift of Mr and Mrs Ethan D. Alyea)

Kenneth M. Newman, The Old Print Shop, N.Y.C., 156

New-York Historical Society, New York City, 10, 11*t*, 230, 253

New York Public Library, 48*t* (Astor, Lenox and Tilden Foundations)

New York State Historical Association, Cooperstown, N.Y., 208, **281**

Old Sturbridge Village, Mass., 233

Parker Brothers, Salem, Mass., 117

Philadelphia Museum of Art, 281 (Bequest of R. Wistar Harvey); 37*t* (Titus C. Geesey Collection); 40 (Baugh-Barber Fund); 80 (A.E. Barber); 126*l* (Given by Mrs William D. Frishmuth); 150*t*, 311 (Given by Mr and Mrs Julius Zieget); 236 (Whitman Sampler Collection: given by Pet Inc.); 242 (Given by Robert L. McNeil Jr, Trusts Gift)

Mrs Dora Raeburn, **109**, 111*t*, 162*t*, **264**, 302

Elizabeth Rainsville, 271, **294**

John Rainsville, 62*l*, 91, 103, 194, 203*l*, 205, 312

References to position on page are in *italic*
References to colour plates are in **heavy type**